# THROUGH THE EYES OF WOMEN

# THROUGH THE EYES
## OF WOMEN
## *Insights for Pastoral Care*

Edited by
Jeanne Stevenson Moessner

Fortress Press
Minneapolis

THROUGH THE EYES OF WOMEN
Insights for Pastoral Care

Where not otherwise indicated Scripture quotations are from the New Revised
Standard Version Bible, copyright © 1989 by the Division of Christian Education
of the National Council of the Churches of Christ in the United States of America.
Used with permission.

Interior design: The HK Scriptorium, Inc.
Cover art and design: Patricia Boman
Back cover photo: by Peggy Zarnek Photography. Standing (left to right) C. Stahl
Bohler, J. L. Marshall, C. Thompson, T. E. Snorton, J. Stevenson Moessner, E. J.
Justes, S. A. Stinson-Wesley, B. L. Gill-Austern, B. J. Miller-McLemore. Seated (left
to right) K. J. Greider, M. Bowman Robbins, M. A. Glover-Wetherington, I.
Henderson, C. Saussy. Not pictured: P. Buford, B. J. Clarke, P. Couture, J. E.
Dasher, B. A. Estock, E. Liebert.

Library of Congress Cataloging-in-Publication Data

Through the eyes of women : insights for pastoral care/ edited by
   Jeanne Stevenson Moessner.
        p. cm.
   Includes bibliographical references.
   ISBN 0-8006-2928-0 (alk. paper)
   1. Women—Pastoral counseling of.  2. Church work with women.BV4445.
3. Women—Religious life.  4. Feminist theology
I. Moessner, Jeanne Stevenson, 1948 -
BV4445 .T57 1996
259'.082—dc20                                                96-18556
                                                                CIP

Manufactured in the U.S.A.                                      AF 1-2928
                                       5   6   7   8   9   10

*To Peggy Way,*
*whose vision guided us,*
*and*
*to all the women who have permitted us*
*to glimpse the world*
*through their lives,*
*and*
*to those who will carry on this work.*

# Contents

Foreword     xi

Contributors     xiii

Acknowledgments     xvii

Introduction     1
*Jeanne Stevenson Moessner*


**PART ONE: THE EYES OF UNDERSTANDING**

1. The Living Human Web: Pastoral Theology
   at the Turn of the Century     9
   *Bonnie J. Miller-McLemore*

2. Female-Friendly Pastoral Care     27
   *Carolyn Stahl Bohler*

3. The Legacy of the African-American Matriarch:
   New Perspectives for Pastoral Care     50
   *Teresa E. Snorton*

4. Pastoral Care and Counseling with Women
   Entering Ministry     66
   *Miriam Anne Glover-Wetherington*

5.  Weaving the Web: Pastoral Care in an
    Individualistic Society                                       94
    *Pamela Couture*


**PART TWO: INSIGHTS FOR PASTORAL CARE**


6.  The Healing Power of Anger                                   107
    *Carroll Saussy and Barbara J. Clarke*


7.  "Too Militant"? Aggression, Gender,
    and the Construction of Justice                             123
    *Kathleen J. Greider*


8.  Sexual Identity and Pastoral Concerns: Caring
    with Women Who Are Developing
    Lesbian Identities                                          143
    *Joretta L. Marshall*


9.  Women and Motherloss                                        167
    *Martha Bowman Robbins*


10. Manna in the Desert: Eating Disorders
    and Pastoral Care                                           179
    *Jane E. Dasher*


11. Hysterectomy and Woman's Identity                           192
    *Beth Ann Estock*


12. Matters Close to the Heart: Pastoral Care
    to Mastectomy Patients                                      207
    *Irene Henderson*


13. Daughters of Tamar: Pastoral Care
    for Survivors of Rape                                       222
    *S. Amelia Stinson-Wesley*

14. Pastoral Care and Older Women's Secrets                    240
    *Emma J. Justes*


**PART THREE: VISIONS OF HOME**


15. Coming Home to Themselves: Women's
    Spiritual Care                                                    257
    *Elizabeth Liebert, SNJM*


16. Women and Community: Women's Study Groups
    as Pastoral Counseling                                            285
    *Paula Buford*


17. Love Understood as Self-Sacrifice and Self-Denial:
    What Does It Do to Women?                                         304
    *Brita L. Gill-Austern*


18. From Samaritan to Samaritan: Journey Mercies                     322
    *Jeanne Stevenson Moessner*

# Foreword

In her Introduction to *Through the Eyes of Women: Insights for Pastoral Care* Jeanne Stevenson Moessner speaks of the gift of new insight often gained in visiting a foreign country. The distance from the familiar helps ". . . see her homeland with new comprehension."

Beckoning the reader to accompany them into unfamiliar territory, the eighteen writers of this book are engaged in seeking new eyes of understanding through their studies, experience, and theological reflection on what pastoral care from the perspective of advocacy for women might look like. These new eyes and their resultant work make a contribution to the field of pastoral care and counseling that will continue to extend the boundaries. This book, along with *Women in Travail and Transition* (Fortress Press, 1991), makes new contributions written from within the life experience of women available for use in study, teaching, and in the practice of pastoral care. Both those who use these materials and those who continue to write them will make available the good news in forms that frequently have not been experienced by women in crisis.

The insights for pastoral care that are shared in this book are also insights wanting and waiting to be heard. The women serving as pastors, pastoral counselors, clinical pastoral education supervisors, and academics who worked them out have spent time listening to one another over a period of four years. They seek to do what no *one* woman could succeed in doing, to have their voice collectively heard by the guild. They are calling for a paradigm shift from care for women as victims to care for women as part of a human web of relationships, as part of a wide cultural, social, and religious context.

In the visions of home in Part Three of this collection, we can read of women caring for one another and creating networks of support and community for one another. As women learn to value one another as sisters and grow in relationship with others, they also learn to value and love themselves as children of God.

From this experience of self-worth and sisterhood, an experience of coming home to themselves, springs new hope for many cultures in which the full humanity of women together with men can become a daily reality. The new eyes for learning that we gain in cross cultural experiences are the same new eyes that give us hope in this book. For here women become the subject of their own healing so that they may truly be partners with God in making "all things new" (Rev. 21:5).

—Letty M. Russell
Yale Divinity School

# Contributors

CAROLYN STAHL BOHLER, PH.D., is Emma Sanborn Tousant Professor of Pastoral Theology and Counseling, United Theological Seminary at Dayton, Ohio. She is an ordained United Methodist clergywoman, the mother of two children, and the author of *When You Need to Take a Stand* (Westminster/John Knox, 1990), *Prayer on Wings: A Search for Authentic Prayer* (LuraMedia, 1990), and *Opening to God: Guided Imagery Meditations on Scripture* (Upper Room, 1977; completely revised edition, 1996). She pastored a church in San Diego, California, and was chaplain of Simpson College in Indianola, Iowa.

PAULA BUFORD, M.DIV., TH.D. CAND., has fifteen years' experience in chaplaincy and pastoral counseling settings. A Southern Baptist minister, Paula holds an M.Div. from Southwestern Baptist Theological Seminary and is a Th.D. candidate in pastoral counseling at Columbia Theological Seminary. She is a fellow in the American Association of Pastoral Counselors and a clinical member of the Association for Clinical Pastoral Education.

BARBARA J. CLARKE, PH.D., is Associate Professor of Biology at the American University in Washington, D.C. She is also a Candidate for Holy Orders in the Episcopal Diocese of Washington, D.C., and is currently enrolled at the Episcopal Divinity School in Cambridge, Massachusetts. She has worked as a hospital chaplain and as a lay minister in her diocese.

PAMELA COUTURE, M.DIV., PH.D., is assistant professor of pastoral care at Candler School of Theology. She is author of *Blessed Are the Poor: Women's*

*Poverty, Family Policy, and Practical Theology* (Abingdon, 1991), and coeditor with Rodney Hunter of *Pastoral Care and Social Conflict: Essays in Honor of Chas. V. Gerkin* (Abingdon, 1995). She is ordained by the United Methodist Church.

JANE E. DASHER, M.DIV., is interim assistant director of chaplaincy services at Grady Memorial Hospital in Atlanta, Georgia. At Grady, she serves as head of staff at Hughes Spalding Children's Hospital and is a Supervisor in Training with the Association for Clinical Pastoral Education, Inc., through the Georgia Association for Pastoral Care. Jane specializes in providing care to women and children in the areas of pediatrics, neonatal intensive care, general perinatal care, and psychiatry. Ordained in the Presbyterian Church (USA), she is the 1993 recipient of the Presbyterian Writers' Guild Scholarship for creative writing.

BETH ANN ESTOCK, M.DIV., is the Associate Minister at Druid Hills United Methodist in Atlanta, Georgia. She has worked as a chaplain at a medical center as well as at a state mental health hospital. She enjoys spending time with her family, Jeff and Hannah Joy, working in her garden, and pursuing her interests in women's issues and urban ministry.

BRITA L. GILL-AUSTERN, M.DIV., PH.D., is Associate Professor of Pastoral Care and Practical Theology at Andover Newton Theological School in Newton, Massachusetts, and a pastoral psychotherapist in private practice. She is an ordained United Church of Christ minister and has served as a parish pastor for eight years in Pennsylvania and California. She received her M.Div. from Harvard Divinity School and her Ph.D. from the Graduate Theological Union in Berkeley.

MIRIAM ANNE GLOVER-WETHERINGTON is an Assistant Professor in Pastoral Psychology at the Divinity School of Duke University. She has worked both in campus ministry and Christian education as an ordained Southern Baptist. After becoming a Member of the American Association of Pastoral Counselors in 1984, she served as a counselor in three pastoral counseling centers, a rape crisis center, and a clinic.

KATHLEEN J. GREIDER, PH.D., is Assistant Professor of Pastoral Care and Counseling at the School of Theology at Claremont. She serves as a pastoral counselor at Christian Counseling Service in Redlands, California, and is an ordained United Methodist clergywomen with experience in both parish ministry and in-patient mental health services. Her book, *Reckoning with Aggression: Feminist Investigations in Power, Violence, and Justice,* is forth-coming.

IRENE HENDERSON, DIPL. THEOLOGY, is Director of Clinical Pastoral Education and Associate Director of Pastoral Services at South Carolina Baptist Hospital, Columbia, South Carolina. She is an ordained Southern Baptist minister and a certified Clinical Pastoral Education Supervisor. Irene has worked as a chaplain in several hospitals and nursing homes.

EMMA J. JUSTES is professor of pastoral care and pastoral theology at Northern Baptist Theological Seminary. Emma is ordained in the American Baptist Churches U.S.A. and is a member of the Society of Professional Church Leaders, American Baptist Churches. She is a member of the Editorial Committee of the *Journal of Pastoral Care.*

SISTER ELIZABETH LIEBERT, SNJM, PH.D., is Professor of Spiritual Life and Director of the Program in Christian Spirituality at San Francisco Theological Seminary. A member of the Sisters of the Holy Names of Jesus and Mary, she is also on the Christian Spirituality faculty of the Graduate Theological Union. She has authored *Changing Life Patterns: Adult Development in Spiritual Direction* (Paulist, 1992).

JORETTA L. MARSHALL is on the faculty at Iliff School of Theology where she teaches in the area of pastoral theology, care and counseling. Joretta is an ordained United Methodist pastor, a member of the American Association of Pastoral Counselors, and a workshop and retreat leader. Her book *Pastoral Counseling with Women in Lesbian Relationships* is with Westminster/ John Knox Press.

BONNIE J. MILLER-MCLEMORE, PH.D., is associate professor of pastoral theology and counseling at Vanderbilt Divinity School. A member of the American Association of Pastoral Counselors, she has worked as a hospital chaplain, as an associate minister with the Christian Church (Disciples of Christ), and as associate staff at the Center for Religion and Psychotherapy of Chicago. She is author of *Death, Sin, and the Moral Life* (Scholars, 1988) and *Also A Mother: Work and Family as Theological Dilemma* (Abingdon, 1994).

MARTHA BOWMAN ROBBINS, TH.D., is Associate Professor of Psychology and Pastoral Care at Pittsburgh Theological Seminary and a licensed psy-chologist. Currently a consultant for the Spiritual Development Program at Western Pennsylvania Psychiatric Institute, she spent a month in cross-cultural family therapy training at the Family Centre in Lower Hutt, New Zealand. Martha is author of *Midlife Women and Death of Mother: A Study of Psychohistorical and Spiritual Transformation* (Peter Lang, 1990).

LETTY M. RUSSELL is Professor of Theology at Yale Divinity School. Her books include *The Future of Partnership, Household of Freedom: Authority in Feminist Theology,* and *Church in the Round: Feminist Interpretation of the Church.* She has edited *Feminist Interpretation of the Bible* and co-edited *Inheriting Our Mothers' Gardens: Feminist Theology in Third World Perspective.*

CARROLL SAUSSY, PH.D., is Howard Chandler Robbins Professor of Pastoral Care and Counseling at Wesley Theological Seminary, Washington, D.C. She is a fellow in the American Association of Pastoral Counselors, a member of the Pastoral Psychotherapy Group of Greater Washington, and a former steering committee member for the Society for Pastoral Theology. Carroll is the author of *God Images and Self Esteem: Empowering Women in a Patriarchal Society* (Westminster/John Knox, 1991) and of *The Gift of Anger: A Call to Faithful Action* (Westminster/John Knox, 1995).

TERESA E. SNORTON, TH.M., is Director of Pastoral Services at Crawford Long Hospital, Emory (University) Center for Pastoral Services in Atlanta, Georgia. She is an ordained clergywoman and pastor in the Christian Methodist Episcopal Church and a certified supervisor in the Association for Clinical Pastoral Education. Teresa is also on the adjunct faculty in the Pastoral Care Department at the Candler School of Theology and the cofounder of the National Center for Excellence.

JEANNE STEVENSON MOESSNER, M.A., DR. THEOL., is adjunct Assistant Professor of Practical Theology at Columbia Theological Seminary with occasional teaching at Samford University in Birmingham and Candler School of Theology in Atlanta. She is a member of the American Association of Pastoral Counselors, a former missionary, a candidate for ordination in the Presbyterian Church (PCUSA), and a mother of two children. Jeanne is author of *Theological Dimensions of Maturation in a Missionary Milieu* (Peter Lang, 1988) and co-editor of *Women in Travail and Transition: A New Pastoral Care* (Fortress, 1991).

S. AMELIA STINSON-WESLEY is the founder and former director of Response: A Religious Response to Violence against Women and Children. A graduate of Meredith College and Duke Divinity School, she is an ordained minister in the Western North Carolina Conference of the United Methodist Church.

# Acknowledgments

The vision for this volume became a reality with the assistance of significant eyewitnesses. For the editorial discernment of Cynthia Thompson and Timothy Staveteig, the contributors are profoundly grateful. For the technical expertise of Bill Washburn and Kathleen Herrington of Columbia Theological Seminary and Pamela McClanahan and Lois Torvik of Fortress Press, we are indebted. We give special thanks to President Douglas Oldenburg and Dean James Hudnut-Beumler; they greatly assisted us in so many ways. The financial grants from the Griffith Theological Research Foundation and Columbia Theological Seminary enabled the nineteen women who wrote this book to assemble in collaboration. Through the perceptual lenses offered by members of the Society for Pastoral Theology, these women sharpened their focus.

# Introduction

JEANNE STEVENSON MOESSNER

## WINDOWS TO THE SOUL

When the eyes are covered by cataracts, impaired with old age, blind, it is then that the eyes of the soul must inform us completely. Teresa E. Snorton recounts an experience with her grandmother, one hundred and three years old. It is from this story that the title of this collaborative work, *Through the Eyes of Women: Insights for Pastoral Care,* has been taken.

"Eyeball to Eyeball, Nose to Nose"
When my children were little I used to play a game with them, "Eyeball to eyeball, nose to nose." The game was actually a gesture of affection—somewhat of a modified "kiss." Both my sons expressed great joy at this game, and as a mother I experienced the sheer joy of showing love for my children through such physical closeness. As some Native American cultures believe that the eyes are the windows to the soul, likewise I also felt a spiritual connection with my sons when we got "eyeball to eyeball, nose to nose."

My one-hundred-and-three-year-old grandmother recently had surgery—an amputation of one of her legs because of an unhealed, and now gangrenous, burn to the lower part of her leg and foot. The family was anxious about the decision to proceed with the surgery, primarily because of her age. We wondered not only whether she could survive the surgery but whether she would heal properly and beat the odds against infection and pneumonia during the recovery period.

About four days after surgery, I sat at the foot of my grandmother's hospital bed. My mother, an aunt, and an uncle were in various places in the room. We were greatly relieved that she had indeed survived the surgery, and so far there were no signs of trouble. Our greatest worry was around the fact that my grandmother refused to eat. She simply did not want anything and would not

1

take more than one or two bites of anything. Her firm position was a reflection of her strong will and personality that all of us knew in personal ways and accepted with humor.

As I sat at the foot of her bed, a conversation ensued. After a few moments, my grandmother motioned for me to come closer, so she could see me. Her eyesight had been failing over the years, and the cataracts made her vision very poor. I moved closer, only to be beckoned by her to "Come a little closer." Again I moved closer, again she beckoned. By the time we had finished, there I was "eyeball to eyeball, nose to nose" with my grandmother. I was so struck by the moment, because as I felt her breath and her gaze upon me, I realized I had never in my forty years of life been this close, physically, to her. As a child, she had been larger than life for me—strong, confident, assertive and aggressive in a time when women were expected to be less so. More recently, as a young adult, I had still regarded her as larger than life—now because of her age, her wisdom, and her remarkable memory.

But now, "eyeball to eyeball, nose to nose," I felt as though I were looking into the soul of a woman whose life had shaped the lives of many, including mine. Interestingly enough, the conversation we had was about my grandmother's mother. Story after story, memory after memory floated out of my grandmother's mouth, some of which I have already forgotten. But what sticks with me, what will not go away, is the spirit of my grandmother that floated out of her and into me that day as we sat "eyeball to eyeball, nose to nose" and I "saw" the world, her world, through her eyes during those moments, and a rich vision it was.

## A Pastoral Focus

This volume will look into and through the eyes of women. The insights will come not only from the women who wrote the chapters but from those who gave their life stories. Through the eyes of women, there is a new way of seeing the world community, a new perspective on suffering, a new lens by which to view the self.

It is in visiting a foreign country and gaining a distance from the familiar that a traveler can sometimes really see her homeland with new comprehension. This sourcebook, *Through the Eyes of Women: Insights for Pastoral Care,* is a map to the territory of women's experience, some of which will be familiar, some unfamiliar. While many regions will be covered—community issues, public policy, physical crises, emotional passages, anger, aggression, sexuality, loss of mother, violence, self-esteem, spirituality—the journey is by no means exhaustive. It is informative and transformative by offering a new lens and a mirror.

When I was a missionary schoolteacher in an international school in [West] Germany in 1977, I heard some missionaries who had been conducting relief efforts in Cambodia speak of the scarcity of food in the refugee camps. Since it was a day before my furlough and I was near a major European city, I found myself back in my hometown in the United States within twenty-four hours. Forty-eight hours had elapsed between hearing of the refugee work in Cambodia and attending a football brunch at a private club in a major southern city. As I passed through the dining rooms after the brunch, I noticed large quantities of leftovers—meats, eggs, breads—on the plates of the departed guests. Nausea over the contrast of what I had just heard and what I was now seeing overcame me. The shock was intensified in realizing I was not just now seeing the waste of food. I had been seeing it and doing it all my life. I had not known the different levels of seeing. The eyes of understanding had been opened only through a journey into the unfamiliar.

In 1993 a group of women serving as pastors, pastoral counselors, Clinical Pastoral Education supervisors, and academics met after the meeting of the Society for Pastoral Theology in Atlanta to put together this sourcebook on caring for and with women. These eighteen women had met over a period of four years to share their visions. Their collaborative work will reflect changes not only in North American and European societies but in ministry within those cultural contexts as well. This collaborative work is designed to encourage church leaders, to better equip pastoral counselors, to inform lay leaders, and to serve as a textbook in pastoral care courses around the country. It is designed to be used in training centers for the American Association for Pastoral Counselors and for the Association of Clinical Pastoral Education as caregiving in a variety of contexts and settings is envisioned. The contributors have written with a pastoral focus to promote critical "seeing" among pastors, counselors, and the laity on the different ways of caring. This pastoral approach reflects biblical themes, reexamines traditional doctrines, exposes ideological illusions, and reenvisions the life of the church. Women's resistance in the face of evil and women's creativity in the crush of culture are highlighted.

This cooperative effort challenges by example the academic guild's tendency to be as monolithic and individualistic as the culture it critiques. The response by a senior colleague after an earlier collaborative effort was as follows: "Now, when are you going to write your own work?" Ironically, many of the collaborators had already written solo works or were simultaneously writing individual works. The "either/or-ness" of the collective endeavor was never seen. Although a collective effort receives a low rating in the point system on a tenure track, working together has been a proactive statement to that system with its elevation of individual achievement. The answer to our colleague: "This collaborative volume *is* our own work."

Our methodology in writing has included circulating the chapters among contributors, giving help and feedback to one another. Another colleague's response to that method was the warning: "Don't give away your best stuff." When the contributors met in 1993 to give away their "best stuff," this personal story was told:

There was a woman who went through infertility treatments for seven years: laparoscopies, hysterosalpingograms, artificial insemination, surgeries, in vitro fertilization, drug therapy, hoping and waiting. She yearned for another child, especially a daughter. She sat with her husband in adoption agencies, adoption workshops, home studies; she filled out forms for the agencies, had yearly physicals, and updated financial statements—for seven years—only to wait and hope.

Now, in another state, there was a woman, a young woman, who had a child, born early, two pounds and fourteen ounces, a high-risk premature baby girl. This mother, because of her age and her circumstances, could not care for the child. She drove through several states with one of her parents to Georgia, leafed through the yellow pages of the phone book, picked an agency, and chose a family that had been waiting with that agency for seven years.

On a day in 1992 these two women met. They decided their lives were a match. Ten days later, in the parking lot of an apartment complex, in the presence of a social worker and a birth grandparent, the baby girl was placed tenderly in the backseat of the social worker's car. The birth mother lingered for moments. The adoptive mother held back. Then, in the rain of that February afternoon, they embraced. Weeping, they said to each other, "Thank you." "Thank you." For they were giving to each other the best that they had to give.

If the goal of our collaboration could be summarized in one statement, it would be that of giving hope to women in the midst of despair. It is to maintain, without glamorizing or glorifying suffering, that pain is not the end of the story. It is to stand with collective and particular insight. It is to assert our resilience as women in this process. It is to challenge and even change the sexist conditions that contribute to women's despair. It is to offer and encourage a new vision.

A student at Candler School of Theology in a class on the pastoral care of women gave the following response to the question: What constitutes hope in the midst of despair?

What constitutes hope for me more than anything else is the women who have gone before. The women who have found their voices and spoken and written about themselves and for and about other women. Sometimes the more I know about the inequality and oppression of women's lives, the more I love the foremothers, for their courage and honesty and intellect and emotional capacity and wisdom. We can find them in history and tradition—thanks especially to the more recent academicians who have rediscovered them and

brought them back to attention, at least to the attention of those who are looking and listening.

And the women today who are writing and researching and creating and
discovering—these bring me hope. Women writing their own lives into the disciplines of psychology and theology especially, these have been my lifelines
sometimes. They counter the infinite number of voices out there that say
"Here's your place, stay in it."

Will women change the church, will they merely be absorbed, or will the
church change them? I believe as women continue to enter the church there
will be change, just as there is change, at least in women's consciousness,
because women practice and publish in the disciplines of psychology and theology.

This collaborative effort is one of those "lifelines" particularly to those who
have not always felt a part of mainstream Protestantism. As churches and
theological institutions look at issues of gender, culture, family, and sexuality, we who specialize in these issues as pastoral counselors, pastors, and
academicians want to share our insights with the churches, pastoral guilds,
and religious institutions. This, in short, is the purpose of this volume.

In Germany in the fall there is a festival of thanksgiving, "das Dankfest"
or "das Erntefest," a time to thank God for the bounty. This is the Sunday
on which the produce and fruits from the parish gardens are placed on the
altar of local churches. In some ways, this collaborative effort is such an
offering. We women are committed to bringing the best of our labors as an
offering to the church, our respective guilds, the academy. We bring our
theological diversity as contributors. Although we do not always agree with
one another, we have agreed to support each other's speaking through
writing.

As in the Dankfest, we come with what we have produced, grateful for
our training and experience in our varied areas of expertise. We have been
given advantages that most of the world's women still do not have. This
book is our Erntedankfest. We trust that others will be nourished by the
fruits of our labors.

# Part One
# The Eyes of Understanding

Pastoral caregivers have traditionally viewed the individual as a "living human document." Looking at the context of the solitary life, we find that the metaphor of "living human web" better represents an understanding of the person-in-relationship. This relatedness includes not only other persons but connectedness with society, family systems, public policy, institutions, and ideologies. These ideologies and cultural factors influence counseling techniques, pastoral care goals, and clinical methodologies. While Bonnie Miller-McLemore expands the metaphor of "living human web," in an overview of the field of pastoral care Carolyn Bohler illuminates cultural illusions and biases toward females that penetrate the pastoral context.

Bonnie Miller-McLemore carefully illustrates the pastoral theological shift from a focus on care as counseling the individual as "living human document" to care as part and parcel of a broad social, religious, cultural, and economic context. Feminist, womanist, and black theologies have often offered a critique of the more traditional individualistic focus. Pastoral care from feminist and womanist perspectives challenges us to look not only at those who are experiencing the web as support system but at the victims caught in the web as entanglement. Pastoral care concerns itself as well with those who are spinning the patterns.

Carolyn Bohler offers ten guidelines as she develops a female-friendly approach in collaborative caring. She adeptly analyzes gender assumptions and biases in pastoral care.

A web of extended relationships is important to the African-American woman; she is a person of "community," as discussed by Teresa Snorton. The controlling image of "matriarch" is examined with an awareness of the realities of sexism, racism, and classism in the lives of black women. Snorton modifies the image of matriarch and replaces it with the image of womanist to allow for more effective and liberating pastoral care.

Emerging clergywomen face a network of tangled contradictions: Christian encouragement and societal restrictions, God's call to ministry and people's resistance to that call, redemption into Christian community and servitude to outmoded norms. Miriam Anne Glover-Wetherington looks at the pressures and the confusion that external contexts (placement processes, internships, collegial and personal relationships) can create for women entering ministry.

An ideology and idolatry of self-sufficiency has further torn and weakened the societal safety net which has the potential to undergird those in poverty and isolation. Pamela Couture argues that twentieth-century pastoral care has contributed to the spread of individualism with its "individual psychology as status quo" emphasis. Couture suggests a broad, social ecological framework for pastoral care that would tend to the intersections of cultures, public policy, community institutions, families and individuals, and theologies. Attention to this larger system weaves a web of support much like a social safety net. The peripheral vision of a congregation or of a caregiver can only be enhanced by this broader framework of seeing.

# 1

## The Living Human Web:
## Pastoral Theology at the Turn
## of the Century

BONNIE J. MILLER-MCLEMORE
*Vanderbilt Divinity School*

After completing academic work in religion and psychology, I found myself teaching pastoral care at a seminary. In making that transition I experienced two surprises. The first was the jolt of moving from the academic study of religion and social science to the peculiar discipline of pastoral theology. Although I had had clinical training and professional experience in chaplaincy, pastoral psychotherapy, and the church, I had never had an actual course in pastoral care or pastoral theology, nor had many of my courses emphasized pastoral or congregational practices. This gap between the study of religion and its practice was not just a personal quirk. Anyone who leaves the university religion department, degree in hand, and crosses the threshold of the seminary to teach will inevitably face professional dissonance. More specifically, pastoral theology is expected to be more oriented to ministerial practice than other theological disciplines; at the same time, it has struggled with the ambiguities of its identity midway between academy and the church. The routine use of the psychological sciences in the last few decades, while helpful, has also complicated the struggle.

The second jolt was encountering a student body that was approximately 50 percent women and 50 percent non-Caucasian. Despite my personal interest in listening to other voices, none of my graduate school courses in the early 1980s had required a text by a woman or by a person of color. In a society increasingly aware of the ways in which gender, race, class, and

This chapter is a revision of the article "The Human Web: Reflections on the State of Pastoral Theology," copyright 1993 Christian Century Foundation. Reprinted by permission from the April 7, 1993, issue of *The Christian Century*, 366–69.

worldview shape our ways of knowing, my good intentions quickly proved to be insufficient in working with such diversity.

Both shocks represent significant issues in pastoral theology. It is a field that is still trying to clarify its identity in relation to the academy and the church and its methods in relation to the social sciences. And now it must do so while taking heed of many new voices that are contributing new perceptions of pastoral care. Both issues deserve further attention. In this chapter, I will look at each in turn. For those invested in pastoral care, counseling, and theology, this discussion is essential, I believe, to securing the place and the future of the field.

With both issues, this chapter is more an invitation to dialogue than an exhaustive attempt to define the field and to delineate solutions to current methodological, theoretical, and practical problems. Here I simply initiate a conversation that, fortunately, successive chapters confirm, illustrate, expand, and qualify. While the first issue—the relationship between ministry, pastoral theology, and the academy—is not directly related to the focus of *Through the Eyes of Women: Insights for Pastoral Care* on women and pastoral care, this issue is still important as it influences the future of the field and women as part of that. Furthermore, the devaluation of religion and religious institutions in the twentieth century is related to the devaluation of the feminine and the identification of the church with the feminine in its attention to emotion, care, nurture, and religious piety. The marginalization of the field of pastoral theology and theology more generally is intertwined with this characterization—certainly a problem about which women in pastoral care and theology ought to have concern.

## Bridging the Gap between Academy and Church or Falling into It? A Crisis of Identity

Whereas biblical studies experienced the impact of modernity in terms of historical-critical approaches to Scripture, the field of pastoral theology experienced it in terms of the emergence of psychology and sociology as disciplines. For the past four decades pastoral theology's toehold in seminaries has depended to a considerable degree on its use of clinical psychology. Pastoral theologians may have felt uneasy about the ethos of pop psychology and self-analysis, but they flourished within it. Whereas in 1939 few theological schools offered counseling courses, by the 1950s almost all of them did. And 80 percent listed additional courses in psychology and had at least one psychologist on the staff. Similarly, in the clinical world in the 1940s only a few Protestant hospitals employed full-time chaplains; by the 1950s almost 500 full-time chaplains were serving general hospitals and 200 served in mental hospitals. As historian E. Brooks Holifield observes,

"In a relatively brief period, . . . pastoral theologians had secured their place in academia." Ministers interested in counseling had an expanding range of institutions in which to serve (Holifield 1983, 270–271, 273).

During this time, those in pastoral theology learned a great deal from psychology about understanding and respecting the inner experience of others. In the 1960s and 1970s, Carl Rogers's *Counseling and Psychotherapy* (1942) was a standard text in theological seminaries, and the fundamentals of empathic, reflective listening were a staple of introductory pastoral care courses. In the 1970s and 1980s, Howard Clinebell's variation on this theme, *Basic Types of Pastoral Care and Counseling* (1966), replaced Rogers's as the conventional textbook for introductory courses. Although the first edition situates modern pastoral care within the longer history of pastoral ministry, the majority of the text devotes itself to individual counseling techniques for an array of problems. Students learn to understand, interpret, support, evaluate, probe, and advise—six "appropriate responses" in situations of crisis intervention, supportive counseling, marriage enrichment, grief care, and so on (Clinebell 1984, 94–96). If there was any challenge to this approach, it was over the question of how directive to make the nondirective style, particularly when moral and religious judgments might qualify the psychological assessment.

At the same time, the widespread use of psychology fostered nagging questions about how pastoral theology could be both a genuinely theological and a scientifically psychological discipline. In 1973, in *The Living Human Document*, Charles Gerkin names this dilemma the "root question facing the pastoral care and counseling movement" (Gerkin 1973, 11). His answer, which proposes a dialogical, hermeneutical method of psychological and theological investigation of human experience as the primary text of pastoral theology, became one of the most well-liked and commonly endorsed characterizations of the field.

Gerkin and the distinguished pastoral theologian Seward Hiltner and others have found the "correlational" approach of Paul Tillich and "revised critical correlational" method of David Tracy helpful models for understanding the task of pastoral theology as an interdisciplinary endeavor. For Tillich, the questions raised by human existence, often helpfully named and analyzed by the human sciences, must be correlated with the answers of the Christian tradition. Tracy revises Tillich's one-directional juxtapositioning of "situation" and "message" by asserting that both the human sciences and theology suggest questions and answers; hence the dialogue is multidirectional. The human sciences not only provide answers, they may qualify those of religion. Persons who adopted this solution to Gerkin's "root question" have explored a variety of topics and clinical cases by matching texts in the sciences with Scripture and theological doctrine.

Nonetheless, neither Gerkin's text nor correlational methodology alone could dispel the persistent identity crisis. This confusion was readily apparent in the assorted job titles. Those in the field may teach pastoral care, pastoral counseling, pastoral psychology, pastoral theology, practical theology, religion and psychology, psychology of religion, religion and personality, religion and culture, and most recently, ethics. As these titles reflect, the discipline has been roughly divided between those who emphasize practical care and counseling approaches, those engaged in the critical correlation of theology, religion, and the social sciences, and those involved in the empirical social-scientific study of religious experience. Meanwhile, the use of psychology has generated stereotypes of the field as oriented to skills and feelings and as therapeutically shrewd. Among clergy, this approach has generated an almost unhealthy reliance on psychological jargon and counseling techniques rather than on theological language, pastoral mediation, and congregational care. For this overemphasis, there is some reason for critique.

To look to the future, it is crucial not to forget the past. Early participants in the pastoral theological movement, finding propositional theology remote and barren, turned toward the vivid color and textures of clinical cases. In place of a transcendent doctrinal theology, traditionally imposed on believers in their religious crises with little or no sensitivity to their own experience or religious understandings, pastoral theologians found theological meaning in the lived moments of human suffering and joy. In contrast to religious generalities deduced from Scripture and church doctrine, religious truth was deeply inductive. It emerged out of reflection on personal struggles, with clergy working as mentors rather than as judges.

Part of the appeal of psychology has been its ability to bridge the distance between human suffering on the one hand and theology, philosophy, and ethics on the other. During my own graduate years, clinical training in both chaplaincy and pastoral psychotherapy was one way to link academy and church, although it received no official academic credit. When I began teaching I tried—against the pressures of institutional structures—to maintain positions both in the seminary and in a pastoral counseling center. Without some kind of pastoral practice, I realized, my efforts in theological education were going to become a noisy gong, attempting to achieve a worthy goal but always lacking the one essential element of religious experience. I have also gradually recognized that my insistence on multiple roles had something to do with an approach to work typical of many women who resist the rigid, classificatory boundaries of most professions. It is not unusual for women to enter interdisciplinary fields, to attempt to integrate divergent foci such as psychology and spirituality, and to hold down more than one job at once.

I was intrigued, however, that few of my colleagues, mostly men, in other fields felt this same tug. Why shouldn't those being interviewed for seminary positions in biblical studies, ethics, or theology be asked about their pastoral practice? How do other seminary faculty resolve the question of the gap between academic theory and ministerial practice?

Pastoral theology discovered in the social sciences fresh models of how to relate theory and practice. In many respects, figures such as Freud, Heinz Kohut, Elisabeth Kübler-Ross, and M. Scott Peck write like sophisticated practical theologians. It is no small coincidence that when a friend in the midst of a marital crisis reached for a book, he bought one of Anne Wilson Schaef's popular titles. Kübler Ross's *On Death and Dying* has been recommended more frequently by pastors and chaplains than any one religious or theological text. While these books may have what some might call "a religious flavor," they are written by psychologists from a distinctly psychological point of view, sometimes with rather unprofessional excursions into religious speculation. But therapeutically oriented books have reigned in part because they offer clarification: they translate theories of human nature, fulfillment, and anguish into understandable terms. Pastoral theology took up this helpmate both to its benefit and to its detriment. In a word, although it avoided theological abstraction and academic trivialization, it was lured toward technique, theological vacuousness, and an individualistic, subjectivist orientation.

In addressing the Society for Pastoral Theology in 1994, Liston Mills claimed that at last the pastoral theology that arose on the crest of modern psychology is no longer an up-and-coming movement. It is no longer caught in the exciting, yet precarious moment of creating a new field. Pastoral theology is, he said, an established and respected discipline with both the stability and the increased responsibility that comes with this. Those in the field have to live with the ambiguities of its heritage.

## A SHIFT TOWARD CONTEXT, COLLABORATION, AND DIVERSITY

Most pastoral theologians and educators would still assert that empathic listening skills and sensitive individual counsel are prerequisites for ministry. But significant changes are afoot, symbolized both by the apparent decline in the popularity of Clinebell's text and the publication of a revised edition of it (1984). Most pastoral educators and practitioners have added to their repertoire the theories of more recent schools of psychology such as family systems and object relations theories. More critical, however, are a number of other changes: the focus on individual counseling and eductive listening has come under increasing criticism from a variety of angles; the prevalence of counseling courses has waned; "pastoral theology" has replaced "pastoral psychology" as the overarching theme; and the notion of care has returned to center stage, with counseling regarded as an important but not comprehensive speciality. Ultimately, almost everyone acknowledges the limits of the therapeutic paradigm and talks about sharpening our understanding not just of theological paradigms but of the social context as well, through the study of sociology, ethics, culture, and public policy. Specialized professions that rely on therapeutic paradigms, such as chaplaincy and pastoral psychotherapy, will be understood increasingly as only two of the manifestations of pastoral theology.

The focus on care narrowly defined as counseling has shifted to a focus on care understood as part of a wide cultural, social, and religious context. Initial examples of this change can be found in the new interest in congregational studies and in the ambiguous developments in pastoral psychotherapy. The world of parish ministry has offered an ill-sanctioned, little recognized wealth of insight for learning. Recent congregational studies have also begun to confirm the congregational nature of pastoral care. Aware of the limits of relying primarily on one-to-one counseling and the expertise of the pastor, pastoral care curriculum has focused increasingly on how congregations provide care and on clergy as facilitators of networks of care rather than as the chief sources of care. For instance, Roy Steinhoff Smith, professor of pastoral care at Phillips Theological Seminary, requires students to work together in small groups in his introductory courses to evaluate their different congregations as "caring communities." Not only do students need role play of individual counseling sessions, they need to study the ways in which clergy and members of religious institutions create and sustain networks of care. In a study of congregations and pastoral care, Don Browning concludes that while parishioners want and expect a minister to arrive when they face life-shaking crises and transitions, such as illness and death, this represents only a part of the broader care of the congregation (Browning 1988, 107–108). More often, a great deal of informal care takes place through diverse intercongregational activities, such as choir practice, women's circles, coffee hour, and Bible study. Although the minister must learn how to listen in individual counseling, equally essential to providing adequate pastoral care is the task of "facilitating the natural patterns of care that emerge in healthy congregations" and creating new avenues of care that build upon the special gifts and needs of individual members and the "psychosocial kinship groups" of the congregation as a whole.

Similarly, illustrative shifts are occurring in pastoral counseling. On the one hand, pastoral psychotherapy has also ceased to be a movement. It has acquired the status of a recognized clinical profession. On the other hand, in part because of its relationship to religion and the congregation, it does not have the kind of recognition accorded secular therapeutic professions. And yet, at the same time, from the perspective of those in secular circles, pastoral counseling lacks a clearly distinct identity in its affiliation with religion and the "pastoral." Confirming the place and importance of religion and theology in therapy continues to present challenges. Despite the notable contributions of clinical pastoral education and pastoral psychotherapy, many chaplains and pastoral therapists have tenuous relationships with seminaries and congregations. As one avenue around this impasse, some in the past two decades have turned, or returned perhaps, to age-old traditions of spiritual direction better understood within Catholic circles, now partially reconceived through the knowledge and practice of therapeutic modalities. On this score, recent books such as Elizabeth Liebert's *Changing Life Patterns: Adult Development in Spiritual Direction* (1992) and the work of Henri Nouwen, Eugene Peterson, and others, are important contributions.

Nonetheless, as pastoral theology curriculum in seminaries broadens, as the clinical identity of pastoral counseling solidifies, and as American health care reforms evolve, those in pastoral counseling training centers will have to address multiple questions about their appropriate ministerial, educational, and institutional place in relation to the congregation, the academy, and society. To be taken seriously by other mental health disciplines as well as by insurance companies and governmental structures, pastoral psychotherapy must develop its own evaluative criteria. To be taken seriously by churches and seminaries, it will have to affirm its connections and contributions to ministry and theological discourse. And to be taken seriously by people of color and by white women, it will have to include, even if only to a limited extent, social analysis of oppression, alienation, exploitation, diversity, and justice in its clinical assessment of individual pathology.

As I will develop further below, this final demand to attend to the wider cultural context, partially fostered by liberation perspectives, may be the most critical. At this point, let me delineate the ways in which a feminist perspective radically reorients perception and understanding. Black feminist bell hooks argues, and I agree, feminists have frequently been careless in failing to clarify agreed-upon definitions of feminism. Without them—with an "anything goes" attitude that feminism can mean anything anyone wants—we lack a solid foundation on which to construct theory and engage in meaningful praxis. Beneath its many current forms and definitions, some of which are too focused on rights, personal autonomy, and social equality, feminism is, in a word, a radical political movement. Hooks writes,

> Feminism is a struggle to end sexist oppression. Its aim is not to benefit solely
> any specific group of women, any particular race or class of women. It does not
> privilege women over men. It has the power to transform in a meaningful way
> all our lives. (hooks 1984, 26)

To call feminism simply a movement to make men and women equal
reduces and even confuses its full intent, especially when sexual equality in
the midst of difference remains an elusive ideal and discounts the weight
of other inequities. Feminism reclaims the lost and denigrated voices of
women and strives to eradicate the underlying cultural biases, including
imperialism, economic expansion, and others, that sustain sexism and
other group oppression. A feminist perspective demands an analysis of
structures and ideologies that rank people as inferior or superior according
to various traits of human nature, whether gender, sexual orientation,
color, age, physical ability, and so forth. Hence, to think about pastoral theology and care from this vantage point requires prophetic, transformative
challenge to systems of power, authority, and domination that continue to
violate, terrorize, and systematically destroy individuals and communities.

This emphasis on confronting systems of domination has been instrumental in creating the shift in pastoral theology from care narrowly defined
as counseling to care understood as part of a wide cultural, social, and religious context. These two highly significant, related developments and commitments are perhaps most evident in a variety of recent publications in
the field such as James Poling's *The Abuse of Power* (1991), Pamela
Couture's *Blessed Are the Poor?* (1991), Larry Graham's *Care of Persons, Care
of Worlds* (1992), and my own *Also a Mother* (1994). These are the kinds of
text most likely to come under consideration in introductory pastoral care
courses. All of these books, to varying degrees, challenge systemic structures
and ideologies of patriarchy, individualism, self-sufficiency, rationalism,
materialism, and so forth. They argue for alternative theological understandings of the social, cultural context as essential for adequate caregiving.
Many in pastoral theology have traditionally harkened back to Anton
Boisen's powerful foundational metaphor for the existential subject of pastoral theology—*"the study of living human documents rather than books"*
(1950, cited by Gerkin 1984, 37). Today, the "living human *web*" suggests
itself as a better term for the appropriate subject for investigation, interpretation, and transformation.

When I first pictured the "living human *web*" as a central theme of pastoral theology, I was thinking more of the three-dimensional net that a
process-theology-oriented college professor etched on the flat classroom
blackboard than the musty, sticky, annoying webs spun by insidious and
numerous spiders in our old and not so clean house. Within the limits of
chalk, blackboard, and his own imagination, John Spencer sought to illus-

trate the dense, multitudinous, contiguous nature of reality as he saw it over against the static interpretations of reality of much of Western philosophy and religion. As I tried to understand why I believed what I believed and to formulate fresh theological constructions of my own, this raw depiction made a great deal of sense to me. It still does.

While I did not consciously or intentionally make the connection, my use of the term "web" also results in part from feminist discourse. The most specific example that comes to mind is a book by Catherine Keller, *From a Broken Web: Separatism, Sexism, and Self* (1986), a theologian also significantly influenced by process theology through the work of John Cobb. *From a Broken Web* refutes thousands of years of misogyny embedded in Western myths, philosophy, religion, and psychology. Her thesis is that sexism and separatism—the view of the self as essentially separate from others—are intricately interlinked in this history. By sheer force of iconoclasm—juxtaposing hated images of women and images of monsters, serpents, spiders, dragons, Medusa, Tiamat, Tehom, or the "deep" in Genesis (which Keller sees as the Hebrew equivalent to Tiamat), the "oceanic" in Freud—Keller reveals how repulsive, how frightening, the powers of interconnection and the wisdom of women have been made to appear. Distorted fears of enmeshment, entanglement, and loss surround the relationality represented by the female and the mother in Western history. The resulting animosity and fury toward women, monsters, serpents, spiders, dragons, Medusa, Tiamat, Tehom, the "oceanic" has entailed the repression and banishment of connection itself.

By contrast, Keller asserts, the "self-structure of separation is a patriarchal artifice"; the "web is not originally a trap" (Keller 1986, 137). Using revised creation myths, object relations theory, process metaphysics, and feminist theology, she spins the new meanings of the connectivity of selfhood, religion, and all life. While aware of the limits of any one metaphor in a metaphysics of relationality, the image of the web "claims the status of an all-embracing image, a metaphor of metaphors, not out of any imperialism, but because, as a metaphor of interconnection itself, the web can link lightly in its nodes an open multiplicity of images" (Keller, 218). What she calls "arachnean religion" involves the spider's genius of repairing the web that the separative self has broken, "spinning oneness out of many and weaving the one back into the many" (Keller, 228).

Obviously, Keller's work is dense, highly technical, and not without its flaws; for my purposes, the important point is this: an alternative mythos resurrects the interconnectivity of selfhood. This mythos and the theology connected to it have funded a new approach in pastoral theology. More specifically, this means, for example, that public policy issues that determine the health of the human web are as important as issues of individual emotional well-being. Psychology serves a less exclusive, although still important, role, while other social sciences such as economics or political science become powerful tools of interpretation. In a word, never again will a clinical moment, whether of caring for a woman recovering from hysterectomy or attending to a woman's spiritual life, be understood on intrapsychic grounds alone. These moments are always and necessarily situated within the interlocking, continually evolving threads of which reality is woven and they can be understood in no other way. Psychology alone cannot understand this web.

The move away from psychology is not without its drawbacks. Maxine Glaz has provocatively observed that the newly critical perception of psychology in pastoral theology may be part of an "impetus to avoid issues of gender." Just when women in pastoral theology begin to find feminist psychology an incisive tool for reconstructing pastoral care and theology, the "people of a dominant perspective emphasize a new theme or status symbol" (Glaz 1991a, 12, 29). Glaz is right: we have some cause for concern about this change as a covert attempt to disempower the new participants in the pastoral theology discussion.

Women in pastoral theology would do well to retain the power of psychological analysis. First, to move beyond psychology too quickly is to underestimate the power of men like Freud and psychological definitions of human nature and fulfillment as culture- and consciousness-shaping forces. Moreover, new resources, such as Jessica Benjamin's *Bonds of Love* or Luise Eichenbaum and Susie Orbach's *Understanding Women*—to name just a few—challenge conventional understandings of female desire in Freud and others. They provide fresh insight into intrapsychic need and interpersonal dynamics. Feminist psychology and therapy, joined by psychologies attuned to different ethnic groups, will continue to be vital tools. Indeed, women in pastoral theology need to correct the subtle biases of some theologians who dismiss too rashly all of modern psychology as individualistic and inept in social analysis. In truth, the use of recent psychology by pastoral theologians and by feminist theologians, as Keller herself reveals, will continue to reshape fundamentally the ways in which we think about selfhood, the needs of children, human development, religious behavior, and other phenomena. If those in theology understand mutuality better than they used to, feminist psychology is at least partially responsible.

Glaz's criticism points to the difficulty of bringing diverse voices into play. Criticism of the individualistic focus of pastoral care has come in part from feminist theology and black theology. Few books in pastoral theology have addressed cultural issues of gender, race, and class. Even the otherwise thorough, well-documented history of pastoral care by E. Brooks Holifield sees women, slaves, and "others" primarily as the objects of care, rarely as caregivers themselves, and never as the source of new ideas (Holifield 1983). Some, like Clinebell, have tried to revise their basic texts to add new sections on "transcultural" perspectives (Clinebell 1984). David Augsburger's *Pastoral Counseling across Cultures* (1986) has received wide acclamation.

However, such books represent—as the authors acknowledge—dominant perspectives. Augsburger's definition of an otherwise helpful idea, "interpathy," is a good illustration of the problem. He uses the term to encourage entering into a "second culture" with a respect for that culture "as equally as valid as one's own" (Augsburger 1986, 14). Many feminists and people of color have pointed out that the subordinates in a society already intimately know the foreign realities of at least two worlds, that of their own and that of the dominant group or groups. And they have often given the second culture undue credibility and deference. Augsburger's interpathy is absolutely necessary, but it is a trait more relevant for the dominant culture than for those in oppressed groups. They have been "embracing of what is truly other" for a long time.

By contrast, the first step of those in the "second culture" is to affirm their own realities as worthy of equal respect. For many women, well trained in sensitivity to the needs of others and insensitive to their own suppressed desires, it is less a matter of bracketing and transcending one's own beliefs in order to feel as the other feels than of identifying for themselves what they feel and want at all. Significantly, even more than Caucasian women, African-American women, Asian women, and others must arbitrate between multiple, often hostile, cultures. For women, then, interpathy into the foreign beliefs of another culture necessarily implies envisioning distorted thoughts and feelings of repulsion, violence, fear, hatred—a problem Augsburger fails to note in his development of the concept (racism and sexism are conspicuous in their absence in the book's index).

With a few significant exceptions, women in pastoral theology have come up through the ranks of higher education approximately one generation behind women in religion and theology such as Rosemary Radford Ruether and Elisabeth Schüssler Fiorenza. A few women, such as Peggy Way and Sue Cardwell, have significantly impacted the field, although this occurred less through publications than through their compelling personal styles of teaching, speaking, and counseling. One possible reason for the lag in the more active participation by women is the proximity of pastoral theology to the church and the conservative nature of congregational life. Despite the pastoral nature of much feminist theology and careful treatments of specific issues in pastoral care such as abuse or spirituality, there was no book by a single author on pastoral theology from a woman's or a feminist perspective until quite recently. With Valerie DeMarinis's *Critical Caring: A Feminist*

*Model for Pastoral Psychology* (1993), the advent of a new era has commenced. Pivotal articles by Christie Neuger (1992) and Carrie Doehring (1992) suggest that further developments are only a matter of time.

These problems are partly less severe for black theology because of contributions from scholars with longer tenure in the academy such as Archie Smith (1982) and Edward Wimberly (1979). Still, wider recognition and reliance upon their work has been slow in coming. And until the recent publication of *WomanistCare* (1992), the participation of African-American women has been almost entirely missing from the discussion. Furthermore, *WomanistCare* is not explicitly presented as a book in pastoral theology. Meanwhile, more general books in theology such as Emilie Townes's *A Troubling in My Soul* (1993) are helpful resources and hopeful signs on the horizon for understanding care from a womanist perspective.

What will it mean for the practice of pastoral care to bring new voices into play? *Women in Travail and Transition: A New Pastoral Care* offers an initial indication. Edited by Maxine Glaz and Jeanne Stevenson Moessner, the book includes the work of five authors in ministerial settings and four in the academy. It aims to nurture intellectual acuity in the midst of pastoral practice. Chapters on new pastoral understandings of women and new pastoral paradigms are the brackets for other chapters on work, family, and alternative family forms, women's body, sexual abuse, battered women, and women's depression. Almost every man who has read this text in my courses testifies that it powerfully illumines women's lives. Women students want to send multiple copies to their ministerial colleagues, men and women alike. These students have heard a "cry," as one student expressed it, that they had never heard or understood before; they begin to hear in a different way.

Emma Justes states that if clergy "are unable to travel the route of hearing women's anger, of exploring with women the painful depths of experiences of incest and rape, or enabling women to break free from cultural stereotypes that define their existence," they should not be doing pastoral counseling with women (Justes 1985, 298). This claim suggests limits to empathy that people in Carl Rogers's time never suspected. When those involved in pastoral care do not know how to recognize the realities of violence toward women, they foster further damage and violence. Particularly in situations of sexual abuse, for example, the problem in pastoral response is not too little empathy but too much indiscriminate empathy by an uninformed pastoral caregiver that surfaces long-repressed feelings that overwhelm rather than help the person in need (Glaz 1991b). All pastoral caregivers must sharpen their sensitivity to the stress that women experience as wage earners and homemakers (Miller-McLemore), the economic devaluation of women in the workplace and women's poverty (Couture), health issues of concern to women, and the implications of female images of God for self-esteem (Saussy).

But these kinds of understandings are merely a beginning. The authors of *Women in Travail and Transition,* all white professional women in mainline faiths, invite "companion volumes written by nonwhite, ethnic, non-middle-class women within Western culture and by other women elsewhere throughout the world" (Glaz and Moessner 1991a, vi). No Hispanic, Asian, African, or American Indian pastoral care and theology has been published, although Robert Wicks and Barry Estadt have recently edited a "brief volume" of the "*experience* and *impressions*" of pastoral counselors involved in ministry in ten different countries (1993). Few texts deal with the pastoral agenda for men that might include issues such as the fear, anger, and grief over role changes and vocational confusion or tensions between work and family. Protestant pastoral theology and related clinical associations have all but ignored rich traditions and histories of pastoral theology and spiritual direction in Roman Catholic, Jewish, evangelical, and other circles.

We cannot predict what difference other stories and traditions will make to general formulations of the field or in pastoral practice. When we admit that knowledge is seldom universal or uniform, and truth is contextual and tentative, we discover a host of methodological, pedagogical, and practical problems. If the field of pastoral theology can no longer claim unity in thought and mind, what commonalities of approach define the field as distinct and relevant? In many ways, teaching and ministry become harder, professors and clergy more vulnerable. We find that we do not yet have the right texts to assign in our classes or the right answers in the pastoral office. Pastoral theology's trademark of empathy for the living human document is confounded by the limitations of empathy in the midst of the living human web. Sometimes a person must admit an inability to understand fully the lived reality of the oppressions suffered by another. There may be boundaries beyond which empathy itself cannot go.

We do know that we can no longer ignore an author's or a parishioner's identity and cultural location. A "living human web" cannot simply be "read" and interpreted like a "document." Those within the web who have not yet spoken must speak for themselves. Gender, feminist, and black studies all verify the knowledge of the underprivileged, the outcast, the underclass, and the silenced. If knowledge depends upon power, then power must be given to the silenced. In part, the pastoral theology movement began with this claim: Boisen, having suffered an emotional breakdown and finding himself inside a mental hospital, refused the marginalized, ostracized status of the mentally ill patient. He claimed the importance of what he learned about health, spirituality, and theology as learning that could occur from nowhere else than inside the experience of illness and suffering. This lesson—that we must hear the voices of the marginalized from within their own contexts—is one that pastoral theologians have known all along, even when Boisen claimed the validity of his own mental breakdown (1952), but perhaps never articulated in quite the way that it is now being addressed in this book and more widely.

## WHERE TWO OR THREE ARE GATHERED

Seven years after teaching my first introductory course, I finally created a course this spring with which I am fairly satisfied. Among its central objectives, it retains an emphasis on good listening skills, empathy, and moral and religious guidance; it adds an investigation of the networks of care in religious institutions; and it includes a study of diverse perspectives and of the interconnections between intrapsychic understandings, social analysis, and theological reflection. My satisfaction, I realize, is likely to be short-lived. The pressures on religion and higher education are immense. Entire religion departments in some universities have been shut down, and departments of religion and psychology and pastoral theology have sometimes been the first area cut. Likewise, the steady decline in numbers and monetary well-being of mainline denominations is already having an effect on seminary funding and constituencies. The reallocation of health care monies has affected and will continue to affect clinical pastoral care in hospitals and pastoral counseling institutions. Pastoral theology, however, has weathered rather well the challenges of the two fundamental crises described in this chapter. It has survived turmoil over its identity crisis and has actually done better than many other disciplines in theology in respecting a pluralism of voices.

Women in pastoral theology have much to contribute. Distinct from the claim in the preface of *Women in Travail and Transition* that "no individual woman in our field could undertake the complete project" (Glaz and Moessner 1991a, vi), now several women in the field are qualified to draft a book on pastoral care and women. Yet it is less clear that any individual woman would want to do so. In this volume, then, the choice to coauthor in the broadest sense becomes ever more deliberate and intentional. Most of us realize that this collaborative endeavor is more than, perhaps better than, what anyone might have written alone.

Pragmatically, our time and energies are already quickly consumed by the extra responsibilities of representation, mentoring, and so forth, that are typical of women in previously male-dominated professions. More important, feminism has learned the dangers of attempting to speak for all women in some generic sense. Our united effort defies mathematical and empirical logic that contends that "1 + 1 = 2." One plus one becomes something entirely new, different, and more than the mere summation of its parts. Our shared meals, correspondence, phone calls, and late-night hotel room conversations affirm a religious truth that "where two or three are gathered in my name, I am there among them" (Matthew 18:20).

The benefits of cooperation are evident both in terms of content and in terms of method. The collective text taps into areas of expertise that each author has developed out of particular passions and experiences. Few of us could address adequately, with the kind of depth and insight demonstrated here, the wide range of critical issues that this book covers. Into the web the authors weave issues thus far overlooked in the care of and care by women, many of them clandestine matters about which women, particularly women in churches, have not spoken freely, openly, and honestly—anger, aggression, eating disorders, hysterectomy, rape, lesbianism, aging. Most of the authors are different from the women who participated in the first collaborative effort. There has been a more intentional inclusion of non-European-American perspectives.

True, the main voices remain European-American, and other yet unexplored topics will come to the minds of our readers. Nonetheless, this volume in pastoral care is moving in the right direction. Like *Women in Travail and Transition*, it sustains the conversation between women in the academy and those in practices of pastoral care. Every chapter holds the tension between psychological analysis of the internal processing of personal experience and social analysis that situates individual issues within a more complex web of human interaction that includes divine intervention and grace.

Methodologically, participating in this volume did not mean dispatching twenty-five pages, written in the solitary confinement of one's office, to the editor and the publisher. Unlike many edited books, this book is written with the purpose of the entire book and the work of each other in mind. Individual chapters have been circulated among us for shared commentary. Even as I write, the conversations of my sisters at our meeting during the Society for Pastoral Theology ring in my ears. Just as feminist therapeutic theory defines differentiation as individuation in connection to others, the authors, while separately focused on individual areas of expertise, write in close connection to and knowledge of each other.

This approach is not one most of us learned in our respective institutions of higher education; academic rewards and dictates of professional survival often forbid it. Nonetheless, the choice to collaborate affirms the priority and value of relationality and working together to create a reality greater than any of its parts.

More broadly speaking, pastoral theology in general has much to contribute. The methods of pastoral theology have demonstrated the value of "thick description" as a powerful beginning point for all the fields of theological study (Geertz 1973, 3–30). "Thick description" means seeking a multilayered analysis of human strife, including detailed, intricately woven, "experience-near" rather than "experience-distant" readings of the "living human document." Standing explicitly between academy, church, and society, those in pastoral theology know intimately the limits of academic exercises and the necessity of religious experience in the creation of theology. They have found in the psychological sciences a lesson in practical theorizing. Better than most others in religious studies, they understand some of the problems and the possibilities involved in using the social sciences as a tool of analysis. They know the difficulties of marginalization. And they have grasped with greater ease than many in theology the importance of claiming one's own, often silenced, subjectivity.

Second, pastoral theologians, women and men alike, know the limits of knowledge apart from sensitive listening to the context, finding in the voices of women and people of color new ways of knowing and being. In the formation of The Society for Pastoral Theology itself, they have struggled to make white women and men and women of color central to the construction of the field, and not just other subgroups within its evolution, as has happened in some of the other theological societies. They know the tensions and conflicts of actually respecting and mending the living human web. On both scores, pastoral theology is challenging theology and theological education to reconsider its foundations.

## BIBLIOGRAPHY

Augsburger, David W. 1986. *Pastoral Counseling across Cultures*. Philadelphia: Westminster Press.
Boisen, Anton. 1952. *The Exploration of the Inner World*. New York: Harper & Brothers, Harper Torchbooks.
Browning, Don S. 1988. "Pastoral Care and the Study of the Congregation." In Hough and Wheeler, eds., 103–118.
Clinebell, Howard. 1966; rev. and enl. 1984. *Basic Types of Pastoral Care and Counseling: Resources for the Ministry of Healing and Growth*. Nashville: Abingdon Press.
Couture, Pamela D. 1991. *Blessed Are the Poor? Women's Poverty, Family Policy, and Practical Theology*. Nashville: Abingdon Press.
DeMarinis, Valerie M. 1993. *Critical Caring: A Feminist Model for Pastoral Psychology*. Louisville, Ky.: Westminster/John Knox Press.

Doehring, Carrie. 1992. "Developing Models of Feminist Pastoral Counseling." *Journal of Pastoral Care* 46, no. 1 (spring 1992): 23–31.

Geertz, Clifford. 1973. *The Interpretation of Cultures.* New York: Basic Books.

Gerkin, Charles V. 1973; 1984. *The Living Human Document: Revisioning Pastoral Counseling in a Hermeneutical Mode.* Nashville: Abingdon Press.

Glaz, Maxine. 1991a. "A New Pastoral Understanding of Women." In *Women in Travail and Transition: A New Pastoral Care,* edited by Maxine Glaz and Jeanne Stevenson Moessner, 11–32. Minneapolis: Fortress Press.

———. 1991b. "Reconstructing the Pastoral Care of Women." *Second Opinion* 17, no. 2 (October 1991): 94–107.

Graham, Larry Kent. 1992. *Care of Persons, Care of Worlds: A Psychosystems Approach to Pastoral Care and Counseling.* Nashville: Abingdon Press.

Holifield, E. Brooks. 1983. *A History of Pastoral Care in America: From Salvation to Self-Realization.* Nashville: Abingdon Press.

Hollies, Linda H., ed. 1992. *WomanistCare: How to Tend the Souls of Women.* Joliet, Ill.: Woman to Woman Ministries.

hooks, bell. 1984. *Feminist Theory: From Margin to Center.* Boston: South End Press.

Hough, Joseph C., Jr., and Barbara Wheeler, eds. 1988. *Beyond Clericalism: The Congregation as a Focus for Theological Education,* 103–118. Atlanta: Scholars Press.

Justes, Emma J. 1985. "Women." In *Clinical Handbook of Pastoral Counseling,* edited by Robert J. Wicks, Richard D. Parsons and Donald E. Capps, 279–299. New York: Paulist Press.

Keller, Catherine. 1986. *From a Broken Web: Separatism, Sexism, and Self.* Boston: Beacon Press.

Liebert, Elizabeth. 1992. *Changing Life Patterns: Adult Development in Spiritual Direction.* Mahwah, N.J.: Paulist Press.

Miller-McLemore, Bonnie J. 1994. *Also a Mother: Work and Family as Theological Dilemma.* Nashville: Abingdon Press.

Neuger, Christie Cozad. 1992. "Feminist Pastoral Theology and Pastoral Counseling: A Work in Progress." *Journal of Pastoral Theology* 2 (summer 1992): 35–57.

Poling, James Newton. 1991. *The Abuse of Power: A Theological Problem.* Nashville: Abingdon Press.

Rogers, Carl R. 1942. *Counseling and Psychotherapy.* Boston: Houghton Mifflin Co.

Saussy, Carroll. 1991. *God Images and Self Esteem: Empowering Women in a Patriarchal Society.* Louisville, Ky.: Westminster/John Knox Press.

Smith, Archie, Jr. 1982. *The Relational Self: Ethics and Therapy from a Black Church Perspective*. Nashville: Abingdon Press.

Townes, Emilie M. 1993. *A Troubling in My Soul: Womanist Perspectives on Evil and Suffering*. Maryknoll, N.Y.: Orbis Books, 1993.

Wicks, Robert J., and Barry K. Estadt, eds. 1993. *Pastoral Counseling in a Global Church: Voices from the Field*. Maryknoll, N.Y.: Orbis Books.

Wimberly, Edward P. 1979. *Pastoral Care in the Black Church*. Nashville: Abingdon Press.

# 2

# Female-Friendly Pastoral Care

CAROLYN STAHL BOHLER
*United Theological Seminary*

To be female-friendly in our caring requires a deep awareness of how it is to be a woman in our current culture. It often requires naming cultural assumptions or biases for females, so that they do not see their situations from only their own individual experiences. Pastoral care that is female-friendly does not hurt women: It does not leave emotional scars in its attempt to alter family dynamics, for example. Care includes preventive measures such as providing a theology, from nursery education onward, that teaches equality of females and males and responsibility to use our God-given freedom wisely. Female-friendly pastoral care is simultaneously male-friendly. This chapter focuses on females; attention to particular effects of pastoral care upon males is needed—that belongs in a different book. Care that is biased for either gender hurts both and is certainly not preventive care for the long haul. Males are hurt when gender assumptions are made about females, just as males are restricted by stereotypes or prejudiced assumptions about males.

Much of feminist theology and psychology initially concentrated on critique; it had to, to grasp what it was that created pain or was just plain wrong. After more than two decades of critique, we have gradually gained more of a sense of what to do—feminist *constructive* theory and practice is now being proposed and implemented. In this chapter, I provide twelve suggestions for what to do to be female-friendly in pastoral caregiving. Ten are guidelines for what to do in counseling itself. The last two are preventive care measures. The goal is for all persons in the church to receive care that is given with compassion and without blame.

One way to think of female-friendly pastoral care is to consider the difference between "peace" and "peace with justice." During the last decade

27

this distinction has been made by denominational bodies as we have attended to world problems. We have recognized that it is not sufficient to stop wars. The goal is to have justice for all persons. To insist that current fighting stop, when that halt means the continuance of gross injustice for a segment of the population, is to conclude that one segment of the population should sacrifice its own rights to justice. Peace with justice implies a resolution of injustices, a reordering of society on a more just foundation for all.

When families seek out pastoral care, they have often been in upheaval for a while. They are likely to be grateful for any kind of peace. If they can just make it through the particular crisis or life stage apparently intact, they may consider the counseling helpful. However, that new stability may be at the expense of an individual's (perhaps mother's) self-esteem (if that one shoulders blame for the way things were). Or, one person may make major changes without other family members making equally large behavioral changes. Female-friendly care is likened to the goal of "peace with justice," for no one person bears the burden of blame or takes an unfair percentage of responsibility for change. Along with the new resolution to the conflict, there is an increase of justice in the family itself. All know it.

Just as women had critiqued psychoanalytic and humanistic psychotherapies in the 1970s (Bardwick 1971; Franks and Burtle 1974; Rizzuto 1979; Strouse 1974; Williams 1974), over the past decade women family therapists began to notice gender biases in the therapy they were practicing, and these therapists began to seek to correct those biases (Walters et al., 1988; McGoldrick, Anderson, Walsh, 1989). Many of the suggestions in this chapter are based on critiques and suggestions made by these family therapists (and informed by the critiques of the prior decade). Because pastoral care so rarely consists of formal counseling, and even more seldom includes the luxury of whole families in counseling, I am making my recommendations for pastoral care broadly conceived. After choir practice, a father may ask the pastor to talk with his wife about the way their daughter is behaving. The pastor may never actually get the whole family together to talk (although that would be advisable), but *how* he responds to the initial cry for help from the father could be friendly to all members of the family, or it could be gender-biased.

## GUIDELINES FOR COUNSELING

### 1. Listen!

Listening to a person, hearing what she is saying, is an ability that takes sincere effort. To listen requires that we move our own assumptions out of the way.

A forty-year-old student, the mother of two teenagers, was talking with a fellow student in a counseling course who was specifically assigned to "listen to her." She explained that she was three months pregnant and greatly worried about her own health and the health of the future child. She had recently consulted with various professionals, all of whom verbalized concern about everyone in her family except her. They were worried about the adjustment of the older children and the effect of another baby on her husband's work, for example. She was shaken, fearful, angry, resentful, sad, and confused. She shared her vulnerability—even her fear of dying. The "listening" student asked whether he might pray *for her,* and she agreed. They closed their eyes, and she heard him start praying using these words, "Lord, help this baby, in this mother's womb." By the end of the prayer, the woman almost screamed. She was betrayed again. The student, who had been given the task of listening to her, did not hear her at all. His prayer showed concern for the baby, but he never mentioned the panicked mother who had already felt unheard by others and who was quite fearful for her own health and even life. After the prayer, this woman, vulnerable as she was, cared enough for the fellow student (and any other women with whom he might pray) to explain the great error the student had just made. Stunned, he realized he had not listened to her at all—he had projected *his* interests, ideas, and longings onto this woman whom he had objectified and reduced to a "pregnant woman."

Elizabeth Bernstein and Carol Gilligan comment that "fairness and listening are not concepts that are typically associated with each other. To be treated fairly is commonly viewed as a right; to be listened to, a wish or a need." Yet the authors, referring to their research, point out that "fairness and listening appear to be intimately related concepts" (Bernstein and Gilligan 1990, 147). The forty-year-old woman above was not listened to. A number of professionals did not hear her. This led her to experience unfairness. It was unfair to ignore her in order to focus solely on the lives of others; *she* was in a state of crisis.

### 2. Expect Inner Conflict between Care for Self and Care for Others

All persons sort out how to care for themselves and the people they love. For females, this sorting process is often accomplished with deep ambivalence. We have internalized a strong need to consider others' desires and interests above our own (Gilligan 1982)—so much that at times we are not sure what we ourselves do desire or want—we are so busy picking up cues from others.

A fifteen-year-old girl explained to her youth pastor that she was shaken up when someone she actually knew, a man in his mid-twenties, developed AIDS. The teenage girl mentioned that she had been having sexual intercourse with her boyfriend for over a year but that they had never taken any precautions for birth control or AIDS prevention. She realized that to care for herself, not to get AIDS and not to get pregnant, would require thinking through how to consider God's role in health and sickness and how to understand the causes for events that happen. She suddenly realized she was not taking responsibility to prevent pregnancy or illness. It dawned on her that she had "sort of blamed God" when people got sick, but, realizing that she and people she knew were acting in ways that easily could lead to diseases (and pregnancy), she began to realize that humans were also causes of events in their own lives.

The youth pastor desperately wanted to help this girl. He wanted her to know that she was just too young to be having sexual intercourse. He wanted simply to tell her to stop. But he knew that she was asking him an even larger question, which, if dealt with properly, could lead to her decision to care for her body more wisely not only through this crisis but also in future years. He named the theme of conflict, helping the girl to state openly her commitments to herself, to others, and even to God. He encouraged her to see that she was not being required to make an "either/or" choice between others and herself; decisions that benefited one also would likely benefit others. The pastor took the girl seriously. Her focus—ambivalence regarding whom to care for—was heard and named.

This theme is reflected by many females in our culture. We need to talk with someone who is willing to hear that ambivalence and appreciate its grip. Discussion of this inner conflict can help the female to recognize her right to consider herself. She may even discover a sense of responsibility (to God) to include her health and desires in her discernment process.[1]

Another woman, who was twenty-two, actually named these questions to the same youth pastor: "Can you be true to yourself without hurting someone else? Where does the responsibility for hurt lie?" This young woman was clear that she wanted to go to graduate school, but that would mean leaving her boyfriend, who was more serious about their relationship's longevity than she was. She did not want to hurt him, but she was also sure that she was going to graduate school. It was not sufficient to applaud her for paying attention to her own wishes. The conflict with which she wrestled had to be taken seriously, heard, named, and pondered, so that she could genuinely process her view of morality.

Pastors may grow weary of facing this ambivalence. It may seem that the female should see more quickly that she needs to consider herself, as well as others, when she makes decisions. Well-meaning pastors may lecture the female about how to think, advising her what to do, or prematurely reassure her that she will choose wisely. These are unfriendly modes of "caring." The female needs to be heard in her ambivalence. She needs to have her conflict respected as long as it endures. *The inner conflict is the "problem" as much as the decision is the "problem."* The challenge for a female may not be the one decision (what sexual behaviors to follow or how to relate to a boyfriend). She may be sorting out her orientation toward that basic internal conflict between care for self and care for others, a conflict that will never go away.

### 3. Expect Resiliency as Well as Despair, Relief as Well as Pain

Just as we pastors need to hear despair and pain, when that is a woman's experience, if we listen, we will hear resilience and relief expressed by women, too. In our rush not to avoid the despair, we may miss the particular woman before us, who is relieved or feeling freed and who now wants from us only a confirmation of her experience.

Imagine a particular woman who is in pain; she is one of many who was abused as a child and assaulted again as an adult. She moved in and out of various relationships until she found—and made—a genuinely healthy one. She has been in that relationship for almost a decade. A year ago she went to her pastor to ask for assistance in facing issues created by the childhood and early adulthood abuse. The pastor made a counseling referral to a professional therapist, and the woman has been receiving a good deal of help. However, the woman continues to talk occasionally with the pastor. Every now and then the pastor feels impatient, wondering how long this process of healing will take. The pastor thinks, at times, that the woman, currently in a healthy relationship, should just get on with her life and appreciate her current joy. A female-friendly pastor needs to remind herself or himself that healing takes time. This woman still has a soul-tugging need that requires her to keep working to heal long-buried hurt. While healing can and does occur, it often takes a long time. Pastors' patience is required.[2]

Now imagine another particular woman whose resilience after a crisis surprises us. She is relieved, freed. It is important *not* to impose the expectation of despair or pain onto this woman if that is not her experience. Beth Ann Estock points out that although many women experience grief with a hysterectomy, some experience relief. Likewise, numerous women experience, as their dominant emotion after an abortion, relief. Yet, given the propagandistic literature, one might be led to believe that loss or regret is the only response. If a woman expresses a mild sense of loss, some regret, and a desire for ritual closure to a crisis such as a hysterectomy, abortion, mastectomy, divorce, or abuse, the female-friendly pastoral caregiver needs to take that woman seriously with her stated experience. It is horrible to be relieved of a burden, only to have supposed caregivers tell you that you must feel remorse, guilt, pain, or grief over that for which you do feel relief.

One woman receives a "promotion" at work and is excited. It is just what she has wanted. Another is "depressed," anxious not about her ability but about whether she really wants that new job, for she likes what she is doing. Our culture presses her to want to keep "climbing ladders," never to be satisfied. Something is wrong, we often think, if she is content. Clearly a pastoral caregiver is remiss if he or she decides in advance a particular woman's response to a promotion. Whether a woman faces a promotion or a crisis involving her body, a spectrum of emotions could be felt.

### 4. Balance Personal Responsibility with Systems' Influences

If the youth pastor of the teenager described above *only* tells the girl that she must immediately either stop having sexual intercourse (and other risky ways of touching) or use a condom and birth control, that pastor is thinking too individualistically, not taking into consideration the girl's context. The pastor is correct to be alarmed and would be offering wise, important, advice, but if that is all the pastor does, it is not enough. The girl is in a *relationship* with her boyfriend; he needs to be counseled too. She is in a *relationship* with her parents. They, as well, need to be the focus of the youth pastor's attention. In fact, the youth group and the church itself are systems in which this girl is greatly affected. All these systems need to be attended to, for these sets of people give her a variety of mixed messages that help to maintain her current behavior.

The girl may hear in church that Mary submitted to God's will, and she may come to believe, as many women have, that she should be passive. She may watch and hear older people, concluding that they don't have or don't enjoy sex, so she had better get it when she's young.[3] She may figure out that males' opinions often count more than females', especially regarding contraceptive decisions, as she talks with her girlfriends (Gerrard, in Kelley 1987). She may observe that males have more authority: What they say in school and church classes seems to be taken more seriously than the voices of females. She may actually have been told that males cannot control themselves sexually. Sexuality may have been so equated with intercourse that she doesn't realize there are other ways to touch intimately that do not jeopardize health or risk pregnancy. She no doubt has heard mixed messages about who is responsible for initiating certain sexual behaviors.

The youth pastor needs to name the possible misconceptions (clarifying the facts) and to point out the systems and gender issues, so that the girl does not believe that she is alone in her situation. It is so easy, even today, for a girl to blame only herself and to be unaware of the huge resistance on the part of others to a change in *her* behavior. In caring for the girl, the youth pastor will need to consider the resistance the girl will face in taking his advice. It is not enough to tell her what to do, that resistance must be considered simultaneously. If she is treated only as an individual, given advice, and then does not follow that advice, not only is she in danger of acquiring AIDS (or other illnesses) and of becoming pregnant. She is also likely to feel worse about herself because she did not implement the pastor's advice. She needs to be aware of and know that the pastor recognizes the huge pressure she is pushing against as she claims her voice, values, and behaviors. She certainly could be aided if the pastor talked with the youth group and the whole congregation about issues of sexuality, power, authority, and gender bias (Brown and Bohn 1990; Countryman 1988; Heyward 1989; Washington 1987; McFague 1993; and Bohler, *Stand,* 1990).

Of course, this particular young woman cannot wait for her systems to change before she begins to protect herself. Her context should be transformed; it is currently setting her up to be hurt. However, right now *she* must be transformed, whether anything else changes or not. The urgency of the individual behavior must be challenged while the seriousness of the context is addressed by the pastor and the individual.

Cyclical causation, popularized through family systems therapeutic theories and methods, has been very helpful for seeing how individuals are embedded within their systems. Rather than saying to person X that her talkativeness causes person Y's quietness (or to person Y that her quietness causes X's talkativeness), X and Y are seen as participating in a cycle of behavior. One's quietness sets the stage for the other's talking; simultaneously, the talkativeness sets the stage for the quietude. Neither is the cause of the other's behavior. The two work together, *equally* maintaining their set of behaviors. This analysis has been helpful to understand all sorts of connected behaviors. "Enabling" has been a popularized aspect of this analysis. People (often women) will announce that they are "enablers," meaning that they help to maintain the cycle of their spouse's (or friend's) drug addiction, or addiction to gambling, eating, or even abuse. Those who make such announcements are seeing themselves in a system and taking responsibility, even blame, for its continuance.

There are drawbacks, however, to this strict systemic model. We see this through the lens of a case study reported by a seminary student. A seventy-year-old woman is currently being abused by her husband. She had been married thirty years to a man to whom she felt equal and who treated her with respect. She is alarmed and dumbfounded by the growing mistreatment by her second husband, to whom she has been married for eight years. She tries to please him, so that he does not become angry. Nothing she does will placate him. He has begun to attack her physically when he gets irritated. Afterward he becomes outwardly remorseful. She is ashamed to get help, then grateful for his many attempts at wooing her back toward trusting and loving him. The cycle of tension, abuse, and remorse continues.[4]

Thinking only at the level of family systems neglects both the individual and the *larger* systems, which are components of the family's context. To say that this woman and her husband are *equally* responsible for this cycle ignores many facts. She may "maintain" the cycle, but the consequences of her stopping the cycle are drastically different for her than his stopping the cycle would be for him.

Imagine a ride at an amusement park in which everyone stands against a circular wall. The lever is pulled. As the machine spins, all stay pushed out against the wall because of centrifugal force. The ride goes around and around. We could say that anyone can get out of the circle by stopping the ride and getting off. (That is, intervention can occur at any point in the cycle.) However, in our society, each person is not given equal access to the machine's lever. Some, often women, are in greater danger than others if they leave their position. Many would risk their safety or make themselves vulnerable to harsh economic or relational consequences.

In the case of the seventy-year-old woman and her husband, the family systems cycle analysis misses a major fact: There is not equal power between the participants in the cycle. She knows that; she was widowed before. Her husband is quite appreciated in their community. She may have a hard time even being believed, if she seeks help. It is not easy to step off the cycle.

Some pastors are still inclined to ask a woman like this what she is doing to encourage, permit, enable, or accept the abuse. *This line of questioning with its assumptions about enabling must stop.* We pastors need to think con-textually, to consider the family, *and* we must also think about the *larger* contexts, bigger than families—churches, cultural messages, economic sys-tems—which "enable" the male, in this case, to continue his behavior unchecked.

If the pastor were to see the family cycle of behaviors, but *also* saw the gender power differential in the church and community, the pastor could name it. In this way the woman is not left wondering why (in her mind and also in the mind of the pastor) she is inept, unable to follow through. The pastor can lead the woman to resources, so that she can be prepared for a strong and wise departure, if or when she chooses that. The pastor could try to assist the husband to seek counseling and healing too.[5]

### 5. Take Everything into Account

To take everything into account is clearly impossible, but this suggestion is stated boldly so as to force us pastors to think. Larry Graham has shown in his work *Care of Persons, Care of Worlds* (1992) how what he calls a "psychosystems" approach to pastoral care functions. One does not attend just to the individual or to the family system but also to the community and even the environment. In order to be female-friendly, we think of as many factors as possible that might bear on the situation. This was evidenced in the situation above, with the older woman and her husband. The pastor had to move outside an analysis of the individual and of the family system to see a picture large enough to grasp how interventions could be made.

I observed family systems counseling, watching (through a one-way mirror) a family that consisted of a mother, a preteen boy, and two smaller children. They lived in a housing project that was considered by many, including the mother, to be unsafe. She worked an afternoon-evening shift, so she required her children to come directly home from school and stay inside the two-bedroom apartment until she arrived home at nine. It was out of love that she was afraid to let her children step outside their front door. The counselor tried a variety of behavioral and family systemic approaches to enable the children to cooperate more fully during their time at home. The counselor did occasionally ask the mother whether there was any possibility of a move. In fact, one reason the mother was working so hard was that she was trying to move to a place that would be safer.

However, if the counselor "took everything into account," it would be impossible just to talk and work at the level of the family. To be effective, it would be imperative to find out more about the housing project and to act politically and socially to make a safer environment. It is important to name the dilemma for the family, which is not only the children and how they get along but is also political. Another step is to take action, as a pastoral caregiver, on a broader scale.

One woman, who is a church pastor, indicates that she experiences this frustrating situation on a regular basis in her pastoral ministry. She feels powerless to alter the situation. A counselor at a counseling center may feel all the more isolated from the community. However, the individual cannot be counseled effectively unless the context is considered. If the context is named and considered a significant factor in the situation, at least the "problem," and potentially the "solution," is reframed. However, if the pastor actually gets involved in trying to bring about contextual improvement, how much more effective!

Pastoral care that stays only at the level of thinking about individuals and families is not enough. Caregivers who are female-friendly will have to be as committed to systems analysis and transformations as we are to helping individuals and families within those systems. Pastoral caregivers do not need to become social workers. But we can actually talk to social workers, meet with housing authorities, and write to politicians. A good medical doctor refers patients to a specialist but also works with the specialist for treatment. We can connect our neighborhood involvement with our counseling.

To actually manage to get safer dwellings, by working for better employment practices and gun control laws, by reducing racism, and by making changes in welfare and tax laws, would be female-friendly pastoral care. The changes would definitely help this family, for example. However, I maintain that our *working* for the changes is also therapeutic for the family, even before the results are evidenced. To tell them that they do have some capacity to change their situation but also that they do have realistic limits, based on their context, is one thing. To be visibly working to expand those very limits in their context exemplifies not only our concern but our conviction in that therapeutic position.

A congregation in Albuquerque, New Mexico, decided that to care for the women in its midst who were being physically and emotionally damaged by chemicals in their workplace, the congregation would have to work to change the laws and heighten public awareness of the hazards.[6] They provided female-friendly pastoral care that was not focused upon only one woman or family but literally changed the lives of hundreds of women. The concern *began* with the pain of several women, but this pain was not met with the expectation that the cure was private. Societal change was the answer. Instead of being blamed for their pain, the women were empowered to speak up and to act.

### 6. Observe and Expand Divine Images

During the past fifteen years a large number of books have called us to challenge the metaphors that we use for the Deity (Christ and Plaskow 1979; Daly 1973; Jones 1987; McFague 1982; Morton 1985). Space does not permit a lengthy explanation of this important female-friendly dimension of pastoral care. I simply want to mention three reasons that pastoral caregivers need to notice and expand metaphors for the Deity used by parishioners.

First, these metaphors give a clue to the understanding of God's power and human responsibility which is assumed. If the person prays to an "Almighty Heavenly Father" and then proceeds to ask for all sorts of things, it could be that her "god" is unconsciously Magic Wand. She wants God to have all the power and to understand herself as having only the responsibility of waving the wand. Pastoral care can make that unspoken divine image explicit, teasing out her beliefs about power and responsibility. It may be that God as Jazz Band Leader would better fit the woman's experience. This new metaphor would be a good "fit" if she feels responsibility for the "music" of her life, yet also believes there is a "Leader" who is responsive to every note she makes and who makes suggestions for the next. The shift in divine metaphor may help her to take more responsibility and actually affect her behavior.

Second, as Valerie DeMarinis (1993), Carroll Saussy (1991), Annie Imbens and Ineke Jonker (1992), Carolyn Bohler (*Prayer*, 1990), and others have demonstrated, how females conceive of the Deity affects their self-esteem. DeMarinis tells the story of Heather and Henry, six-year-old twins, who are asked to draw "a picture of God" in their church school class. God had been described in the Sunday school class as "Father and Provider," so Henry's picture, which resembled their father's, was applauded, while Heather's, which showed God to have two faces, one male and the other female, received a large red-penned X over the whole paper. Her parents acted promptly when they observed the effect on Heather. They all became involved in seven months of therapy to resolve some of the effects of this crisis (1993, 67–71). Seldom do most of us consider counseling in such a matter. However, virtually every female and male in our culture is affected by gender-biased assumptions about the image of the Deity. Males and females are all wounded or burdened by that bias.

The pastoral caregiver does not need to get into "theological" or so-called "feminist" discussions about metaphors for the Deity to help people. He or she can notice what metaphors the women do use. Then, the caregiver can ask about the assumptions of God's power implicit in the metaphor. If God is "Lord," how does the woman "divide up" responsibility and power between Lord and herself? If God is Justice Maker or Infinite Comforter, what does that imply for *her* self-esteem? We can *explore* metaphors that would be congruent with the woman's faith and her experience as a female. After the exploration, the woman could choose to reclaim her original images, but she would have thought through the consequences of those choices.

The exhilaration when a "Yes!" metaphor emerges for a woman is marvelous to witness. A parishioner-friend who was diabetic and I held intense dialogue for four years as she faced medical emergencies such as eye surgeries and the amputation of a leg. She telephoned me one day with a metaphor that aptly captured God's power and influence in her life. She had felt that her faith should allow her to move past limits, yet the medical doctors kept telling her to face limits. Her metaphor for the Deity: Divine Physical Therapist. Her human physical therapist knew more intimately than any human what were her actual limits, yet helped her to push those as far as possible. God would do likewise, but knew her even more intimately. She came up with an image of God she could believe in, a God to whom she could pray only after searching for several years. It was not just theological discussions about what God could and could not do that helped; her greatest discovery was a metaphor that *pictured* that God for her. This woman currently employs many divine metaphors and keeps adding them as she lives and prays, for they give richness and vibrancy to her prayer life.

The female-unfriendly pastoral caregiver is oblivious to divine metaphors or imposes divine metaphors on women, intentionally or unintentionally. The female-friendly caregiver is ever attentive to see and gently expand girls' and women's understandings of the Deity and to help them find what metaphors fit their understanding of God.

### 7. Evoke the Authority of Females

Does the pastor pray for a care seeker? Or does the pastor ask the care seeker how she experiences the Deity? Does the caregiver ask questions and give advice? Or does he or she reflect what the care seeker says, empathically entering into the frame of reference of the speaker? These options convey different views of the pastor's authority. Praying for someone claims one's own authority as pastor, just as advice-giving and questioning keeps the authority with the caregiver. Focusing upon the female's way of experiencing and relating to God recognizes her authority in spiritual matters. Hearing *her* validates her authority.

Edward Wimberly's book *Prayer in Pastoral Counseling* (1990) has been helpful to students in my Introduction to Pastoral Counseling course as well as courses that focus on prayer. In the examples he provides in his book, he does not only pray with people, when that seems appropriate, but also has "prayer conversations" before praying, to discuss the meaning and desire to pray. By discussing prayer, rather than just leaping in to "give" one, Wimberly moves toward enabling parishioners to experience their own authority. He is respecting their authority, not using his to intrude upon theirs. When, as happened once in the cases he presents, a woman decided to pray aloud at the end of his prayer, Wimberly rejoiced—his authority was not threatened but seemed to be shared with hers.

However, DeMarinis's *Critical Caring* (1993) suggests another step that can be made with regard to evoking authority in female care seekers. DeMarinis manages to get her clients to share how *they* relate to the Deity, whether that is through writing poetry, sewing, dancing, praying, or singing. DeMarinis, as the counselor in her book's case illustrations, uses her authority to evoke the authority of the females. Based on the clients' ways of relating to the Spiritual Presence, she helps them to create rituals, poems, prayers, fabrics, or whatever is relevant as part of the therapy process itself. This practice avoids "offering" prayer or even asking the care seeker to "pray." It focuses upon the spirituality *of the seeker,* conveying the importance of the seeker's authority.

If the pastoral caregiver sees herself as an "archaeologist," searching for a buried treasure, then she may dig with question after question, assuming the authority of one who will find the treasure and present it to the parishioner.[7] The authority is in the hands of the pastor. If the caregiver sees himself as a "solace provider," one who needs to convince the care seeker that "things will be all right," or that "God will take care," that is an enormous weight of authority on the caregiver's shoulders.

However, if the pastoral caregiver is a "truthful, accurate mirror," then the pastor gives back all of what he sees—potentials and limitations. No reassurance, if the situation is ambiguous; no advice, when the decision is the woman's to make; no question, when it is, after all, the seeker who is questioning. Rather, there is a reflection of what is made obvious. For example, let us say that after a woman explains her situation, I respond to her with this reflection:

> You are very worried about the outcome of your marriage. You and your husband have stayed together for over twenty years, though you realize you don't really enjoy each other's company. You are both incredibly devoted to your children. Life is orderly, neat. Your futures are planned, together. But you want intimacy—you want a friend. You would like for me to tell you what to do, so you won't have to face this horrible in-between state of not knowing. Yet, deep inside, you know that this decision and how to talk with your husband is yours (with God's help). I see you as caring, lonely, and as painfully aware of your emptiness.

My response is one that evokes authority in the woman. I do not take authority from her, nor assume that I have it to give her. She has it. I name it.

## 8. Consider Talking with Family Members Separately as well as Together

Family systems theory and my own verification in practice convinced me a long time ago that we should not create a triangle in which one member of a couple feels more comfortable talking with us than she or he does with her or his partner. Our task is solely to enable the two to talk with each other. They can best do that if we frustrate their avoidance of talking with each other. By insisting upon talking with couples together, we are careful not to build an alliance with one member of the couple who feels a special relationship with us which the other does not share. Also, each person sees us relating to the other; each is guaranteed that we are being fair.

However, women in classes have persuaded me that, while systems theory reasoning is plausible *most* of the time, sometimes women (and men) need to be able to talk with the pastor privately. Sometimes women can't speak when their husbands (or friends) are present.

If a man has physical, economic, social, or emotional control over a woman, he may talk calmly to the woman in front of the counselor but go home and return to abusive behavior. He may make the woman "pay" for what she said in the counseling. To assume that they have to learn to talk with each other (not to me) is to make the prior assumption that they are each free to do that without fear of the consequences.

This factor is at work not just with couples but also with parents and children. When we are working with an adolescent who is being abused at home, if we insist upon seeing the family together, our very counseling may contribute to the adolescent's pain. The family is made to look good, for they are getting help, yet behavior during counseling is guarded, for fear of revelation of the abuse.

I realize that most pastors do not have time or expertise to see many families in formal counseling. However, they do become involved in short-term counseling, whether it is premarriage preparation or counseling at a time of crisis. To name the natural possibility of seeing people separately at the beginning of that counseling makes any request they may make for an individual session not seem too unusual or too threatening.

It is not just with abuse that separate sessions may be needed. Some women have become so "tongue-tied" in their relationships that they need much silence and private space to gather their words. They need to be heard before they can be expected to speak.

Still other women have secrets that they have never told: maternity issues (genetic paternity, abortions, adoptions), their own genetic identity, early childhood traumas, even longings never shared. Many of these women want to tell, eventually. They want to tell someone; the pastor may be that someone. Not seeing the women (or men) alone may be a barrier to that speech.

We still need to avoid becoming too connected with one member of a family; also, we should not carry messages to other members that should be communicated by the speaker. Yet we need to stay alert to the chance that private talk may be therapeutic.

### 9. Use Imagery and Metaphors Intentionally in Counseling

Even though verbal ability is a sex difference in our culture, with females from an early age scoring higher than males (Macoby and Jacklin 1974, 351), women often experience themselves at a loss verbally with men, especially in counseling. It can be that a woman has "lost" many so-called "logical" arguments, so that she has become pessimistic about one more in front of the caregiver. Or she may have a hard time claiming her right or authority to speak (Bohler, *Stand,* 1990).

It is very useful to shift modes of expression in the counseling, to use imagery more intentionally. Peggy Papp capitalizes on this in what she calls "couples choreography" (Papp 1983, 142–164). She asks each member of a couple to have a fantasy of the other member, then to include themselves in that fantasy. They share these images, even acting them out at times. For example, one spouse may imagine the other as calling for help in the middle of a swimming pool. When asked to include himself or herself in the image, that one says he or she is emptying the pool with a teaspoon! This image is much stronger than simply saying that he or she feels "unhelpful." The couple, usually through laughter and tears, grasp much more about the dynamics of their relationship than mere talk would provide. They have shifted to a different mode of communication.

When we hear a parishioner comment that he feels as if he has lost his wife to a "lover," as she is becoming "overly involved" in church activities, it is just as important to explore the husband's use of the metaphor "lover" as it is to check out the wife's time involvement and motivations for church work. The couple's relationship with each other and with the church is in tension—the metaphors they use to conceive of their tension can be used creatively to find viable resolutions.

My teaching at seminary started simultaneously with my learning how to mother an infant. Especially after our second child was born, at times I resented the amount of time and energy my mothering was taking from my teaching. I had seen myself as a "Teacher who Mothers." Some students helped me to talk through my feelings, and lo and behold, a different metaphor emerged: I became a "Mother who Teaches." This made quite a difference in my attitude toward both important dimensions of my life. I probably spent the same amount of time mothering and teaching as before, but my attitude toward both altered.

### 10. Be Careful Not to Blame the Female or to Overly "Protect" the Male

These cautions seem separate, but the two errors are often practiced in counseling as opposite sides of the same coin. For example, family systems therapists have used as a general rule for two decades: "Challenge the pursuer; invite in the one who distances" (Walters et al. 1988, 21) When one person pursues the other, to talk, to be present, to be involved with the children, or to attend church, and the other stays at a distance, away, resisting the involvement, it is likely that the "pursuer" is the more motivated for relational change. The pursuer, too, has more likely been the female (in a male-female relationship). If the pursuer is told she is to stop the pursuit, while the distancer is gently invited to participate more fully, the first is blamed, while the second is overly protected. The sin of commission is seen as greater than the sin of omission.

Often it is the woman in a relationship who wants counseling. She is even willing at times to be called the "identified patient" in order to obtain help. She has often worked very hard to get her partner or family to see the pastor (caregiver). Because she initiates the counseling, seeks change in the family, and may be the most aware of hurting, emotionally, she is willing to see herself as a part of the problem. Thus, it is tempting for the pastor to buy the identification of her "pathology" as the primary problem of the family.

Theorists and therapists from various schools of psychotherapy have blamed women: Women, according to Sigmund Freud, flee from their femaleness in their desire to obtain a penis, most fulfilled when they finally get one, through the birth of a male child; women, according to Erik Erikson, should take on their biologically based role to protect the planet with arms control, as they are simultaneously attentive to birth control; "mothering objects" should be good enough—not too doting, not too distant, according to object relations therapists. Family systems theory and practice sought to be gender "neutral," because dynamics between people were considered most important. But this approach, too, resulted in unintentional (and sometimes significant) blaming of females (Walters et al. 1988; McGoldrick, Anderson, and Walsh 1989).

Most pastors would not dream of intentionally blaming one member of a family for the whole situation within that family. However, our culture is so attached to female blaming, especially mother blaming, that it takes enormous efforts to wean ourselves from this practice.

For example, Elizabeth Bernstein and Carol Gilligan, who are noted for their interest in the moral development of females, suggest that some teenage girls look to their mothers to model assertiveness with fathers (Bernstein and Gilligan 1990, 25). The researchers observed girls who at age ten were forthright in their opinions become less sure, at least linguistically, by ages twelve to fifteen (Bernstein and Gilligan 1990, 14–15). These researchers want girls to be able to maintain their voices. They encourage adult women to speak up to their husbands and colleagues, as role models for these teenagers. However, never in their essay do the authors suggest that the husbands and men should not objectify the wives and colleagues, or that men need to listen more intently to the women, if they expect their daughters not to relinquish their voices. Here, in a chapter that has the distinct purpose of helping girls, women are subtly blamed. Men are not named as part of the problem, except that women are to speak up to them more strongly. Blame is very subtle, seen to be so natural, that both the women who receive it and those who give it often do not realize that blame has happened.[8]

When females are blamed, in theory or in practice, this is often in conjunction with the assumption that males have a fragile ego that should be protected, although it has never been clear to me why. I am convinced that once we in our society expect as much maturity in males as we do in females, we will be released from the burden of the (untrue) myth of the fragile male ego.

In *The Gift of Sex,* a book that has been helpful to many female-male couples because it sincerely seeks to get Christians to recognize the goodness of sexuality within marriage, the authors explain with great caution that the size of the penis "has little to do with sexual pleasure or satisfaction" (Penner and Penner 1981, 48). However, the authors, Clifford and Joyce Penner, consistently use the word "sloppy" to refer to a woman's PC (pubococcygeus) muscle, after it has been stretched by several childbirths, if the woman has not exercised it "properly" (Penner and Penner 1981, 61–62). Here the male ego is assured, yet the female is subtly blamed for not having "exercised" her "sloppy" muscles after childbirth.

It can be honestly said that the man and the woman can explore together how they can express their sexuality and that they can both be fulfilled, no matter what the size of any parts of their bodies—if they don't blame each other and if they truthfully explore. It can also be said that nothing can be done about leg size, finger size, mouth size, or penis size, but exercises can indeed help strengthen the PC muscle, just as watching one's weight can help adjust one's stomach size.

It is not gender-biased to say that in this case the woman can do something about her pelvic floor muscles. The man cannot do anything about his penis size. That is a fact. It *is* gender-biased to refer to the female muscle as sloppy but to tell the man his organ size is of little importance.

Many other examples can be given in which females are blamed, while males are protected. Patty Davis has shown that women carry a "Burden of Empathy," being expected to have the automatic capacity to empathize with their children, even when the women are in the midst of enormous crises that require a survival level of functioning. Males are seldom *expected* to be so empathic and are not blamed by counselors if they are not. Rather, they might be gently taught how to empathize (Davis 1993, 29–38).

In still another arena, women are often expected to work the "second shift," taking responsibility for the house and child care (Hochschild 1989). If there is a problem with these areas, the woman, the man, and the counselor may all look to the woman, blaming her. The man may be invited to participate more fully, and he is usually complimented when he does.

Similarly, care for elders, which is needed at home more often today since stays at hospitals are less lengthy, is often expected to be provided by a female. A male feels proud of himself if he "helps out"; the female blames herself (and others do, too) if she cannot help as much as she (or others) thinks she should. Clearly these are generalizations. There are many instances when these uncritical assumptions are not made. However, this blaming, protecting/inviting process is still rather prevalent in so-called "caring" environments.

## PREVENTIVE CARE

Whether it is in expanding gender role expectations, conceiving of the Deity in meaningful and healthy ways, considering full contexts with what seem at first to be individual problems, or grasping the inner conflict when faced with decision making, the practice of pastoral care can be female-friendly. However, caregivers could prevent some problems if they were more intentional about education. The two suggestions that follow would be gifts to females (therefore males too) in the congregational context. Although they are presented as "education," they are clearly preventive pastoral care, female-friendly style.

### 11. Think of the Impact on Females
### When You Provide Education in Church

I was expected by the education commission in my church to help a fourth-, fifth-, and sixth-grade Sunday school class that I teach to memorize the "books of the New Testament." It occurred to me that as a way to help them remember the books, we could act out a play in which the books would come alive and talk to each other. I decided to write such a skit, placing it within the dream of a child who was to memorize those books. Within the dream I included the *Gospel of Mary* and the *Gospel of Thomas*, two important gospels that have been discovered and were very crucial to the early Christians but were not included in the canon. Mary and Thomas leave the stage before the end, so as not to confuse the dreaming child, whose Bible does not contain those gospels which "did not make the team" a long time ago.

I had some mild concern about whether anyone would object to education of the children that included extracanonical biblical resources. (I did tell the pastor.) There was not a voice of concern raised. Several people commented that it was good to think about how the Bible was consolidated. The children had fun and took the process of canonization quite naturally—it made sense to them.

One lesson I wanted to teach was that the "Word of God" is a living word, muted or fulfilled by humans. Frankly, I think that educators must convey this, if we are to be female-friendly. Pastors and Sunday school teachers must be honest and courageous to tell the truth—especially about our biblical sources.

Once the children grasp that certain books were chosen to be included in the canon, they can also grasp that certain emphases have been chosen by biblical authors and redactors. For example, it is not unusual to hear a boy or a girl ask why Jesus had only male disciples. There are a variety of ways to answer this. One option is not to answer but to allow the children to come up with ideas as to why we have only male disciples recorded in the Bible. Another is to talk about what it means to be a disciple and who else in the Bible (including women) did follow Jesus. Or we can discuss who it is that *names* the twelve disciples. Certainly Jesus did not say he had "twelve." We do. It is important to pursue all these questions if we are serious about female-friendly pastoring.

### 12. Name Sexuality and Sexual Issues Often and Clearly in the Local Church

The supposed "taboo" regarding the mention of sexuality in church settings hurts females. It is females whose bodies and lives are drastically affected by pregnancy, yet most pastors lull themselves out of seeing the drastic impact of this fact. I have at times wondered how fast our secular laws and our behavior on sexual matters would alter if, at the moment of the conception of a fetus, the male who was involved would grow a permanent P (for parent) on his forehead and would be required to provide complete child care and support for the next twenty years, or be considered a criminal if he did something to stop the conception from becoming a baby.

I do not consider a reversal of the current situation any solution at all. This scenario would obviously be ludicrous, but so is the way things are now. Many a woman is abandoned, after she becomes pregnant, and if she considers an abortion, some, even sometimes those who abandon her, consider her a criminal. Yet this same society that publicly often insists that females bear their children, and care for them, also creates situations in which the female must provide the financial support for herself and the children or be ridiculed for being on welfare.

Pamela Couture shows how our secular—and religious—culture encourages male responsibility for financial support, as long as the male is in the household. But whenever he chooses to leave, or never to join the mother and child, the female is expected to take sole care of herself and the child (Couture 1991, 27–48).

Several years ago I gave a lecture to about five hundred clergy and laity at the beginning of a training event in southern Ohio. I was told to speak to the topic, "What ministers can do to teach sexuality education in the local church." Unfortunately, contrary to my expectations, almost none of those who attended the event, which was primarily for training volunteers to do a variety of jobs in their local churches, knew what my topic would be before they arrived. When I completed my talk there was utter silence. In my mind, I scanned what I had said, wondering what had offended people.

I led one of the workshops that followed the lecture. The pastors and the laity who dared to attend that workshop were enormously helpful in getting me to realize the depth of fear regarding mentioning sexuality in churches. However, they did believe that sexuality must be discussed and healthy sexuality taught. In fact, three pastors in that group had remorse over having not said anything to a pregnant teenager in each of their current congregations. One verbalized his intent to provide sexuality education in his church—as soon as he was informed that he would be reappointed (in the United Methodist system). The others laughed in agreement.

What kind of female-unfriendliness is this? To know the consequences of an avoidance to be misery for a teenage girl and perhaps her offspring, yet to continue in that avoidance, is *deplorable*.

Silence in the area of sexuality is unfriendliness. It is maintaining oppression and pain; it is gender-biased.

Male and female clergy can be "female-friendly" in their preventive and attentive caregiving. Each of the twelve suggestions given here would benefit all persons in relationships, precisely because if followed, these suggestions lead to justice. Justice is healthy for all in a system.

It has been humbling for me to have my eyes opened by therapists, students, and theorists who have shown me that what I thought was good pastoral care was not good enough—it was gender-biased. (Even as I tried to be fair, I hurt the female.) I invite the reader to be willing to be humbled through implementing these suggestions. I also invite you, the reader, to stay *alert*, to watch yourself as you care, to observe assumptions or habitual patterns, ever asking yourself whether you have been blinded in any way. You can open the eyes of others.

## NOTES

1. Gilligan's vintage work (1982) shows the recurrent theme of conflict between attention to others and self. She demonstrates a three-stage process that begins with attention to survival, then care of others, and, finally, if a female matures to this level ethically, inclusion of self in the sense of justice.

2. Chapter 3, "Karen: Survivor of Sexual Violence," in Poling, *The Abuse of Power*, provides a story that gives a sense of the length of time needed for healing. Many resources for the healing person were needed: therapist, small group at church, pastor, etc. See also chap. 6 in DeMarinis (1993) for an outstanding presentation of a case that includes the help of a priest, Our Lady of Guadalupe, and a Mexican-American consultant, as well as a pastoral psychotherapist.

3. A junior high student actually mentioned to me that she had held this opinion, prior to a sexuality education retreat that she had just completed. After the retreat, she knew differently and was relieved that she did not need to rush her sexual activity.

4. Resources for domestic violence can be found at many local shelters. Two books especially for pastors are Rita-Lou Clarke, *Pastoral Care of Battered Women* (1986), and Carol J. Adams, *Woman-Battering* (1994).

5. More counseling centers are succeeding in providing therapy for perpetrators. See Poling, *The Abuse of Power*.

6. This project is now a part of the South West Organizing Project, 211 10th St. SW, Albuquerque, New Mexico, 81102, which publishes a newsletter, *Voces Unides*.

7. This example derives from a teaching experience in which a student asked question after question, even after our class had encouraged him to try some empathic responses. When he presented a case on audiocassette with fourteen consecutive questions, never responding to the parishioner's answers, I asked the student what image he had of himself. His answer, immediately, was "archaeologist." We all laughed with relief. His method *fit* his metaphor: Dig, dig, dig! He would need to consider his metaphor *before* he could make any alteration in his method.

8. It would be interesting to study whether boys also look to their mothers to stand up to their fathers and whether boys and girls look to their fathers to stand up to their mothers.

## BIBLIOGRAPHY

Adams, Carol J. 1994. *Woman-Battering*. Minneapolis: Fortress Press.

Bardwick, Judith. 1971. *Psychology of Women: A Study of Bio-Cultural Conflicts*. New York: Harper & Row.

Bernstein, Elizabeth, and Carol Gilligan. 1990. "Unfairness and Not Listening." In *Making Connections: The Relational Worlds of Adolescent Girls at Emma Willard School*, edited by Carol Gilligan, Nona Lyons, and Trudy Hanmer, 147. Cambridge: Harvard University Press.

Bohler, Carolyn. 1990. *Prayer on Wings*. San Diego, Calif.: LuraMedia.

———. 1990. *When You Need to Take a Stand*. Louisville, Ky.: Westminster/John Knox Press.

Brown, Joanne Carlsson, and Carole Bohn, eds. 1990. *Christianity, Patriarchy, and Abuse: A Feminist Critique*. New York: Pilgrim Press.

Christ, Carol, and Judith Plaskow. 1979. *Womanspirit Rising: A Feminist Reader in Religion*. San Francisco: Harper & Row.

Clarke, Rita-Lou. 1986. *Pastoral Care of Battered Women.* Philadelphia: Westminster Press.

Countryman, William. 1988. *Dirt, Greed, and Sex: Sexual Ethics in the New Testament and Their Implications for Today.* Philadelphia: Fortress Press.

Couture, Pamela. 1991. *Blessed are the Poor? Women's Poverty, Family Policy, and Practical Theology,* 27–48. Nashville: Abingdon Press.

Daly, Mary. 1973. *Beyond God the Father: Toward a Philosophy of Women's Liberation.* Boston: Beacon Press.

Davis, Patty. 1993. "Women and the Burden of Empathy." *Journal of Pastoral Theology* 3 (1993): 29–38.

DeMarinis, Valerie M. 1993. *Critical Caring: A Feminist Model for Pastoral Psychology.* Louisville, Ky.: Westminster/John Knox Press.

Franks, Violet, and Vasanti Burtle. 1974. *Women in Therapy: New Psychotherapies for a Changing Society.* New York: Brunner/Mazel.

Gerrard, Meg. 1987. "Emotional and Cognitive Barriers to Effective Contraception: Are Males and Females Really Different?" In *Females, Males, and Sexuality: Theories and Research,* edited by Kathryn Kelley, 237. Albany: State University of New York Press.

Gilligan, Carol. 1982. *In a Different Voice: Psychological Theory and Women's Development.* Cambridge: Harvard University Press.

Graham, Larry Kent. 1992. *Care of Persons, Care of Worlds: A Psychosystems Approach to Pastoral Care and Counseling.* Nashville: Abingdon.

Heyward, Carter. 1989. *Touching Our Strength: The Erotic as Power and the Love of God.* San Francisco: Harper & Row.

Hochschild, Arlie. 1989. *The Second Shift: Working Parents and the Revolution at Home.* New York: Viking.

Imbens, Annie, and Ineke Jonker. 1992. *Christianity and Incest.* Minneapolis: Fortress Press.

Jones, Major J. 1987. *The Color of God: The Concept of God in Afro-American Thought.* Macon, Ga.: Mercer University Press.

Macoby, Eleanor Emmons, and Carol Nagy Jacklin. 1974. *The Psychology of Sex Differences.* Stanford, Calif.: Stanford University Press.

McFague, Sallie. 1993. *The Body of God: An Ecological Theology.* Minneapolis: Fortress Press.

———. 1982. *Metaphorical Theology: Models of God in Religious Language.* Philadelphia: Fortress Press.

McGoldrick, Monica; Carol Anderson; and Froma Walsh, eds. 1989. *Women in Families: A Framework for Family Therapy.* New York: W. W. Norton & Co.

Morton, Nelle. 1985. *The Journey Is Home.* Boston: Beacon Press.

Papp, Peggy. 1983. *The Process of Change.* New York: Guilford Press.

Penner, Clifford, and Joyce Penner. 1981. *The Gift of Sex: A Christian Guide to Sexual Fulfillment.* Waco, Tex.: Word Books.

Poling, James Newton. 1991. *The Abuse of Power: A Theological Problem.* Nashville: Abingdon Press.

Rizzuto, Ana-Maria. 1979. *The Birth of the Living God: A Psychoanalytic Study.* Chicago: University of Chicago Press.

Saussy, Carroll. 1991. *God Images and Self Esteem: Empowering Women in a Patriarchal Society.* Louisville, Ky.: Westminster/John Knox Press.

Strouse, Jean, ed. 1974. *Women and Analysis: Dialogues on Psychoanalytic Views of Femininity.* New York: Grossman Pub.

Walters, Marianne; Betty Carter; Peggy Papp; and Olga Silverstein. 1988. *The Invisible Web: Gender Patterns in Family Relationships.* New York: Guilford Press.

Washington, Mary Helen. 1987. *Invented Lives: Narratives of Black Women 1860–1960.* New York: Doubleday & Co.

Williams, Juanita. 1974. *Psychology of Women: Behavior in a Biosocial Context.* New York: W. W. Norton & Co.

Wimberly, Edward P. 1990. *Prayer in Pastoral Counseling: Suffering, Healing, and Discernment.* Louisville, Ky.: Westminster/John Knox Press.

# 3

# The Legacy of the African-American Matriarch: New Perspectives for Pastoral Care

TERESA E. SNORTON

*Crawford Long Hospital, Emory University*

Madeline was a Euro-American woman in her mid-forties, a student in a program of Clinical Pastoral Education (CPE) where I was the supervisor. She had brought for reflection and discussion her pastoral visit with a fifty-year-old African-American woman. Madeline had said more than once during the presentation, "Her faith is so strong." She finally confesses, "I don't know what I could possibly offer her as a chaplain. Her faith in God is so strong!" As an African-American, CPE supervisor, this was not the first time I had heard such a statement.

Pastoral care to African-American women is typically informed by the same conceptual understandings that inform pastoral care to Euro-American women. The latter is theoretically based on traditional pastoral care constructs and contemporary feminist theology and theory. Recent theorists and theologians, particularly those with a womanist perspective, have noted the limitations of such an approach to the African-American woman. The African-American woman's historical reality makes her experiences socially, politically, psychologically, and spiritually different from those of women of European descent in this culture.

Like my womanist sisters, as a pastoral care provider and educator I believe an accurate understanding of the African-American woman's experience is essential to the task of responding responsibly to the pastoral care needs of those women. Of particular concern to me is the appropriate pastoral response to African-American women whose experience has required them to be "strong, persevering, and determined." The sociological concept of matriarch has often been used to describe them. The woman whose entire survival has been dependent on her ability to transcend the difficulties of her life can at first glance appear to have little need for pastoral care, except perhaps just compassion or empathic support. A close study of the

African-American matriarch (both as a person and as a concept) can expand the perspectives of pastoral care providers, in order that they take the next step with these kind of very strong, persevering women—a step closer to their deep spiritual need to be heard, to be valued, to be cared for beyond an admiration of their skill at "holding it together in the face of the worst odds."

## THE CONCEPT OF MATRIARCH

The concept of matriarch to describe the strong African-American female figure was brought into the sociological mainstream by the Moynihan report, officially titled *The Negro Family: The Case for National Action,* authored by Daniel Patrick Moynihan as a part of the investigative processes of President Lyndon Johnson's war on poverty in the mid-1960s. The report, which drew considerable criticism from African-American sociologists and leaders, concluded that the African-American family was more pathological than other (white) families, in part because of a "black matriarchy." This pattern was noted as having a detrimental effect on the black family, because women were dominant, resulting in a further castration of black men and their sense of power. This conclusion was challenged on several points. First, statistical data of the 1960s indicated that the rate of deterioration in the black family (as measured by out-of-wedlock births) was no more than that among white families (Giddings 1984, 326). Second, the conclusion that black men were disempowered by the assumed power of black women was challenged as being myopic, minimizing the impact of racism on black males and erroneously relocating the disenfranchisement of the black male in the black community generally and in the black male-female relationship specifically. Finally, as Paula Giddings writes: "What appeared as matriarchy, many argued, was in reality something else" (Giddings 1984, 327). Giddings, Staples, and others pointed to the many realities that indicate the pervasive lack of power of the African-American woman both in the black community and in culture as a whole. Only recently has the black community been willing to assess honestly the impact of sexism within its own walls, although the exploitation of African-American women has been at the hands of white men, white women, and black men (perhaps in that order in terms of severity).

If the notion of black matriarchy is a myth, as asserted by Robert Staples (Giddings 1984, 327), what then is this phenomenon of the African-American woman who appears to approach the world and her life experiences with a sense of strength? More important, how does this historic legacy of an African-American matriarch influence how the pastoral care world views these women and responds to their needs?

Patricia Hill Collins writes extensively about the "controlling images" used within American culture to describe black women and subsequently to justify racist, sexist, and classist attitudes toward them. She lists four such images: the mammy, the matriarch, the welfare mother, and the Jezebel (Collins 1991, 67ff.). The mammy is the "good" mother, dutifully taking care of other people's (white) children. This nurturing figure (often caricaturized by a hefty, bosomy character in the media) is faithful, caring, and appropriately submissive to and respectful of her employers. Her strength is valued, but only because she is dependent on the benevolence of "her" white family.

On the other side of the spectrum is the controlling image of the matriarch, the "bad" mother, who in her own African-American home wields power, dominates the male (and ultimately drives him away by such dominance), sacrifices for her children to meet their physical needs (but neglects their emotional and socialization needs through her absence). Cheryl Townsend Gilkes reminds us that the emergence of this negative image of the black matriarch coincided with the rise of the feminist movement. Matriarch, previously a "muted theme," became a racialized, controlling image to exclude black women from the claims of women as a whole for more power (Collins 1991, 73–74).

The third controlling image of the African-American woman is that of the welfare mother. Collins describes this further objectification of the black woman as a modern reworking of the image of the slave woman as breeder. Within this image the fertility of the African-American woman is viewed as problematic and hence the white culture's business to control:

> While the matriarch's unavailability contributed to her children's poor socialization, the welfare's mother's accessibility is deemed the problem. She is portrayed as being content to sit around and collect welfare, shunning work and passing on her bad values to her offspring. The image of the welfare mother represents another failed mammy, one who is unwilling to become "de mule uh de world." (Collins 1991, 76)

The fourth controlling image is that of "Jezebel, whore or sexually aggressive" (Collins 1991, 78). This image not only supports the denigration of black women but reinforces the other three, justifying the social, political, and interpersonal sexism toward black women. It brings us back full circle to the image of mammy, the preferable one where the black woman is submissive, non-sexual, and dependent.

This historical and conceptual understanding of the images ascribed to African-American women is important to the activity of pastoral care. First, it places in cultural context the unique position of black women in the social hierarchy. Second, it points us to a deeper understanding of the perceived presence of the matriarch figure as the one encountered by chaplains and pastors in the pastoral care setting. Let us look at one way of interpreting the interface of these images within the pastoral care event.

The "mammy" is beholden to the "master and mistress" of her employment. They know little about her personal life and spiritual life, for she is a one-dimensional figure, a servant who serves. Only when service is disrupted is consideration given to the broader context of who she is beyond the "master's or mistress' house." And then, such consideration is usually regarded as an inconvenience and an imposition to the provision of her service. In order not to risk dismissal or reprimand, the "mammy" keeps quiet about her own spiritual wonderings and minimizes any real personal problems or concerns, lest her effectiveness as servant be called into question. The collusion between "mammy" and "mistress/master" enables the continuation of the servant/employee relationship on a superficial level and a denial of or distancing of her other life as a person from her life as a domestic. The "good mammy" has no concern for herself, just for her charges.

The matriarch, on the other hand, is "Sapphire" (the name used by Toni Cade Bambara), the figure who has the problems—her man, her children, and often her health (that is, high blood pressure, heart disease, diabetes, cancer, gynecological problems). Her interpersonal qualities as an aggressive, bitchy, overbearing, permissive, self-sacrificing woman are generally determined to be the causal factors of her problems. There is little room for her spiritual searching, and affirmation given for her total dependence on a God who will see her through in spite of her "arrogant" self. This dependence moves her back toward the image of "mammy," the more socially acceptable submissive, dependent paragon of black womanhood. Healing of the soul is seen in the ability to move to this place of total reliance and away from the state of self-reliance.

The welfare mother and the Jezebel have such obvious problems that society is able to focus on the external "error of their ways" in response to their problems. Their "blatant" participation in their own "sin" can become a focus of pastoral care to the exclusion of looking at the spiritual impact of life as a marginalized, stereotyped person. The resignation or hopelessness of the welfare mother or Jezebel who expresses her own troubledness makes any expression of strength difficult for the care provider to hear and, if expressed, somewhat incongruous with the reality of being victimized in such profound societal and interpersonal ways. The cure of the soul in these instances is seen as the confession of one's sins, its subsequent forgiveness, and the commitment to a new way of life.

If the above represent, in any accurate way, the impact of the four controlling images of African-American women on the perceptions of the pastoral care provider, then it is no wonder that the "matriarch" is often viewed as already having great spiritual strength and access to the spiritual resources for her own healing. She has many problems; however, traditions of faith and culture have taught her that her only recourse in this life is to look Godward. Her testimony of faith in the midst of crisis is admirable indeed—if one is guided by the controlling image of matriarch.

While these conclusions of the impact of these controlling images on pastoral care may seem to be exaggerated, Collins expresses well the impact of these images on culture as a whole:

> Taken together, these four prevailing interpretations of Black womanhood form a nexus of elite white male interpretations of Black female sexuality and fertility. Moreover, by meshing smoothly with systems of race, class and gender oppression, they provide effective ideological justifications for racial oppression, the politics of gender subordination, and the economic exploitation inherent in capitalist economies. (Collins 1991, 78)

Pastoral care as a discipline cannot claim exemption from the cultural impact of racism, sexism, and classism, for if these attitudes are not explicitly embraced in theory and practice, they certainly are implicitly inherited and must be examined within our praxis of pastoral care. Jacquelyn Grant reminds us that the only way for African-American women to do theology (and hence for others to theologize with them) is to do so out of the tridimensional realities of racism, sexism, and classism (Grant 1989, 209).

There are at least two assumptions, then, that must be re-examined within the constructs of pastoral care. First, it is inaccurate to assume that the matriarchal image is indeed what it appears to be—an overbearing, aggressive "I can handle anything" woman. Second, the expressions so commonly heard from these women, while on the one hand can be profound professions of faith are in reality much more. To be more effective in ministry with the African-American woman means being willing to learn more about this "womanist" person, and then to hear her language of faith as an indicator of both her pastoral need and her spiritual strength rather than just as the latter.

## A NEW UNDERSTANDING OF MATRIARCHY

Alice Walker's concept of "womanist" as opposed to "feminist" is a good beginning point for our reframing of the notion of matriarch. Jacqueline Grant comes to this conclusion, utilizing Walker's idea: "A womanist then is a strong Black woman who has sometimes been mislabeled as a domineering, castrating matriarch. A womanist is one who has developed survival strategies in spite of the oppression of her race and sex in order to save her family and her people" (Grant 1989, 205). This womanist has learned through experience that strength is a requirement, not a luxury, in her life.

Life as womanist in the African-American context begins early. Because the qualities characteristic of the womanist are as essential as food, clothing, and shelter in terms of survival, they must be cultivated early. This is an important reality for the pastoral care provider to embrace. The womanist person developmentally represents an individual whose training is embedded in a family and cultural tradition of several generations. Unlike her Euro-American counterparts, the young womanist must strive to continue the tradition of strength modeled by her elders. The Euro-American female, in terms of social and individual development, has strived to surpass the social condition of the prior generation of women. Each Euro-American generation has worked to become more "liberated" from the patriarchal traditions and sexist constraints of society.

While liberation for the African-American woman has been an important ideal, that understanding of liberation has not required her to separate herself from the traditional image of the "strong woman" who can survive the perils of being black and female. Julia A. Boyd, psychotherapist, says: "This legacy of Black-womanhood-sameness is a blessing and a curse. The blessing is that in our ethnicity and our womanhood we share a sense of connection and we have a history that can be traced to queens and rulers of empires. . . . The curse is that we're expected not to deviate from the mold of how we are supposed to be as Black women" (Boyd 1993, 34). A study conducted by Gloria Joseph supports the premise that African-American mothers are regarded as role models by their daughters (Joseph and Lewis 1981). Individualization and autonomy are less important for the womanist than for the feminist.

In *Talking Back*, bell hooks further emphasizes the importance of community for the African-American woman. Hooks affirms that the idea of self is "not a signifier of one 'I,' but the coming together of many 'I's'" (hooks 1989, 30–31). To be an African-American woman individually is interwoven with the collective generations of women of our same culture, both the "ancients" and the "bloodmothers, othermothers, and women-centered networks" of our own community (Marshall 1959). And in this culture, "resilience" is one of the recurring psychological themes undergirding the "affective, cognitive and cultural flavor of the Black perspective" on life (White and Parham 1990, 56ff.).

The adaptive training of black females begins early. Gloria Joseph calls this process a "mother/daughter collaboration" in which one is taught skills for both physical and mental survival. Among these skills are those of strength and independence, essential because "precarious circumstances growing out of poverty and racism" means black women "might have to eventually become heads of their own households" (Ladner 1979, 3). Often the lessons are so covert that one might miss them, except for their telling impact on how one is expected to respond to life's difficulties.

A poignant illustration is an encounter between the two main fictional characters in Terri McMillan's *Mama*. In one scene the mother, Mildred, has to tell her eldest child, Freda, that there is not enough money to get all the Christmas presents out of layaway. Mildred asks Freda, who is now a "big girl" at the age of twelve, to do without her gifts until after New Year's, so that the younger children can enjoy Christmas. Freda readily agrees, "Yes, Mama, I can wait," knowing that her mother is depending on her to help with this crisis. Both mother and daughter yearn to hug each other, but, as McMillan writes:

> A plastic layer had grown over that part of Mildred's heart and it refused to let her act on impulse. She never showed too much affection because that made her feel weak. And she hated feeling weak because that made her vulnerable. Who would be there to pick up the pieces if she let herself break down? Mildred felt she had to be strong at all times and at all costs. (McMillan 1987, 37–38)

In that instance, Freda learns that the proper response to disappointment is to be strong, to be accepting and to move on. While the matriarch is predominantly a myth of mainstream culture, the womanist is a reality.

## THE QUANDARY FOR THE WOMANIST

Psychosocial and spiritual difficulties arise for the womanist around the mixed responses she receives for her strength and resilience. In a chapter on "Racism and Feminist Theology," Barbara Hilkert Andolsen notes, "Black women . . . have been condemned for strength developed in the fight for survival in a racist society" (Andolsen 1986, 103).

Johnetta Cole, in her book *Conversations: Straight Talk with America's Sister President*, Johnetta Cole makes an essential point:

> These pervasive stereotypes about African-American women also have unfortunate consequences in terms of our own behavior. Oftentimes they put us in a defensive position and make us feel guilty about our accomplishments and for exhibiting healthy attributes. To be nurturing and caring is good, as it is to be self-sufficient, independent. . . . But in the case of the African-American woman, in displaying these positive qualities she is likely to be viewed (and thus treated!) as a Mammy, a Jezebel, a Sapphire [matriarch]. (Cole 1993, 71)

Some African-American women have attempted to work their way out of this quandary by aspiring to the "cult of true womanhood." Joseph describes this cult as Eurocentric and in direct contrast to the Afrocentric understanding of womanhood. Yet the African-American woman, whose strength is both blessing and curse societally, may see as her only option to embrace the ideology of this "cult"—the true woman is self-contained within her nuclear family, with specific and separate roles for men and women, and with an economic dependence on men, in such a way that motherhood is one's true occupation (Joseph 1991, 43–44). This woman's spirituality is subordinate to and dictated by that of mainstream culture. Here, woman can be both weak and strong, with the certainty that someone will take care of her, if the need arises.

It would seem that the womanist would experience some sense of liberation through the ideology of the "cult of true womanhood," for here she could lay aside the edict to be strong and experience more fully her vulnerability. This is often the invitation of the pastoral care provider to her. However, the womanist, in reality, often lacks the economic and social resources to embrace such a posture. Flexible sex roles, outside-the-home employment, and a responsibility to and for one's extended family are certainties and necessities for most African-American women. Hence they could not in reality be more vulnerable by being more self-focused.

## The Coping Style of the Womanist

How has the womanist managed to function out of a position of strength in the face of adversity and without the option of being vulnerable? One might expect that the person whose existence was under these terms would be likely to succumb to stress rather than utilize strength as a coping style. There are at least four aspects to the African-American woman's coping style—expecting the worst, surrendering to God, sparing others, and affirming one's strength in the community of faith.

African-American women seem to have a particular way of viewing life and its difficulties that empowers them to function this way. In *Sisters of the Yam,* bell hooks comments on the paradoxical notion of positive thinking among such women. For black people, positive thinking means expecting the worst. Of this kind of cynicism, hooks says:

> It often has the quality and magic and sassiness that comforts. It's tied up with our sense of being able to look on the rough side and *deal.* . . . Since the "worst" rarely happens, there is a sense of relief when we find ourselves able to cope with whatever reality brings and we don't have to face debilitating disappointment. (hooks 1993, 62)

The womanist therefore braces herself for ultimate disaster, so coping with the actuality of daily disappointment has less impact on her psyche and on her sense of self. Even in life-and-death situations, the death-embracing ethos of the black culture enables the womanist to stare in the face of death, sometimes with barely a tremble.

Faith becomes an essential component in this coping strategy. The womanist shifts her focus from the finitude of life to the transcendent nature of the human experience. This is not really a "pie in the sky," "otherworldly" attitude but rather a survivalist stance. The historical experience of slavery embedded in the black culture the concept that eventually God would intervene on behalf of the suffering but that in the meantime the sufferer can be sustained by the belief in God's presence in the midst. The exodus narrative of the Old Testament is a fundamental metaphor for the African-American culture. So, in the face of adversity, the womanist draws on this faith to sustain her. Writing of her grief experience after the deaths of several family members, Bridgett Davis explains why she could not openly grieve those losses: "Also, it seemed a betrayal of faith, of a belief in God to totally surrender myself to grief" (Davis 1990, 221).

Davis's account of her own experience highlights another coping skill of the African-American woman, that of "sparing others." She writes:

> In the early days, I fought myself not to break down. I wouldn't cry. I wouldn't talk about it. I wouldn't give in. . . . I didn't want to lose control. My primary incentive was to spare my mother the heartbreak. . . . She had been so strong throughout these tragedies, even though I know she feels a deep pain that those of us around her can't comprehend or save her from. To breakdown and give my mother someone else to worry about was a selfish indulgence I didn't think I deserved. (Davis 1990, 221)

Self-indulgent behavior is abhorrent to the womanist. The cultural norm that a "self" exists only in the context of a "community" means the womanist's feelings must be monitored for and tempered according to their impact on others. It is not that the womanist does not have feelings of fear, dread, sadness, and so on, she simply doesn't express these feelings on behalf of herself as an individual. To do so would be to set oneself outside or over against the community.

Finally, there seems to be at least one other coping phenomenon common to the womanist experience. The reader might be tempted to think that that womanist's sense of strength is a false sense in view of her lack of power in the broader society. Quite the contrary, for the strength of the womanist has a real and particular value within the black culture. This is especially true of her spiritual strength. Delores Williams reminds us of how the women of the church, particularly those designated the "mothers of the church," are exalted for their strength and wisdom:

> She is often called upon to be a healer of relationships within the congregation. She is well-versed in and knows how to pass along the highest values for living the Christian life. Her power and influence often extend beyond the church into her community, because she has been empowered by one of the central authority agents of the community—the African-American church—to provide care and nurture to the children of God. (Williams 1993, 79).

This affirmation of strength and its link to one's spirituality reinforce the womanist's manner of responding to life's difficulties with strength.

## NEW PERSPECTIVES ON PASTORAL CARE TO THE WOMANIST

How then does the pastoral care provider enter into relationship with the womanist? Most pastoral encounters occur around some type of crisis or developmental transition in life. Individuals usually seek or respond to pastoral care because of their need to make meaning out of these kinds of experiences. How does the pastor or chaplain or pastoral counselor engage with the womanist?

First, a word of caution. The strength of the womanist is often so attractive that the pastoral care provider could be tempted to want to receive strength from the black woman rather than to nurture her and critique her. In my estimation, this kind of admiration is not helpful, because it leads to a reversal of roles. While I do believe in the concept of mutuality within the pastoral relationship, I cringe when I hear a pastoral care person say of a black woman in the person's care, "She ministered to me as much as I did to her." That kind of statement is reminiscent of the image of the African-American woman as "mammy," who even in her moments of need continued to give and to care for others. The pastoral care person must remain in a functional role with the African-American woman. Admiration of her story and of her tenacity is fine, as long as one does not switch places with her or enter into one's own countertransference.

The second notion for the pastoral care provider is to recognize that the pastoral relationship will be reflective of the larger world. The realities of race, gender, and class will be part and parcel of the pastoral interaction. Boyd says, "Therapy that covertly denies the validity of a woman's ethnic and cultural experiences is not therapy" (Boyd 1990, 231). It *will* make a difference if you are white, male, or of a different class from your African-American patient, client, or counselee. Boyd continues to say that it is essential to recognize and acknowledge the imbalance of power that exists in such relationships, not only on the therapeutic level, but also on the cultural, social, and political levels. The helper "can begin to equalize the division of power by becoming knowledgeable about . . . the world of women of color" (Boyd 1990, 231). The norms and standards of mainstream, Euro-American culture are not the same as those for the African-American.

To be an effective pastoral caregiver requires one to step out of one's own culture and into that of the womanist. "Black women are highly aware of the racist labeling that is used to define their person and environment, and are therefore legitimately cautious in seeking professional therapy" (Boyd 1990,

230). A necessary question for the pastoral care provider is: "To what extent is my care to this particular African-American woman influenced by the "controlling images" (that is, Mammy, Matriarch, Jezebel, the Welfare Mother) traditionally used to describe black women in general?

Next, the pastoral care provider should be sure not to label the womanist's coping style as "denial." The womanist is all too aware of her precarious existence. She neither denies nor minimizes her troubles. She reinterprets them. What this means is that at a basic human level, the womanist experiences the same emotions as anyone else. Culturally, she has learned to ascribe a different value to those feelings which move her too closely to her pain, too closely to despair and hopelessness. Bell hooks subscribes to the notion that the sociopolitical status imposed on the African-American woman leads to her "addiction to being tough" (hooks 1993, 62).

There has to be a safe place, however, for the womanist to express her deeper feelings without having to give up her strength and without feeling too vulnerable. Vulnerability is highly valued in the discipline of pastoral care. Yet it is extremely risky for the womanist, who, outside the pastoral care moment, must continue to contend with sexism, racism, and classism. Further, it will not make sense to the womanist to speak only of her feelings. It will be difficult for the womanist to separate her desires from her perception of how they impact and affect her "community." This difficulty is not necessarily due to a lack of boundaries or a lack of autonomy or to a dysfunctional enmeshment. In reality, the womanist cannot afford too much self-focus, lest she erode her capacity to continue to survive in an unfriendly, insensitive or hostile world. In addition, her survival is dependent on being part of a community where there is some level of acceptance and belonging. She must, then, in some way maintain her responsibility to the "others" of her community even when she is sick, tired, confused, or distressed. Even when circumstances make it impossible for her to carry out physical responsibilities, it will be extremely important for the womanist to maintain a level of emotional and spiritual responsibility to or for her loved ones.

In "Releasing Our Womanist Song," Gale Kennebrew-Moore points to a process that can assist the womanist in appropriating socially necessary behavior (being strong) with one's own finitude and need for healing (vulnerability). She identifies the "critical voices" of our personal and social histories as the origin of the need to stay strong. The distorted states mentioned by Kennebrew-Moore can be paralleled with the "controlling images" identified earlier:

> In my theology, when we listen to our critical voices we have a distorted understanding of our purpose and meaning of our existence. The spirit of God within us motivates us to seek harmony with ourselves. The sole purpose of

critical voices is to maintain our current state of distorted understanding, purpose and existence. (Kennebrew-Moore 1991, 164)

The womanist's healing is dependent upon some resolution of the tension between exhibiting socially acceptable behavior and attending to one's own needs. According to Kennebrew-Moore:

> The process of releasing our womanist song is a struggle between the spirit of God within us striving for harmony and our critical voices that seek to maintain our current state of distorted understanding. . . . Healing occurs as we realize, verbalize (to ourselves, others and God) our critical voices, beliefs and actions that maintain our painful existence and keep us from releasing our womanist song. (Kennebrew-Moore 1991, 164–165)

An egalitarian, Womanist Christology is one resource for the releasing of this song of the African-American woman. (One should note that all African-American women are not Christian. Many are Muslim, Jehovah's Witness, and of countless other faith traditions.)

Jacquelyn Grant describes Womanist Christology as constructive and liberating. Unlike their Euro-American sisters, African-American women have not had as a primary concern the sexist language of the Christian tradition, particularly concerning images of God and Jesus. The maleness of Christ is not paramount to African-American women, in the same way that the portrayed "whiteness" of Christ did not prevent African-Americans in history from embracing the notion of salvation through Christ. Therefore, for African-Americans, "if Christ is the Savior of all, then it is the humanity—the wholeness—of Christ which is significant" (Grant 1989, 219), not his maleness or his race.

The constructive, liberating power in this focus on the humanity of Christ enables the womanist to identify her *response* to her suffering (through sadness, grief, anger, fear, or any other set of emotions) within the context of her faith rather than experience it as being outside or contrary to her faith. Typically, the contemporary church tradition identifies more with the suffering of Christ to the exclusion of also identifying with Christ's *affective responses* to suffering. A Womanist Christology is therefore one that can engage in a process of expanding one's understanding of one's own faith stance by expanding one's sense of who Christ is as a human model. Thus, when the critical voice says, "Be strong. Thou shalt not cry," the womanist is aided in recalling that Jesus cried. This image will be more meaningful for the womanist than the notion of her "need" or "right" to cry. In addition, for the womanist who is striving to be "Christlike" in a crisis, her own definition of such a virtue can be expanded to integrate human emotions.

On a conceptual level, this means that part of the task of the pastoral care provider is to assist the womanist in moving from "first order religious language" to "second order religious language" and then on to "third order theological reflection." This process is one of examining the theological phrases, narratives, Scriptures, and liturgies (first order language) for their basic meaning (second order language) and then "reflecting upon the way in which judgements are made" in view of what the womanist says *and* what it means to her (Jennings 1990, 862). To only respond to what she says is a myopic and limited pastoral response. To get at what she means, and then how she makes use of these beliefs and meanings, is essential. The role of the pastoral care provider is to facilitate an expansion of faith to a deeper level, rather than remain at the surface of faith expression.

This kind of pastoral process is a universal process on one level. To do effective pastoral care means to engage in a meaning-making and reflecting process with our helpees, regardless of their race or gender. However, for the African-American woman, the process may look and feel different because of the impact of racism, sexism, and classism on her belief system. When the womanist says, "God will not place any more on you than you can bear," it is not enough to hear and admire how this woman has survived the various burdens and crises of her life, but also tantamount that the pastoral care provider engage with her around how this belief makes sense to her in view of the realities of discrimination, poverty, imprisonment, illness, premature death, and so forth, especially the ways in which these have been realities in her life. Healing will come through her struggle with making meaning out of the contradictions between her faith stance and her life experiences.

In summary, the legacy of matriarch is a powerful one that can inform our pastoral care to African-American women. It is essential to understand the history of the concept of matriarch and its power as a "controlling image." I have attempted to suggest in this chapter a way of modifying that image of matriarch and replacing it with the more positive, liberating image of womanist. I use this nomenclature not as a way of labeling African-American women nor of generalizing their experience but as a reinterpretation.

The womanist utilizes a coping style that includes "expecting the worst," finding sustenance in the presence of God, "sparing others" from her pain, and deriving a sense of empowerment from the African-American church's affirmation of woman's strength. This style emerges in response to a culture that both praises and criticizes the African-American woman for her strength. Many an African-American woman has said, in response to accolades, "It's not me, but the Christ within me," as a way of giving account for their strength. To spiritualize one's strength makes the asset more socially acceptable in a culture that tends not to value the African-American woman and her attributes.

While the womanist is a strong figure, the pastoral care provider is still required to "pastor" the womanist, not just admire her or receive from her. This must be done with a high level of awareness of the sociopolitical realities of sexism, racism, and classism in the lives of black women. Further, it is important that the pastoral care provider avoid utilizing such labels as "denial" to explain the womanist's lack of verbalization of her distress or need. It is also important to remember that the womanist is a person of "community." She will not perceive of herself as a separate "I" in the same way as the Euro-American woman. Careful attention to her story and to her extended relationships is important, as is the acceptance of her sense of responsibility for others as valid.

Finally, the pastoral care provider can facilitate whatever kind of healing is needed for the womanist by assisting her in a process of meaning-making and reflecting on the elements of the faith system that she utilizes in a crisis or transition. The religious phrases, stories, rituals, and Scriptures drawn upon should not only be examined for meaning and application but also critiqued for their contradiction with the womanist's actual life experiences. It is only then that our pastoral relationship with the womanist can truly be said to move beyond the "controlling images" of culture and society to engage with the soul of a woman whose very life has been shaped, hampered, hindered, and impacted on every level by those same images. The title of a book by theologian Renita Weems sums up the pastoral need of the African-American womanist: "I asked for intimacy . . . ."

## BIBLIOGRAPHY

Andolsen, Barbara Hilkert. 1986. *Daughters of Jefferson, Daughters of Bootblacks: Racism and American Feminism.* Macon, Ga.: Mercer University Press.

Bambara, Toni Cade, ed. 1981. *The Black Woman: An Anthology.* New York: Random House.

Bell-Scott, Patricia, et al., eds. 1991. *Double Stitch: Black Women Write about Mothers and Daughters.* Boston: Beacon Press.

Boyd, Julia A. 1990. "Ethnic and Cultural Diversity in Feminist Therapy: Keys to Power." In E. C. White, ed., 226–234.

———. 1993. *In the Company of My Sisters: Black Women and Self-Esteem.* New York: Penguin Books.

Cole, Johnetta B. 1993. *Conversations: Straight Talk with America's Sister President.* New York: Doubleday & Co.

Collins, Patricia Hill. 1990. *Black Feminist Thought: Knowledge, Consciousness, and the Politics of Empowerment.* New York: Routledge & Kegan Paul.

————. 1991. "The Meaning of Motherhood in Black Culture and Black Mother-Daughter Relationships." In Bell-Scott et al., eds., 42–60.

Davis, Angela. 1981. *Women, Race and Class.* New York: Random House.

Davis, Bridgett M. 1990. "Speaking of Grief: Today I Feel Real Low, I Hope You Understand." In E. C. White, ed., 219–225.

Edelman, Marian Wright. 1990. "The Black Family in America." In E. C. White, ed., 128–150.

Giddings, Paula. 1984. *When and Where I Enter: The Impact of Black Women on Race and Sex in America.* New York: William Morrow & Co.

Gilkes, Cheryl Townsend. 1983. "From Slavery to Social Welfare: Racism and the Control of Black Women." In Swerdlow and Lessinger, eds., 288–300.

Grant, Jacquelyn. 1989. *White Women's Christ and Black Women's Jesus: Feminist Christology and Womanist Response.* Atlanta: Scholars Press.

Hollies, Linda H., ed. 1992. *WomanistCare: How to Tend the Souls of Women.* Joliet, Ill.: Woman to Woman Ministries Publications.

hooks, bell. 1981. *Ain't I a Woman? Black Women and Feminism.* Boston: South End Press.

————. 1984. *Feminist Theory: From Margin to Center.* Boston: South End Press.

————. 1993. *Sisters of the Yam: Black Women and Self-Recovery.* Boston: South End Press.

————. 1989. *Talking Back: Thinking Feminist, Thinking Black.* Boston: South End Press.

Hull, Gloria T.; Patricia Bell-Scott; and Barbara Smith, eds. 1982. *But Some of Us Are Brave.* Old Westbury, N.Y.: Feminist Press.

Hunter, Rodney J., ed. 1990. *Dictionary of Pastoral Care and Counseling.* Nashville: Abingdon Press.

Jennings, T. W., Jr. 1990. "Pastoral Theological Methodology." In Hunter, ed., 862–864.

Joseph, Gloria I. 1991. "Black Mothers and Daughters: Traditional and New Perspectives." In Bell-Scott et al., eds., 194–206.

Joseph. Gloria I., and Jill Lewis. 1981. *Common Differences: Conflicts in Black and White Feminist Perspectives.* New York: Doubleday & Co.

Kennebrew-Moore, Gale. 1991. "Releasing the Womanist Song." In Hollies, ed., 159–179.

Ladner, Joyce. 1979. *Labeling Black Children: Some Mental Health Implications.* Vol 5. Washington, D.C.: Institute for Urban Affairs and Research, Howard University.

Marshall, Paule. 1959. *Brown Girl, Brownstones.* New York: Avon Press.

McMillan, Terri. 1987. *MAMA.* New York: Washington Square Press.

Staples, Robert. 1973. *The Black Woman in America.* Chicago: Nelson-Hall.

Swerdlow, Amy, and Hanna Lessinger, eds. 1983. *Class, Race and Sex: The Dynamics of Control.* Boston: G. K. Hall.

Walker, Alice. 1983. *In Search of Our Mothers' Gardens: Womanist Prose.* New York: Harcourt Brace Jovanovich.

Weems, Renita. 1993. *I Asked for Intimacy.* San Diego: LuraMedia.

White, Evelyn C., ed. 1990. *Black Women's Health Book: Speaking for Ourselves.* Seattle: Seal Press.

White, Joseph L., and Thomas A. Parham. 1990. *The Psychology of Blacks: An African-American Perspective.* Englewood Cliffs, N.J.: Prentice-Hall.

Williams, Delores S. 1993. *Sisters in the Wilderness: The Challenge of Womanist God-Talk.* Maryknoll, N.Y.: Orbis Books.

# 4

# Pastoral Care and Counseling with Women Entering Ministry

MIRIAM ANNE GLOVER-WETHERINGTON
*Duke University*

As a professor of pastoral care at a seminary, I teach women who are going into ministry, and sometimes I hear from former students. Motivated by their stories and by my own clinical training and experience,[1] I offer this chapter as a resource for the pastoral care of both seminarians and women in the early years of their ministry. Since the issues for women entering ministry pervade all spheres of life, many differing kinds of people are in positions to offer them either assistance and pastoral care or some form of hindrance. Pastors, chaplains, supervisors, pastoral counselors, professors, denominational and seminary administrators, seminary friends, ministerial colleagues, and family members all play important parts in the nurture of entering clergywomen. Accordingly, in this context I will refer to all such people as pastoral caregivers. I hope this study will be used not only by clergywomen themselves but also by all the pastoral caregivers in their lives.

One June in the early 1990s, a young minister and former student of mine phoned me. During her studies at Duke Divinity School for her master of divinity degree, Shirley had taken one of the pastoral care courses I taught. Now she was saying she had been having a rough time recently. She had quit her first church position. She still felt called into the ministry and did not know what to do now. She had seen a counselor in her home state but was in North Carolina for the summer and would like to talk with me.

I readily agreed to see Shirley. She had been a fairly quiet student, but she had caught my attention by doing well in picking up on underlying emotions and in being in touch with her own feelings. Her strengths included a basic authenticity and a genuineness of caring that was willing to be involved with the pain of others. While Shirley's Christian faith came across with a quiet directness, her faith was not simplistic or magical.

Shirley had told me that she had problems at times managing her anxiety. She struggled with low self-confidence. She seemed somewhat surprised whenever I affirmed her gifts and skills in pastoral care. I had told her that one of her "growing edges" in ministry preparation was to have a more realistic (and positive) appraisal of her work. At her graduation, I was pleased that some church would have her guiding presence in its life. What had happened now in her first church since her graduation?

That summer, I began to sort through Shirley's overreadiness to blame herself and to develop my own picture of what had happened. Her Methodist district superintendent had placed her as an assistant pastor, working with a senior pastor who did not want her. The pastor seemed overcontrolling and overly critical. He did not allow flexibility for Shirley to do her ministry in a slightly different way. He criticized her if she actually took her weekly day off and for not being dynamic and driven. In response, she worked so many hours she had little time to build any support network. She went to her district superintendent for advice, but she still felt stuck and hopeless. Feeling isolated, exhausted, and not seeing any other way to go, she checked herself into a hospital for depression. When she was discharged, a Methodist church mediator suggested that the pastor change some of his patterns in the staff relationship. But when the mediator left, the pastor told Shirley that he planned to change nothing and that she should leave. She resigned. The pastor was then able to have as his assistant the layman he had wanted all along.

While Shirley was relieved to be out of that situation, she did not realize until later that some people would interpret both her hospitalization and her resignation as signs that the problem was basically in her. Hurt and confused, she went to live with her parents. At that point her self-esteem was so low that she did indeed place blame primarily on herself. Understandably, her Conference Relations Committee sought information and guidance from Shirley's therapist about whether to accept her back into the Methodist system and place her in a church. Her therapist wrote that although she was better, he could not guarantee that she would not become overstressed in a ministry position again. Basically he saw her as fragile. She appreciated the help he had given her to work on some previously unresolved childhood issues, but his lack of confidence in her made it difficult for her to continue to trust him. Shirley came to see me, asking for counseling help and a second opinion. She hoped that she could work through enough with me that I could honestly write her committee that she was ready for a church.

Shirley is an example of why, even in this decade, pastoral caregivers still need to focus on the contexts of women seminarians and ministers.[2] Her story shows how a variety of contextual elements can come together destructively in a particular situation. Not everyone will have the kind of public markers of crisis (hospitalization and sudden loss of job) that occurred in Shirley's situation. Instead, many women will experience a more private pain and a more subtle diminishment of what they are called to do. Obviously, each person's story will be shaped by unique factors, unique factors in the clergywoman or seminarian and unique factors in the situation and people around her. But if we as pastoral caregivers know the kinds of things for which to look, we are less likely to pass over them without even seeing them.

These kinds of things caregivers do and do not notice are based in part on factors such as cultural expectations and clinical training. When culture and clinical training share the same blind spots, caregivers can unintentionally neglect major dimensions of reality. This neglect can easily be overlooked because the caregivers believe they are basing their perspectives on sound "clinical experience." But clinical experience, like all other forms of research, is shaped by the researcher's expectations. Barbara Hargrove notes that there is no purely "objective" research:

> There are no facts that speak for themselves. They always represent pre-existing ideas and expectations, even if there is no attempt to skew the results. Neither qualitative nor quantitative research can escape this fact, any more than we can escape the fact that our own presence in any research situation may have some effect on the results we find. (Hargrove 1987, 396)

This chapter invites pastoral caregivers to reconsider how their own assumptive frameworks are influencing the way they evaluate women entering ministry. The next section describes the tendency of many pastoral caregivers to focus on inner, long-term, stable personality characteristics. The second major section examines the pressures that external contexts (placement processes, internships, collegial relations, and personal relationships) can exert on women entering ministry.[3]

## LONG-TERM, STABLE PERSONALITY CHARACTERISTICS

The training of many pastoral caregivers has been deeply influenced by aspects of modern psychology. One of the assumptions of many forms of psychology is that people's problems are basically intrapsychic (Greenspan 1983; Poling 1991; Graham 1992; Patton 1993). I was not surprised to hear Shirley report that she had worked with her therapist mainly on unresolved feelings from her childhood. Even though these feelings had developed in relationship to her family and external experiences, their existence in 1992 was within Shirley. Their present presence was internal. All people have parts of their identity or personality characteristics that are stable and long-term within them. Whenever some part of them keeps them from being and doing what God wills them to be and do in the present or for the future, then examining these intrapsychic and often unconscious parts of themselves can be helpful.

Shirley's situation would have been difficult for any young minister. Still, as part of our work together, Shirley and I discussed alternative ways in which she could have dealt with the situation better. While she repeatedly took considerable initiative (more than I have outlined here), she had stopped short of doing everything possible to involve people in the Methodist system to help her. Shirley described for me how she believes some of her omissions of action did reflect patterns that stemmed from childhood experiences.

As children, Shirley and her brother experienced a traumatic injustice. When they went to their parents for help, their parents chose not to take them seriously. No empathy was offered; no one stood up for them when they were too young and powerless to stand up for themselves. Even worse, Shirley and her brother were blamed for the injustice done to them. Shirley had worked with this incident in her previous therapy and had an understanding of how that experience had influenced her to have not enough confidence that her voice would be heard, especially by those with more power. This pattern is one of which Shirley should stay aware. She needs to be aware in situations in which her voice is indeed again not being heard. At these times she needs to recognize that now that she is an adult, she has more options and resources than she did as a child, even in a society that resists hearing women's voices and restricts women's options.

Of course, other clergywomen's internal problems will differ from Shirley's. Given the appalling statistics on domestic violence and sexual abuse, it is reasonable to expect that many women (and men) seminarians will have had traumatic experiences. In addition, the gender role socialization we take so much for granted often distorts both men's and women's ideal development into the body of Christ. As a result, women and men both are taught to discount women's work and women's perspectives. Women are often taught that to be assertive is to be labeled "unfeminine," "not able to get along," or a "bitch." Pastoral caregivers need to inform themselves both about childhood crises, about the destructive aspects of gender roles, and about how caregivers can act to prevent so much damage being done to our children and youth. Pastoral caregivers need to know how to help women find release from whatever resulting internal characteristics keep them from the full exercise of their spiritual gifts (1 Corinthians 12; Ephesians 4:11–16).

Crises do not, of course, end with childhood. In seminaries, just as in churches and in society as a whole, are women who as adults have lived through sexual abuse, rape, domestic violence, divorce, eating disorders, role confusion and overload, the devaluing of identity and work, miscarriages, menopause, mastectomies, hysterectomies, healthy births, and the death of children. All of these events can wound the woman's self and world perceptions. But even in this section about effects on the individual, it is crucial to remember that in any kind of abuse the societal perspective is essential. Contextual factors play a role in the existence and extent of abuse, in the tendency to minimize the problems, and in the rewounding of the survivor through society-engendered shame. Pastoral caregivers need to look at many of these childhood and adult issues and discuss how the inner hurts can be survived or healed in community, not stopping short with an internal focus.

As helpful as I hope internal insights will be to Shirley and to others, they are not enough. If Shirley is led to believe that the results of her childhood pain were the sum and substance of her present difficulties, then her therapy did her a disservice. To hold a person responsible for more than her share of a difficult situation communicates to that person that she is sicker and more fragile than she really is. If a person's self-confidence and appraisal of reality is undermined in the name of "helping" her, then the therapeutic diagnosis may to some extent become a self-fulfilling prophecy (Neuger 1991, 146–161).

An extended example of this tendency for psychology to consider intrapsychic interpretations more basic and "deep" than contextual interpretations can be seen in the "fear of success" debate in the psychological literature (Glover-Wetherington 1992, 119–173). In the early 1970s Matina Horner proposed that in addition to the desire to succeed and the fear of failure there was also a "fear of success." Her hypothesis was advanced to explain why people (especially women) who were on the verge of or in the process of succeeding sometimes seemed to sabotage themselves. She theorized that if women were taught in childhood that they were not supposed to succeed, then the fear of success could become a relatively stable, long-term personality characteristic (Horner 1972, 157–175). In other words the problem, while originally stemming from outside the person in childhood, affected the woman in the present because it had become a part of her intrapsychic composition.

Horner's hypothesis set off an avalanche of research. Various measures of "fear of success" were attempted and researchers found what they called "fear of success" in both men and women, especially when people were tested in reference to activities that were not traditional for their gender. Women in ministry, like women in medical school or law, meet the qualification of being in an activity traditionally thought of as male. Consequently, some of these researchers might have suggested "fear of success" as the explanation of what happened to Shirley. When she went to the hospital and when she resigned, was she self-sabotaging herself because of her inner fear of success?

The research about "fear of success" did not itself succeed in establishing that such a construct existed. The most convincing explanation for the findings that did emerge was that the source of people's anxiety about success was *not* a long-term, stable personality construct. Instead, the fears were a more realistic awareness of subtle ways that our society penalizes men or women who step outside traditional gender roles. The combined effects of all the penalties for going outside the role boundary served to maintain that role boundary. In other words, in the light of *role boundary maintenance theory,* the present source of the "problem" was not internal but existed in the person's context (Condry and Dyer 1976, 72; Tresemer 1977, 49–82).

Ironically, the very research that tried to prove that "fear of success" existed is itself an example of the subtle penalties society imposes. Later reflection on the process led several theorists to note the strong motivation there had been for psychologists to find a reason *inside women themselves* for women's difficulties in nontraditional occupations (Condry and Dyer 1976, 76; Tresemer 1977, 50; Eccles 1987, 167). If women themselves are the only ones who can be held responsible for inequities in the workplace, then the society can be let off the hook. If "fear of success" had been found to exist, then women like Shirley could be given a label and told they should get over their internal problems if they are to be fit to work in a traditionally male context. One penalty for attempting to go into a "man's" field might well be to be given a pathological label. Theory claiming to be "only descriptive" became itself an enforcer of traditional norms.

The God in whose image people are made is a God of community. What our culture refers to as individual identity is actually composed at its very core of relatedness. Identity can never be purely individual. Consequently, any advice to clergywomen simply to ignore their context and base their identity only within themselves is unhelpful and often punitive. Such advice can discourage women from a careful understanding of the realities of their lives. These realities include the sinful, negative effects and the redemptive possibilities of their communal contexts.[4] Internal processes should *certainly* be taken into account; but they are *neither more basic nor more important* than the actual relations in which the person continues to be involved.

## READING THE SIGNS: SORTING OUT THE AMBIGUITIES

Although learning about the inner distortions, wounds, and maladaptations of seminarians can be of great usefulness, it is important that the pastoral caregivers in a woman's life do not stop short with the intrapsychic. Christians are not called to a one-on-one privatized relationship between some falsely conceived "separative self" (Miller-McLemore 1991, 75–80) and a god to be found within ourselves. Inevitably, our contexts, with both sinful and redemptive elements, are a part of our most intimate lives before God and part of our ministerial formation. Because our culture over-emphasizes individualism, pastoral care to women entering ministry needs to insist that these women learn to identify specific ways that even their private feelings and inner dialogues inevitably participate in the lives of the conflicting communities in which they are immersed.

Pastoral colleagues need to assist the emerging clergywoman to discern in her own experiences many confusing, tangled contradictions: Christian encouragement and societal penalties, God's call and people's resistance to affirm the call, redemption into community and bondage to sinful norms. How shall particular Scripture passages be applied in a specific situation? It is not a simple matter to sort out: Which tensions represent calls of God to move beyond a woman's prior sense of reality (Matthew 9:16–18; John 4:4–42)? Which tensions are temptations to retreat into the familiarity of well-worn paths that feel less risky (Matthew 16:21–26; 25:14–30)? Which tensions result from commitments to faithful Christian service and belief even in the face of ridicule or exclusion (Luke 4:21–30; 9:22–26; 14:25–27; John 15:18–21; Romans 1:16–17; 2 Corinthians 1:3–11)? Interpreting communities can use these scriptural passages either redemptively or destructively. Furthermore, whether a perspective is faithfully Christian cannot be discerned only by whether it is "feminist" or "traditional."[5] All Christians, certainly including women entering ministry, need to be part of a continuing, prayerful, community dialogue that seeks to read God's signs even in the swirling ambiguities.

To provide a beginning framework for sorting out ambiguities, this section on societal pressures has four subsections. The first, on placement, will take an overview of attitudes toward clergywomen and how those attitudes affect both whether or not women can find ministry places and what types of positions are available for women. The subsection on internships concentrates on how ambiguous attitudes create subtle put-downs or penalties in small daily church interactions. The third area examined is that of women's relationships to seminary and ministerial colleagues. The fourth subsection carries the study of relationships over to interactions with families and romantic friendships.

### Trying to Go Where You Are Not Wanted: Placement

One of the important features of Shirley's story was that she was placed in a church in which the pastor did not want her. In her situation, apparently the pastor already had in mind a particular man, not just any man, with whom he wanted to work. Even so, given the common resistance to clergywomen, it would have been surprising if her gender were not at least a partial factor. Part of the difficulty for women entering ministry is not knowing to what extent resistance to them is based on their gender or on performance factors that they can work to improve.

The church is both the formative context out of which women do or do not experience their calls to ministry and the community in which most women seminarians hope to serve and lead. In regard to the contexts of the tensions for women seminarians, the church is the beginning and the end. While I affirm that ministry should be a call from God, in present society it has also become a job, a means of economically supporting oneself and one's family. To deny or restrict financial income to women in ministry is a direct way to impose negative consequences on them.

In the last several decades many churches have thought of women ministers as "new."[6] Protestant denominations vary greatly both in their official attitude toward women in ministry and in their type of placement system. Despite this variety, in most denominations women interested in ministering receive mixed signals from their churches.[7]

The leadership of the Southern Baptist Convention, some Pentecostal or "holiness" groups, and conservative Presbyterians officially interpret the Scriptures as not permitting women as priests or as full pastors. The impact of these interpretations of Scripture vary with the form of church government and the character of the discourse, but the presence of mixed signals remains.[8]

Even in churches in which the denominational leadership has supported women in ministry, placement problems remain. These problems include both the initial, entry level, placement after seminary, and the changing to a different church in subsequent placements. Women tend to stay marginalized in their second and subsequent placements either as assistant pastors or as pastors in smaller, more rural, or more troubled churches (Carroll, Hargrove, and Lummis 1981, 125–130; Hoch 1996).

In denominations that do not guarantee ministry positions, women ministers of all types may simply not be offered church calls when it is time for them to move (Carroll, Hargrove, and Lummis 1981, 115–118, 125–132; Lehman 1987, 37). By being ignored, women can "fall between the cracks" and be forced to take secular employment. When they do so, their voices drop out of the ministerial statistics and research studies. These clergywomen may well, however, in their grief, hurt, confusion, and anger turn to pastoral caregivers. Faced with this type of situation, Shirley asked for advice and support.

Several studies of women's placement difficulties considered the question of how to facilitate the placement of qualified clergywomen. While differences in clergy deployment practices do affect women ministerial candidates, the way that informal "old boy" networks or "cousin" systems overlap the formal systems results in strong similarities in actual function (Carroll, Hargrove, and Lummis 1981, 111–112). One similarity, present formally or informally in all denominations, is the role of regional denominational leaders, such as bishops, executive presbyters, conference or executive ministers, directors of mission, and executive directors or directors of church-minister relations at state conventions. Many denominational leaders reject affirmative action and take a "neutral" stance toward appointing or helping women find church placements. Carroll, Hargrove, and Lummis comment:

> For women to be placed it is necessary for judicatory officials of all denominations to be more than pleasant but inactive in support of women clergy; rather, they need to be active advocates if women are to find jobs. (Carroll, Hargrove, and Lummis 1981, 122)

The role of the local congregation is the second major focus in considering the placement of women. Even in the Methodist appointment system, increasingly the trend has been to give consideration to the preferences of the laity. Even laity who say they believe that women should be ordained and even those who have previously experienced a woman as minister are often either opposed to or deeply ambiguous about calling a woman to their own church. Both clergy and laity are also generally opposed to affirmative action plans (Carroll, Hargrove, and Lummis 1981, 111–112, 122–124, 147–149; Lehman 1987, 320–321).

Edward Lehman provides a helpful framework in which to understand some of these ambiguities. He summarizes social psychologists' usage of the term "attitude." Attitudes toward women in ministry can be studied by looking at three components:

> Perceptions of clergy women are the "cognitive" dimension, feelings of attraction and aversion are the "affective" or emotional dimension, and preferences to act one way or another toward female clergy are the "behavioral" dimension. (Lehman 1987, 320)

Attitudes can be seen as more complex than simply "for" or "against." Not only do congregations have members who differ with one another in their perceptions of women as clergy, individual church members can have multifaceted attitudes. So even when lay people say they are willing to have women perform any particular ministerial functions, these same laity often prefer to have a male as their own pastor (Lehman 1987, 320–321; Carroll, Hargrove, and Lummis 1981, 142–144).

The minority of laity who do not want women clergy at all are willing to be more vocal and aggressive in their resistance. They are able to have a marked effect on the decision of the congregation as a whole. People whose perceptions support the idea of women in ministry are usually more concerned about keeping harmony in the congregation than they are about taking a stand in favor of calling a woman pastor. That is to say, the people whose cognitive and affective attitudes toward clergywomen are positive are usually willing to discriminate against women in the church's actual hiring practice (behavioral dimension) (Lehman 1987, 320–321).

Church members who experience one clergywoman positively do not necessarily generalize their changed attitude toward women as pastors overall. Instead, they sometimes are quite proud of their particular woman for being so unusually gifted and exceptional that she can make it in a man's profession. They may still assume (cognitive attitude) that most women would not be competent in the job. Consequently, women beginning a pastorate at a church that has had a woman as pastor before still cannot count on finding a lack of gender stereotypes in the congregational attitudes (Lehman 1987, 320–321, 325; Hoch 1996).[9]

Changing lay attitudes sufficiently to open more pastorates to women will need to involve more than simply persuading a majority of the laity that individual women can do outstanding ministry. While sexist distortions of Scripture and language have been challenged, many Christians resist the changed perception of the world that the new insights would bring. Lehman reflects:

> Religious sexism is in many ways but an extension of secular sexism. . . . Most people's sex-role socialization takes place long before they make religious commitments, and the stability of their personal attitude structures usually requires this type of consistency. (Lehman 1987, 322)

Subtleties of ambiguity can be seen even in the ways that many people advocate a "balance" of genders in the ministry of a local church. On multiple minister church staffs, "balance" seems to mean having both male and female ministers, but with many people preferring to have the senior pastor be a man. Clergy and laity also support a "principle of alternation" of gender, meaning that in one-pastor churches a man should follow a woman as pastor. There is not, however, the same advocacy in favor of women pastors following men pastors. The reason that people have given for being worried about having two women as pastors in a row was that they did not want the church to "be typecast as one that only has women clergy" (Carroll, Hargrove, and Lummis 1981, 148–149). When the question is asked what people mean by a type of church that has only women clergy, we are brought back to cultural stereotypes in which women have a lower stand-

ing than men. Because of that general perception, work that becomes identified as women's work will likely experience a decrease in status
(Broughton 1989, 6–7; Schaper 1990, 22, 38).

All of these various forms of laity ambiguity about women in ministry
are not surprising given the context of our culture. Pastoral caregivers
should remember that women entering ministry will frequently encounter
laity who have such ambivalent attitudes. These laity may sound supportive of women in ministry in the abstract, but they may not be supportive
in actual practice or on specific occasions. When the clergywoman senses a
negative reaction and attempts to check out her perception, the ambiguous
lay people may deny all but their positive feelings and behaviors. That
denial may leave the seminarian to doubt her own perceptions. Even if,
however, she values her own perceptions, she is left without an easy or
direct way of addressing the resistance she experiences.

### Developing Ministerial Identity and Confidence: Internships

The context of the church is vital to women seminarians long before
they graduate from seminary and face the fundamental issues involved in
placement. The church plays a significant role in whether women are able
to hear the initial urging of the call to ministry (see note 8). The church is
also the major context in which women seminarians will develop their ministerial identity and professional confidence. I will use the word "internship" to include the variety of church involvements—formal and informal;
paid and volunteer; before, during, and after seminary—in which women
try on and grow into ministerial roles and identity. The dynamics discussed
are also involved in a new minister's first church placement after seminary,
which continues to shape ministerial identity and confidence.

Not all men in seminary are preparing for the pastorate. But men in
seminary are likely to have considered it. While some women enter seminary with the sense of a call to the pastorate, many, especially midlife
women, seem to have initial difficulty seeing themselves in that role. These
midlife women are more likely to have come to seminary "with personal
and spiritual goals" than with a clear decision to seek ordination. Lack of
role models, lack of encouragement, as well as active discouragement and
messages about "appropriate" gender roles can be obstacles for women
deciding for the parish ministry (Carroll, Hargrove, and Lummis 1981,
222; Charlton 1987, 307).

Knowing women who were affirming calls to ordained ministry helps
seminarians hear their own call (Howe 1982, 165).[10] But few women who
eventually seek ordination do so out of a feminist motivation to change
church and society. Most state that their motivation is based on a call of

God. More clergywomen than clergymen rated a call to "administer the sacraments and perform other priestly acts" as predominant in their decision (Carroll, Hargrove, and Lummis 1981, 44–46, 95–98, 225; Royle 1987, 333). Women reflecting on their ordinations seem more likely than male ministers to describe the service as a significant experience of the grace of God. These anecdotal sources suggest that for some women the process of moving toward ordination may involve their deeply personal relationship with God. Rather than being predominantly conceived as a career choice, ministerial education may for these women be a powerful, integrative, personal pilgrimage.

Because of this tendency to be intimately and deeply involved with the call to ministry, women are likely to bring their whole sense of identity to their experiences in field education, Clinical Pastoral Education, and initial church placements. Seminary women are likely to be searching in these experiences either to hear the call of God more clearly or for validation of that call. To bring such a pilgrimage into ministerial training is in many ways the ideal for ministerial formation. But by investing more of themselves in the process, women also are placing more of themselves at risk. Pastoral caregivers need to recognize and affirm the significance of the process for women.

The development of ministerial identity and professional confidence comes out of an interplay between the interns' perceptions of themselves and the perceptions of other people about the particular intern. In describing how women often face the task differently from men, Martha Gilmore, Associate Director of the intern program at Perkins, sheds light on struggles like Shirley's (Gilmore 1987, 10). Shirley's crisis occurred while she was still in the process of developing professional confidence. Her pastor's and later her therapist's appraisal of her differed substantially from the positive aspects of her own self-perception. This conflict undermined her self-confidence.

A part of every intern's identity both in her own eyes and in the eyes of the congregation is the meaning of her gender identity in our culture. Since our culture still images the ministry as a male profession, women themselves may have ambivalent feelings about performing ministerial functions, even when they believe that Scripture supports the ordination of women. The question is not only, "Will I be able to function as a minister?" There is also the question, "If I succeed in performing ministerial functions well, will I still feel like a woman and will people still consider me acceptable as a woman?"

For example, often by the time a woman preaches her first sermon in an internship, she has already had classroom opportunities to build confidence in exegesis and preaching delivery. She is particularly likely to be anxious, however, about how she will be perceived as a woman who is preaching. Will the congregation think not only that she is an odd preacher but also that she is an odd woman (Gilmore 1987, 11)? Judging on the basis of comments made after worship, congregations do struggle with how to understand such an oddity as a woman preacher. Women often feel "patronized, discounted, and cheated" by comments they receive on their preaching:

> These reactions run the gamut from being curious, reserved, fascinated, aloof, to pleasantly surprised, enthusiastic, proud and delighted. Some view her adoringly. Others find her sexually attractive. Typical comments: "You're a lot prettier than the Senior Pastor." "You're the first preacher I ever saw wearing lipstick." "Do you have legs underneath that robe?" Often, sexual slurs imply that being a woman and preaching are incompatible, that female sexuality is bad and could well defile the sanctity of the pulpit. Parishioners further discount her sermon calling it "a little talk" or "a nice speech." (Gilmore 1987, 11)

My own first sermon (about 1970) was described in the bulletin as a testimony. Following the service, my pastor came up to me and said with intense surprise something to this effect: "You sounded almost like you were preaching." Even superficial, positive comments may be discouraging to women interns.[11]

The role conflict is accentuated for women when they try to shape replies to these varied comments. Most churches consider it a ministerial function to interact warmly, with caring, to congregational members following a worship service. A blunt response to inappropriate comments will probably be regarded as indicative that something is wrong with her. She may be considered defensive, hostile, overly sensitive, or "just not knowing how to get along with people."

When comments about a woman's attractiveness are given to her in a lighthearted way at church, she is expected to thank the people for the compliment or to tease them back in an innocent way. This expectation is rooted in the cultural evaluation that the "first duty of a woman is to be pretty."[12] So when members of the congregation comment on the intern's good looks, they are returning to safer, more familiar ground, on which to evaluate her as a person who is always first a woman.

Faced with responding to smiling, friendly people whose basic perceptions of the ministry and of women are incompatible, interns often feel they are in a "catch twenty-two." Do they act out the role of the friendly, obliging woman who loves to receive sexual compliments and light flirtations? Do they challenge the presuppositions of the comments in a public setting with not much time to be sure the other parties have understood them or feel understood by them? Experienced women who have resolved much of their ministerial identity and who have well-developed communication skills can still feel some discomfort or annoyance when faced with these comments. Such comments given to seminary interns who are in the process of trying to develop their ministerial identity can make them feel out of place in the ministry or can lead to feelings of inadequacy.[13]

Gilmore describes some women interns as getting trapped into a "fear cycle." Because they are afraid of being rejected, women interns can put extra pressure on themselves to work hard to the point of overachievement. When they put too much of their reliance on themselves, they can become "tense and defensive." Gilmore believes that a crucial part of the gospel is the human need to rely on God for salvation rather than ourselves. That salvation is God's freeing power. Ministers, men and women, need to experience this power personally as well as in their ministry. Gilmore documents the need for those supervising the intern to affirm her so that she can experience God's power through them, freeing her from the bonds of the fear cycle (Gilmore 1987, 9, 11–12).

Gilmore continues by looking at the problems that can emerge for the woman intern in her relationship with the field instructor (usually male) who supervises her. If either or both of them move into a father-daughter model of relationship, she may be treated as if she is fragile and in need of protection from the opinions of others or from her own emotions. Such a model deprives her of realistic feedback that she needs to learn from her actions or to explore her needs. Instead of protecting the intern, this type of supervisory relationship actually functions to undermine her self-confidence. Sometimes, however, the field instructor or Clinical Pastoral Education supervisor is so afraid of playing a father role that he overly avoids affirmation and withdraws emotionally from the intern. At times his withdrawal might be triggered by his perception that she is overly demanding or dependent. But if he withdraws, he might not even discuss his perception with her to check for its accuracy. This stance can confuse the intern in her evaluation of both her ministry and her relationship to the supervisor (Gilmore 1987, 13).

The intern will likely feel guilty if the relationship with the supervisor is inadequate. Women are socialized to place high value on personal relationships and to assume that they have the primary responsibility for ensuring the quality of their relationships. This socialization carries over in the woman intern's relationship with her field supervisor. If the relationship is not one of respect and trust, the woman intern is likely both to evaluate her internship as a failure and to blame herself for it. She is unlikely to wonder about her field supervisor's competency or whether he is confusing some of his issues with her issues (Gilmore 1987, 12).

These same cultural patterns make managing sexuality a different experience for women and men interns. The cultural expectations for women place added stress on female interns:

It is with alarming frequency that women travel completely through internship in silence and in pain regarding sexual issues. Certainly male interns
report stories of sexual propositions and attraction, but none experience them
in the same way as women. Males may indeed feel uncomfortable or embarrassed, but not ashamed and responsible. (Gilmore 1987, 14)

One of my students was clear that she was not responsible for her supervising pastor's propositioning her. But she still decided not to tell anyone
in her denomination for fear that she would not be believed and that the
pastor would criticize her to her district superintendent in retaliation. Her
fears seemed well grounded. When she came up for a denominational committee review, other people could not understand why that particular pastor was making things so difficult for her. The student thought that his
actions were due to her having clearly and briefly turned down the man's
advances. Another of my students felt she had to change denominations
when she did report her pastor's sexual assault. She was both blamed and
not believed by her church. Recent research about the frequency of clergy
sexual abuse has not yet changed the response given to most women who
report clergy misconduct (see Heggen 1993; Fortune and Poling 1994).

A further source of difficulty may be that "men perceive less friendliness,
but more sexuality than women when observing women's social interactions." If men are taught to interpret as sexual what a woman intends to
be merely friendly, then misunderstandings are likely to occur (Saal, Johnson, and Weber 1989, 263). While this pattern operates in congregations, it
has particularly plagued the old style of Clinical Pastoral Education supervision. When women chaplain interns did not interpret a situation in a sexual way, they were often told by their male supervisors that they were "not
in touch with their sexuality." Many of the women who participated in
Clinical Pastoral Education in the 1970s and 1980s look back on that
experience with the realization that what passed then as authoritative
supervision might now be considered sexual harassment. At the least, it
was a poor supervision that elevated the needs and problems of overly sexualized men in our culture to the status of universal human realities.[14]
Anecdotal evidence indicates that this pattern of supervision has been
challenged from within Clinical Pastoral Education structures and has
been on the decline in recent years. But nurturers of women entering ministry should remember that it is still possible for a woman to encounter this
type of confusing and perhaps abusive supervision in some phase of her
ministry training.

A final area of the relationship of the church to the intern relates specifically to the intern's development of leadership or authority. Knowing specific leadership skills is not sufficient in and of itself to become a leader. If
congregational members do not think of women having genuine leadership

or authority, they will not respond to leadership skills and cues from a woman the way they would respond to the identical initiatives taken by a man (Coger 1985, 16–18).[15]

Claiming power is closely related to developing confidence in ministerial identity and functioning. Theologically, it would be described as affirming one's spiritual gifts and believing that God might choose to accompany and empower one's actions. Seen in this light, not only do interns need to "claim their power," they need to learn to feel comfortable with exercising a more direct power than women are generally accorded. Women may have internal difficulties in claiming this power:

> Women are socialized to act vulnerable, passive, tender, gentle, supportive, powerless. . . . Socialization and structures of society reinforce these definitions. . . . Some women hide their power because they do not believe being powerful is consistent with being female. They act apologetic and discount their strengths. Many women genuinely experience themselves as powerless. . . .
>
> . . . One way a woman blocks the development of her power is that she fails to believe that her opinions are important and accurate. Often women do not trust their perceptions until they are validated by someone else. (Gilmore 1987, 16)

Certainly, when women come for pastoral counseling, any ways in which they are sabotaging themselves by not claiming or developing their spiritual gifts need to be examined. The messages of their early childhood and of our present culture need to be analyzed. In one study, 60 percent of the women ministers surveyed thought "that they are being blamed for going against the tide" (Richmond, Rayburn, Rogers 1988, 68; Glover-Wetherington 1992, 119–173; Pfost and Fiore 1990, 15–24; Worell and Remer 1992; Neuger 1991, 146–161). Pastoral counselors need to be aware that women seminarians may be pressured not to see themselves as potentially competent leaders.

When one woman intern told her field instructor that she was nervous, he responded to her by saying, "Don't get hysterical." Was the woman intern's emotion expressed inappropriately or was the supervisor uncomfortable dealing with emotions? The field instructor's use of the word "hysterical" implies that he thought there was a pathological element in the woman intern's expression. The very history of the word "hysterical" indicates a tendency of the male medical establishment to see women's emotions as naturally tending to the pathological (Gilmore 1987, 16–17).

Other examples that Gilmore gives have to do with a pointed lack of direct response to a woman's comments. Women reported saying something in a meeting and being "met with silence." In that situation, silence can be a powerful means of communicating that the comment or the one making it will not be accepted. One woman told of her experience in the local ministerial alliance. In discussions, whenever she made a statement the comment would be ignored. Later one of the male ministers would repeat the same statement, and the group would then discuss it. After this pattern had gone on for some time, the woman confronted the group with her observations. As the group discussed the situation, the men were eventually willing to admit their attitudes to themselves and to her: "The group acknowledged their reluctance to hear what she said because of their resistance to her being part of the group. This opened the way for dialogue" (Gilmore 1987, 16–17). Certainly, most women interns would experience the need to confront a group of male ministers in this way as being highly stressful. Shirley's fear that her voice will not be heard has a long, ongoing basis in experience, not just a birth in childhood experiences. If pastoral counselors ignore or discount the importance of either past or current societal pressures for women entering ministry, they are not helping them deal with the full reality of the situation.

### Collegial Relationships: Tokens and Zoo Exhibits

A man in one of my classes was honest enough to include in his class journal his realization that he would resent any of his women seminary friends "getting ahead" of him. He made this admission with some surprise and some embarrassment. My guess is that, unlike this student, most clergymen who would resent a clergywoman succeeding would not recognize their own reaction as a subtle message to women to stay in their place. Instead of the student's embarrassment over his own competitive resentment, it seems likely that these clergymen would place the blame for their discomfort on the actions and person of the clergywomen who had succeeded. The "problems" of which they might accuse her could range from her being driven, manipulative, pushy, phony, castrating, unfeminine, and "just not a team player." Instead of realizing that they were withdrawing support from her, they might project that she was ignoring them or putting them down.

Clergywomen's and women seminarians' relationships with their male colleagues are understandably diverse. An obvious source of tension would be those relationships with men who believe that the Bible and God are opposed to the ordination of women. But relationships with men students who support women in ministry can also be difficult because of mixed signals, ambivalent attitudes, and polarization (see Glover-Wetherington 1992, 223–224; Rogers, Rayburn, and Richmond, "Outlooks," 1988, 27; Rogers, Rayburn, and Richmond, "Women in Religious," 1988, 22). Pastoral caregivers in church, clinical, and seminary contexts need to model how to discuss differences without attacking or putting down people who are misinformed on gender issues, who have other perspectives, or who are ambivalent.

While some seminaries have around 50 percent women, women in other seminaries are still a decided minority. Whatever their seminary experiences, however, women in ministry can still be seen as "tokens" in the contexts of local churches and ministerial meetings. Kanter suggests that some of the attitudes and behaviors that have been assumed to be characteristic of women because of their gender may actually be situational responses to being in a "token" group. Out of her study of corporate business structures, Kanter specifically speculates that "fear of success" could be better understood as the token's fear of visibility.[16]

Coger, using Kanter's categories, describes three main patterns of relationship between tokens and dominants in a skewed group. In the first pattern, *boundary heightening,* the dominants are fearful that they will lose their common bond, and so they accentuate the difference between themselves and the tokens. Sometimes this difference is enacted by the dominants having meetings to which the tokens are not invited (Coger 1985, 20). In my experience, if asked later why the tokens were not included, the dominants may respond in a number of ways that accentuate the naturalness of the dominants wanting to be together and cast the token asking the question in the role of a pushy interloper. Responses may include: "We did not know that you were interested"; "Please understand that we have known each other so much longer and have a deeper friendship with one another"; "This was just an informal gathering. We wanted to be able to let our hair down with the boys"; or "Well, it was our idea to do something special for the group, and so we thought we would plan it and present it as a surprise."

There are also more subtle ways that dominants can send messages that the tokens are not part of the dominant group. Sometimes the dominant group of men may in the presence of token women talk more than usual about traditional male themes, such as sports or off-color, sexualized humor. The men may also turn to the women and apologize for their language. By this action the dominants make clear that their language is the accepted norm or culture for the group. By implication the woman is seen as an intruder or special case who takes extra time away from the normal interactions of the group. She is told indirectly that acceptance of these group "traditions" is a condition of her entry into the group (Coger 1985, 20). While some clergy groups do have this culture of off-color humor or language, ministerial groups that avoid such language can certainly find other ways to do boundary heightening. In the 1970s one of the male pastors in our Baltimore ministerial group persistently called me (the only woman in the group) "honey" or "sweetie."

The second pattern of relationships between dominants and tokens is *loyalty tests.* If the tokens want admission into the group, the dominants ask for reassurance that the tokens will "not turn against them." These loyalty tests can take several forms. Men may "invite" women to join them in jokes or comments that put women down. The token woman may be expected to state her preferred identification with the men rather than to be like "most women." She then becomes a special case who does not serve to challenge the men's right to be the dominant group. To show "due appreciation" for having been included in the group at all, the tokens are usually also required not to question the status quo in other ways as well. In another loyalty test, token women may be expected to take being teased or kidded to provide humor for the group (Coger 1985, 20).

Obviously, if a woman accepts these loyalty tests she is involved in supporting and continuing negative stereotypes of women. What she "wins" in partial acceptance by the dominants is countered by what she looses in self-esteem and identity with other women. If she is not willing to pay this price, she is denied the collegial support that comes automatically to new clergymen (Coger 1985, 20–21).

*Competition* is the third area that Kanter describes as characterizing patterns of relationship between dominants and tokens. The male student whose journal writing is noted above was observing this pattern in himself. As a part of loyalty tests, women are expected to describe women as incompetent. If, then, a token succeeds more than a dominant, then the dominant considers himself humiliated and the woman will be punished by the withdrawal of collegial support. Peers who are resentful because they feel they have been humiliated do not tend to be supportive in the future. Because men consider women's success threatening to them, they discourage women from excelling in notable ways (Coger 1985, 21).

One of the most difficult situations for clergywomen is when some or all of the dominants in the skewed group consider themselves feminists and are on some level supporting women in ministry. One woman minister on a "liberal, socially conscious staff" described the problem: "It's harder to get the issues out on the table when he denies there is a problem" (Coger 1985, 24). Part of the tension for the women is that the men who consider themselves beyond the possibility of unconscious sexism are often the men who are the women's closest male colleagues and friends. The ambiguities and mixed messages of those friendships can be confusing.

Because of being a token, women ministers are sometimes not seen as individual people with particular hopes and interests. Instead, the woman minister is treated as a representative of her "kind." As tokens, clergywomen receive extra public attention. Coger explains what Margaret Howe means in saying that women in ministry are treated like "zoo exhibits." Each time that a clergywoman preaches or conducts a funeral or wedding some of the congregation may use their evaluation of her "performance" to judge whether any women belong in ministry (Nason-Clark 1987, 334). Knowing that they are always being scrutinized this way, women clergy can easily slip into becoming overachievers who drive themselves excessively. In many communities women pastors may also serve as "'visible walking targets for the pain, confusion, and grief that people feel over the changing roles of women and men in society at large'" (Howe quoted in Coger 1985, 16). These two unrequested roles, symbolizing all women in ministry and even, for some people, representing all gender changes, obviously place added stresses on women entering ministry.

Pastoral caregivers who work with seminarians and clergywomen would benefit from an understanding of the societal pressures on "tokens" and "zoo exhibits." Women may initially wonder whether all their frustrations should be attributed to something being wrong inside themselves (see attribution theory: Basow 1986, 163–166, 192, 244–245; LaNoue and Curtis 1985, 337–356; Frieze et al. 1978, 333–334; McHugh, Frieze, and Hanusa 1982, 467–479). If pastoral carers use overly individualistic counseling theory and theology, they are likely to support the tendency to a distorted self-blame. Caregivers need to help women identify reality and decide how to deal with it.

### Parenting, Marriage, and Romance

The previous sections describe how placement, internships, and collegial relationships can pressure women to stay in traditional role boundaries. The more personal home relationships can also serve as powerful parts of this role boundary maintenance system. Here I discuss this group of possible external, relational pressures on women entering ministry by looking briefly at parenting, marriage, and the friendships of single women.

*Marriage and Parenting.* Many of the pressures on married clergywomen were similar to pressures on married clergymen: the need to balance parish and private life, the lack of privacy, the need for personally supportive relationships, difficulties for clergy couples, difficulties for two career marriages, spouse sometimes resentful of time spent in ministry, pressures of parenting, and conflicting role sets (Carroll, Hargrove, and Lummis 1981, 189, 193–194; Mehl 1984, 293). Both men and women who were single parents and ministers felt role overload and conflicting time pressures pulling them between the needs of their children and of their churches.

Women who are a part of clergy couples are more likely to report that their husbands are understanding about the demands of the ministry than are clergywomen married to nonordained husbands (Carroll, Hargrove, and Lummis 1981, 193, 202). But if they work in the same parish as their husbands, they may feel their ministerial leadership is discounted and considered subordinate to their husbands' ministry (Carroll, Hargrove, and Lummis 1981, 196; Rayburn, Richmond, and Rogers, "Stress, Religion, and Marriage," 1988, 54–56).

Other significant differences for women came when in spite of their seminary and church responsibilities, people expected them to continue in homemaking and parenting as if they had no other responsibilities. In churches served by clergy who were married with children, parishioners were more likely to wonder how the clergywoman could combine her ministry with being a mother than they were to worry about the clergyman balancing the responsibilities of being a minister and a father. Clergywomen reported greater strain than did clergymen during the years when their children were young (Carroll, Hargrove, and Lummis 1981, 192, 195; Mehl 1984, 295). A clergywoman who divided the parenting more evenly with her husband might be evaluated as not a good mother and socially rejected. For most women in our culture, to be considered a bad mother is a blow to one's self-esteem and identity and, consequently, serves as an emotional punishment.[17]

The temptation for women clergy is to attempt to combine higher parenting expectations with a need to excel to prove themselves acceptable as seminarians and ministers (Rayburn, Richmond, and Rogers, "Women and Men," 1988, 2; Rogers, Rayburn, and Richmond, "Outlooks," 1988, 25, 27–28; Rogers, Rayburn, and Richmond, "Women in Religious," 1988, 23). The initial appeal of this superwoman image then confronts the exhaustion that results from "superwoman's" difficulty saying "no," setting limits, and separating professional and private time.[18]

When midlife women decide to enter seminary, the responses of their husbands are significant influences shaping the marriages. Mehl reported on fifteen midlife marriages:

> Most of the husbands said they would help out,[19] but the tasks usually remained the wife's responsibility, and this led to much frustration and anger. "I felt I had to keep the home up. He was good at asking, 'Can *you* manage?'" (Mehl 1984, 293)

If the husband's response was to be actually supportive, it needed to be more than toleration. Support included willingness to change his own level of involvement in his career and at home. When husbands were not understanding, not flexible in renegotiating home responsibilities, and not supportive in actions as well as in words, marital crises occurred (Mehl 1984, 293–295).

*Single Women.* Single clergywomen do not have the "excuse" of a family to justify their need for private and social time. Young, single clergywomen in rural placements were the most likely group to suffer from loneliness. The problem seemed to be in finding enough compatible friends outside the church with whom the women could relax and be themselves, not always on stage in the pastor role. While about 94 percent of clergymen are married, only about 55 percent of clergywomen are married. Do women clergy find it particularly difficult to combine ministry and marriage, or do they "have higher expectations of the kind of equitable marriage relationship they wish to enter?" (Carroll, Hargrove, and Lummis 1981, 190–191, 198–199). To what extent does their singleness express their own preference? To what extent is their singleness a result of being labeled undesirable because they are in a profession considered nontraditional for women? If this latter reason is a significant factor, then being rejected in romantic relationships is a silent way society penalizes women and tries to maintain traditional role boundaries (see Pfost and Fiore 1990, 15–24).

## Decoys and Detours: Formation in Christian Ministry

Pastoral counseling specialists have often emphasized that it is the relationship between caregiver and care seeker that "heals." Sometimes the analogy is used of the caregiver "reparenting" the care seeker. But that analogy provides too small a theoretical framework because it assumes that the primary or only problem is that the internal "normal" growth into individual maturity has been distorted or derailed. In reviewing the recent debate about seminary structures and goals, Barbara Wheeler asserts that, from a theological viewpoint, ministerial formation must involve more than an individualistically conceived "psychological maturity" (Wheeler 1989, 14, 18). Her analysis has important implications for pastoral care.

The focus of most of this study has been on possible, current, external pressures on women entering ministry. Pastoral caregivers working with these women need to consider the power of these forces to create pain and confusion. Silence about the ambiguities of the present teaches women that it is their inner unresolved issues that are solely responsible for their anxieties and depressions. Overly individualistic pastoral care can be a subtle decoy, distracting the woman and her caregivers from problems in the realities around her.

Fortunately, Shirley was able to use her first therapy as a detour instead of a permanent decoy. Its excessive individualism sidetracked her for a while, but she was able to overcome its paralyzing effects and use its insights in a positive way. As she did more connecting with people who affirmed her gifts and treated her more collegially, her own sense of God's call to the pastorate was confirmed.

A focus exclusively on the internal is not only detrimental to the care seeker. It can also cloud pastoral caregivers' awareness of the larger context of their own actions. All forms of pastoral care with women entering ministry, including pastoral counseling, inescapably participate in the process of ministerial and ongoing Christian formation. What communities shape the perspectives of the caregivers about formation? As pastoral caregivers (whether professional specialists or colleagues and friends), we are called to help the care seekers more clearly envision and live into their communal destiny in God. By drawing the reality of that future into the present, we are allowed to participate in God's redemptive activity.[20]

As a part of these formations, *pastoral care specialties, including spiritual nurture, clinical pastoral supervision, and pastoral counseling* themselves work as powerful, shaping environments. These caregivers have a strong, but often hidden, influence on the professional ministerial culture. From a secular viewpoint, they serve a gatekeeping function on the profession of ministry, especially on their own pastoral care specialties. Their assessments, expressed both in written and oral evaluations and recommendations, impact professional inclusion and rejection. Pastoral care or counseling that overemphasizes the intrapsychic and neglects both current contexts and eschatological community will unwittingly itself become part of the current contexts that discourage and debilitate women called to ministry.

## NOTES

1. As in all research, my own background serves inevitably as a perspective lens. While the pastorate was not open to women in my denomination, one of my congregations blessed me with ordination. I have served as a campus minister, as a minister of education and youth, and as a pastoral counselor. The settings in which I worked as a pastoral counselor have included a rape relief center, a clinic providing therapy for an HMO, and three pastoral counseling centers.

2. Charlton is among those who caution against the assumption that so much progress has been made that seminaries are no longer sources of problems for women. She understands that assumption to be a blind spot that will keep us from further study of seminary contexts (Charlton 1987, 312–313).

3. The initial research was done as part of my dissertation. There I discuss the methodological problems of the study and give more detailed descriptions of the sources (Glover-Wetherington 1992, 174–293).

4. For additional insights into the centrality of human relatedness, see Fulkerson (1994, 4–11); Miller-McLemore (1993); Moltmann-Wendel and Moltmann (1991, 36–37); and the discussion of Pannenberg in Glover-Wetherington (1992, 26–118).

5. Pastoral caregivers need to be aware of the diversity both of feminist and of traditional approaches. Women can receive destructive pressure to conform from

both feminist and traditional groups. See the womanist critique of feminism (hooks 1981; Williams 1986, 42–58). Fulkerson notes the neglect by her own academic feminist community of women in other communities and that feminist declaration of "women's experience" does not adequately address "race, class, and sexual particularity." The practical impact of a Scripture passage on the lives of women depends on how it is construed and enacted by a particular faith community (Fulkerson 1994, 3, 13–116).

6. Both in the New Testament churches and through the centuries there have been more women in church leadership and ministerial roles than is commonly recognized. See, for example, even such nonfeminist scholars as Stagg and Stagg (1978); Talbert (1987); and Bainton (1978).

7. Carroll, Hargrove, and Lummis 1981, 111–112. While the research for this study is now over ten years old, it remains one of the most careful and comprehensive studies done on women in ministry. Hoch (1996) finds that issues for women entering ministry have not changed significantly from those described by Carroll, Hargrove, and Lummis.

8. Large studies were sponsored either by individual denominations themselves or by ecumenical groups interested in advocating women clergy. There is little research on lay attitudes in denominations whose officials discourage women's ordination (Lehman 1987, 323). The scarcity of research does not mean that these groups are unimportant.

For example, at present, the Southern Baptist Convention (SBC) is still the largest American Protestant denomination. In the SBC, some women may never recognize God's call to them, because women in fundamentalist congregations are being taught to regard as misguided any sense of call to ordained ministry. SBC moderate churches have been more willing to ordain women than to call them as pastors. Still, in 1990 Southern Baptist women in seminary, whether they intended to be ordained or not, often had unrealistically positive hopes of being called to church positions when they graduated (Glover-Wetherington 1992, 278–279, 285–288; Anders 1983, 427–436).

Another example of much needed research is Fulkerson's post-structuralist exploration into the relationship between Pentecostal mountain women and their faith tradition. Outsider feminist observers might casually conclude that these women are hopelessly "unliberated" and stuck in a community that depreciates their abilities and roles. But Fulkerson finds the situation more intricate. While still engaging in the self-denigrating language their faith culture expects, these women have indeed found the gospel new wine that confronts the debilitating and sinful structures of their society. By the way that they have lived into certain aspects of their tradition, they claim the authorization of the Spirit who calls them to be preachers and interpreters of Scripture. The contradictions and ambiguities of their position in their community result in some situations in continued, evil abuse. But their way of enacting Scripture also creates a place of grace for them in which they can respect and affirm God's work in them and their work in God (Fulkerson 1994, 239–298). It is important for pastoral caregivers to look for these subtleties and ambiguities and not too quickly to categorize contexts.

9. Lehman (1987) mentions nothing about any of the churches he studied reporting having had a negative experience with a woman pastor.

10. In 1994 one of my students was the daughter of a woman pastor.

11. A study of nonseminarians "found some evidence to indicate that women were more negatively influenced by feedback that was positively toned, yet irrelevant with respect to their performance, than men" (Roberts and Nolen-Hoeksema 1989, 725). Whether or not other studies would replicate this finding, this study does point out that "positively toned, yet irrelevant" feedback can be discouraging. This is the type of feedback that many women seminarians receive.

12. The value represented by this saying is frequently repeated in advertising and stories presented in the media.

13. The need for women seminarians to have advanced skills in balancing role expectations parallels Kanter's study of women managers in large corporations (Kanter 1977, 219).

14. These observations are based on the underground conversations of many women involved in clinical training during this time. Confused and sometimes angry, these women often turned to one another to try to sort out what was really happening. More recently, I have heard confirmation of this perspective from male supervisors who now see their past behavior as having been a problem.

15. Johnson describes several types of power and how gender roles are related to them. She names legitimate power, referent power, expert power, and informational power (1978, 301–320). Fulkerson incorporates a more complex power analysis as an integral part of her understanding of human interactions (1994).

16. "Skewed groups" have a preponderance of one type (the "dominants") and up to 20 percent of a group that Kanter calls the "tokens." Some evidence indicates that even when the proportion of women is larger than 20 percent, some of the characteristics of skewed groups may be evident in the male-female dynamics (Kanter 1977, 209, 221; Coger 1985, 4–5. See also Carroll, Hargrove, and Lummis 1981, 198; Charlton 1987, 313; and Royle 1987, 348–349). The effect of changing ratios on group relationships needs additional study. It has applications not only to situations of gender difference but also to groups defined by differences in race or culture.

17. While Reeves does not conduct a separate study of clergywomen's family relationships, many of her reflections on role conflicts are applicable to those situations (1983, 14–16).

18. Some evidence indicates that women clergy have good skills for coping with stress (Richmond, Rayburn, and Rogers 1988, 69; Rogers, Rayburn, and Richmond 1988, "Outlooks," 28; and Rogers, Rayburn, and Richmond 1988, "Women in Religious Professions," 21-22). Other researchers found indications that women have more difficulty than their male clergy counterparts at setting limits on their work (Carroll, Hargrove, and Lummis 1981, 189–191, 201).

19. During the 1970s, Ellen Goodman in her newspaper column described the implications of men "helping out" at home. When the "helping out" term is used, the responsibilities are still assumed to belong to the woman. The husband is thought to be deserving of special praise and appreciation, while the wife's contribution is taken for granted.

20. For the emphasis on the importance of the eschatological future in forming our present identities I am indebted to Pannenberg (Glover-Wetherington 1992, 26–118; see also Fulkerson 1994, 4).

## BIBLIOGRAPHY

Anders, Sarah Frances. 1983. "Women in Ministry: The Distaff Side of the Church." *Review and Expositor* 80: 427–436.

Bainton, Roland H. 1978. *Women of the Reformation: In France and England.* Minneapolis: Augsburg Publishing House.

Basow, Susan. 1986. *Gender Stereotypes: Traditions and Alternatives.* Pacific Grove, Calif.: Brooks/Cole Publishing Co.

Broughton, Patricia. 1989. "Welcome to Women-Church! Where Have We Come From and Where Are We Going?" *Daughters of Sarah* 15: 6–7.

Carroll, Jackson; Barbara Hargrove; and Adair T. Lummis. 1981. *Women of the Cloth: A New Opportunity for the Churches.* San Francisco: Harper & Row.

Charlton, Joy C. 1987. "Women in Seminary: A Review of Current Social Science Research." *Review of Religious Research* 28: 305–318.

Coger, Marian. [1985] 1991. *Women in Parish Ministry: Stress and Support.* Washington, D.C.: Alban Institute.

Condry, John, and Sharon Dyer. 1976. "Fear of Success: Attribution of Cause to the Victim." *Journal of Social Issues* 32: 63–83.

Eccles, Jacquelynne S. 1987. "Gender Roles and Women's Achievement-related Decisions." *Psychology of Women Quarterly* 11: 135–172.

Fortune, Marie, and James N. Poling. 1994. *Sexual Abuse by Clergy: A Crisis for the Church.* Decatur, Ga.: Journal of Pastoral Care Publications.

Frieze, Irene H., et al. 1978. *Women and Sex Roles: A Social Psychological Perspective.* New York: W. W. Norton & Co.

Fulkerson, Mary McClintock. 1994. *Changing the Subject: Women's Discourses and Feminist Theology.* Minneapolis: Fortress Press.

Gilmore, Martha. 1987. "Women Developing Confidence in Internship: No Easy Task." *Perkins Journal* 40: 9–17.

Glaz, Maxine, and Jeanne Stevenson Moessner, eds. 1991. *Women in Travail and Transition: A New Pastoral Care.* Minneapolis: Fortress Press.

Glover-Wetherington, Miriam Anne. 1992. "The Significance of Systemic Paradigms for Pastoral Care with Women, M.Div. Seminarians." Diss., Southern Baptist Theological Seminary.

Graham, Larry Kent. 1992. *Care of Persons, Care of Worlds: A Psychosystems Approach to Pastoral Care and Counseling.* Nashville: Abingdon Press.

———. 1989. "Prophetic Pastoral Caretaking: A Psychosystemic Approach to Symptomatology." *Journal of Psychology and Christianity* 8: 49–60.

Greenspan, Miriam. 1983. *A New Approach to Women and Therapy: How Psychotherapy Fails Women—and What They Can Do about It.* St. Louis: McGraw-Hill Book Co.

Hargrove, Barbara. 1987. "On Digging, Dialogue, and Decision Making." *Review of Religious Research* 28: 395–401.

Heggen, Carolyn. 1993. *Sexual Abuse in Christian Homes and Churches.* Scottdale, Pa.: Herald Press.

Hoch, Ann. 1996. "Observations by the Director of Student Life and Associate Director of Field Education, Duke Divinity School." Unpublished interview. Durham, North Carolina.

hooks, bell. 1981. *Ain't I a Woman: Black Women and Feminism.* Boston: South End Press.

Horner, Matina S. 1972. "Toward an Understanding of Achievement Related Conflicts in Women." *Journal of Social Issues* 28: 157–175.

Howe, Margaret E. 1982. *Women and Church Leadership.* Grand Rapids: Zondervan Publishing House.

Johnson, Paula. 1978. "Women and Interpersonal Power." In Frieze et al., 302–320.

Kanter, Rosabeth Moss. 1977. *Men and Women of the Corporation.* New York: Basic Books.

LaNoue, Joan B., and Rebecca C. Curtis. 1985. "Improving Women's Performance in Mixed-Sex Situations by Effort Attribution." *Psychology of Women Quarterly* 9: 337–356.

Lehman, Edward C., Jr. 1987 "Research on Lay Church Members Attitudes toward Women Clergy: An Assessment." *Review of Religious Research* 28: 319–329.

McHugh, Maureen C.; Irene Hanson Frieze; and Barbara Hartman Hanusa. 1982. "Attributions and Sex Differences in Achievement: Problems and New Perspectives." *Sex Roles* 8: 467–479.

Mehl, L. Guy. 1984. "Marriage and Ministry in Midlife Women." *Journal of Religion and Health* 23: 290–298.

Miller-McLemore, Bonnie J. 1993. "The Human Web: Reflections on the State of Pastoral Theology." *The Christian Century* 110: 366–369. A revised form of this article forms the basis of chapter 1 of this volume.

———. 1991. "Women Who Work and Love." In Glaz and Moessner, eds., 63–85.

Moltmann-Wendel, Elisabeth, and Jürgen Moltmann. 1991. *God—His and Hers.* New York: Crossroad.

Nason-Clark, Nancy. 1987. "Are Women Changing the Image of Ministry? A Comparison of British and American Realities." *Review of Religious Research* 28: 330–340.

Neuger, Christie Cozad. 1991 "Women's Depression: Lives at Risk." In Glaz and Moessner, eds., 146–161.

Patton, John. 1993. *Pastoral Care in Context: An Introduction to Pastoral Care.* Louisville, Ky.: Westminster/John Knox Press.

Pfost, Karen L., and Maria Fiore. 1990. "Pursuit of Nontraditional Occupations: Fear of Success or Fear of Not Being Chosen?" *Sex Roles* 23: 15–24.

Poling, James Newton. 1991. *The Abuse of Power: A Theological Problem.* Nashville: Abingdon Press.

Rayburn, Carole A.; Lee J. Richmond; and Lynn Rogers. 1988. "Stress, Religion, and Marriage in Women." *Journal of Pastoral Counseling* 23: 54–56.

———. 1988. "Women and Men Religious Leaders and Stress." *Journal of Pastoral Counseling* 23: 1–5.

Reeves, Joy B. 1983. "Role Conflict and Resolution: The Case of the Christian Feminist." *Journal of Pastoral Counseling* 18: 11–19.

Richmond, Lee J.; Carole A. Rayburn; and Lynn Rogers. 1988. "Stress within Religious Leadership Roles: What Counselors Need to Know." *Journal of Pastoral Counseling* 23: 67–71.

Roberts, Tomi-Ann, and Susan Nolen-Hoeksema. 1989. "Sex Differences in Reactions to Evaluative Feedback." *Sex Roles* 21: 725–747.

Rogers, Lynn; Carole A. Rayburn; and Lee J. Richmond. 1988. "Women in Religious Professions and Stress." *Journal of Pastoral Counseling* 23: 21–24.

———. 1988. "Outlooks of Seminarians and Ministers on Women in Ministry." *Journal of Pastoral Counseling* 23: 25–30.

Royle, Marjorie H. 1987. "Using Bifocals to Overcome Blindspots: The Impact of Women on the Military and the Ministry." *Review of Religious Research* 28: 341–350.

Saal, Frank E.; Catherine B. Johnson; and Nancy Weber. 1989. "Friendly or Sexy? It May Depend on Whom You Ask." *Psychology of Women Quarterly* 13: 263–276.

Schaper, Donna. 1990. *Common Sense: About Women and Men in the Ministry.* The Alban Institute.

Stagg, Evelyn, and Frank Stagg. 1978. *Women in the World of Jesus.* Philadelphia: Westminster.

Talbert, Charles H. 1987. *Reading Corinthians: A Literary and Theological Commentary on 1 and 2 Corinthians.* New York: Crossroad.

Tresemer, David Ward. 1977. *Fear of Success.* New York: Plenum Press.

Wheeler, Barbara G. 1989. "Practical Theology: Notes on a Common Enemy." Unpublished manuscript: "Remarks at a Meeting of the Faculty of the Episcopal Divinity School, Cambridge, Massachusetts, September 7, 1989."

Williams, Delores S. 1986. "The Color of Feminism: Or Speaking the Black Woman's Tongue." *Journal of Religious Thought* 43: 42–58.

Worell, Judith, and Pam Remer. 1992. *Feminist Perspectives in Therapy: An Empowerment Model for Women.* New York: John Wiley.

# 5

# Weaving the Web:
# Pastoral Care in an
# Individualistic Society

PAMELA COUTURE
*Candler School of Theology*

Hear these words, addressed to the congregation at Baptism:

*Pastor:* Will you nurture one another in the Christian faith and life and include these persons, now before you, in your care?
*Congregation:* With God's help we will proclaim the Good News and live according to the example of Christ. We will surround these persons with a community of life and forgiveness that they may grow in the trust of God and be found faithful in service to others. We will pray for them that they may be true disciples who walk in the way that leads to life. (*United Methodist Hymnal,* Baptismal Rite II)

℡hese are grand promises of genuine care of one another. Yet in the individualistic society in which we live, we often believe that we are our best selves when we are autonomous, neither intervening in the lives of others nor inviting others to comment on ours. A further paradox thrives in our own discipline: we seek to be healers, yet many social theorists would say that the very methods and assumptions of the twentieth-century pastoral care and counseling movement have contributed to spread the contagious disease of individualism. This disciplinary paradox is cradled in a broader cultural dilemma: our ambivalence about the role of the individual.

On one hand, on the basis of the Christian belief in the worth of the individual and of the Enlightenment assertion of the rights of man (*sic*), Americans have stressed the importance of the individual as a lever against the abuse of power in hierarchically organized society. Our constitutional com-

A version of this article was originally published as "The Context of Congregations: Pastoral Care in an Individualistic Society," In *The Journal of Pastoral Theology,* June 1992. Reprinted by permission.

mitment to individual worth and individual rights sets the stage for egalitarian claims by women and people of color.

Since World War II, however, even as women and people of color staked
their claims with new urgency, the hand has turned: the commitment to
the individual has been transformed from social criticism into status quo.
In legal discourse and in culture, arguments on behalf of the rights of individuals that provided leverage for individuals within disenfranchised
groups against larger power structures became arguments on behalf of
individuals regardless of larger purposes and commitments (Glendon
1991). This transformation has created a prominence of individualistic values in personal growth, family life, social institutions, including the church,
and public policy. As we face the twenty-first century, these individualistic
values have become the basis not only for personal and interpersonal
lifestyles but also for national and international economic practices. The
consequences of economic individualism, consequences including various
kinds of human suffering that can be attributed to the narrowing of the
middle class and the growing distance between the haves and the have-
nots, are already forcing the hand of individualistic society. These consequences create a changing situation within which pastoral caregivers and
congregations will need to minister.

This ministry calls us to no less than a reworking of the theoretical base
upon which pastoral care and counseling in the twentieth century has been
constituted. We can appreciate the gains of the twentieth-century movement by placing this turn to the individual in care and counseling in its historical context. However, the story of a particular woman, Ellen, helps to
demonstrate the limits of the psychology-theology correlation and individualistic assumptions in interpreting her plight; her story will also help to
introduce the concept of social ecology as an alternative to the correlation
between theology and psychology. A social ecological theoretical foundation challenges us to think about the individual not only as she is formed
in the nexus of intrapsychic, interpersonal, and family dynamics but also
as she is held secure or let loose by public and ecclesial policies and the
beliefs of the culture in which she lives. I dedicate this presentation to
Ellen, the counselee whose life taught me to perceive the terrifyingly multilayered vortex of the individualism with which we live.

## ELLEN

Stories of women such as my counselee Ellen are becoming increasingly
commonplace. Ellen was a spunky young woman from a working middle-

class family who had average intelligence and a measure of artistic ability. She told her story something like this:

She had had a relatively happy childhood until her mother died of cancer when Ellen was seventeen. In her grief, Ellen, like so many other children, attempted to fill her mother's tasks and "make a home for her father" in order to secure her father's attention and affection. Her father began to date and established a new relationship about which Ellen felt the usual ambivalence. When he married two years later, he asked Ellen, the youngest of his four children, three of whom lived in a neighboring state, to move out on her own. Unhappily, Ellen rented her own apartment and got a menial job in an auto parts store.

As she tried to establish relations with her father and her stepmother, they revealed a family secret: she was not the biological daughter of the father who had raised her but had been conceived when her mother had an affair. This news sent her into a state of confusion, for she was now doubly uncertain whether she could look to her father for love and support. In the midst of the loneliness and insecurity of the situation, she became suicidal, was hospitalized, and lost her job. Hospitalization, in the belief system of the family, was a sign of Ellen's weakness, an indication that it was time for her to shape up and stop pitying herself. After the hospitalization, her father told her that it was her turn to care for her thirty-five-year-old, somewhat mentally retarded sister, and brought Julia to live with her. In Ellen's words, "I could not put her out as I had been put out." Ellen's mental health improved, but her medical history was now burdened with a damaging preexistent condition. She found another service sector job that provided minimal medical coverage. As she began to put her life back together, she attempted to establish her own permanent relationship, became sexually involved, and, as the relationship began to deteriorate, became pregnant. Despite the fact that she was a practicing Roman Catholic, she chose to have an abortion, firmly convinced that she could not provide a home for Julia and for a baby.

## THE INDIVIDUAL AND SOCIAL ECOLOGY

In our case conferences Ellen was considered a borderline personality disorder; theologically, she had little trust in grace from humans or from God. The most striking aspects of Ellen's situation, however, cannot be contained by that diagnosis but are better interpreted through a social ecological perspective, one that accounts for Ellen's familial and social supports and interprets the impact of cultural beliefs and social institutions, including governmental policy and the congregation, on Ellen's life.

Most of us take for granted a series of supports, all of which deteriorated beneath Ellen. The possibility for family support disintegrated through a series of circumstances: her mother's untimely death, the unsuccessful reconnection with her father, and the physical and emotional distance of her two emancipated siblings. Only Julia, her mentally disabled sister, represented an emotional family connection, making Ellen extremely ambivalent about separating from Julia when the economic and relational stresses of their roommating became overwhelming. Because of her social-structural position, Ellen's service sector job did not provide the salary or benefits, in particular, access to adequate medical insurance, that most middle-class people, until now, have been able to take for granted. In addition, Julia's marginal mental retardation placed her in the no-help-land just above the access line of programs targeted for the mentally disabled. Despite Ellen's yearning for emotional connection and her clear need for material and social support, she lived by the cultural belief in self-sufficiency and reasoned as a good, unmarried American woman is expected to: she would make it on her own apart from her family, without a family wage that could support two persons, and without the social benefits that would allow her and Julia access to emotional, mental, and physical health care. She found it extremely difficult to hold the other members of the family responsible for participating in providing support for Julia. In the absence of a familial or social-structural safety net, the only decision about which she felt repeatedly firm was her decision to have a legal abortion, a decision available to her in this country, ironically, because of the philosophy of individual rights.

Lately, individualism has been popularly—and narrowly—associated with personal growth and the breakdown of families (Blankenhorn 1995; Couture 1995, 546–547). Self-sufficiency, however, is a broader ideology supporting the abandonment of people like Ellen by the society in which she lives. The appeal to self-sufficiency and personal responsibility undergirds family policies such as divorce settlements, child support, and welfare reform and plays a significant role in this nation's health care policy. For example, when approving divorce settlements, judges often assume that mothers must become economically self-sufficient but do not assume that fathers will participate in child care. Even if such gender role equity were assumed, lower-income families would not emerge from poverty, much less flourish, after divorce and separation, because they have so few familial resources to reorganize.

The poverty of children in this country is one of our most significant public problems; yet the primary value undergirding child support policy affirms "the personal responsibility of the parent," leaving children whose families have disbursed and whose parents are barely surviving with little social safety net. In contrast, according to Sheila Kamerman and Alfred

Kahn who have conducted international comparisons of child support, countries with social insurance for children, which include most other industrialized countries, base their policies on a value of "doing good by the children" (Kahn and Kamerman 1988, 363). The Welfare Reform Act of 1988 created a workfare program that requires mothers with children over age three to become "self-sufficient"—to become employed or lose benefits—but gives only lip service to creating access to adequate child care (Hacker 1988, 30–35). When church and public policy makers gathered at the Carter Center to talk about the role of congregations in health care, the primary message of James Mason, former director of the Centers for Disease Control and Assistant Secretary for Health in the Department of Health and Human Services, centered around the value of "personal responsibility"—in other words, if every individual changes his or her lifestyle to reduce unhealthy behaviors such as smoking, drinking, eating fatty foods, having sex, and so forth, a majority of our health care problems would be solved (Mason 1990, 26–29). Alternatives such as cleaning up the environment or creating access and equity in an affordable health care system were not mentioned as significant issues for the church.

The ideology of self-sufficiency is even an international export. After communism faltered in Eastern Europe, according to John Kenneth Galbraith, we disregarded human suffering for the sake of dismantling an opposing ideology. In an article entitled "The Rush to Capitalism," Galbraith wrote (and note the metaphors for healing): "We are exporting a casual acceptance of—even a commitment to—human deprivation, to unemployment, inflation, and disastrously reduced living standards. This is even seen as essential therapy: out of the experience of unemployment and hunger will come a new and revitalized work ethic, a working force eager for the discipline of free enterprise. . . . In one ardently expressed view, which I heard just a few days ago from a business adviser recently returned from Poland, such deprivation—unemployment, low wages—will cause foreign investors and entrepreneurs in years ahead to come in for the rescue. Only a few years of suffering and all will be well. This, I choose my words carefully, is insanity" (Galbraith 1990, 51–52). Galbraith went on to point out that just as socialist distribution could not exist without free enterprise, capitalism cannot serve its people unless it is built on a network of social supports.

Let us return to Ellen. Ellen and her family adhered to the cultural belief that "dependency" is bad and "self-sufficiency" is good. They believed that Ellen should be self-sufficient even though she maintained heavy responsibilities for her dependent sister with no familial and social-structural support. Under the burden of this belief, which Ellen and her family participated in, and its enforcement through our public policy system,

Ellen's increasingly fragile self deteriorated. When she became suicidal the second time, while she was in care with me, a counselor-in-training, at a fee of $15 which Ellen paid regularly, she was hospitalized briefly for a maximum of three days under a provision of state support for crisis care. She was placed in a room with a loud, delusional psychotic, and, although she knew she needed care, she pleaded to be released to the relative tranquillity of her own home. Thereafter she came under the care of a new psychiatrist with whom I consulted. Despite the fact that Ellen was increasingly anxious and had a history of suicide attempts, the psychiatrist suggested that she remain in therapy with me, whom she trusted; that she needed—again, note the metaphors—to be "worked" rather than "supported"; that her medical insurance situation almost eliminated the possibility of hospitalization; but that hospitalization would be bad for her anyway because it would support her feelings of inadequacy and she needed to feel competent and become self-sufficient. While this suggestion was well grounded in psychiatric theory, it also was well grounded in the economics of the situation. I have always wondered whether the psychiatrist would have given me the same advice if she had been an upper-middle class person with medical insurance and family resources that could cover the cost of hospitalization and the usual fees for psychiatric services.

Significantly, when Ellen became suicidal her death instrument of choice was the noose. Unlike a privatized form of suicide such as swallowing sleeping pills, the noose is associated with social rejection, the death of one who is unfairly forced outside the safety of community, whom the social system refuses to support, who is deemed expendable: whether one thinks of the hanging of the moral character in the western movies or the history of the lynchings of poor blacks, the noose becomes the symbol of the social outcast. Her place of choice was the bathroom: the place in which we expel the waste we create. Ellen, as a poor woman trying to be self-sufficient against all odds, knew herself to be expelled from the family and society she so desperately wanted to participate in. She tenaciously attempted to hang on to the lifeline of family and social-system support by also taking into the bathroom a telephone with which to call me, a person at the bottom of the barrel in the mental health profession, while Julia, simultaneously distanced and present, was banging at the locked bathroom door. The irony of individualistic society is that as individualism has become the status quo, individualistic society has cast out not only the common good but also the individual.

What difference can the congregation make as part of the social ecology that cares for a person such as Ellen and for a society and culture seduced by self-sufficiency? What became abundantly clear in Ellen's case was that one-on-one pastoral counseling was not enough; Ellen and Julia needed familial and social-system support. Ellen clung for several years to pastoral counseling as her fragile lifeline, rarely missing a session or a payment. It is rare, however, that people with such limited resources as Ellen's would remain in touch with the professionalized care and counseling movement over a period of years. I would argue that these persons go unserved not only because of the institutional and economic limits of chaplaincy and counseling but also because the therapeutic movement only partially meets their needs. The efficacy of verbal, meaning-oriented counseling was limited by Ellen's social environment.

In Ellen's case the participation of her local congregation provided the turning point in her healing. She contacted her congregation for help in two ways. Firmly resolved that the abortion was her only option, but in grief at each anniversary of the abortion and the delivery date, Ellen approached her priest in order to seek consolation and absolution. She never got to the point of confessing that she had had an abortion because of the priest's off-putting responses to her underemployment and sexual involvement. He, too, implicitly emphasized her need for self-sufficiency. As she talked about Julia, however, he was wise enough to ask the religious order connected to the parish to intervene on Julia's and ultimately Ellen's behalf. The sisters contacted Julia and helped her find a transitional living environment. No longer holding herself responsible for Julia's welfare and free to seek connection with other siblings (who had also housed Julia), Ellen was able to initiate a move to another state where she found a job and lived with another sister and her family. Ultimately, however, Ellen's anxiety was too great for that family system to contain; but in the new state she was treated in a residential hospital for over a year. After this massive intervention which was provided by more adequate social-system support, at her last contact with me, she was able to live and work independently while maintaining connections with various members of her family.

Members of local congregations, as in Ellen's case, may have the wisdom to perceive the social ramifications of particular problems; they also may have the resources to intervene in a person's social environment in helpful ways. I am reminded of a time when I was a seminary student and attended a program for chaplains and pastors conducted by Paul Pruyser, author of *The Minister as Diagnostician*. When Dr. Pruyser asked for case examples for the audience, I asked for assistance with a situation involving my neighbor, the wife of a schoolteacher and a mother of seven children, four of whom were not yet in kindergarten. She had recently been taken to the emergency room with a symptom that acted like an impending heart attack. Her cardiovascular system was fine, the doctors told her, but she had a condition that was harder to treat than heart malfunction: stress. I don't remember Pruyser's response, but I do remember the chaplains' interpretations of this woman's psychological problems and the outcry that occurred when someone suggested that she was experiencing a relatively understandable reaction to limited financial resources and the constant presence of four preschool children. Despite this minority view, a grandfather who served as associate pastor of my church approached me afterward and said simply, "It sounds like this woman needs a babysitter." He arranged to admit the children to the church's preschool several days a week at substantially reduced fees, providing preventive medicine for my neighbor's problem.

Congregations have traditionally provided material and social resources to persons in need. These congregational practices challenge the theory of pastoral care, which has become truncated by "individual psychology as status quo," to give equal weight to the possibility that providing support within the material and social environment of a sufferer is a significant and appropriate part of the healing process. In addition, in congregations in which people are not primarily in material need, the congregation may activate its latent meaning-oriented healing processes. Some psychological and spiritual care may be deprofessionalized, helping to overcome pastoral care's institutional and economic limits. According to a congregational study recorded in *Second Opinion,* sharing groups in an upper-middle-class Lutheran congregation made significant strides in overcoming self-imposed self-sufficiency. Persons who lived with the loneliness of chronic disease and persons who suffered from the detachment common to medical providers met face-to-face. As they explored how the riches of Lutheran theology intersected with their personal struggles, they overcame their isolation (Anderson 1990, 90–107).

Although providing material, social, emotional, and theological support is appropriately the domain of the congregation, congregations cannot be expected to become full-service social organizations. The appeal frequently made by big government—to fill the void in declining governmental services by asking congregations to increase the kinds of charitable practices in which they engage—may be theologically inviting, but inflating the congregants' expectations of themselves easily creates burnout and a renewed sense of helplessness among parishioners-citizens who are overwhelmed by the problems facing society. Congregational social service cannot fully round out the practice of care, especially in the context of present economic trends.

The most fundamental challenge that the congregation can provide to individuals and to a society who have invested in the ideology of self-sufficiency is in the arena of meshing the beliefs and practices of theology. The ideology of self-sufficiency is permeated with a theology of works that expects the individual to be grandiose. Attempting to live up to the socially reinforced belief that one is the god of one's own universe, an individual is led to deny the network of support that sustains that universe. Deluded into the apostasy that all that one has earned one has attained on one's own merit, an individual who is his or her own god and his or her own creation is justified in abandoning other individuals and ignoring the common good. This individualistic but practiced theology creates the dissonance between explicit theological declarations, such as baptismal vows, and the implicit expectation that these vows will not become practiced theology. Congregational care is consistent with the explicit theological declaration and challenges individualistic beliefs as this care is practiced.

The contradictions between the theological assumptions of congregational life and the theology embedded in individualistic society are substantial. Congregations exist only by the grace of a transcendent but intimate God. Creation, including natural and social environments, provides an abundant nest in which congregations are gathered. In Baptism, the care of children becomes the responsibility of all of the adults in the congregation. Baptism affirms that more than one or two adults are needed to raise a child. As the body of Christ, the congregation proclaims that no feeble individual exists in isolation; rather, brokenness is taken into the body and made whole. Sorrow and grief as well as celebration and joy are shared with the neighbor and lifted to God. No one person needs to "do it all," but each can do a part, knowing that the community together can accomplish what individuals alone could not dream of. The congregation is a community of friends who delight in one another, who help one another, and who hold one another accountable. Too often, however, congregations have ignored or reveled in creation, without tending it.

## CARE AND "THE WEB"

As caregivers, we can become seers who, from a particular vantage point in society, can interpret the relationship between the suffering of individuals and the structures and policies of our social ecological web. Pastors and congregations are primary caregivers, even among the caring professions. Pastors, congregations, and those who specialize in care and counseling are often the first to discover where people really hurt. This bird's-eye view of human suffering in congregations suggests that we could make a great contribution to the mending of the society whose safety net has become so torn. We are able to identify the pain of distorted childhoods and dysfunctional families, but we can also see firsthand the suffering created by social (and ecclesial) policies and ideology. We cannot do this, however, simply by adding social concerns that are not directly tied to the practice of care to a correlation of theology and psychology. Too often, pastoral caregivers feel they ought to be involved in social concerns and "add social concerns and stir," to paraphrase a feminist line, creating a backlog of "ought to dos" and "ought to knows" and "ought to be involved in" and contributing to their own sense of helplessness and withdrawal. Rather, I am suggesting that we need to reformulate the basic commitments of our discipline. If we were to create a social ecological foundation for pastoral care and counseling, we would correlate theology not only with the implicit theology and practice in psychology, family systems theory, and general culture but also with the theology implicit in social institutions, including the congregation and government, and the ecclesial and public policies and practices they produce. A social ecological framework for pastoral care would include attention to the potential sources and practices of care, and their implicit and explicit theologies, in culture, public policy, the formation of community institutions, families and individuals, as these dimensions of care intersect with one another. Such a framework would also help the primary caregiver offer a critique of larger systems as they create undue suffering. Without a broad, social ecological framework, we will not be prepared to interpret the suffering created by our shifting economy or to reach those persons experiencing downward and upward mobility.

Many pastoral care texts attend to the importance of culture and society, but few, if any, help us become concrete about mending our social nest. In particular, to offer adequate care beyond the 1990s we will want to become as expert about public policies affecting the family and health as we are about the workings of various personality types. If we attend to policy issues that most closely impinge upon our work, we will discover that policy makers are well aware of a number of programs that could reduce poverty and suffering, particularly among children. For example, in the area of family policy, Head Start works. Social insurance for children of divorced and separated families works. Identifying parents by their Social Security numbers, so that they pay child support as regularly as they pay their taxes works. A national health insurance plan that would provide access to preventive health care for all families would be less expensive than our present Cadillac-or-nothing care, would reduce the federal deficit, and would also help to abate the intensity and complexity of the problems of the people who will seek care from congregations and pastors in the 1990s. Variations of all of these programs have been effective in other countries. Not only would we want to be prepared to advocate for the kinds of policies and programs that have been proven effective but we would want to improve access to that support. If congregations were helped to interpret the relationship between the sufferer, themselves as primary care providers, and public and ecclesial policy makers; if they were helped to interpret the reciprocal relationship between charity and policy; if they learned to seek the implicit and explicit theological bases upon which decisions are made, they would help to create, maintain, and provide access to successful programs and policies. The congregation would discover that in the face of overwhelming distress, it is not helpless, nor must it bear all the suffering of the world on its own shoulders. As such, pastoral caregivers and congregations could care for both individuals and the public good as a prophetic witness against an individualistic society that would just as soon abandon both.

## BIBLIOGRAPHY

Anderson, Douglas. 1990. "The Physician's Experience: A Journey through Illness." *Second Opinion* 13: 90–107.

Blankenhorn, David. 1995. *Fatherless America: Confronting Our Most Urgent Social Problem.* New York: Basic Books.

Couture, Pamela D. May 17, 1995. Review of *Fatherless America,* by David Blankenhorn. *The Christian Century* 12:17, 546–547.

Galbraith, John Kenneth. October 25, 1990. "The Rush to Capitalism." *New York Review of Books* 37, 51–52.

Glendon, Mary Ann. 1991. *Rights Talk: The Impoverishment of Political Discourse.* New York: Free Press.

Hacker, Andrew. October 13, 1988. "How Fair Is Workfare? Getting Rough on the Poor." *New York Review of Books* 35:15, 30–35.

Kahn, Alfred J., and Sheila B. Kamerman, eds. 1988. *Child Support: From Debt Collection to Social Policy.* Newbury Park, Calif.: Sage Publications, 363.

Mason, James O. 1990. "Health Care in the U.S.: Facts and Choices," *Second Opinion* 13: 26–29.

# Part Two
# Insights for Pastoral Care

Insights for pastoral care of women arise out of a matrix of specific issues. The suppression of women's anger and aggressiveness in a society that prefers women silent and invisible is one of these issues. Carroll Saussy, Barbara Clarke, and Kathleen Greider expose society's attempts to exterminate women's anger and aggression. Women may need to recover long-repressed anger, uncover rage, and express this in a safe circle. The church more often than not has failed to be a safe circle with teachings such as "Anger is a sin." Carroll Saussy and Barbara Clarke maintain that anger expressed is not only a healing power but a mode of connectedness, a form of caring, and an impetus for social change.

Kathleen Greider perceives the elusiveness of aggression and looks at being on the "giving end" as well as the "receiving end" of aggression. She develops a range of aggression, from violence to assertiveness, and discusses its suppression and expression.

Four of the chapters reclaim the significance of the body and further reduce the mind-body dualism in religious thinking. Jane Dasher, Beth Ann Estock, Irene Henderson, and Amelia Stinson-Wesley claim this moment in the history of Christian doctrine to underscore that the body is important. They combat the legacy of Aristotle who claimed that women are mutilated males. They counter the docetic tendency in theology as they affirm that Christianity is fully human. Eating disorders, hysterectomy, mastectomy, and rape are theological issues. A bruise, a wound, a physical invasion, violence are theological matters. Removal of a breast and loss of the womb are spiritual issues. The importance of the woman's body is at the heart of the Christian faith. We recall that the crux of the Christian tradition centers on a God who entered the world through the body of a woman.

As we speak of the human web, as pastoral theologians we focus our attention on the victims caught in the web, and we work in the hope that the web can provide a safety net. Older women who have carried secrets in silence for all their lives particularly need the safety net provided by a sensitive, facilitating caregiver. Emma Justes enumerates how these secret experiences have deeply shaped women's lives. The secrets range from instances of sexual abuse, denial of sexual identity, instances of rape and incest, secrets of paternity, and cases of battering. As we move toward a new care of women, we affirm not only the expression of healing anger and positive aggression but the emergence of the secret stories when a woman as narrator chooses to tell them. This can be done only in the context of collaborative caring.

Insights for pastoral care of women arise also out of silences. Joretta Marshall speaks into the silence surrounding sexuality. In a more general way, she examines how sexual orientation, identity formation, and Christianity converge in pastoral care. In a more specific way, she focuses on women who self-identify as lesbians. Martha Robbins helps to break the silence surrounding every woman's most formative relationship: the mother-daughter relationship. Taking issue with the way the dominant culture judges the bonds between women in general, and mothers and daughter in particular, Robbins reflects on both motherlines and motherloss.

It is in hearing the speechlessness of segments of society that we are able to see into the silences. "The hearing ear and the seeing eye—the LORD has made them both" (Proverbs 20:12).

# 6

# The Healing Power of Anger

CARROLL SAUSSY
*Wesley Theological Seminary*
*and*
BARBARA J. CLARKE
*The American University*

How often do women celebrate their gift of anger? We, the authors, believe that anger well used is an essential ingredient in one's personal odyssey as well as the motivating element in work for justice. Anger well used is a gift to be celebrated. Most people, however, find it difficult to appreciate and express intense anger or rage, let alone cherish such troublesome experiences. Some people, particularly older women who have been socialized to be "nice ladies," are not even aware of much of their anger.

The purpose of this chapter is to explore the complicated and much misunderstood emotion of anger— more specifically, to look at women's anger and its relationship to their faith and spirituality.

How can women be helped to identify and claim their anger or rage so that its expression can result in self- and other-healing? How can they counter society's tendency to view women's anger as pathological?

First, we will briefly discuss the problem of anger in women's lives. Then we will explore the Bible's treatment of anger. Much of the problem with anger for women stems from the conflicting ways in which the biblical witness has been both expressed and interpreted, resulting in considerable misunderstanding as to what the Bible teaches about anger.

The authors of this chapter are Caucasian, middle-class women who know that we cannot speak for all women. We cannot speak for women of other races or cultures or classes. Different cultures have different styles of expressing anger.

Our claim is that in the United States and in countries around the world, anger is a problem. Both the unawareness of anger and the inability to express it constructively are major areas of concern.

Throughout the chapter the expression "self-in-relation" is used rather than "self" in order to counter an overemphasis on autonomy and to emphasize the crucial significance of relationship in every person's journey toward wholeness (Jordan et al. 1991).

## WOMEN AND ANGER: THE PROBLEM WRIT LARGE

Women who experience intense anger or rage struggle for ways to express creatively these legitimate, sometimes energizing, sometimes paralyzing feelings. At other times they need help in sorting out where the anger comes from. The anger may be a reaction to an immediate or recent experience of having been rejected, trivialized, or abused. However, the anger could be a projection of the hurt that originated in painful experience suffered in the past which resulted in repressed rage. Something happening in the present touches the buried pain, and blame is projected onto an available target.

Anger can be constructive—a message that change is demanded. Anger can be destructive—an act of verbal or physical violence that damages relationship. Women, so often abused, know firsthand that anger sometimes means physically damaging or destructively lashing out at people who deserve to be treated with respect—namely, themselves. What women too often have not learned is that the expression of anger can be empowering and re-creative.

The message that women receive from many men, from religious institutions, and from society in general is that their expression of anger is inappropriate. As Jean Baker Miller points out, a dominant group never wants subordinates to express anger and uses its power to keep such expressions down. The angry persons then see themselves as weak, unworthy, with neither right nor cause to be angry (Miller 1991, 182).

Consequently, when angry women counter cultural taboo and express their powerful emotions, they are often uncomfortable themselves and keenly aware of the discomfort of others. It is all too easy for women to allow their acute anxiety about expressing anger to soften or even mute their angry voices. They may choose to repress the anger; they may decide to "let their anger out." However, unless they are supported by persons who respect them in all of their anger, as they storm their way through outrageous, oppressive experiences, they often "split." That is, they bracket their anger, restraining themselves from fully expressing it, and focus instead on the effect their anger is having on others.

Finding the balance between a responsible, mature concern about the effects of one's behavior on others and an overconcern for the emotional life of another requires both knowledge of oneself and discernment of what is happening in any particular relationship. Both women and men need to assess how the expression of their anger will affect their relations. Neither men nor women ought to take more responsibility for the feelings of those with whom they are angry than rightfully belongs to them.

In other words, if a person is angry with a partner and speaks forcefully and truthfully about her perception of the behavior that has evoked the anger, she need not bear responsibility for the effect her forceful speech has on her partner. However, if a person speaks in a way that intends harm, disrespectfully demeaning her friend, she will have further work to do because of the damage done to her partner and to the relationship as well as to her image of herself-in-relation. People who base their behavioral decisions primarily on how their communication or gesture will be perceived by the other, rather than on what would constitute an honest expression of their true feelings, fall into what has been described as co-dependent behavior.

When women forgo or suppress their authentic feelings of justified anger for the sake of the other, they may experience a mixture of relief and frustration and might well continue to be labeled "angry women." If this denial of feeling becomes a pattern in their relationships, they seldom find satisfying ways of being freely themselves, women who are both angry because of personal or social offense and who are passionate for justice. Conversely, many women hide some of their anger from themselves and from others and are never able to identify the source of their pain. These women may come to a professional counselor or pastoral caregiver with diffuse symptoms of malaise.

Another complicating factor in the difficulty that persons have in naming their anger is that anger is rarely experienced in isolation from other emotions. Carol Tavris has pointed out that "our emotions are not especially distinctive. They tend to come in bunches like grapes, and it is very rare to find a single emotion causing trouble on its own" (Tavris 1982, 96).

For example, suppose a woman is convinced that a person has not understood what she attempted to communicate and in fact has distorted what she tried to say. She may first feel *confused;* she may feel *insecure,* because she thinks she has been lacking in making herself clear; perhaps *hurt* because she does not think she was taken seriously; surely *frustrated,* sensing that communication has been obstructed; conceivably *fearful* that a project she thought was to be a mutual venture is not likely to be workable; *sad* and *disappointed* that what she hoped would be a working relationship will not be; and, yes, *angry* at what she may sense to be intentional blockage. Some sorting out is required before she can understand just what she is experiencing and what she wants to do as a result of that experience. If anger is an important part of the "bunch" of feelings, and anger is considered "off limits," she may block the whole cluster of feelings and be left with numbness, deadened in apparently unrelated emotions as well. In many cases alcohol or some other substance abuse is the path people take when they consider feelings of anger or fear to be off limits. Alcohol can block all feelings, leaving a person emotionally numb.

Anger clusters with prior feelings and is considered by many to be a secondary emotion. Scratch the surface of anger and you have an earlier feeling: pain, fear, frustration, hurt, or sadness. Yet because many people deny much of their anger, they may be in touch only with the primary emotion. "No, I'm not angry. I'm hurt."

In addition to the difficulty involved in sorting out clusters of feelings, anger is problematic because it always involves an interpretation. For example, if the person incessantly ringing your doorbell is in crisis, you may well share the intensity of her feelings when you open the door. You enter into or share her crisis. If, however, the person is a neighborhood crank who prattles on about insignificant details, another set of feelings surfaces when you open the door. You make an interpretation about the reason for the intrusive, relentless ringing of the bell.

Belief systems themselves can trigger anger, and beliefs can change. Witness the anger expressed by activists on both sides of the abortion debate. Lived experience has undoubtedly resulted in some persons changing sides. In many cases angry feelings are triggered by irrational beliefs that must be changed if one is to use anger well.

If a woman is angry because someone has offered her constructive criticism, her task is to review her need to perform perfectly and thus protect herself from criticism, a need that most likely goes back to an excessive need to win parental approval in early childhood.

In our efforts to explore anger with women, we designed a worship service for a local Women Church gathering on this subject. We reflected on the fact that feeling words often are seen as antithetical: joy/sorrow; love/hatred; elation/depression; fear/courage; hope/despair; disappointment/encouragement. What is the antithesis of anger? When asked what they considered to be the opposite of anger, the group of eighteen women gave intriguing answers. We ask our readers the same question: What do you consider to be the antithesis of anger? Ponder the question before reading further.

One woman in the group said that the opposite of anger was despair; another said death. Other suggestions were quite different: equanimity, serenity, peace, security, happiness. Still others suggested hopelessness, fear, stuckness. To search for what might be considered the antithesis of anger and not come close to a consensus underscored the complexity and confusion we share about a profoundly significant emotion.

Still another complication in naming anger is the fact that women receive conflicting messages concerning anger not only from society but also from the Bible and the church. The Bible admonishes one to be slow to anger and teaches that "anger is overwhelming" (Proverbs 27:4). Anger is to be avoided. Yet the Bible is rich with images of God's anger, people's anger, and Jesus' anger. Anger is to be expressed.

Many of the images of God's anger are found in the Hebrew Bible. The times when God is described as angry are times in which God has been upset with the failure of the Hebrew people to act kindly and with justice. The churches have tended to call this justifiable anger (Baloian 1992).

It would appear from an examination of the Bible that for God to express anger is acceptable, even expected. But is it acceptable for people, particularly women, to express anger? What can we glean from the biblical witness? What happened when human beings in the Bible expressed their anger? These are among the questions to be addressed.

## A BIBLICAL THEOLOGY OF ANGER

To discuss women, the Bible, and anger in search of an encouraging word with regard to the expression of anger is extremely difficult. Examination of the treatment of women in the Bible, in itself, has the potential to generate anger in women. Women are raped, murdered, and sacrificed by men who are their fathers and brothers (Trible 1984). These are situations over which the women had very little control. Not being in a position to make choices about one's life puts women (and men who are powerless) in an onerous predicament.

Societal injunctions against anger, or the exhortation to control one's anger, are based on the assumption that one is in a position to make choices about how one is to live one's life. There are times when women and men have minimal choices about needs such as housing, employment, schooling, and health care. Anger is often a human response to deprivation of basic needs. Everyone needs the freedom to express anger in appropriate ways and in appropriate contexts. The choice of expression and action should then be judged on one's conformation to standards of justice and love (Trible 1984, 164).

How are we to understand the Scriptures in relationship to anger? Although the Bible gives ambiguous messages about the rightness or wrongness of anger, there is sufficient evidence in the Bible that expression of anger is appropriate and necessary when one is confronted with oppression and abuse. Examination of both the Hebrew Scripture and the New Testament reveals that anger is expressed in many diverse circumstances with varying outcomes.

### Hebrew Scripture

Many of the images of God's anger are found in the Hebrew Bible, in which there are more than four hundred references to God's wrath or anger (Campbell 1986, 33). Over half of the occurrences relate to situations where people have failed to act justly, with kindness. Other times are instances when Israel has been rebellious against Yahweh's will (Baloian 1992, 191–210).

However, how does one understand the instances when God appears as "a sinister and irrational force which seeks people out in order to victimize them?" (Campbell 1986, 4). Certainly in these cases it is difficult to see how God's anger leads to connectedness with God's people. Instead, God's anger appears arbitrary and destructive, the very features of anger that make it so problematic to deal with constructively. In trying to answer the question initially posed, we must consider the context in which these stories occurred and the writers who recorded them. How much of this "destructive God" reflects the societal norms of patriarchal and retributive justice? (Although beyond the scope of this chapter, a feminist biblical hermeneutic would be helpful in putting God's "irrational" anger in perspective.)

We prefer to interpret God's anger in the Bible in the context of the overall theme that permeates the Bible—God's passion and love for God's people. The passionate God expresses anger when people fail to do what God requires—to do justice and to walk kindly. It would appear from an examination of the Bible that for God to express anger is acceptable, even expected. But is it acceptable for people to express anger?

The presence of the psalms of lament in the Bible are an indication that, yes, it is acceptable for people to express anger. Yet the laments, many of which express anger particularly at God, are often overlooked, specifically in liturgical practice. A whole, loving relationship, including a relationship with God, is possible only when one is able to express fully one's feelings of joy, fear, and anger. Not to express a part of oneself is ultimately destructive to the relationship. The psalms of lament provide an outlet for the expression of anger at God, at the cruelty of life, at one's misfortunes. An example of how the lament psalms can be used to aid women in expressing their anger is seen in the following excerpt from the diary of an eighteenth-century woman who experienced years of spousal abuse and whose oldest daughter was incestuously assaulted (Zub 1992, 58–59).

Who is this cruel oppressor? This grievous rod in the hands of the High and Lofty One, by whom I am thus sorely chastised? It was not an enemy; then I could have borne. Neither was it he that hated me in days past; for then I would have hid myself from him. But it was the man mine equal, my guide, my friend, my husband! (Bailey 1989, 73)

These words hauntingly echo those of Psalm 55:12-14:

It is not enemies who taunt me—I could bear that: it is not adversaries who deal insolently with me—I could hide from them. But it is you, my equal, my companion, my familiar friend, with whom I kept pleasant company.

Perhaps more instructive to us would be the stories of specific people who expressed anger. Following are accounts of how three biblical people, two women and one man, expressed anger over their predicaments. The outcomes of their expressions of anger are decidedly different.

Hannah, the mother of Samuel, was transformed by her expression of anger. The favored wife of Elkanah, Hannah was barren. Peninnah, Elkanah's other wife, had several sons and daughters; she made Hannah's life miserable. (The portrayal of antagonism between two women, particularly over the ability to bear children, is a common motif of the Old Testament writers.) Elkanah could not understand Hannah's distress and asked if he were not better than ten sons; Hannah remained silent. Since her barrenness was viewed as God's will, Hannah reasoned that if God had "closed" her womb, then God could "open" it.

Standing before the temple gate, Hannah prayed that God would give her a child, preferably a boy. If God heard her prayer, she would give her son up to the service of God when he was weaned. Praying silently with moving lips, she was accused by the priest Eli of being drunk; he told her to go away. Hannah responded that she was not drunk; rather, she was pouring out her vexation and frustration to God that she was barren.

Hannah named her son Samuel. It is true that Hannah had to give Samuel up, but *she* decided when it was time to wean him, and *she* did so, and *she* took Samuel to the temple as *she* had promised.

Transformed from a woman with no voice to a woman who named the truth about herself to Eli (Killen 1992, 374–375), Hannah was empowered. She was clearly angry with Peninnah for flouting her fertility in her face. Our assumption is that she was also angry with her husband for not understanding how she felt about her childlessness, although he may have simply accepted it. Hannah's anger empowered her to act to achieve justice for herself. Anger can enable the self to heal, restore, change a situation that is harmful, wrong, or unjust.

While Hannah's anger was transforming, the outcome for Miriam, another woman who expressed displeasure, was not as positive. From the beginning, as a nameless child, Miriam showed initiative and courage in her successful effort to save her baby brother, Moses. She became Miriam the prophet, leader of song and community celebration, and leader of the people out of Egypt. Before long, though, Miriam's leadership was terminated.

Miriam had in mind an inclusive model of leadership. When it seemed that she, as well as her other brother, Aaron, was not being consulted in the decision-making process, she complained. The story was presented by the writers of Exodus as a jealousy issue between Miriam and her new sister-in-law, the Cushite woman. According to the story, God got angry and gave Miriam leprosy. Women are not supposed to exercise their leadership authority. Further, if women express their anger about being excluded, they are punished. For a woman to exercise such authority in a patriarchal culture has great potential to lead to her suffering, if not her martyrdom.

But what happens when a man complains to God? To answer that question, we turn to the story of Job. Job was a man who had it all. He had great abundance in land, flocks, a wife, seven sons and three daughters. He was considered to be a righteous man, well respected in his community. He had faith in God and, in turn, was favored by God.

Then, for no readily apparent reason, Job lost it all—property, possessions, children, his health. Because it seemed as if Job acquiesced to his treatment, society and the church have taught people to be as "patient as Job." Anyone who advocates such behavior based on Job's story has not read beyond the second chapter of the Book of Job.

Job's friends had encouraged him to admit his guilt for the sins that he had obviously committed. But Job refused. Instead, he challenged God to show him how he had erred. Job used language that called God into court. Job was exceedingly angry. Did God punish Job? No. Instead, God appeared in court and in the end restored Job's wealth and family to him. In the process, God chastised Job's friends for not having "spoken of God what is right." Job expressed his rage at his unjust treatment and, eventually, had his wealth restored.

These three stories are paradigmatic to the situation that prevails today. If women are allowed to express anger, it is usually only when they are fulfilling their womanly functions of child bearer, mother, or wife—just as Hannah did. On the other hand, for women in leadership positions to express their anger and indignation about being unfairly treated results in their punishment, as in Miriam's case. However, men are rewarded when they express anger, as Job was rewarded. How much has changed over the thousands of years since these stories were first told?

Although the climate for women in leadership positions seems to be improving, there is still considerable resistance to women claiming their full humanity. Failure to deal constructively with anger is a block to spiritual and psychological growth for both women and men.

### The New Testament

The passionate God of the Hebrew Scriptures is made manifest in the life and actions of Jesus, the incarnate revelation of God. Several years ago a friend of ours, looking for something to believe in, decided to reread the New Testament. She maintained "in her heart" that Christ was at the center of what was important. To her surprise, what she found was an "angry young man." It seemed to her that nothing much pleased Jesus—he was particularly angry with the "establishment."

Jesus was trying to teach those in authority a better way, but they seemed to choose not to listen. Jesus called them "a brood of vipers." Regrettably, our friend did not trust her own perceptions of what is in the Gospels. She was still a captive to the church's presentation of "sweet Jesus" and believed that there was nothing in the church or the Bible for her. It was twelve years later, and recovery from an almost fatal illness, before she came back to the church.

How many have been deprived of the transforming love of Jesus, the Christ, because of the failure of the churches to preach and teach the full Gospel? Jesus' expressions of passionate anger provide an empowering example to us today as we attempt to live fully into the gospel.

The shape of Jesus' person and mission is seen clearly in the incident of healing in the synagogue on the Sabbath (Mark 3:1–6). Jesus encounters a man with a withered hand and is moved to heal him. Jesus' enemies seize the chance to accuse him of breaking the law. When they refuse to answer Jesus' question about the lawfulness of saving life on the Sabbath, Mark records that Jesus "looked around at them with anger . . . grieved at their hardness of heart. . . . The Pharisees went out and immediately conspired with the Herodians against him, how to destroy him."

Several illustrations of anger are at work here, both the anger that destroys and the anger that works for change. Initially a group of people are on watch to catch Jesus doing something against the law. Is this not an angry reaction to a man who threatens one's sense of security? "They watched him . . . so that they might accuse him." The same plotters refuse to answer a basic gospel challenge: can the law ever be used to prevent one from doing good? Their silence angered Jesus. What he did with his anger was to reach out to heal a sufferer. In reaction to his creative use of anger, he received the anger of hatred. Jesus must be destroyed.

In other words, Jesus' anger at injustice is fair warning to women and men. If you express your justice anger, the powers that be may well work to destroy you with their hatred anger. Those who could not hear Jesus' message chose anger that led toward enduring hostility and eventually to the death of Jesus. Jesus chose anger that leads eventually to freedom, a freedom he won by using anger to bring about change.

Carter Heyward suggests that one "re-image anger as an alternative to discouragement." Jesus does not withdraw; he does not make false peace. Jesus pushes on" (Heyward 1982, 56). That is a paradigm for a healthy expression of anger.

The model of how Jesus expressed his anger needs to be before us as we attempt to interpret other biblical discussions of anger such as those of Paul.

> So then, putting away falsehood, let all of us speak the truth to our neighbors, for we are members of one another. Be angry but do not sin; do not let the sun go down on your anger, and do not make room for the devil. . . . Put away from you all bitterness and wrath and anger and wrangling and slander, together with all malice, and be kind to one another, tenderhearted, forgiving one another, as God in Christ has forgiven you. (Ephesians 4:25–27, 31–32)

This passage spells out the dilemma. On the one hand the reader is told to be angry; on the other, to put away anger. But the passage is not as contradictory as one might think. The passage demonstrates the main thesis of this paper: that anger, well expressed, is a sign of love and caring and a means to greater connection.

Unfortunately the churches through the centuries have chosen to emphasize "put away anger," overlooking the "be angry" companion part of the text. To "speak the truth in love" may require that one express one's anger. If one represses one's anger and lets the "sun go down on it," then the seeds for grudges, bitterness, and the contamination of friendship are sown. It is an act of love to risk the expression of anger. This is the witness of Jesus and Paul.

## On Using Anger Well

What women (and of course men as well) need is a whole new way of seeing themselves and their role in relationships. In rewriting their "job descriptions," women are rewriting their "life descriptions." Lesbians are finding the support they need to claim their sexual orientation, their relationships, and when they choose, to raise children. Heterosexual women are no longer assuming that their goal in life is to stand by a man and take major if not full responsibility for the lives of children. (Just as heterosexual men no longer assume that they must be the primary breadwinner, nor the less emotionally engaged parent. They need not protect themselves from becoming vulnerable in relationship to a woman or a child.)

Some older women feel profoundly challenged: they recognize how patriarchy has deprived them of genuine self-expression; they realize that it is late for them to choose career and lifestyle the way they see younger women doing; and they struggle to overcome envy and resentment. They want to be generative and supportive, but at the same time they feel cheated and sometimes depressed.

Alexandra Kaplan's use of a definition of depression as a description of a generic woman's life in this society is startling (Kaplan 1991, 210). She cites experts on depression who offer a personality pattern typically found in the depressed person (Arieti and Bemporad 1978, 139). Depressed persons are driven to please others, to meet the expectations of others. Consequently they lose touch with themselves, neglecting to listen to their own wishes and blaming themselves for their unhappiness and lack of fulfillment.

A person who lacks a sense of herself may well describe her life as unhappy, futile, and unfulfilled. These polite words, however, may mask a deeper anger and rage. How can a person begin a new life who has "de-selfed" through years of trying to please, serve, and be accepted? Because many women have muted their anger for so long, have learned well to conform to societal expectations that they be "nice," they need safe places where they can indeed listen to their own wishes. They need to recover the long-repressed anger, reclaim their rightful rage, and express their true feelings within safe and caring relationships. For some, this requires bewailing the messages they heard in home and church that estranged them from the power of their anger.

Groups provide a safe and powerful place where women can help women reclaim their anger. Perhaps an essential step in their recovery of their selves-in-relation is the projection of their rage onto the men in their lives. What may seem inappropriate projection to those who are quick to label such women "male bashers" is in fact essential to women's recognition of their entrapment in patriarchal culture and norms. Focusing on their wants and needs, on their true selves-in-relation, is a subsequent step. This sequence of recovery is often perplexing to family members who fear that in the initial stages of recovery, their angry spouse or daughter or sister is getting worse rather than better.

Group work may need to be paired with individual therapy for women damaged by seriously abusive childhoods. Survivors of abuse can experience a re-creation with the help of skilled women therapists who facilitate the recovery of their true self-in-relations. (Very traditional women who have internalized a fragile sense of self may initially seek to work with a male therapist because they disvalue women. They assume that female therapists are weak and vulnerable and not powerful enough to receive their rageful projections. While their individual work may be done with a woman-friendly male therapist, they ought to be encouraged to join a women's group. On the other hand, many women may need a female therapist with whom they can feel safe in expressing anger. Male therapists who are aware of gender issues may also help women break social barriers in expressing anger at a "more powerful member" of our culture.) The difference between the journey of such women and the processes of normal recovery of anger, though vast, is mostly one of degree. While the depth of the deprivation determines the method of intervention required for healing, the goal is the same: *discovery and empowerment of the true self-in-relation through a reclamation of anger and rage at disrespect and abuse.*

Not all women require either a therapeutic relationship or a women's group. They may need only one or two profoundly mutual relationships that result in the blossoming of true selves-in-relation.

To use personal anger well requires self-respect and especially respect for one's experience of anger. This takes time and effort to recognize and better understand the experience of intense anger and, through that understanding, to arrive at a considered choice of response.

For example, a woman was offended by a strong sense that she was not wanted in a working group assigned by the appointed leader of her organization. The subgroup leader said straight out: "*You* don't belong *here.*" However, others in the group noted that she did in fact belong in the group and she stayed, feeling bruised and discouraged, deeply inhibited, but not safe enough to confront her "superior."

Over the next few months, she was painfully aware of several other slights: a memo not answered; a meeting at which she felt unheard and invisible. Finally, she mustered the courage to make an appointment to confront the man about what she perceived as rejecting behavior. On the morning of the meeting, a secretary called for him to cancel the appointment, setting a later date. The aggrieved woman's sense of being trivialized and disrespected mounted.

Finally the moment came when she walked into an office and initiated a confrontation, her body filled with apprehension. What she learned was that her colleague had himself felt manipulated and disrespected by the head of the organization, who had made in his absence what this man considered arbitrary decisions that negatively affected his role in the company. The fact that the woman was assigned to his work group was a relatively minor one of those decisions. The "offending person" was self-absorbed at the initial event when the woman interpreted his behavior as demeaning. When she finally confronted him, he looked genuinely abashed and in fact was in tears as he explained himself. Her anger, well expressed, was followed by compassion and empathy and the beginning of a new relationship.

Not all attempts to express one's anger end as well. However, it is most often the effort itself that effects significant intrapersonal change. *Doing something* in the face of perceived oppression is often more important than the results of one's activity. Being proactive rather than passively brooding

over mistreatment can result in a stronger sense of self-in-relation and consequently more solid self-esteem. The major conclusion by a group of psychologists who researched self-esteem was that self-esteem primarily
reflects one's tendency to choose coping over avoidance when faced with
conflicts that evoke fear and anxiety (Bednar et al. 1989).

To use social anger well requires respect for one's sisters and brothers and
a fundamental belief in justice for all. Anger used well can be a profoundly
religious experience. Such expression obviously takes time and effort. One
needs to focus one's energy on a particular injustice to be righted. More
than individual effort, social change takes community organizing and steady
work for justice.

The following story was reported in the New Orleans *Times-Picayune* on
the twentieth anniversary of a tragic fire that killed thirty-two persons in a
barroom in the French Quarter (*Times-Picayune,* June 24, 1993, 1 and A-
8). No safety violations played a role in the burning of The Upstairs
lounge, "a place one police official called a hangout for homosexuals and
thieves." The most lethal fire to burn in New Orleans in nearly two hundred years, the fire was declared an act of arson. The suspect, never
charged, later committed suicide. The fire mobilized the gay and lesbian
community of New Orleans, until then closeted. They coped publicly with
their grief.

> The trauma also set that community on the course it follows today—one that
> begins with public acknowledgment of its identity, and progresses toward
> legal and social action to end discrimination against gays. . . . Some recall that
> the Catholic Church refused to allow memorial services in St. Louis Cathe-
> dral because the victims were homosexuals, and the story of that rejection still
> circulates.

The article describes the movement from fear and intimidation to bold
action on the part of Charlene Schneider, a lesbian activist and bar owner,
who at the time was determined to hide from cameras.

After conducting memorial services for the victims of the fire, Reverend
Troy Perry, founder of the Metropolitan Community Church, suggested
that those among the three hundred mourners who wanted to avoid cameras could leave by a back door. Schneider reports that "most people went
through the front door of the church, and you knew that day that things
would never be the same."

> Within weeks of the fire, A Gay People's Coalition had formed offering coun-
> seling, a health and VD clinic and a "gay switch board" number.
> "I believe the fire was the catalyst for the anger to bring us all to the table,"
> Schneider said.

Schneider recounts the subsequent gay rights work that has transformed the gay and lesbian community in New Orleans: demonstrations, gay pride celebrations, political action for candidates favoring gay and lesbian civil rights, and finally the passage of an ordinance forbidding discrimination in housing, public accommodations and jobs, and a mayor's advisory committee on lesbian and gay issues.

While the first illustration involves an everyday event in the life of a career woman, the second points to tragic social evil, at once systemic and individual. The arsonist was likely a homophobic person driven by hatred. The homophobia was fed by deeply rooted prejudice and fear of difference. What the illustrations share is that in both situations, a moment of truth came when a person or persons knew that change was needed and that action was imperative.

Whether one is working on personal assertiveness and change or social justice issues, perhaps the ideal response is to express anger directly and responsibly to the target of one's anger when the emotion arises. Yet research indicates that only 9 percent of 535 women reported that they would express anger to the person who triggered their anger (Thomas 1993, 90). There are undoubtedly many reasons why women are reluctant to express their anger, such as fear and intimidation. There are also race, age, and class reasons that have been mentioned. Sometimes the context itself makes it difficult, if not impossible, to express anger directly. Does one stand up in a public setting and confront the speaker or preacher? Does a single voice or even group chant in front of the White House mean shelter for the homeless people in Lafayette Park?

More often the angry person feels ill prepared to use anger well. What angry people need first is an understanding of their anger, which may require individual therapy, group work, or transforming relationships—any one of which will include a reinterpretation of their socialization processes. They need conviction that anger can be precisely what God requires of them if they are to love themselves and their neighbors. They need skill in handling their anger, which takes time and practice. Above all, they need friends who share their conviction that well-used anger leads to a rich and satisfying life and that collective anger well used creates communities of justice.

We conclude with Beverly Harrison's prophetic claim that anger is not the opposite of love; rather, it is a powerful mode of caring both for our interpersonal relations and for persons we may not even know. Anger waves a red flag that something is wrong in our own relationships; anger cries out that something is wrong in the world around us. Harrison boldly claims that "all serious human moral activity, especially action for social change, takes its bearings from the rising power of human anger" (Harrison 1985, 14).

## BIBLIOGRAPHY

Arieti, S., and J. Bemporad. 1978. *Severe and Mild Depression: The Psychotherapeutic Approach.* New York: Basic Books.

Bailey, A. A. 1989. *Religion and Domestic Violence in Early New England: The Memoirs of Abigail Abbot Bailey.* Edited by Ann Taves. Bloomington, Ind.: Indiana University Press.

Baloian, Bruce Edward. 1992. *Anger in the Old Testament.* New York: Peter Lang.

Beattie, Melody. 1987. *Codependent No More: How to Stop Controlling Others and Start Caring for Yourself.* Center City, Minn.: Hazelden Foundation.

Bednar, Richard L.; M. Gawain Wells; and Scott R. Peterson. 1989. *Self Esteem: Paradoxes and Innovations in Clinical Theory and Practice.* Washington, D.C.: American Psychological Association.

Campbell, Alastair V. 1986. *The Gospel of Anger.* London: SPCK.

Daly, Mary. 1984. *Pure Lust: Elemental Feminist Philosophy.* Boston: Beacon Press.

Harrison, Beverly. 1985. *Making the Connections: Essays in Feminist Social Ethics.* Carol Robb, ed. Boston: Beacon Press.

Heyward, Carter. 1982. *The Redemption of God: A Theology of Mutual Relation.* Lanham, Md.: University Press of America.

————. 1989. *Touching Our Strength: The Erotic as Power and the Love of God.* San Francisco: Harper & Row.

Hopkins, Denise Dombkowski. 1990. *Journey through the Psalms: A Path to Wholeness.* New York: United Church Press.

Jordan, Judith V., et al. 1991. *Women's Growth in Connection: Writings from the Stone Center.* New York: Guilford Press.

Kaplan, Alexandra G. 1991. "The 'Self-in-Relation': Implications for Depression in Women." In Jordan et al.

Killen, Patricia O'Connell. 1992. "Rediscovering Women's Authentic Voices of Faith." *Sewanee Theological Review* 35,4: 374–375.

Miller, Jean Baker. 1991. "The Construction of Anger in Women and Men." In Jordan et al.

Nathanson, Donald L. 1992. *Shame and Pride: Affect, Sex, and the Birth of the Self.* New York: W. W. Norton & Co.

Russell, Letty M. 1992. "A Quest for New Styles of Ministry." *Sewanee Theological Review* 35,4: 344–353.

Saussy, Carroll. 1995. *The Gift of Anger: A Call to Faithful Action.* Louisville, Ky.: Westminster John Knox Press.

Schaef, Anne Wilson. 1986. *Co-Dependence: Misunderstood—Mistreated.* Minneapolis: Winston Press.

————. 1987. *When Society Becomes an Addict.* New York: Harper & Row.

Tavris, Carol. 1982. *Anger: The Misunderstood Emotion.* New York: Simon & Schuster.

Thomas, Sandra P., ed. 1993. *Women and Anger.* New York: Springer Publishing Co.

Trible, Phyllis. 1984. *Texts of Terror: Literary-Feminist Readings of Biblical Narratives.* Philadelphia: Fortress Press.

————. 1989. "Bringing Miriam Out of the Shadows." *Bible Review* 5,1: 14–25.

Weems, Renita. 1988. *Just a Sister Away: A Womanist Vision of Women's Relationships in the Bible.* San Diego: LuraMedia.

Winter, Miriam Therese. 1991. *WomanWisdom: A Feminist Lectionary and Psalter.* New York: Crossroad.

Zub, David John C. 1992. "God as the Object of Anger in the Psalms." In *Church Divinity Monograph Series,* edited by Francis S. Tebbe. Notre Dame, Ind.: Graduate Theological Foundation, 47–63.

# 7

# "Too Militant"? Aggression, Gender, and the Construction of Justice

KATHLEEN J. GREIDER
*School of Theology at Claremont*

## INTRODUCTION

In Whitney Otto's novel *How to Make an American Quilt* (1991), Glady Joe Cleary and Hy Dodd are sisters and avid quilters. They are inseparable, despite the fact that twenty years ago, when Hy's husband James was dying, she had a brief, devastating affair with Glady Joe's husband, Arthur. While confronting Arthur, Glady Joe cleared her vanity table of atomizer bottles and makeup jars with one sweep of her arm and then kept searching the house for things to throw: cups, bowls, vases.

A week after the betrayal and throwing frenzy, Glady Joe started to glue the shards of glass on the walls of the laundry room. Arranging the pieces in intricate patterns, transforming them into art, gave Glady Joe a sense of purpose and calm. When the laundry room walls were filled and looking like three-dimensional Persian carpets, she began on the den, then the kitchen. Arthur pleaded with her: "This is really creepy, you know, . . . Couldn't you just toss that stuff out?" (Otto 1991, 41). Years later, the walls remain "an anathema" to Hy. She refuses to use the laundry room and den, and goes into the kitchen only because the walls remain unfinished, as if the artist had run out of materials (Otto 1991, 21). Once Hy said to Glady Joe, "It's just that the effect is so . . . " "So what?" demanded Glady Joe. "I don't know . . ." said Hy, "busy or aggressive or . . . I don't know," and Hy dropped her eyes to the floor (Otto 1991, 42–43).

The intense complexity of aggression is portrayed graphically in the story. Aggression reveals and obscures, terrorizes and mobilizes, destroys and creates. Pastoral caregivers and people who come for pastoral care are faced with the challenge of coming to terms with aggressive impulses, often without much guidance from church or society.

123

My interest in aggression arises most fundamentally out of a personal and communal faith question with which I have wrestled nearly all my life: Where shall I and other people of faith find the power to respond to the biblical call to do justice, and how can we employ that power justly and without using it for violence? The Judeo-Christian faith calls its followers communally and individually to do right by one another, and it is important to me as a pastor and a scholar to use the resources of psychology and religion to help create right relationship in both social and personal life. The diminishment of injustice depends upon psychological analysis and strategizing no less than upon social analysis and strategizing. These reflections on aggression are part of that larger project.

In this chapter, I argue three main points. First, aggression is part of human createdness, not inherently negative, but a resource that can be used for good and for ill. Second, although greater facility with aggression is a crucial part of psychospiritual health for both women and men, most theories about aggression's origin, meaning, and value serve to undermine women's aggressiveness. Third, aggression often plays an essential role in the justice making important to many religious individuals and communities of faith. I am analyzing my own Euro-American, female, liberal Protestant, middle-class context, in interaction with other cultures. I welcome hearing from readers how aggression is understood and functions in their cultural contexts.

## WHAT IS AGGRESSION?

There is much scholarly and popular discussion—but little agreement in either context—about the origin, meaning, and value of human "aggression."[1] This lack of agreement reflects, I believe, both deep ambivalence about aggression and the complexity of aggression itself. Aggression's elusiveness can be attributed in part to its being resident in the unconscious, often not visible directly but only through its manifestation in dream, emotion, and behavior. Aggression's elusiveness also reflects denial and repression of it: aggression is often relegated to unconsciousness. Because of its rootage in and banishment to the depths of the psyche, aggression has about it a numinosity and mysteriousness not easily captured in words.

Although aggression often leaves people speechless, use of the word by English-speakers reveals diverse meanings. "Aggression" is often equated with harm and violence. But in everyday speech one finds examples showing that aggression can be positive—for example, medical professionals normally are expected to fight disease aggressively. "Aggression" is used to refer to a destructive instinct, to behavior learned in cultural context secondary to frustration, and to an expression of the life force.[2]

For me, none of these theories are satisfying in themselves. There are communities where human behavior does not emerge in stereotyped patterns of violence, and so I am not convinced by the theory that aggression is a destructive instinct. There are instances where aggressive action occurs that is not necessarily secondary to frustration or some other circumstance but might be primary—for example, a person's bold self-assertion in discussion or athletics. Finally, it risks naiveté to define aggression as an expression of power of the life force without quickly wrestling with the contradiction that human beings often express aggression in ways that do intentional as well as unintentional harm to the life force.

Some researchers, especially the most scientific, deal with the wide range of meanings in theory and in popular usage of aggression by ascribing it to "fuzzy thinking" and error. In contrast, feminist and depth psychological methodologies prize ambiguity, complexity, and even conflict in theory if they better illuminate human experience. My research—based on review of literature, on interviews and case studies, and on clinical evidence—indicates that the complexity in language and conceptualization reflects (rather than causes) complexity and ambiguity in a specific realm of human experience that English-speakers try to capture in the word "aggression." Each of these theories, and the different meanings attributed to aggression in popular discussion, tell a part of the truth about aggression. Therefore I have formulated a description of "aggression" that seeks to integrate these diverse insights.

The most foundational meaning of aggression in English is suggested by etymology: "aggression" comes from the Latin *aggredi*, to go forward, to approach. My working definition is that aggression is one primary expression of the life force, of the drive to survive and thrive, embodied in positive and negative movement toward and engagement with goals, persons, objects, and obstacles. Since the life force is not individualistic—that is, human beings need both personal and social life to survive and thrive—both individuals and groups can be aggressive. Aggression can take emotional, cognitive, or physical forms. Aggression has different meanings and effects in particular and relational contexts. In general, however, aggression manifests in a gamut of feeling-thoughts and behaviors, including, for example, initiative, anger, assertion, militancy, wildness, confrontation, rage, and war (Fromm 1973). Motivations for expressing aggression include, among others, desire for essential self-expression, meaningful connection with others, response to frustration, defense against threat, and intent to harm. But foundationally, aggression is always an expression of a biological and psychospiritual drive to survive and thrive, although this essential meaning is frequently deeply unconscious and not easily recognized because of aggression's costs and stigma. It is crucial to note that, nearly always, forms and rationales for aggressive expression are of mixed value and meaning. Aggression's ambiguity and relationality prevent simple hierarchies of acceptable and unacceptable aggressive behavior. I address below the discernment of aggression's values and violences.

I will suggest a hypothesis of aggression's etiology, function, and development, beginning with infancy.[3] At birth, all living things are endowed with a drive to survive and thrive. From a theological point of view, the living creation as a whole is endowed by its creator with such a drive to survive and thrive. Full understanding of this drive eludes both science and philosophy. At minimum, it seems composed of two primary, essentially interrelated expressions that, in and between humans, have been called "love" and "aggression." These two primary forces can be seen in infants, who have at birth both the sentiment (love) to engage others and the force (aggression), especially through their ability to cry, to influence the powerful others around them to meet their needs. The drive to survive and thrive is a life-promoting and therefore sacred part of the creation. Thus, both love and aggression can be honored, preserved and, in the ecological sense, conservatively utilized.

The complex issues related to the proper relation of love and aggression are introduced in the first chapter of the biblical text (Genesis 1:28), establishing the magnitude of this topic for religious reflection. The biblical injunction to "be fruitful and multiply . . . and fill . . . and subdue . . . and have dominion" fundamentally concerns how aggression and love shall be exercised. Embedded in the creation story, this divine call to love and aggression is delivered in the text not only in the hearing of the first woman and man but also, narratively speaking, in the "hearing" of the whole created order. In this way, it predicts the struggles for fruitfulness, multiplication, filling, subduing, and dominion that absorb the attention of most of the living beings in creation.

Throughout the life span, insofar as conditions are favorable—that is, whenever threats to the self and its affiliations are not too great—aggression and love are "fused." Aggression and love are fused, not in the sense of being rigidly welded to each other but of being indelibly associated, like blood relatives.[4] That is, aggression and love are interrelated in the beginning and, when the person or group is not under duress, continue to be affiliated aspects of the personal and collective psyche. When functioning in this essential unity, aggression and love cannot be fully differentiated. However, an approximation of their particular contributions might be that love is "desire" and aggression is "movement."

Love and aggression function in this "braided" way because, under favorable conditions, a mixture of love and aggression most effectively ensures personal and collective survival and fullness of life. When integrated, the one cooperatively enlivens, seasons, and tempers the other: aggression enables love to move toward the thing desired, love enables aggression to desire the thing toward which it moves. Love has gumption in it, aggression has affection in it. Without this intermingling, love might be passive, aggression might be only self-serving; with this intermingling, aggression is more likely to be constructive, love is more likely to have backbone.

From a spiritual and theo-ethical point of view, this original fusion of aggression and love might be thought of as one expression of the essential holism of the human person, a desirable expression to be sought as a way to keep body, mind, and spirit in unison. If life begins with an indissoluble relationship between aggression and love, then that becomes a guideline for what it means to be created and act in the image of an awesomely powerful God—divine power is imaged only insofar as power is exercised out of the original harmony of love and aggression. Indeed, a powerful congruence between love and aggression certainly forms one promising root of humanity's capacity to do justice. This blending of love and aggression might underlie the paradoxes of what has been called "tough love," of what theologian Mary Hunt describes as the "fierce tenderness" that characterizes deep friendships (Hunt 1991, 22–23), and the irresistible power of satyagraha—the "soul-force" of nonviolence.

Aggression and love, then, might not be essentially distant from or contrary to each other. But clearly aggression and love can become split, even opposed. Like relationships between blood kin, the relationship between love and aggression cannot be severed, but it can become exceedingly tenuous and thin. As with family, I suggest that love and aggression can become estranged and turn violent when the survival or thriving of one's self and/or that which is valued (people, groups, things, places, principles) is or seems to be threatened.

Perhaps it happens first in infancy when newborns' aggression and love may feel to them unrelated, fierce, even ultimately powerful—one unable to temper the other. The intense degree of their desire and the uncontrollability of their movement likely seems to infants—at least, at times—to have the power to drive away the caring ones upon whom they are utterly dependent, putting their survival at risk. This psychological theory about infants' interior reality may shed light on why biblical images of God as loving father of the prodigal son and mother hen of restless chicks have such power as metaphors: perhaps there is a usually forbidden truth in the notion that the divine parent, holding love and aggression in tension, will not reject or even rebuke aggressive wanderings but will lovingly gather them in as part of the whole fabric of life together.

As babies grow, interpersonal, social, and existential stresses will unavoidably give rise to a conflict between love and aggression. For example, the beloved parent does not respond quickly enough to their hunger, and they wail in a grating rage, long after food is presented. Or, babies' arms and legs flail in excitement but then bump hard surfaces and cause pain to the child. Children's hearts are broken by the vicious taunts of supposed friends, and they must choose between retaliation, retreat, or reconciliation. For too many children, just as their bodies and spirits begin to mature, an adult whom they have been taught to respect now aggressively assaults them with emotional, sexual, and physical violence. Further, and ironically, in most Euro-American cultures, girls and boys are psychosocially crafted to mirror the feared split between love and aggression, boys taught to embody aggression and girls taught to embody love.

In adulthood, too, as the old ballad puts it plainly, "we hurt the ones we love." In the case of existential threats, adults hurt the ones they love because there is no appropriate target anywhere for the vulnerability they face. Often a person hurts a loved one as a rejoinder to hurt caused by the loved one. Both are enveloped in a conflict between their personal need to survive and their desire to see loved ones survive. Most often, human beings hurt the ones they love because intimates are less threatening targets than those who actually cause the distress. Such cases demonstrate human faith in the close relationship between love and aggression. Individuals regularly count on the fact that, within reasonable limits, they can be difficult with significant others. A person risks being irritable with friends because she trusts that they can feel for her both aggression and love and stay relatively close. Finally, if split love and aggression make it so common that people hurt the ones they love, then it is not a far stretch at all to understand the relative ease with which people hurt the ones who do not live so near to heart. Human beings are engaged in a complex dialectic, moving away from one another despite the desire for connection and moving toward one another despite the desire for safety.

Thus, aggression can lead to violence, but aggression is not equal to violence. When threatened, both love and aggression can become violent. Human beings can, and do, sometimes love one another to death. Violence happens when there is too great a threat against the drive to survive and live well. Violence can result when either love or aggression is thwarted or threatened. Thus, parents are filled with the urge to destroy those who harm their children, and the victimized may eventually kill abusers who keep them under physical and psychospiritual lock and key.

There are several implications of the hypothesis about aggression's origin and value that I have been proposing. First, aggression just is. It is a given aspect of human createdness, part and parcel of the drive to survive and thrive. Human beings do not have a choice about whether or not they will be aggressive.

Second, people are generally deeply ambivalent about aggression because aggression is so ambiguous and multivalent. That is, mixed feelings about aggression (and about power in general) rightly reflect aggression's mixed values, the reality that aggression can be all at once positive and negative. Aggression's ambiguity contributes to the atmosphere of taboo that surrounds aggression in many societies. Under these conditions of complexity and taboo, it is a psychospiritual achievement, a sign of maturity, to hold on to some consciousness of the essential relationship between love and aggression and to develop the ability to reweave these aspects of the psyche that social and existential forces tear apart.

Third, individuals and communities do not have a choice about being aggressive, but there are crucial choices of consciousness and conscience about how they shall express aggression. Aggression acquires negative and positive values according to how it is used, consciously and unconsciously, emotionally and behaviorally. Individuals and communities must consciously endeavor to have an anchor line in both the positive and the negative aspects of aggression if aggression's power to help is to be accessed even while its power to harm is curbed. There is no generally applicable rule to save the painstaking work of discerning the meaning and value of aggression in each circumstance. I have been working with the following guideline: in my view, aggression is used negatively when it is directed toward wasteful and/or unconscious violence[5]; aggression is used positively when it is directed toward the affirmation of life and well-being in both its personal and collective dimensions. Or, perhaps a derivation from the Golden Rule is more to the point: be aggressive unto others as you would have them be aggressive unto you.

Finally, aggression is better known for the harm it does than for the good it does. But from a depth psychological point of view, aggression plays some very particular, central roles in psychosocial maturation and well-being, some of them quite contrary to, and often obscured by, aggression's bad reputation. I want to point out three of aggression's life-affirming contributions.

Aggression seeks to end violence at least as much as it is the cause of violence. Aggression has long been thought of as a cause of violence. Yet, in the case of physical self-defense, the right to be aggressive against another in order to end violence is protected by law. Similarly, the "laws" of the psyche—personal and collective—recognize the need and right to defend against psychospiritual violence as well. The seemingly unprovoked and unpredictable violent aggression of individuals often has the greater power to grip public attention. But aggression—whether negatively or positively expressed—is more often a predictable reaction to and a defense of self and/or others against the high level of violence in the environment.

Psychoanalyst Karen Horney criticized Sigmund Freud for positing a human instinct of destructiveness; she said he erroneously did so because he did not take into sufficient account that there are reasons in the environment to be destructive.[6] Hostility is a reaction to hostility in the psychic, relational and social environment, she countered, not evidence of an instinctual destructiveness in essential human nature. She defended her claim with this metaphor: "If a tree, because of storms, too little sun or too poor soil, becomes warped and crooked, you would not call this its essential nature" (Horney 1952, 68).

Furthermore, aggression is fundamental to relationality. Aggression often is conceptualized as pushing others away, and this often is its effect—sometimes necessarily, sometimes needlessly. But aggression is at least as often an attempt toward meaningful, honest engagement. Although the aggressive effort to make a substantive contact can take desperate and even violent forms, such as picking a fight, it may as often take more benign and even beguiling forms, such as an energetic exploration of differences. Aggressive living, such as spontaneity, gusto, and adventurousness, teaches boundaries (those of self and others) and safety. D. W. Winnicott points out that children and adults need opportunities to play at being aggressive. Play can teach several crucial lessons. The real injuries aggression can cause are sometimes revealed in play. Conversely, play can also show that not all aggression is destructive or fatal: the self and others can survive some aggression and destructiveness. Further, when aggression is truly playful, it can impart to self and community the benefits of a healthy sense of power and agency (Winnicott 1971, 65–85).

Even more foundationally, Winnicott says, the exercise of aggressiveness teaches human beings that others exist. This is most concretely true for the newborn, who discovers the world outside itself when its thrashing legs and arms collide with people and things. Thus, Winnicott says, aggression establishes externality (Winnicott 1975, 214–218). Without aggressive living, a person learns less about the world outside herself, and fantasy fills in the gaps—for example, a woman may imagine that people will be hurt by even her least little aggression, even though she has little direct experiential evidence for this belief.

A final, crucial point: aggression is as involved in repair as it is in destruction. Aggression is usually fearfully thought of as being destructive, that its inevitable end is irreparable damage. But it can be a conscious recognition of one's own capacity for destructiveness that gives a person the humble spirit necessary for mediation and reconciliation in one's personal and social relationships. The path to reparation is long and arduous and, how-

ever constructively people may employ aggression, there is no way to reparation except through aggression's real costs to self and others. These real
costs are often quite different from the alternately panicky or nonchalant
damage estimates frequently applied to aggression's effects. The approach
to aggression most likely to avoid violence and build up peace is not to
sidestep aggression but to cultivate a conscious and relational exploration
of positive and negative aggression—ambition and hate, assertiveness and
violence—neither exaggerating or minimizing aggressiveness. Only in this
way can the real costs of aggression be discerned. These real costs ought to
lead, not to a sense of shame, but to a sense of real guilt, a sense of remorse
appropriate to the violence of aggression as it really is. Winnicott puts it
more simply: a feeling of concern arises, based in a feeling of love (Winnicott 1965, 73–81).

Once beyond a false sense of either guilt or self-righteousness, there is a
possibility that an authentic impulse to set things right might arise. Real
ownership of one's participation in the problems associated with aggression might increase real personal and collective ownership in the efforts to
make reparation for the real costs of aggression. This is a paradoxical
moment: one must claim one's violence in order to make true peace. Those
who know their aggression closely can both take responsibility for their
contribution to tearing things down and have renewed confidence in their
ability to contribute toward building things up again.

## "TOO MILITANT"? PSYCHOSOCIAL PERSPECTIVES ON WOMEN'S AGGRESSION

One of the great and tragic violences practiced in dominant, Euro-
American cultures is the extermination program that is aimed at women's
aggression. Almost always, women's aggression is ignored, mocked, or vio-
lently punished. This program has been so successful at stunting positive
conscious and unconscious images of aggressive women that, in general,
even among women's most ardent supporters and the most radical of
women themselves, women's aggressiveness is "attractive" only when it is
publicly judged as having been exercised on behalf of others, preferably
white men and children, and/or against other women's aggressiveness.
Even then, it is a risk.

The appellation "too militant" is one of the major weapons in the extermination program against women's aggression, I suggest, and is one of the
most widely effective forms of pressure against a woman's self-definition
and enjoyment of her aggressiveness. The mere phrase has wielded the
power of definition over the popular conceptualization of feminism: to be

feminist is to be "too militant." There are many women who would call themselves feminists if to do so did not automatically mean, in their own eyes as well as in the eyes of others, that they had become "too militant."

The theories offered to explain the meaning and function of the psycho-social blockades against women's aggressiveness are numerous and complex. I can only briefly mention a few here. Teresa Bernardez has observed that the suppression of women's aggression has been rationalized as a necessary part of women's mothering: women have been socialized to be nonaggressive, it is argued, so as to protect the children in women's care and thus the future of the human race (Bernardez-Bonesatti, 1987, 215). Women's aggression is "too militant" because it might detract from the myths and reality of women's social role as nurturer of posterity. Here the fear of women's destructiveness is acknowledged to be based not just in unconscious fantasy, a common claim that I will discuss next, but also in consciousness of women's actual power, both creative and destructive.

This argument is specious, since it incorrectly assumes that aggressiveness is inherently self-centered, nonrelational, and violent. As I have argued above, aggressiveness has a part in love and helps establish otherness; many positive features of women's aggression would and do serve to further mothering and other forms of nurturance. The rationalization and argument is also unconvincing, since the defense of the young is nearly the only situation in which women's aggressiveness receives any sanction.

More convincing perhaps is the second argument, that women's aggressiveness is repressed because women and men have unconscious fears and fantasies of women's omnipotence as well as of women's "destructiveness" (Lerner 1988, 54–55). This theory rests upon speculation about earliest psychological and relational life, during which most children are cared for almost exclusively by women. Theorists suppose that children's profound dependence on women during those years results in both cherishing and trying to destroy powerful mothering women, who seem to the children so utterly capable of cherishing and destroying them. This theory suggests that in adult life these same children deny women positive as well as negative aggressive strivings so as to try to ensure that, finally, the power inherent in the infantile maternal imago can be controlled, dominated, even revenged (Lerner 1988, 11). Here the notably gendered quality of being "too militant" is illuminated: women are more likely than men to seem "too militant" perhaps because women more exactly symbolize the awesome power inherent in the infantile maternal imago.

But there are questions that make this explanation less than satisfying. What if dependence is not so threatening to everyone as has been assumed? What if infants are able to see and appreciate mother as neither omnipotently caring nor omnipotently destructive? Or what if not only separation-individuation but also relationship-differentiation describes maturation?[7] Then the effort to emulate maternal aggression might be as natural as the effort to triumph over it. Further, certainly gender has some effect upon the strength of this threat from women's aggression and the ability to cope with it: if primary relationship to women during early psychological life sends females and males into different primary tasks in regard at least to "gendering"—girls into identification and boys into differentiation—might it also lead, as the means to shaping their own power, to a girl relishing women's aggression as much as to the boy acting out against it?

These questions and conjectures reveal limitations in the understanding of women's aggression and the psychosocial significance of its repression, thus allowing for a third possibility: certainly the significance of women's aggression and its repression is related to adulthood fears and losses as well as to childhood fears and losses. Specifically, women's aggression represents the potential or real loss of privilege and power resulting from the disturbance of dominating and subjugating social structures, and the repression of women's aggression may seek consciously and unconsciously to avoid or revenge any threat to the status quo. Women's aggression can be an accurate articulation of injustice done and an exposing of its effects in private and public life. If it is true, as Jean Baker Miller argues, that the suppression of women's anger is inextricably linked with—indeed, is a tool in—the sociology of oppression (Miller 1991, 182–183), how much more is the suppression of women's aggressiveness essential to the psychosocial dynamics of denial and resistance that keep in place the collective pathology of unjust systems. Perhaps this is at the core of what it means to be "too militant," since the appellation often is invoked not to open dialogue but to demean and dismiss any person or group that is demanding or impatient or unsentimental in calling for social self-examination in regard to systems of power.

When it focuses too exclusively on the past, psychological theory obscures present psychosocial dynamics in the environment relevant to the significance of women's aggression and its repression. More significantly, too exclusive a focus on the private relational dynamics of individuals and families derails attention from a critique of the psychosocial dynamics that defend against efforts to find more just and healthy patterns of social and relational development. This is not a weakness only of classical schools of thought. In my opinion, neither feminist psychologies nor feminist theologies are doing enough to help women or men understand the significance of aggression in its cultural context and to use aggressiveness holistically and ethically. If aggression is dealt with at all in these disciplines, it is usually equated with violence—too often and inadequately with male violence—and critiqued as such.

Even when it sets out to do so, feminist theory has trouble looking women's aggression in the eye. Psychologists Dorothy Cantor and Toni Bernay have published their findings from research interviews with prominent women politicians concerning the politicians' leadership capacities and its development (Cantor and Bernay 1992). Bernay and Cantor's interpretation of their findings is that three elements comprise the "Leadership Equation": "Competent Self," "Creative Aggression," and "WomanPower" (Cantor and Bernay 1992, 17–34). They also report that the notion that "you can use and enjoy your creative aggression" is one of the "basic secrets" of leadership and one of the "enabling messages" that during childhood foster leadership in young girls (Cantor and Bernay 1992, 236–238). They borrow Karen Horney's definition of "adequate aggressiveness" to define "creative aggression."

> By this I mean the capacities for work, including the following attributes: taking initiative; making efforts; carrying things through to completion; attaining success; insisting upon one's rights; defending oneself when attacked; forming and expressing autonomous views; recognizing one's goals and being able to plan one's life according to them. (Horney 1967, 228)

In light of the lack of attention to aggression in research for, by, and about women, this is a promising direction. However, it soon disappoints. The distinction between "Creative Aggression" and "WomanPower" is not clearly drawn by Cantor and Bernay. It seems to rely on an interpretation of aggression as self-interested and of power as being more altruistically focused on social life. In this they perpetuate what I believe is a false dualism but a dualism meaningful in the fear and repression of women's aggressiveness. Indeed, they say little at all about what creative aggression actually is, or how it is fostered psychologically except to provide the reader a helpful but brief and fairly predictable discussion of how women might use their anger more creatively. In contrast, they devote a chapter to the exploration of WomanPower and never acknowledge any relationship between aggression and power. Overall, the effect is to suggest again that women's aggressive power is at least most interesting and perhaps even most acceptable when it is oriented away from self-interest and toward the benefit of others, an unfortunate effect, since I sense it goes against the authors' intent. Finally, commending "creative aggression" seems to imply that all destructive aggression is wrong, perhaps "too militant." Yet there are some things that need to be destroyed, such as systems of oppression: is there no healthy and ethical way psychically to explore "creative destructiveness"?

The silence in feminist theory about women's aggression is disempowering and unethical. Silence about aggression not only fails to connect women to, but actively separates them from, aggression's capacity to contribute to antiracism and antisexism work. Moreover, women's silence about aggression may amount to complicity with and benefit from aggression's capacity—as exercised by women and men—to keep injustice in place. Women's willingness to wield the appellation "too militant" and other forms of indiscriminate pressure against women's aggressiveness might be understood as an effort to distance ourselves from any responsibility and/or capacity for social violence and reform: a lack of aggressiveness or militancy helps keep in place unjust systems from which privileged women benefit.

One of the things that accounts for this silence about aggression in feminist theory is, I suggest, the multivalence of aggression as it is encountered in the intersection between social location and psychological location. To break the grip of silence in feminist theory about aggression would mean voicing the complex connections between a woman's level of consciousness about, command of, and comfort with her aggression and the exigencies of her social and psychological privileges and marginalization. More specifically, a woman with some access to privilege and its securities, her own or others, may be able to benefit vicariously from the aggressiveness of others and thus afford a distant psychological relationship with her own marginalization and aggressiveness. On the other hand, a woman who has little privilege to lose and not much security is more likely to at least be aware of her marginalization and aggressiveness and perhaps more able to access the lifesaving qualities of her aggression in ways beneficial to herself and her affiliations. For example, white women's complicity in slavery and contemporary forms of racism might be related to white women's tendency to have a distant relationship with both the violent aspects of their aggression and with their aggression's value in antiracism work. In contrast, African-American women tend to have greater access to their aggression because of the everyday necessity of overt and covert defiance of racism and, in the face of racism, the challenge of constructing dynamic, death-defying personhood and community.

White women will be hampered from claiming and expressing the positive aspects of aggression as long as they are defended against a disciplined consciousness of what they gain through nonaggressiveness and confusion about aggression. Euro-American, middle-class women who, like me, have had some measure of privilege to temper our marginalization, have not regularly needed to be aggressive to survive or been encouraged to be aggressive for fun. Consequently, women of privilege do not regularly have a lot of conscious relationship with or access to the forms of everyday aggressiveness that lie between survival and fun.

In light of this observation, it is interesting that the late 1980s and early 1990s have produced several artistic explorations of women's aggression that have garnered a fair amount of popular attention. Some of these explorations have been of aggressive, justice-minded, even militant, white women. These provocative images are more useful than dangerous because, as art, they give women and men the opportunity to explore in fantasy the interrelationships between aggression, gender, and violence; I will suggest below that fantasizing about aggression is one essential aspect of a healthy and less harmful psychosocial relationship to aggression.

These images of women's aggression are being soaked up like rain on parched ground. Even women who could not unequivocally love the film *Thelma and Louise* found the film's script and scenarios popping up in their conversations and imaginations (Scott 1991). After seeing the movie *Fried Green Tomatoes*, a group of middle-aged and older women in a tiny, unsophisticated parish in a conservative region of New England surreptitiously changed the name of their United Methodist women's circle to Towanda (Avnet 1991).[8] Clarissa Pinkola Estés's book *Women Who Run with the Wolves: Myths and Stories of the Wild Woman Archetype* ended up in the middle of the *New York Times* best-seller list in the first week following its publication (1992). Perhaps it is even more telling that the company distributing audiotapes of Estés's work, which also sells tapes of Robert Bly's work, reports that in their sales the Wild Woman has been outselling Iron John ten to one (Krier 1992).[9]

## Aggression, Gender, and Militancy: Tentative Suggestions, Future Directions, Concluding Observations

A greater conscious relationship with aggression might increase the ability not only to register and take responsibility for the costs of aggression's violences but also to envision and employ aggression's constructiveness in a more militant—that is, firm and persistent—approach to social reform. Further, it may be fruitful to study militancy through the lens of women's experience precisely because women have long been discouraged from the most stereotypical and destructive modalities of militancy—militarism, for example—and encouraged to repress any other militancy. Thus, women's militant impulses and images, in large measure long consigned to the depths of the psyche, might return from repression and unconscious process imbued with ancient, less violent, and more creative characterizations and symbolizations of militancy's qualities, hazards, and values, ready for consideration.

Militancy's actual and potential excesses and dangers are extensive. Militancy's underside is well known, and, consequently, I will not detail its costs in this essay. However, unblinking attention to militancy's violences is an essential aspect of any full discussion of militancy's value. Neither can I fully explore here what militancy is, or what unique forms of aggression it represents, or what standards or processes of judgment might be used to distinguish between militancy that advances life and that which advances death; that is another work.

Here I can only claim in the most preliminary way that if the extent of aggression's violences is fully acknowledged, then the conclusion is inescapable that militancy is sometimes necessary to defend life against death. There have been and likely will be times again when a militantly aggressive defense is needed because the violences exacted are so many and so imminent. A militant aggressiveness can be an expression of the personal and collective human will to survive.

Just as aggression is not equal to violence, militancy is not equal to violence. Womanist theorist bell hooks says that "the spirit of militancy" is commitment to struggle against that which threatens life. The spirit of militancy enables human beings to put their lives on the line in passionate resistance and to take other related risks (hooks 1990, 185–191). Militancy can contribute to healthy rebelliousness, making people more able to "step out of line," to "talk back" in a substantive way, when "I-ness" and "we-ness" are under siege (hooks 1989, 5–9). Cecil Murray, pastor of First African Methodist Episcopal Church in Los Angeles and high profile community leader especially after the 1992 uprising, says he does not preach violence, but, because of the reality of racism, he does preach militancy. In an interview with the *Los Angeles Times Magazine* he says: "You've got to push, push, push. . . . When I get to the door [of opportunity and access], I want the door to open. And if it doesn't open, I want the right to kick it in" (Easton 1992, 15).

For people and communities of faith, militancy is sometimes necessary not only as an expression of psychological self-esteem but of spiritual "faith-esteem," making persons more able to stand by their prayerfully considered beliefs. As feminist liberation theologian Dorothee Soelle puts it, militancy can support religious individuals and communities toward giving up a "helpless, self-pitying, 'We can't do anything about it' position" (Soelle 1990, 88–89).

If faith is to be responsive to suffering and not become self-satisfied, Soelle says, faith sometimes needs to be militant like the militancy of Jesus' faith, that took the form of "a degree of steadfastness" (Soelle 1981, 18). This is akin to the insight of Latina theologian Elsa Tamez, who says in her study of the Epistle of James that James calls his readers to a "militant patience," which means "to persevere, to resist, to be constant, unbreakable, immovable" in their work against oppression (Tamez 1990, 53). Sœlle says that the militant element of faith (faith is not all militancy, of course) contributes toward a faith that "is not reserved and detached" but rather takes the form of "a passionate and unbroken interest in life" (Sœlle 1981, 17). In imitation of Jesus' willingness to engage the powers and principalities, faith's militancy is embodied in "a clear, resolute fighting spirit" (Sœlle 1990, 88–89). Faith's militancy is, in part, a willingness to put one's life on the line, but otherwise, Sœlle says, faith's militancy is nonviolent in the "strictest sense": it fights against "anything that hurts or damages another human being" (Sœlle and Steffensky 1985, 93).

Again, a fuller exploration of the positive aspects of aggression's militancy is beyond the limits of this essay. However, in conclusion I want to suggest that there are healthy and ethical paths through which women can explore and employ aggression's creative destructiveness and fruitfulness and through which the value of militancy might be claimed and embodied. Since militancy's oppressiveness can be traced in large measure to an unwillingness to reckon consciously with aggression (especially its potential for positive expressions), I believe that consideration of militancy is safe only as part of a reflective relationship to aggression's many aspects (especially its potential for negative expression). I can only point here in conclusion to a few of these methods and must leave fuller discussion of these, too, for another time. These suggestions are not especially inventive except, perhaps, for their attempt to show their particular usefulness to women for curbing aggression's violence and employing aggression's usefulness. In general, the paths toward positive aggression seem to take women through both more intensive or in-depth use of common modes of human experience and/or through aspects of human experience commonly shunned.

Fantasy is probably the single most satisfying, efficacious, easily available, and cost-effective pathway toward greater capability in dealing with aggression in personal and social life. Importantly, in fantasy women can play, in the Winnicottian sense, with violent aggressiveness without wreaking havoc in the world at large, a special value for women who are overly burdened with fear of aggression's destructiveness (Winnicott 1971, 38–52). If the distinctions and connections between fantasy and relational life can be maintained, in this real inner world women can imaginatively, and with very real psychic and relational effects, "work through" the impulses and responses that they are not yet able to express or are not appropriate to the "outside" world.

Movement—physical, emotional, relational, political—is a way of exploring aggression at the important intersection between mind, body, and spirit. Movement can open up aggressiveness at both physical and emotional levels perhaps because, as Winnicott has observed, in the beginning of life aggression is "almost synonymous" with infantile movement; physical movement echoes the pleasure, rebellion, and release of this "primal" aggressiveness (Winnicott 1984, 91). Physical movement—sports, dance, tai chi—can be an especially provocative way for women to get in touch with buried aggressive physicality and emotionality, especially because in so doing a woman in some measure rebels against the restrictions that sex-role stereotyping places on women's physicality and the aggressiveness expressed through it (Notman and Nadelson 1982, 22–23). Daring to undertake cognitive and relational movement—"getting unstuck"—is also likely to help women access aggressiveness, since the challenge of aggressive strivings often is one of the things that immobilizes women in relationship. Taking some first step out of frozenness can be the first step toward greater health in relationship; self-in- relation theory claims that movement is the essence of growth-fostering relationships (Miller and Surrey 1990, 2). Aggression, because it moves, and moves people in relationship, is one aspect of that health.

Mutuality as a value for aggressive expression is another pathway that may hold special value for women's exploration of the distinctions between positive and negative aggression. The principle of mutuality has received significant attention in psychologies of women and in feminist theory as a core value (Jordan 1991, 81–96). One of the factors that can most increase aggression's capacity to have positive effects, I suggest, is the degree to which women can strive for mutuality in aggressiveness. Specifically, persons must strive to be able to receive and respect someone else's appropriate expression of aggression even as they strive to express their own aggression appropriately.

There are other paths that might particularly enable women's exploration and employment of aggression's potentials: aggression as serving not only the capacity to do but also the capacity to be; aggression as a sign of hope for relationship; aggression as the fruit of a cultivated aplomb; aggression as a means of taking necessary and life-enhancing risks.

With good reason, many people have approached aggression with the feeling that "this is really creepy . . . [can't we] just toss that stuff out?" But if violence is no longer so easily projected, neither can human beings afford to throw away aggression simply because it is broken.

## Notes

1. The wide range of meanings attributed to "aggression" makes it difficult to communicate clearly when using the word. Therefore I use the unqualified "aggression" when I mean to evoke aggression's ambiguity and multivalency. To denote aggression's more specific harmfulness and helpfulness, I use appropriate qualifiers or specific descriptors, such as "negative aggression" or "violence" and "positive aggression" and "vitality."

2. David Augsburger (1993, 1:482–487) offers a brief overview of these theories.

3. This hypothesis rests in large measure on the clinical work of British pediatrician and psychoanalyst Donald W. Winnicott. Although I add and revise a few points based on my own clinical research, in my view Winnicott's theory of aggression is the most profound in the psychological literature. Winnicott's *Deprivation and Delinquency* (1984) brings into one volume most of his writings on aggression. See also "Aggression in Relation to Emotional Development," in Winnicott, *Through Paediatrics to Psycho-Analysis* (1975).

4. As with relationships between blood relatives, the relationship between love and aggression may become strained or extraordinarily distant, but, in my view, it can never be obliterated.

5. In situations of dire and immediate physical threat, violence may be the only possible defense of life. In such situations, it can be argued that violence may be necessary and morally acceptable. Condemnation of all forms of violent revolution may be steeped in racial and/or class privilege (The Amanecida Collective 1987, 69). It is often steeped in gender privilege as well.

6. Karen Horney tells her readers that "doubts" about two aspects of Freudian theory led ultimately to her revision of psychoanalysis: interestingly, those two issues were aggression and gender (Horney 1939, 7).

7. Relationship-differentiation, "a dynamic process that encompasses increasing levels of complexity, structure, and articulation within the context of human bonds and attachment," is discussed by Janet L. Surrey (1991, 35–43). The quotation is from p. 36.

8. "Towanda the Magnanimous, Righter of Wrongs and Queen without Compare" is character Evelyn Couch's aggressive phantastic persona in Fannie Flagg's novel *Fried Green Tomatoes at the Whistle Stop Cafe*, 236–240.

9. Robert Bly's book *Iron John* (1990) has been a popular book among some people interested in the men's movement of the late 1980s and 1990s.

## BIBLIOGRAPHY

The Amanecida Collective. 1987. *Revolutionary Forgiveness: Feminist Reflections on Nicaragua.* A. Gilson and C. Heyward, eds. Maryknoll, N.Y.: Orbis Books.

Augsburger, D. W. 1993. "Anger and Aggression." In Wicks, Parson, and Capps, eds., 1:482–501.

Avnet, Jon (Director). 1991. *Fried Green Tomatoes.* Film. Electric Shadow Productions/Universal Pictures/Act III Communications.

Bernardez-Bonesatti, T. 1987. "Women and Anger: Conflicts with Aggression in Contemporary Women." *Journal of the American Medical Women's Association* 33: 215–219.

Bly, R. 1990. *Iron John: A Book about Men.* Reading, Mass.: Addison-Wesley.

Cantor, D. W., and T. Bernay, with J. Stoess. 1992. *Women in Power: The Secrets of Leadership.* Boston: Houghton Mifflin Co.

Easton, N. J. August 16, 1992. "Rev. Murray's Gospel of Action." *Los Angeles Times Magazine,* 12+.

Estés, C. P. 1992. *Women Who Run with the Wolves: Myths and Stories of the Wild Woman Archetype.* New York: Ballantine Books.

Flagg, F. 1988. *Fried Green Tomatoes at the Whistle Stop Cafe.* New York: McGraw-Hill Books.

Fromm, E. 1973. *The Anatomy of Human Destructiveness.* New York: Holt, Rinehart & Winston.

hooks, b. 1990. *Yearning: Race, Gender, and Cultural Politics.* Boston: South End Press.

——— [G. Watkins]. 1989. *Talking Back.* Boston: South End Press.

Horney, K. 1939. *New Ways in Psychoanalysis.* New York: W. W. Norton & Co.

———. 1952. "Human Nature Can Change." *American Journal of Psycho-Analysis* 12: 67–68.

———. 1967. *Feminine Psychology.* Harold Kelman, ed. New York: W. W. Norton & Co.

Hunt, M. E. 1991. *Fierce Tenderness: A Feminist Theology of Friendship.* New York: Crossroad.

Jordan, J. V. 1991. "The Meaning of Mutuality." In Jordan et al., 81–96.

——— et al. 1991. *Women's Growth in Connection: Writings from the Stone Center.* New York: Guilford Press.

Krier, B. A. August 27, 1992. "A Wild Woman." *Los Angeles Times,* E1+.

Lerner, H. G. 1988. *Women in Therapy.* New York: Harper & Row.

Miller, J. B. 1991. "The Construction of Anger in Women and Men." In Jordan et al., 181–196.

Miller, J. B., and J. L. Surrey. 1990. "Revisioning Women's Anger: The Personal and the Global." Work in Progress, #43. Wellesley, Mass.: The Stone Center.

Notman, M. T., and C. C. Nadelson, eds. 1982. *The Woman Patient,* vol 3: *Aggression, Adaptations, and Psychotherapy.* New York: Plenum Press.

———. and C. C. Nadelson. 1982. "Aggression in Women: Conceptual Issues and Clinical Implications." In Notman and Nadelson, eds., 3:17–28.

Otto, W. 1991. *How to Make an American Quilt.* New York: Ballantine Books.

Scott, Ridley (Director). 1991. *Thelma and Louise.* Film. MGM.

Sœlle, D. 1981. *Choosing Life.* Translated by Margaret Kohl. Philadelphia: Fortress Press.

———. 1990. *Thinking about God.* Translated by John Bowden. Philadelphia: Trinity Press International.

Sœlle, D., and F. Steffensky. 1985. *Not Just Yes and Amen.* Philadelphia: Fortress Press.

Surrey, J. L. 1991. "The Relational Self in Women: Clinical Implications." In Jordan et al., 35–43.

Tamez, E. 1990. *The Scandalous Message of James: Faith without Works Is Dead.* Minneapolis: Fortress Press.

Wicks, R. J.; R. Parsons; and D. Capps, eds. 1993. *Clinical Handbook of Pastoral Counseling.* 2 vols. Mahwah, N.J.: Paulist Press.

Winnicott, D. W. 1971. *Playing and Reality.* New York: Tavistock Publications.

———. 1975. *Through Paediatrics to Psycho-Analysis.* Edited by Masud R. Khan. New York: Basic Books.

———. 1984. *Deprivation and Delinquency.* Edited by Clare Winnicott, Ray Shepherd, and Madeleine Davis. New York: Tavistock Publishers.

———. 1965. *The Maturational Processes and the Facilitating Environment: Studies in the Theory of Emotional Development.* Madison, Conn.: International Universities Press.

# 8

## Sexual Identity and Pastoral Concerns: Caring with Women Who Are Developing Lesbian Identities

JORETTA L. MARSHALL
*Iliff School of Theology*

Pastoral caregivers who seek to empower and support women will be met by women who want to discuss matters of sexuality. Essential to a pastoral perspective is thoughtful reflection on identity formation and sexual orientation. For example, caregivers may be asked to respond to women who are struggling to make sense of internal sexual feelings or who are wondering about their sexual orientation. Apprehension may be voiced by family members who seek pastoral guidance as they speculate about what the disclosure of a relative who has self-identified as lesbian means for their family relationships. Women may turn to pastors with anxiety that has surfaced as they move through the process of verbally acknowledging their lesbian sexual orientation to friends and families. Likewise, there are lesbians who may approach sensitive pastoral counselors to talk about the deep estrangement they experience within their communities of faith. The richness of issues that women who love women bring to pastoral care and counseling is as vast as the number of persons who struggle to be honest and to live with integrity as lesbians.

This chapter focuses on pastoral care with women who primarily are attracted emotionally, physically, spiritually, and sexually to other women or who self-identify as lesbians. Since the goal in this chapter is to examine briefly how sexual orientation, identity formation, and the Christian faith converge in pastoral care, the appropriate starting place is to examine issues of sexuality and identity formation in general. Women who share

This chapter reflects concerns that are part of ongoing research culminating in a book to be released through Westminster/John Knox Press. The work is tentatively titled *Covenantal Partnerships: Pastoral Counseling with Women in Lesbian Relationships* and is scheduled for publication in the fall of 1996.

their lives intimately with other women offer those within the community
of faith the opportunity to think critically and seriously about what it
means to be a sexual being. Second, this chapter proposes that attention be
given by pastoral caregivers to the manner in which sexual orientation
emerges in women's lives. While there is some predictability about the
process through which many women move in self-identifying as lesbian,
precisely what that process looks like is dependent upon the particularity
of each woman's family of origin, community support, class, ethnicity, self-
perception, and a number of other variables. This chapter, albeit limited,
offers some initial reflections on the process that lesbians may face in arriving at an integrated sense of self. Finally, I address some of the specific
concerns that lesbians bring to their churches, to their communities of
faith, and to pastoral care specialists.


## SEXUALITY AND IDENTITY FORMATION

Identity, an ongoing process of development that occurs at both the conscious and the unconscious level, is tied to a number of other aspects in the
construction of the self. Consciously, persons recognize the struggle to
solidify a sense of who they are by the way they fashion commitments,
friendships, intimate relationships, and discernment about vocations. At
the more unconscious level, persons attempt to define who they are as
emotional, physical, sexual, and spiritual beings while they seek to integrate material from families of origin, earliest childhood experiences, and
hidden motivations and agendas. The process of identity formation first
surfaces most clearly during early adolescence, but the movement toward
resolution of identity comes only later in life, perhaps as late as young
adulthood or mid-adulthood. Many theoreticians argue that identity
refinement occurs throughout the entire life cycle (Kegan 1982).

While there are several aspects that contribute to identity, sexuality is
certainly one of the most salient facets in terms of its impact on the deepest internal and external levels of being human. By "sexuality" I mean to
suggest more than how persons engage in physical relationships, although
these are certainly part of the whole. A broader understanding of sexuality
connects it with perceptions and self-awareness as embodied and engendered beings, of core values and beliefs about what it means to be body-
selves, and of the manner in which persons yearn and seek communion
with others. James Nelson and Carter Heyward, two contemporary sexual
theologians, have noted that understandings and experiences of sexuality
also ultimately inform our knowledge and experience of God. Hence, sexuality is intimately connected to more than physical life, pointing toward

the communion of life at its deepest levels—emotionally, physically, sexually, and spiritually (Heyward 1989; Nelson 1978).

As individuals discern what it means to be embodied, to interact with other sexual beings at both intimate and informal levels, they shape and form their identities. Persons relate to one another *through* self-understandings as women and men. Sexuality becomes one of the most significant arenas around which individuals form and integrate various aspects of the self. This does not mean that sexuality is *the most* important or the only integrating aspect of identity, but it is pivotal as it contains some of the most vital facets of our experience with other human beings and in the world. To have an integrated identity means, in part, to have the capacity to think about, reflect, and engage with other human beings as sexual beings.

How persons think about and experience sexuality often becomes a place of intense emotional, physical, spiritual, and sexual energy. Certainly writers like Carter Heyward and Audre Lorde have articulated the richness and depth of sexuality as they talk about "eros" and the energy that is a part of being sexual (Heyward 1989; Lorde 1984, 53–59). This power is evident in the vitality of conversations about diverse sexual topics such as abortion, marriage and sexual fidelity, children's sex education, and homosexuality. Issues related to sexuality can spark intense debate, and even division, within the context of church and society because they are integral to self-understandings and relationships. Since so much is contained within the arena of sexuality I will limit this discussion by defining three terms that are important in conversations about sexual identity and orientation: sex, gender, and orientation. In the process, nuances related to pastoral care with lesbians begin to emerge as each of these words reflects notions of the meaning of an integrated identity (Shively and De Cecco 1993, 80–88).

Sex, a word that has come to signify many things, often raises anxiety in the community of faith. For purposes of this chapter, I suggest that the word "sex" be limited to two distinct meanings. First of all, sex is the word utilized to convey the reality of our creation as male or female. In this sense the word references biological givenness, not necessarily the attributes that have come to be culturally or religiously associated with the particularity of being male or female.

The term "sex" has also come to signify the physical act of intimacy, more specifically of intercourse. Using this word as a verb to refer to specific physical acts has contributed to the confusion of defining sexuality in general, for we are tempted to limit our understandings to this aspect alone. The word "sexual" refers to the human capacity that people have to relate at more than physical levels, but at emotional and spiritual levels as well. All humans have the capacity and yearning to communicate at the deepest levels of their being. Sexuality, in its broadest understanding, refers to this more comprehensive set of characteristics and qualities of human living that engage persons in relationships at physical, emotional, spiritual, and sexual levels.

A common mistake made by well-intentioned pastoral caregivers is to adopt the assumption that homosexuality is only about the way persons engage in the physical activity of "sex." Being lesbian, however, reflects much more than this as it refers to the fundamental perspective that women bring to various experiences of communion and intimacy, including those which are spiritual, emotional, physical, and sexual. Lesbian orientation is central to the way some women communicate with other human beings (women and men) at more than just the physical or sexual level. Hence the emphasis in pastoral care should not be on the activity of "sex" but on the meaning that women bring to this part of their realities as sexual beings and the way in which lesbian women communicate with others at the least and most intimate levels of relationships.

The word "sex," when utilized to specify whether persons are male or female, is often confused with the meaning of gender. This latter term, "gender," refers to the cultural, religious, and communal understandings attached to what it means to be women and men. To recognize that understandings of gender are bound by cultural and religious interpretations and experiences suggests that what it means to be female may differ according to social location and context. Gender identity, then, refers to the internal sense of what it means for a particular person to be a woman. The experience of identifying with a gender occurs early in childhood. The reality is that there is not one "feminine" way to be in the world, but individuals interpret and experience relationships, in part, through the cultural assimilation of what gender has come to mean.

Internalized cultural notions about being female sometimes conflict with other realities in the lives of persons. Gender, having more to do with cultural assignments and roles given to women and men or how persons have been culturally conditioned to think about what it means to be women or men, can become a source for struggle for women who are in the midst of discerning their sexual orientation and identity. For example, the cultural or religious expectation communicated to women may be that they ought to marry men and raise children. However, internal feelings may invite women to find appropriate ways of seeking intimacy with other women. These intimate relationships may or may not involve raising children. Hence, internal gender identity may conflict with external expectations of the culture, of families, or of churches. Times when this conflict is most persistent in the lives of persons are often opportunities for sensitive pastoral counselors to assist women in coming to terms with the dichotomy between internal realities and external messages.

Finally, persons are endowed with sexual orientation or preference as homosexuals, heterosexuals, or bisexuals. Persons internally seek out and experience primary emotional, physical, and sexual attractions and attachments to other sexual beings that are built upon not only sexual but emotional, physical, and spiritual external relationships with others. Primary attractions to persons of the same sex are only one facet of being "lesbian." To self-identify as having a particular orientation indicates something about how persons experience the world and interpret reality. As with any other distinguishing feature of identity (race, class, culture, religious faith), orientation becomes one piece of the lens through which persons experience the realities of life.

There is earnest conversation among scholars in the field of homosexuality about the difference between sexual orientation (implying an internal way of being) and sexual preference (implying a more self-consciously chosen way of being). In some sense the debate centers around understandings of the social construction of lesbianism, issues of choice, and notions of biological essentialism. For purposes of this chapter, I will utilize the more familiar term "orientation" to remind readers that self-identifying as lesbian involves more than sexual activity or choice but centers on a way of being in the world that creates a meaning in and of itself.

It is extremely important to separate sexual orientation from sexual behavior, or to distinguish between self-identity as lesbian and the experience of physical, sexual activity with persons of the same sex. Same-sex sexual activity does not necessarily mean that persons have internally come to lesbian self-identities or that persons have an orientation toward intimate and significant relationships with others of the same sex. Likewise, sexual behavior with someone of the opposite sex does not necessarily suggest that persons are exclusively or primarily heterosexual. The issues are much more complex.

It is true that there are times when same-sex sexual activity actually does reflect other issues that may be under the surface in the lives of individuals. In a similar manner, it is inappropriate to assume that all same-sex sexual activity is pathological. This latter understanding mistakes the richness of God's creation for something corrupt and sinful. Extreme care must be taken as pastoral caregivers attempt to diagnose and work with persons in same-sex relationships.

The question for pastoral caregivers is not whether individuals are having physical or sexual relationships with persons of the opposite or the same sex. Instead, the concern should be whether there is an internal congruence between the emotional, physical, spiritual, and sexual needs of individuals and the way they embody those needs in relationships. What determines the authenticity and appropriateness of sexual behavior is not dependent upon the biologically based sex of persons; rather, genuine intimate relationships require congruence between the internal sense of self and what it means to be faithful persons who embody qualities of love in relationships with others.

Sexual identity formation indicates that a significant aspect of how persons come to understand themselves is through their ability to relate to, reflect upon, and engage one another as sexual beings. Diane Richardson notes: "What is crucial . . . is the particular meaning that individuals ascribe to their sexual feelings and activities, which will depend not only on the specific situation in which sexual conduct occurs but also on the significance of sexual orientation in a particular historical, social, and cultural context" (Richardson 1993, 20). The appropriateness of sexual behavior has more to do with the meanings brought to the context than it does with the sexual activity and behavior in and of itself.

Identity is the synthesis of all aspects of sexuality that enter into the notions of what it means to be a self, not just our physical or sexual behaviors. Sexual identity and orientation should not be the ultimate defining factors in identity, although they may be among the most prominent aspects in shaping relationships with self, God, and others. An identity that is moving toward resolution and maturity is one in which there is congruence between one's internal sense of sex, gender, orientation and the external behaviors that are embodied in relationships.

## SELF-IDENTITY AS A LESBIAN

To self-identify as lesbian is to mark the significant moment when women begin to struggle with and/or claim as part of their internal identities that of being lesbian. For some women, the time in which this first arises is when they discover their feelings of attraction for another woman. For others, self-identity develops gradually as they grow into claiming their lesbianism as part of their total identity. Still other lesbians talk about having always known, from their early childhood, that they were attracted to persons of the same sex.

There are at least two implications in using the phrase "self-identity" in the context of pastoral care. The first suggestion is the reminder that it is erroneous to label someone as being lesbian simply because of suspicions or hunches about a particular person. Pastoral caregivers need to exercise care in respecting the fact that some women may "appear" to others as lesbian but may not internally consider themselves to be so. For example, some women are emotionally connected with one other particular woman and they may even be sharing some kind of physical relationship (hugging one another, for example), but may not consider themselves to be lesbian.

The meaning attached to the word "lesbian" by the person involved in a particular relationship may differ from cultural understandings. Some women who are engaged in primarily physical, sexual, emotional, and spiritual intimacy with other women may talk about themselves as women who happen to be in significant friendships with other women but are not lesbian. Women may be married and still find themselves attracted to other women or involved in relationships of significant depth but still not identify themselves as lesbian. For many women it is not unusual that some level of sexual behavior occurs before they identify with the term "lesbian." Some women who struggle with orientation identity may never come to the point of self-identity as lesbian. Hence, working with self-identified lesbians (those who affirm, accept, and have integrated this orientation into their lives in a more congruent and long-lasting way) is different from working with women who are going through a process of discerning what is appropriate for their relationships. Not all women in intimate relationships with other women should be identified as "lesbian."

The second implication of the term "self-identity as lesbian" emphasizes the fluidness present in notions of sexuality. It is sometimes difficult to articulate to pastoral caregivers the meaning of this fluidness, but it is nonetheless a crucial concept to understand. Saying that sexuality is a fluid reality implies that most persons—straight, lesbian or bisexual—do not experience their sexuality, their yearnings and desires, or their relationships in precisely the same way throughout their lives.

Persons who write in the field of sexual theology articulate this notion of fluidness with some clarity. Carter Heyward, for example, suggests that traditional notions of sexuality as being essential and fixed in our beings have been challenged by theories on the social construction of reality. Hence, not all persons experience themselves as heterosexual or homosexual throughout their lifetimes. Some move through different seasons in expressing their sexuality, participating in same-sex relationships at times while at other times feeling more heterosexual in their relating to others. The way persons interpret and think about sexual orientation and behavior is not fixed and essential, although it may be long-lasting and durable. Heyward's invitation, then, is to develop sexual ethics that center in relationships rather than in essentialism. This attitude recognizes that persons have a high degree of choice and freedom in developing their relationships and making meaning of them (Heyward 1989).

One factor in working with women who are searching to understand their sexual feelings is to recognize this fluidness and relational context for women. Moving away from essentialism (from thinking of sexuality as a given that never changes over time and experience) allows for the fact that women may experience a variety of heterosexual relationships prior to loving another woman. For example, many women have been in traditional heterosexual marriages at one point in their lives and have children they bring into their lesbian families. Simply because persons have been traditionally married, or are currently struggling to make sense of relationships with other women, should not suggest automatically that they are, or are not, lesbian. Instead, what is needed is often the opportunity for women to talk about and work through their notions of sexual identity as they have developed and evolved over time.

Richardson accurately points out that women sometimes "reconstruct" their past in light of their current experiences (Richardson 1993, 122). This does not mean that women falsify the realities of the past or rationalize the present with new images of themselves that are inaccurate. Instead, women often find themselves caught in an attempt to discern the various sexual feelings and experiences from their past and present, integrating them into the totality of self-identity. Some women who have been traditionally married and who are now in lesbian relationships begin to make sense of the past by stating that they have just discovered they really are lesbian and that their past heterosexual relationships were not really honest for them. Other women talk more clearly about being bisexual as a way of self-identity. The careful pastoral caregiver receives these comments in the broader framework of a more fluid understanding of sexuality, refraining from judgment as women interpret and make sense of their past and present.

It is important, likewise, not to fall into the trap of thinking that women are capricious or casual in choosing their relationships. Recognizing the fluidness of relational living suggests that women may approach pastoral caregivers with differences in thinking about what it means to be embodied and to be created as sexual beings dependent upon their present interpretations of themselves and their relationships. This fluid way of thinking should not be interpreted as persons acting out their maladaptive behaviors nor as women being pathologically inclined in their relationships. An understanding of the process through which women move toward self-identifying as lesbian can assist pastoral caregivers in appropriately responding to those who are attempting to understand and integrate their experiences as women who love women.

While there are many ways of thinking about this process, the work of Vivienne Cass seems most helpful. Cass articulates six developmental stages for women moving toward claiming self-identities as lesbians (Cass 1990, 239–266). I would suggest that these not be seen as linear, prescriptive stages through which women necessarily must, nor should, travel. Instead, these stages might be seen as "ideal types" or as different perspectives and interpretations that women bring to their experiences of loving other women, creating meaning in the midst of their relationships (Troiden 1993, 194).

Pastoral caregivers are most helpful when they encourage women to move at whatever pace they find most comfortable in the process. A faithful and caring pastoral presence can be significant in creating stability as women move through the process toward self-identity, arriving at new levels of integration along the way. Again, not everyone moves through the process in similar fashion. Some women will arrive in pastoral care offices appearing to be at the first evolution, while others may be struggling with the latter phases of integration.

It must also be clearly stated that women come to these interpretations of their lives with a variety of ethnic, cultural, class, and gender realities. Hence, no two women move through the process in identical manner, and each woman finds resolution in her particular style. The goal of pastoral care during this process is to be the faithful reminder of God's grace and presence, affirming the journey of women and their attempts to bring theological meaning to their lives and relationships, never completely knowing where the journey will eventually take them. The focus of care must remain on the process of moving toward an integrated sense of identity and not merely on reflections about particular sexual behaviors. The paradigm that follows, of course, is only one way of conceptualizing how many women struggle toward full acceptance of their orientations and lives.

The first of Cass's stages, "identity confusion," surfaces as women struggle with intimacy desires for other women. In approaching a pastoral caregiver, they may talk about these feelings as "confusing." For some women, these emotions arise when they are very young or during their teen years. As girls or adolescents, they may or may not have acted upon their feelings. It is common for attractions to other women not to surface until they are well into young adulthood, or even later. Women have a tendency to arrive at their internal senses of being lesbians at later ages than men who understand themselves as gay. There are several reasons for this delayed questioning, one being the tremendous social pressure on women to marry and raise families. For most women even to begin to question their presumed heterosexual identities requires courage and considerable internal work as well as an opportunity with another woman to risk voicing feelings and experiencing same-sex love. It is not unusual for women to be surprised and to begin to question their heterosexual orientations when they "fall in love" with another woman. For some, this means juggling between heterosexual marriages and the feelings they are experiencing in a specific relationship with another woman.

Pastoral counselors who meet women at this stage must be very careful not to push to premature resolution for women or to suggest that this is a "phase" through which persons are traveling. Caregivers may feel the frustration of not knowing exactly how to be helpful as women may choose any of a number of options in response to these feelings. One of the assumptions to be very careful about in pastoral care is thinking that if women "wonder" whether they are lesbian, then they must not actually be lesbian. Some women will decide that the risk is too great or that there are too many moral directives that prevent them from pursuing their feelings. Others may decide to seek out a relationship with another woman in an attempt to explore their feelings or to participate more fully in a relationship that has begun to emerge. For most women, this moment of wondering becomes an important time to reflect theologically and morally about their life experiences. It is not at all rare for women to seek the assistance of a pastoral person during this stage of confusion. Pastoral caregivers are obligated to remain open to the diverse feelings that women express during this time in their lives.

The second stage, "identity comparison," is identified by Cass as beginning "with the tentative acceptance of a potential homosexual identity ('I may be a homosexual') and finishes with the acknowledgment that such an identity is likely to be applicable to self ('I probably am a homosexual')" (Cass 1990, 248). In other words, women begin to experiment with what it might be like to identify as lesbian, imagining the many losses and fears that accompany such an identity. Persons will choose some way to resolve this stage and move toward the next, or they will decide that they are not able to state honestly that they "probably are homosexual."

Pastoral caregivers can offer opportunities to women as they move through this stage to identify verbally and name some of their potential losses and fears, exploring what each means to particular individuals. Realistic fears that women may have about losing particular relationships with their children, families of origin, spouses, or employers provide rich material as women sift through what it means to pursue lesbian relationships or to form lesbian identities.

The third stage, "identity tolerance," occurs when women intentionally consider what it might actually mean to live as lesbians in the world. At this point women give themselves permission to experience internal feelings in ways that lead to more clarity about their identities and sexual orientations, but it does not necessarily eventuate into full self-acceptance as lesbians. Increasing awareness of potential losses in living as lesbians, as well as a recognition of the attitudes of culture and religion, continues to dominate perspectives and emotions during this stage.

Pastoral caregivers become quite important for women at this stage who are seeking to live faithful lives. Questions about the perceptions and beliefs in their churches, their communities of faith, or on the part of God become important conversation themes during this season of exploration. Often this is a time when women begin to yearn for stronger supportive communities, and, in search of such support, they move toward greater interaction with others who identify themselves as lesbian or gay. This can be an extremely significant time of integration in women's lives as they work through the socialization processes of living as lesbians in the world. Caregivers who assist women in finding supportive church communities and places for engaging with other lesbians and gay-affirmative people and organizations will facilitate the movement of women through this phase.

"Identity acceptance," the fourth stage identified by Cass, arises as women continue to establish clarity about their internal realities as lesbians. From the perspective of increased comfort with themselves as lesbians, women confront issues of self-disclosure in new ways, taking on more positive self-images and being less fearful of sharing openly with others. For many women, these are moments of transformation as they adopt new ways of being in open relationships with others. Most women are very selective in deciding with whom they first self-disclose about their identities or relationships. Cass points out that at this stage women avoid potential conflicts and confrontations with persons who might not be supportive. At the same time, the pressures of remaining hidden and "in the closet" create increasing internal tension. The ongoing internal conversations that women have about with whom to be open and honest consume an incredible amount of emotional energy.

Pastoral counselors at this stage can be most helpful as they talk honestly with women about the realities of self-disclosure and the dynamics of loss and gain. It is never helpful to ignore the griefs that accompany self-disclosure, even when confiding with others may bring new-found friendships and freedoms. Being clear about the inherent losses in self-disclosure and engaging women in planning for self-care through the process of self-revelation can be extremely important. Pastoral persons who not only personally affirm women at this stage but who also assist them in locating supportive communities are invaluable.

In the fifth stage, "identity pride," Cass notes that women often seek out clearly defined lesbian-affirmative places and people while continuing to grow in their positive sense of self-esteem. Often this is coincidental with increased awareness and anger about the rejection they encounter in society and, most particularly, in the church. Women may experience extreme discomfort in places where, up to this point, they had felt comfortable in their quietness about their sexual orientation. For example, women may have spiritual crises as they struggle with what it means to participate in churches that do not affirm their lesbianism or their relationships.

Persons in this stage may hesitate to seek out pastoral caregivers because of the intense anger and distrust experienced in communities of faith. At the same time, many women recognize a deep spiritual awareness during this stage and may want to find pastoral representatives who not only can affirm but can be pro-active in seeking justice in the church and community. There are relatively few pastoral representatives who can assist women in this stage, since women seek caregivers who are willing to become advocates in their churches, denominations, and communities.

Finally, Cass suggests that "identity synthesis" occurs as women experience greater security in their identities and recognize that being lesbian is one significant piece of their total identities. In the previous stages women often focus almost exclusively on their sexual orientation and the feelings that accompany the process. Cass maintains that because women in this final stage are more comfortable with their lesbianism as one part of their identity, it does not become conflated with the totality of who they are. For women in this stage there is a greater propensity to live openly in all the places of their lives, regardless of the cost.

Sensitive pastoral caregivers will find an increased awareness of what it means to be whole persons in working with women at this stage. Issues brought to the counseling context may focus less on what it means to be lesbian and more on the quality of the relationships in which they participate or on other emotional or spiritual material. Women connected to the Christian faith may move toward conversations that reflect theological issues and concerns in new ways, such as thinking about how their issues relate to the broader issues of justice such as classism, sexism, and racism.

Self-consciously claiming lesbian identities suggests that women arrive at the point of recognizing that sexuality is one facet of their total identities, albeit an extremely important piece. It is important to remember that not every woman who begins the journey of self-exploration will eventually self-identify as lesbian. Similarly, not every woman who has an intimate and meaningful physical, sexual, spiritual, or emotional relationship with another woman will self-identify as lesbian. The processes through which women travel, regardless of the eventual outcome in terms of self-identity, become opportunities to explore what it means to be faithful in relationship to God, others, and self.

## PASTORAL CARE ISSUES WITH LESBIANS AND THEIR FAMILIES

Given the backdrop of the previous discussion, it is helpful to turn to particular pastoral care issues that may appear in the context of working with women at various points in the process of self-identity. Again, the concerns and the complexities of lives are as diverse as the individuals and the partnerships with whom caregivers work. However, there are some issues that often become part of the context of pastoral care and a brief articulation of their content seems appropriate. It is important to begin with the person of the pastoral caregiver.

### The Pastoral Caregiver

Pastoral care means not only participating in the activity of sitting with people as they find meaning and direction in the midst of crises but also entering the process aware of the theological, moral, and ethical content present within conversations. Pastoral representatives are not neutral caregivers, particularly when they recognize and confirm pastoral theological perspectives which they bring to the context of care. Questions about sexuality, orientation, families, and relationships offer opportunities for persons to reflect theologically on their lives. It is imperative that pastoral caregivers be as clear in their own perspectives as possible, particularly when working with women struggling with issues of sexual identity and orientation.

There are at least two considerations pertinent to self-assessment in working with women who raise questions and concerns about sexuality. The first aspect involves coming to terms with one's own theological and moral positions on the issue of homosexuality. The most helpful pastoral persons are not necessarily those who agree with the lifestyle and/or sexual orientations of parishioners. Instead, the most helpful caregivers are those who can state clearly where they stand on the issues and who have thoughtfully reflected on the many theological, ethical, and psychodynamic concerns that present themselves around the complexities of sexuality. Pastoral persons who have not yet come to terms with their own positions on homosexuality should responsibly refer women elsewhere in the community. Or, if pastoral persons are extremely opposed to the position of women who approach them, it is most ethical to offer other options for women who seek pastoral assistance.

Ethical accountability requires that pastoral caregivers not use women who approach them on issues of orientation to help pastoral counselors think about where they stand. Clarity on the part of caregivers makes it easier for parishioners and clients to work on the issues they bring rather than assisting pastoral persons in coming to some self-understandings for themselves. Various resources are available that reflect divergent biblical, theological, and ethical perspectives. It remains the responsibility of caregivers to explore this literature critically and thoughtfully prior to providing care related to these issues.

The second consideration for pastoral caregivers relates to self-assessment in terms of comfort levels when working with persons who are self-identified lesbians or who are in the process of coming to some self-understanding about orientation. Caregivers need to assess the presence of homophobia and heterosexism in their internal worlds and in the agencies and churches of which they are a part. Homophobia refers to the internal fear that many persons have in working with others who are lesbian and/or the fear that they have about discovering lesbian or gay feelings in themselves. Often this is talked about in clinical circles as issues of transference and counter-transference. Whatever the frame brought to thinking about homophobia, it is imperative that counselors and caregivers be as clear as possible about their internal comfort levels of being with persons of the same gender or of sitting with persons who raise concerns about homosexual identity.

Heterosexism is a more difficult issue to address in some ways, for it lives in the systems and cultures of which everyone is a part. By heterosexism I mean the structures that actively encourage the formation of heterosexual identities and that actively discourage the formation of lesbian or gay identities and relationships. This is not the same as homophobia, but it is closely related. Pastoral caregivers who may not be very homophobic because of the internal work they have done on their sexuality may discover that they unconsciously participate in perpetuating structures that reinforce heterosexist assumptions. Internal surprise or discomfort with the fact that two women choose to give birth to children and raise them as part of their lesbian family probably means persons have some work to do on heterosexism. Perplexity over why some lesbians are angry that they cannot be considered a "family" when buying insurance or memberships to organizations may mean that caregivers have not thought carefully about the structures that hinder women partnerships from participating in the culture in the same way as female-male partnerships.

There are many avenues for exploring the comfort levels necessary for good work with parishioners or clients. Reading the literature, poetry, and works of self-identified lesbians can assist pastoral caregivers in gaining a perspective on what it means for women who live in the world as lesbians. Going to a bookstore and browsing in the section devoted to lesbian and gay writings offers opportunities for pastoral persons to keep track of internal feelings as others see them looking at these books and may be wondering why they are interested in this section. Listening to women-identified music raises the breadth of diversity in the community of women who love women.

Being open to working with women who are lesbians or who are asking questions about their sexual identity often means being forthright about one's own perspectives. There are times when lesbians appear to be suspicious of pastoral care specialists. The cautious approach of lesbians should not be interpreted as a resistance to the process of counseling, nor should these women be seen as overly concerned about what caregivers think. Instead, pastoral care specialists should recognize how difficult it is for some women to trust those within the community of faith. It is natural and appropriate for women to ask in a direct manner about the perspectives on homosexuality that a particular caregiver maintains. When a caregiver is asked questions about moral understandings of homosexuality or interpretations of Scripture, it is not helpful for the caregiver to respond by wondering why it is important for the parishioner or client to know where you stand. Because women often must struggle to find safe places to talk honestly and openly about being lesbian it is inappropriate for pastoral counselors to display insensitivity by wondering why these might be important questions for women who love women.

Sensitive pastoral care also requires that persons know the resources and organizations within the community that are available and supportive of lesbians. For example, it is essential that caregivers know which churches welcome lesbians and their families, where to obtain the women's newsletter or be put on mailing lists for regional newsletters, what the denominational support systems and contact persons are in the area, where the closest PFLAG meets (Parents and Friends of Lesbians and Gays), or how to locate the names of other networking organizations. These associations provide rich resources not only for women and their families but also for pastoral care persons who may seek assistance and guidance on specific issues.

### The Bible

A significant offering of pastoral caregivers to women struggling to deal with issues of sexuality is to reflect with them about Scripture. It never ceases to amaze me that some pastoral caregivers dismiss biblical passages as if the Scriptures did not exist or were not important for individuals and their families. Pastoral counselors have one of the most pivotal positions in our culture as they avail themselves of the reality that, for many faithful persons, what the Scripture says and how it is interpreted continues to hold meaning. Every pastoral care person ought to have deliberated about the biblical passages that have been utilized in conversations about homosexuality. The questions of interpretation remain dynamic opportunities for every community of faith.

An important aspect in reflecting on the biblical texts is to focus on issues of interpretation. Do persons understand all Scripture to be the literal word of God? How do particular parishioners/clients think about other controversial pieces of Scripture (such as those on marriage and divorce or women in the church)? How does the church or persons who are within the context of the community of faith choose which texts to take literally and which ones to interpret metaphorically? What does it mean for someone to seek out biblical authority? These are questions that cannot be foreign to pastoral conversations. Caregivers should be as comfortable in conversations about biblical interpretation as they are in discussing other matters of significance to persons.

Some of the specific passages that pastoral counselors need to examine are the creation stories from Genesis, the Genesis account of Sodom and Gomorrah (Genesis 19 and its parallel story in Judges 19), the holiness codes found in Leviticus (18:22 and 20:13), and sections from the Epistles (Romans 1:18–32, 1 Corinthians 6:9–11; and 1 Timothy 1:8–11). Many of these texts are utilized by persons who understand homosexuality to be a sin, and the interpretation of these texts often becomes problematic for women who are struggling to discern faithful ways of being lesbian in the context of their religious beliefs. Again, there are several excellent resources in biblical interpretation that can assist pastoral caregivers and women and their families as they struggle to make sense of these texts. Books that offer a variety of perspectives can be available for persons who want to struggle with Scripture and its interpretation.

### A Word about Etiology

Throughout the process of developing self-identities as lesbians, women and their extended family members often raise questions about the causes of homosexuality. The question of etiology might surface in this fashion: What is it that makes or causes persons to be lesbian? Indeed, this matter can consume the emotional energy of many individuals, families, and communities of faith. Dealing with etiology is important not because it is necessary to explain why women are attracted to women but because many persons approach pastoral care specialists to talk specifically about this issue. Faithful people genuinely struggle with the causes of homosexuality in their attempts to come to terms with themselves or others. Astute pastoral caregivers who can bring candor to the discussion of etiology will, undoubtedly, be sought out for conversations on this matter.

There appear to be a number of related issues in considering the causes of homosexuality. One concern is whether all persons are created by God as heterosexual beings or whether, biologically, some persons are created as homosexual beings. Second, the question arises that *if* there is a biological base to homosexuality, does that necessarily imply that persons who identify as being lesbian should be condoned in their lifestyles, or does it mean that homosexuality is an "abnormality" to be reckoned with much as persons might deal with other kinds of "diseases" diagnosed at birth? Finally, how do people understand those who claim to "choose" to live as lesbians but may or may not assume that God has created them this way? These questions, of course, deserve much more attention than can be addressed in this chapter.

In traditional psychoanalytic literature there have been several predominant themes in response to the etiological question. Some suggested causes of homosexuality have included beliefs that homosexuality is a disorder created by an early narcissistic injury or fixation; dysfunctional family relationships result in homosexual ideation; there is some kind of internal gender identity disturbance that leads to or supports homosexual behavior; or a pathological defense against heterosexual relationships has resulted in homosexual behavior. Since 1973 when the American Psychiatric Association deleted homosexuality from its list of mental disorders, care specialists in the field of psychology and psychoanalytic theory have pursued several other avenues in reflecting about the cause of homosexuality. One exploration, centered in biological psychology, contends that there is a genetic link or chemical basis to the creation of persons as either homosexual or heterosexual. Again, there is not space in the brevity of this chapter to focus on these theories, but it is important to know that they exist. Resources in the bibliography at the end of this chapter address some of these complexities.

For some women, the internal sense of being created as lesbian is something they can easily identify at childhood. Hence, the notion that they have been biologically created this way is comforting. Likewise, families who are coming to terms with women who begin to self-identify as lesbian may seek solace in the reality that God has richly blessed creation with a variety of sexual orientations. Lesbians do reflect the richness of God's creation in unique ways. This biological notion, however, must be placed alongside perspectives that suggest that there might be a more fluid sense of sexuality as briefly articulated above.

Women who are farther along in the process of claiming their self-identities often find concerns about etiology less significant. For example, women who are comfortable with their sexuality and who have moved beyond the stage of identity tolerance as articulated by Cass have less tolerance for discussions about the "why" of lesbianism. Instead, they find conversation and reflections about what it means to live in faithful and just covenants with one another to be more meaningful. The nature and the structure of their covenantal partnerships are probably more important for women in care and counseling at the latter stages of identity development than are concerns and questions of causality. Utilizing the developmental process outlined above assists pastoral caregivers in thinking about what etiological concerns may surface as they work with particular persons and their families.

Pastoral care persons offer opportunities to explore with women and their families what it means to be lesbian. For some, it is appropriate to attend to questions of etiology and the conversation will be welcomed; for others, there is little need to talk about "why" they are lesbians, they just are.

### Coming Out

Alongside the process of forming a sexual identity as lesbian is that of "coming out," or making choices about self-disclosure. To come out means to self-identify or to be identified by others as being lesbian. Sometimes this self-disclosure happens quite intentionally, whereas, at other times, coming out may be brought on accidentally as someone "discovers" that another person is lesbian or is in a relationship with another woman. Self-disclosure usually begins with a few trusted friends. From there the circle may be widened to include colleagues, families, churches, or other community contexts. There is no set pattern of coming out, yet there are common concerns that arise throughout the journey.

While moving toward self-identity as lesbian, many women simultaneously go through a process that is sometimes referred to as "coming out to one's self." In other words, the growing internal realization that women have that they may be lesbian or that they want to live in lesbian relationships parallels the process of self-disclosure to others. Discerning how lesbian identity fits into total self-understandings entails revealing to one's self that she is lesbian. Hence, one of the first pastoral concerns to address in counseling is how the process of coming out to one's self is being internalized and made sense of in the reality of particular parishioners or clients.

As persons continue to be comfortable with themselves as lesbians, they seek safe places to talk about their lesbianism, however tentative that identity may be at the moment. At times this sharing will occur only with trusted friends who may or may not respond positively and affirmatively. Working with individuals during this process to assist them in naming the potential losses they face by sharing their sexual orientation with others can be essential. It is highly unlikely that persons will go through the coming out process without experiencing some kind of rejection from someone who has been important and significant in their lives. At the same time, with increasingly positive experiences of coming out, women find more courage to take the risk to tell others and to expand their trusted community.

Pastoral caregivers must remain extremely sensitive in maintaining confidences throughout the process of working with women as they choose about when to come out and to whom. For some persons, coming out may mean the loss of job or the loss of family relationships or the loss of church support. The reality that another person—even a pastoral caregiver—holds the "secret" of lesbian identity often contributes to the fear that women carry. The truth is that some of the most dangerous persons for lesbians who are trying to maintain and manage the secret of their sexual orientation are others who seem not to be bothered by the fact that someone is lesbian and who feel that others should not be bothered as well. Hence, they sometimes take advantage of the privilege of knowing that someone is lesbian and talk about this inappropriately with others. The key for open and caring pastoral persons is never to confuse self-openness with the right to share information that has been given to you with others. When women come out to pastoral caregivers it is helpful to ask verbally who else knows, with whom they are comfortable sharing the information, and from whom they receive support.

As has been mentioned, there are often good reasons why persons choose not to tell others about their emerging lesbian identities. The reality of rejection, the fear of losing relationships, the potential of job loss, or the grief that may be associated with coming out are appropriate reasons for women to choose very deliberately and intentionally about their coming out process. Motivations for keeping the secret are often based on solid reflection and a careful consideration of the losses. At other times a commitment to remain in the closet for some women becomes an unnecessary burden, and pastoral caregivers may become part of the opening of lives by being receptive to self-disclosure. For many women, the fear of coming out is greater than the hope of new freedoms that may accompany the process. Discerning what is appropriate for each particular woman takes time in self-reflection and painstaking deliberation. Experience teaches me that persons move through the coming out process in direct correlation to their internal pain. The greater the internal pain, the more clearly they will seek to be open and honest with others. At the same time, there is increasing pressure in the culture and among lesbian- and gay-affirmative communities to encourage all people to live out and in the open. This can create increased internal pain on the part of women struggling to discern their own processes in the context of the broader community of lesbians and gay men.

Siblings are often the first ones within families of origin to be told by sisters about their lesbianism. Persons seem to find it more difficult and complicated to tell parents, and, consequently, pastoral caregivers may need to participate in extended conversation about the process of coming out to other family members. There are also times when some members of the family are aware of lesbian self-identities, while others within the family may not have been told. This can create genuine tension for all within the family, and pastoral care persons often can become participants in thinking with women about the various levels of coming out within particular families (Strommen 1993).

Moving through the process of coming out raises questions and concerns for spiritual journeys and lives. Craig O'Neill and Kathleen Ritter have written a very helpful book, *Coming Out Within,* in which they examine various ways that spiritual issues become part of the process of coming out. Utilizing the concepts of grief and loss, they engage persons in thinking about spiritual transformation through coming out. Having a resource such as this book available for women and their families can be a tremendous help as persons raise spiritual concerns about their coming out process (O'Neill and Ritter 1992).

### Seeking Community

Lesbians often live on the edges or margins of the various communities of which they are a part. For many, this means never experiencing full acceptance in the contexts in which they live, work, or worship. Women often experience acceptance and openness in one place but not in other places. For example, it may not be safe to talk at work about significant life partners or about friends who self-identify as lesbian or gay, just as some families may remain silent or prefer silence from children who are living as lesbians. There may be relatively few communities in which women live openly. At the same time, women may find solace in PFLAG or other supportive communities living half their lives in the closet and half their lives more openly. A large number of lesbians spend energy screening conversations and being careful about what they say about their personal lives and to whom they speak, trying to remember who knows and who does not.

Experiencing a supportive, affirming, and caring community of faith is often very difficult for women in lesbian relationships for a number of reasons. First, the overt and covert sexism of the church in its tradition and history has been a barrier to various women who seek a community based on feminist principles of mutuality. The emergence of feminist theology in the last several years is helpful to women seeking to find inclusive and justice-oriented communities of faith.

Second, few churches have embraced women who self-identify as lesbians or have offered a place for them to be open about their relationships and commitments. It is not difficult to find churches that lesbians attend. However, the usual pattern is that members of the church may not know that particular women are lesbian, and, in turn, women may feel reluctant to be open about their sexual identities for fear of what self-disclosure may evoke in others. Some people in the church may be aware of the orientation of particular parishioners but encourage them to remain silent about the issues that concern them lest a controversy arise around homosexuality.

Many lesbians look for alternative communities of women to find spiritual nurture and support. These separate communities often become the context for women to experience their lives as blessed and affirmed. Communities of women who are open and who share in their lesbian orientations become rare opportunities for women to feel the freedom to share more completely all of who they understand themselves to be. Dan Spencer has suggested that, "The *ecclesia* of lesbians and gay men will be *a community at the margins:* of the society, the broader church, our communities and families of origin" (Spencer 1994, 398).

Communities of faith that are open and that refuse to be silent on the issues of homosexuality can become sanctuaries where women can reveal the center of their lives with less caution. Part of what is needed from pastoral caregivers who are concerned about justice is a willingness on their part to engage issues of lesbian and gay concerns within the broader communities of which they are a part. In other words, pastoral caregivers who talk openly about sexuality, who are willing to take stands that may not be popular, and who remain committed to seeking justice in the context of their churches will be welcomed by lesbians who are seeking out communities that reflect God's extensive care. Lesbians often seek not only places in which to worship God but communities that work toward justice.

Churches offering sanctuary for women, candid discussions about pain and hope, or prayers that speak to the hearts and concerns of women struggling with lesbian identities will be locations where the good news is embodied and experienced.

### Being Family: Partnerships and Covenants

One of the questions currently consuming this culture is: What does it mean to be a family? With broader conceptualizations of what constitutes families in our culture, the church and those who participate in pastoral care have been challenged to engage with extended families, single-parent families, and blended families, as well as lesbian partners. Relationships between two women offer new dimensions to be brought to ongoing conversations about family.

First, women bring concerns about their primary relationships, especially the other women whom they consider to be their immediate family and the children who might be part of those families. The lack of opportunities for formal conversations about partnerships is one of the adversities many lesbians encounter. In traditional heterosexual marriages the church encourages couples to sit down and talk about what it means to be united in marriage, what their hopes and dreams are for their relationship, how they think about God and the church in the midst of their marriage vows, and other important aspects of their covenantal relationships. Usually this occurs in pre-marital conversations, couples therapy, or marriage encounter groups within the church context. Women in lesbian relationships, however, very rarely experience the opportunity to have such open and honest conversations in the context of their communities of faith.

In similar ways, few lesbian partnerships experience a more formalized covenant service where persons acknowledge and offer blessings for their relationship in ritual moments in their churches. Holy unions or covenant services have been created by lesbians who have sought to bring their relationship into the context of their faith, deciding that the church cannot own the rituals of God's presence. The church has not always welcomed, or known how to participate in blessing covenantal relationships that are not heterosexual but that may still reflect the values of partnerships encouraged in the community of faith. Lesbian covenantal relationships can be guided by the same visions of love, justice, and mutual fidelity in relationships as heterosexual unions. Churches that find ways to honor and bless these covenants add to the richness of the lives of all who participate in them.

As with all other partnerships, there are times when lesbians face particular issues. For example, since lesbian relationships are comprised of normal human beings, their partnerships may encounter addictions, sexual difficulties, struggles over financial realities, or any other number of complex situations. Lesbian relationships are not unique in terms of having struggles and concerns in partnerships. However, since the partnership consists of two women, the dynamics in their relationships may differ from heterosexual couples and it may be more difficult to ask for help. The temptation exists for some lesbians not to talk about the issues of their relationships to persons outside the partnerships. Isolation and silence can be fostered by the fear that persons have of their relationships being interpreted as inherently pathological or not healthy because they are lesbians. Given the negative response toward homosexuality in the culture, it is not difficult to see why these barriers might be present.

These are just a sampling of the questions and struggles that surface in what it means to be a family and how issues of family dynamics are handled in the context of lesbian relationships. Added to these are the concerns that may surface when children are added to the picture: What does being lesbian mean for the mothers who have had children born in the context of previous heterosexual relationships and who are now claiming their identities as lesbians? How do they talk with their children about their relationships? What does it mean for churches to participate in the baptism or dedication of children born or adopted into lesbian partnerships? What does it mean for churches to participate in the lives of children and youth who experience lesbian feelings or attractions? The church family is compelled to respond faithfully to these concerns.

## CONCLUSION

Women who are in the process of coming to terms with their sexual identity deserve pastoral caregivers who can collaborate with them in communal care and self-care. The church can become one of the sanctuaries for women as they journey through development and evolution into becoming more fully human in their relationships with God, self, and others. The relational qualities that persons seek to embody as faithful human beings are those which lesbians also pursue. Genuine pastoral care offers women the opportunity to ask questions, to deliberate, to reflect, and to make movements in their striving to embody right relationship.

## BIBLIOGRAPHY

Berzon, Betty. 1988. *Permanent Partners: Building Gay and Lesbian Relationships That Last.* New York: E. P. Dutton.

Boswell, John. 1980. *Christianity, Social Tolerance and Homosexuality.* Chicago: University of Chicago Press.

Cass, Vivienne. 1990. "The Implications of Homosexual Identity Formation for the Kinsey Model and Scale of Sexual Preference." In McWhirter, Sanders, and Reinisch, eds., 239–266.

Comstock, Gary David. 1993. *Gay Theology without Apology.* Cleveland: Pilgrim Press.

Edwards, George. 1984. *Gay/Lesbian Liberation: A Biblical Perspective.* New York: Pilgrim Press.

Falco, Kristine L. 1991. *Psychotherapy with Lesbian Clients: Theory in Practice.* New York: Brunner/Mazel.

Garnets, Linda D., and Douglas C. Kimmel, eds. 1993. *Psychological Perspectives on Lesbian and Gay Male Experiences.* New York: Columbia University Press.

Glaser, Chris. 1991. *Coming Out to God: Prayers for Lesbians and Gay Men, Their Families and Friends.* Louisville, Ky.: Westminster/John Knox Press.

Heyward, Carter. 1989. *Touching Our Strength: The Erotic as Power and the Love of God.* San Francisco: Harper & Row.

Jung, Patricia Beattie, and Ralph F. Smith. 1993. *Heterosexism: An Ethical Challenge.* Albany, N.Y.: State University of New York Press.

Kegan, Robert. 1982. *The Evolving Self: Problem and Process in Human Development.* Cambridge: Harvard University Press.

Kitzinger, Celia. 1987. *The Social Construction of Lesbianism.* London: Sage Publications.

Lewes, Kenneth. 1988. *The Psychoanalytic Theory of Male Homosexuality.* New York: Simon & Schuster.

Lorde, Audre. 1984. *Sister Outsider.* Freedom, Calif.: Crossing Press.

McWhirter, David P.; Stephanie A. Sanders; and June Machover Reinisch, eds. 1990. *Homosexuality/Heterosexuality: Concepts of Sexual Orientation.* New York: Oxford University Press.

Nelson, James. 1978. *Embodiment: An Approach to Sexuality and Christian Theology.* Minneapolis: Augsburg Publishing House.

Nelson, James, and Sandra P. Longfellow, eds. 1994. *Sexuality and the Sacred: Sources for Theological Reflection.* Louisville, Ky.: Westminster/John Knox Press.

O'Neill, Craig, and Kathleen Ritter. 1992. *Coming Out Within: Stages of Spiritual Awakening for Lesbians and Gay Men.* San Francisco: Harper & Row.

Richardson, Diane. 1993. "Recent Challenges to Traditional Assumptions about Homosexuality: Some Implications for Practice." In Garnets and Kimmel, eds., 117–129.

Scroggs, Robin. 1983. *The New Testament and Homosexuality.* Philadelphia: Fortress Press.

Shively, Michael G., and John T. De Cecco. 1993. "Components of Sexuality Identity." In Garnets and Kimmel, eds., 80–88.

Silverstein, Charles, ed. 1991. *Gays, Lesbians and Their Therapists.* New York: W. W. Norton & Co.

Spencer, Dan. 1994. "Church at the Margins." In Nelson and Longfellow, eds., 397–401.

Strommen, Erik F. 1993. "You're a What? Family Member Reactions to the Disclosure of Homosexuality." In Garnets and Kimmel, eds., 248–266.

Stuart, Elizabeth. 1992. *Daring to Speak Love's Name: A Gay and Lesbian Prayer Book.* London: Hamish Hamilton.

Troiden, Richard. 1993. "The Formation of Homosexual Identities." In Garnets and Kimmel, eds., 191–217.

Weinberg, Thomas S. 1983. *Gay Men, Gay Selves: The Social Construction of Homosexual Identities.* New York: Irvington Publishers.

# 9

# Women and Motherloss

MARTHA BOWMAN ROBBINS
*Pittsburgh Theological Seminary*

Since Adrienne Rich (1976) broke the silence that surrounded the most formative relationship in the life of every woman—the mother-daughter relationship—much has been written about various aspects of that relationship. But only in recent years has the silence been broken about women's experiences of the deaths of their mothers. Hope Edelman's, *Motherless Daughters: Legacies of Loss* (1994) attests to the fact that no matter when a daughter loses her mother through death, divorce, or abandonment, motherloss is a distinctive kind of loss for women, one that has enduring effects on a woman's sense of her self, her relationships, her lifestyle and career choices, and her sense of mortality. In my book *Midlife Women and Death of Mother* (Robbins 1990), I discuss how motherloss also has profound effects on adult women's spirituality, their images of and relationship to God and the church.

When silence is broken, new data about important aspects of women's experience arises. This data gives us insights into what daughters lose and mourn when their mothers die; the dimensions of grief that become exposed as women mourn the loss of their mothers; and the unique ways in which women engage in the mourning process according to where they are in their own development. This new data requires us to examine our underlying assumptions pertaining to grief and mourning; women's development; and the importance of the mother-daughter relationship in the formation of

---

This chapter is a revision of the article "The Human Web: Reflections on the State of Pastoral Theology," copyright 1993 Christian Century Foundation. Reprinted by permission from the April 7, 1993, issue of *The Christian Century,* 366–69.

and redefinitions of female identity and faith. Such an examination challenges us to revise our ways of thinking theologically and acting pastorally
in order to be more effective pastoral caregivers to women who experience
motherloss in their adult years. In this chapter, I will examine some of those
assumptions, propose alternative ways of thinking about this experience,
and then describe pastoral responses that may be helpful to women who
experience motherloss in their adult years. The women quoted throughout
this chapter (with names changed) have been participants in my research
study, class seminars, workshops, and counseling sessions.

> You never get over the loss of a mother. My mother died over twenty years
> ago, and I still miss her. I've just accepted the fact that with each major turn-
> ing point in my life, I have and will continue to rework my relationship with
> my Mom in my heart, how her life and how the loss of her continues to affect
> me. (Amy, age 66)

> A couple of years after my mother's death, I divorced my husband, found a job
> to support me and my two children, and began a master's degree in business
> management. Only when a friend noted that all these changes in my life took
> place after I lost my mother did I begin to reflect that there may be some kind
> of connection. I mean I am only now realizing that I am still grieving the loss
> of my mother in ways that I don't understand. When I spoke to my pastor
> about it, he couldn't understand. He thought I should be over all this by now
> and should just get on with my life. I mean, I was angry. He couldn't hear me.
> . . . And now I find it very hard to know who God is for me. Nothing is like it
> used to be and I didn't know how to sort all of this out. (Barbara, age 36)

> After my mother died, I was the one who became the matriarch in the family.
> Everyone looked to me to bring the family together on holidays, to settle con-
> flicts in the family, and to pass on all she taught us. It's a tremendous respon-
> sibility with lots of power, but I feel the burden of it all. I was with her when
> she died, took care of her when she took sick, so I guess this made me respon-
> sible for the family. I had no one to comfort me, to lean on. So I counted on
> my sisters at church for support. They understood and have been there for me.
> (Josie, age 54)

Amy, Barbara, and Josie acknowledge that the death of their mothers has
had deep reverberations in their own lives and in the lives of their families.
When women approach the age of the mother when the mother died, all
kinds of feelings are unleashed. Josie suggests that she ambivalently
assumed the role played by her mother in the extended family system,
drawing support from some of her church sisters who understood her position. Barbara was upset that her pastor was not able to help her explore the
meanings of her loss and how this loss may be affecting her own sense of
self-in-relation to significant others, the world, and God. While the pastor

was aware of the restructuring of Barbara's life during and after her divorce, he was unaware that tremendous shifts often take place after the death of a parent—shifts that alter family relationships, unwittingly influence life decisions, and affect the next generation. Neither was he aware of how legacies of loss that motherless daughters experience can affect a woman's relationship with God and the church.

## THEORIES OF MOURNING IN CULTURAL CONTEXT

The pastor's remarks to Barbara "to get on with her life" arise from deeply embedded cultural assumptions about grief and the process of mourning, assumptions that prevent "female-friendly pastoral care." In American culture, the loss of one's mother through death during one's adult years has been considered insignificant compared to the loss of a spouse, partner, or a child (Myers 1986). Such a death is expected. It seems more "timely" and natural to us. The death of an adult's parent is not expected to disrupt the daily routine around which the adult woman has oriented her life and sense of purpose. Consequently, an adult woman's expression of intense grief over the death of her mother may be described by many in our patriarchal culture as abnormal—as indicative of the daughter's "dependent" attachment to her mother. While, indeed, some mother-daughter relationships may be grounded in unhealthy dependency interactions, I am referring here to the ways in which the dominant culture judges the bonds developed between women in general and between mothers and daughters in particular.

What a paradox this presents for women! Our culture expects women to care for aging and ill parents, while at the same time expecting women to maintain emotional distance. This paradox reflects the dominant culture's ambivalence about both attachment and grief manifesting, according to Peter Marris, its "tendency to idealize a psychologically impossible self-reliance, at once loving and detached" (Marris 1986, xiv). Because many adult women also have internalized these cultural norms, they are confused by their own responses to their loss. Hence it is no small wonder that women bury their grief behind a wall of silence only to feel that they are inept, weak, or in some ways deficient if grief unexpectedly seeps through the cracks or explodes in outbursts of misdirected anger or implodes in bouts of depression. Buried or frozen grief influences the personality and behavioral patterns of the woman years after her loss. Unresolved grief also affects family interactional patterns over generations.

Likewise, some theories of the process of mourning reinforce the above cultural presuppositions pertaining to loss and grief. "Recovery from loss," according to Freud, is achieved when the adult woman is able to "detach" from her mother by shedding "all memories and hopes from the dead" and "reinvest emotional attachment in other objects" (Freud 1915/1957, 14:255). This view of the nature of mourning supports the notion that development occurs through separation and replacement, which is a more typical pattern in male development. Perhaps this assumption prompted the pastor's remark to Barbara to "get on with her life."

Women's development, as Carol Gilligan suggests, "points toward a different history of human attachment stressing continuity and reconfiguration rather than displacement and separation" (Gilligan 1982, 48). Amy states that many years after her mother's death, she is reconfiguring her relationship with her mother in her heart and that this is often triggered by major life events and transitions. If this is true, then what conception of grief and mourning may be helpful to women?

Proceeding from a different conception of relationship, John Bowlby (1980) describes the process of mourning as the mending of the tear and the weaving together of the narrative of self-in-relation to (m)other that has been broken. Rather than "detaching" and "remembering the loss" to come to terms with reality, the work of mourning for many women focuses on the need to find a positive basis of connection with mother, to remember *realistic* love, and find a means for expressing this love in their present lives (Robbins 1990). Before women can remember a love that is realistic, however, they need to unravel both the positive and the negative bonds of loyalty that wove together the fabric of the mother-daughter relationship. On the one hand, loyalty bonds can bind too tightly, squeezing or restricting further growth, or they, on the other hand, can become the thread of continuity enabling the daughter to explore further and solidify the generational depths of her "motherline" (Lowinsky 1992).

This unraveling is often a long and painful process. Little by little, women recognize, own, and grieve two layers of loss: the first pertaining to the loss of the actual mother and the second pertaining to the losses incurred as she mourns her personal myth of mother (Robbins 1990). Losses grieved by some women after the actual death of their mothers include no longer having a mother or being a daughter; loss of the practical help they gave each other; loss of a mutual dialogue partner, caregiver, companion, friend, or the possibility of ever achieving such longed-for mutuality; changes in extended family interactions; loss of buffer and increased awareness of mortality; and loss of the futures they anticipated with their mothers.

The second layer of loss pertains to daughter's personal myth of mother—those enduring images of the mother that the daughter has accumulated and internalized over the years of their shared history. Optimally, a daughter continues to revise her childhood and adolescent images of mother as she grows into adulthood. In many cases, however, the death of mother awakens those deeply held childhood images of mother that unconsciously may have continued to influence the daughter's current perception of and adult relationship with her mother, significant others, and her relationship with God. Earlier wounds or vulnerabilities incurred from real or perceived inadequate mother-daughter interactional patterns become exposed. In unraveling the bonds of loyalty that undergird the daughter's personal myth of mother, the daughter can either become entangled in the frayed threads or she can separate them out thread by thread to discover their sociocultural and intergenerational roots. The daughter then may be able to recognize her mother—come to know and appreciate her mother in her own psychohistorical reality.

A woman's personal myth of mother is always formed in the context of the dynamics of the entire family system and is maintained by "invisible loyalties" (Boszormenyi-Nagy and Spark 1973) of each family member to the family myth. Family myths are sustained in part by the socioreligio-cultural myth of motherhood in Western patriarchal society. Daughters' perceptions of their mothers' attitudes toward being female as well as of their fathers' attitudes toward women in general and their mothers in particular become part of the formation of their sense of self as female children within their cultural and historical context.

Consequently, the process of mourning cannot be understood apart from the reverberations of motherloss in the woman's psychological, familial, social, cultural, historical, and religious context. How, for example, can anyone understand the grief of Josie, an African-American woman, without knowing what it means to become the matriarch in her familial and cultural context—a context in which racism adds a qualitative dimension to her grief (Boyd-Franklin 1989). As oldest daughter, perhaps she more than her siblings internalized the "myth of the strong woman" and, consequently, was more apt to take over this role after her mother's death (hooks 1993, 104). Josie turned to the elder sisters in her church, "for they knowed what's it to feel `like a motherless child.'They all seen death, death of our fathers, husbands, lovers, and children. They the women who knows how deep our grief as black women runs." Josie found a circle of women with whom to identify and to grieve, women with whom she could begin to name the familial, social, and cultural meanings of her loss, women with whom she could explore her motherline.

Motherlines are essential links to our foremothers through our maternal ancestry. For some women, exploring the legacies bequeathed to them through their motherlines leads them to question those religious beliefs and institutions that perpetuate images of God that oppress women, negating their sense of self worth (Saussy 1991). "The grief that still comes up for me," May says thirteen years after her mother's death, "is that she could not live the life she wanted to live." May's mother had wanted to be a doctor, and despite her father's protest, she worked to obtain the money to begin premed. After her first year, she married May's father, who was supportive of her vocational goals. At least he was until May was born. May continues: "My father wanted mother to stay home, but she insisted on taking me with her to class, which was *very* unusual in her day. All the men in her class made fun of her. Then my father started getting violent and mother went to see her pastor who told her that she had no right to inflict this kind of home atmosphere on her children, that she should obey her husband and then she would be as God wanted her to be. My mother thought God wanted her to be a doctor and a wife and a mother. But no one else affirmed her and when they started using God talk to keep her at home, she began to doubt her desires and gave them up. I'm convinced that part of her died then because she became very depressed."

After speaking about her deep sadness over her mother's life, May continues: "And I am so angry with the church, because I still see that kind of attitude in people there. So I stopped going to church. But I grew up in a family where religious ties were important. So I've found a group of women with whom I worship and pray and celebrate and grieve. The God we worship and talk about is a God who wants to nurture all life, calling us to grow into the fullness of being a woman with all our cycles of birth, bleeding, dying, and rebirth. Some of the women in our group find some of those notions of God in the Hebrew and Christian Scriptures, others find it in ancient stories of the Goddess. I'm still sorting it through as to where I find a basis for my new experience of God. All I know is that I feel good being a woman now, although I still have the pain of the loss of my mother way back then . . . a vital part of her died then. If only she had the kind of support that I have, her life, and my life may have been different."

When asked how her life would have been different, May responded: "I always felt my mother's sadness and depression; I found it difficult to connect with her." When her mother's dream was aborted, her voice was silenced, and her grief froze within her. The mother-daughter relationship was tinged with grief from the start. This perception of her mother was woven into May's personal myth of mother. Indeed, "legacies of loss find expression in continuing patterns of interaction and mutual influence among the survivors and across the generations" (Walsh and McGoldrick 1991, 3).

In the process of unraveling her personal myth of mother, May began to sort through the threads that bonded mother and daughter together in a culture that oppressed women. One thread was her religious ties to her mother and family of origin. While identifying this thread as important to her, she began to search for a place and for persons who could offer empowering images of God and support her in discovering a more authentic expression of faith, a faith that does not deny, denigrate, or idealize her femaleness. At this point, May is connecting with the images of God that give her a feeling connection with the "Primal Matrix" which Rosemary Ruether describes as "the foundation (at one and the same time) of our being which embraces both the roots of the material substratum of our existence (matter) and also the endlessly new creative potential (spirit)" (Ruether 1983, 71). By feelingly connecting with the energy and power of the Primal Matrix, she is being empowered to remember a felt connection with her mother and give birth to herself. Indeed, as Katherine Keller reminds us: "We arise from the matrix; we redesign its elements; we are woven back into the matrix. This is the religious action of reconnecting. As the word itself tells us, matrix is always 'mater,' mother" (Keller 1986, 248). May is "still sorting through" various religious traditions in which to ground these personally empowering images of God. As she does find grounding, she can choicefully reweave these images of God in more complex and richly textured ways—ways that honor her mother and the self she is becoming as she relates to others, the world, and to God.

## THEOLOGICAL REFLECTIONS AND PASTORAL IMPLICATIONS

Many adult women experience more grief over the *lives* of their mothers than over the actual deaths of their mothers. Stated more simply, many daughters grieve intensely the death of their mothers in life. The "death in life" of our mothers is partly due to their being silenced in grief by a culture that continues to deny all forms of "maternal thinking" in personal, cultural, historical, and spiritual life (Ruddick 1989). Consequently, long before their mothers' death, many women experience profound motherloss. "Daughters embody the grief of the dead mother; their grief is multidimensional, intergenerational, and transgenerational" (Robbins 1990, 248).

How can pastoral caregivers help facilitate this process? How can they minister to adult women who mourn the actual deaths of their mothers and the women who mourn profound motherloss? Effective ministry creates both corporate and private spaces for grief to be acknowledged and expressed in all its dimensions and forms.

### Creating Space for Corporate Expressions of Grief

*Women's Study Groups on Motherloss.* Provide an opportunity for women to gather together to speak with one another about their experience of motherloss and how this has and continues to affect their lives. This can be done as part of an ongoing study group or as a retreat experience. Recent books on this topic provide excellent triggers for discussion (Ainley 1994; Edelman 1994; Vozenilek 1992). The convener of such a group can extend the discussion of how women's experience of motherloss has affected their images of and relationship with God and the church. In the sharing of their experiences, the women engage in a process of restorying their self-constructions, God images, and their relationships to significant others (Laird 1989, 427–450). A creative leader can help the group to ritualize the dimensions of their grief, using the images and symbols that both numb and empower women as they share their experiences (Imber-Black 1989, 451–469; 1991, 207–223). As women create this kind of woman space together, they participate in the priesthood of all believers.

*Adult Education Seminars.* Offer adult education seminars on coping with aging and ill parents, including adults who have recently lost a parent. It is important to be attentive to how women and men may describe their situations and experiences differently. Gently but firmly expose and challenge the dominant cultural assumptions that may be reflected in attitudes and behaviors, especially regarding caretaking responsibilities, expressions of grief, and the process of mourning.

*Worship Services.* Create a space in Christian worship services for the expression of grief in all its forms of anger, confusion, doubt, and so forth, during the memorial or funeral service; utilize Sunday worship, especially that which coincides with Mother's Day. While memorial services that celebrate the dead person's life in the light of a resurrection faith ritually enact the heart of Christian faith, it has been my experience that many pastors proclaim resurrection faith to those who are suffering without giving the moments of death, loss, and grief their full due. Whatever range of notions that permeate theological discourse about resurrection, it is clear that a heartfelt resurrection faith is meaningless without the heartrending, mind-baffling, soul-searching experiences that death often provokes. Resurrection talk brought up too quickly denies us the opportunity to embrace our true humanity which is historically embedded even as it is eschatologically rooted.

Similarly, Robert Davidson (1983), a noted biblical scholar, has observed that the use of psalms of doubt, rage, and lament has almost totally been eliminated from Christian liturgy and in most contemporary hymnbooks. He notes, furthermore, that "the one-sided liturgical renewal of today has in effect driven the hurtful side of experience either into obscure corners of faith practice or completely out of Christian worship into various forms of psychotherapy and growth groups" (Davidson 1983, 17). By giving public expression to grief and the dark side of life, the creative use of psalms in worship can facilitate the mourning and transformation of its community. It is important, moreover, in the selection of psalms, themes, and readings that such passages be gender-inclusive in language and imagery.

Mother's Day, a secularly imposed day of recognizing mothers, poses homiletical challenges for pastors. Either the pastor emphasizes the drippy, sentimentalized, and idealized images of mother, reinforcing the dominant culture's myth of motherhood, or the pastor chooses to ignore theologically Mother's Day altogether. Male pastors could invite a woman to give the sermon on this day—one who could offer practical theological reflections on relevant issues pertaining to mothers, such as tensions between work and family, motherloss, the silencing of maternal thinking in the dominant culture, and so forth. Not only should the liturgy be gender inclusive in language and imagery but also it could creatively incorporate concrete symbols that evoke a sense of continuity with one's motherline. Pastors could invite members of the congregation to bring a cherished symbol of their mothers to be placed near the altar. Alluding to these symbols during the service would provide a way for participants to honor corporately the rich legacies of their mothers whether alive or dead. Some acknowledgment of the grief that some members of the congregation may be experiencing on this day would also be important.

### Creating Space for Personal Expressions of Grief

*Pastoral Visitations.* Visitations with daughters whose mothers have died can be helpful not only soon after the loss but even years later. Pastoral caregivers could invite the woman to share stories about her mother's life. If the mother had been a member of your congregation, or if you knew her personally, you could recall with the daughter cherished memories of her mother. Perhaps a photo of her in the room can be an entry into such a conversation.

As you listen to the woman's story, you may note in particular how she tells the story. What are the meanings or insights that she has gleaned from reflecting on her mother's life and death? Are there any expressions of feelings, such as regret, anger, sadness, bitterness, peacefulness, joy, or loneliness? Or is the emotional tone of her storytelling flat? Such flatness may be due to fear that recounting memories of her mother will trigger emotions too difficult to handle. It has been my experience that most women speak more freely about the impact of their mothers' lives and deaths on their own lives when the person listening has shared the experience of motherloss while acknowledging that every experience has its own uniqueness. It is more difficult for women to speak to men about the depth of their experience, as they fear they will be misunderstood and misjudged by prevailing cultural attitudes toward women's relationships with women in general, and mother-daughter relationships in particular. If the daughter chooses not to speak to you about her mother, honor her choice. Ask her whether she would be interested in meeting with other women who have had the experience of motherloss.

*Pastoral Counseling Situations.* Whether you are working with an individual woman, with couples, or with families, it would be well early in your conversation to inquire about any recent or past losses, how she or they dealt with them, or how her or their family of origin dealt with significant losses. As is often the case, your counselees may make no conscious connections between their "presenting problem" and recent or past losses. Your inquiry, however, will have sown a seed that may later take root. Such a suggestion assumes that you have some theoretical framework for understanding how death affects the family system. Are you aware of intergenerational grief patterns and how you may identify these?

In addition, pastoral caregivers and counselors need to address afresh the following questions and seek the necessary information, education, and training in pastoral skills that would enable them to reenvision their responses to become more effective in helping women who experience motherloss in their adult years. What are your notions of grief and the mourning process? What are the cultural assumptions behind these notions? Do you think it is different for men and women in grieving a same sexed parent? How? How would you handle a woman's anger at the church for perpetuating notions of God that contributed to her mother's "death in life" and the daughter's grief over this aspect of her loss?

Would you be able to identify "frozen grief" or someone who hasn't grieved a past loss? How would you differentiate delayed grief from reactivated grief triggered by an anniversary, milestone events, or life cycle transitions? Would you recognize unhealthy signs of mourning, and would you know how to help a person get professional help if needed?

How do you understand death, loss, grief, and the mourning process theologically? Do you feel you can really listen to someone whose theology, lived faith experience, and images of God are different from yours without trying to impose (or evangelize) your theology, faith, or images of God on the bereaved person? At a time when a woman may be questioning her beliefs, challenging her own faith and or images of God, it is helpful to acknowledge her doubt and the concomitant feelings of confusion, anger, guilt, and so forth. Her ways of knowing and believing are in transition.

Neither you nor the bereaved person can fully know what God or faith will mean for her after she works through this transition. It is important that the bereaved woman know that it is *normal* for significant losses to usher in some major shifting in how she sees her self in relation to others, to the world, and to God. You can assure her that you will walk with her through the process; you can pray with her, using images, words, or Scripture that speak to *her* reality, staying close to her own images or words.

Indeed, women are beginning to break the silence, give public expression of their grief, and collectively engage in the activity of remembering their mothers. When grief is given collective public expression, it pierces through the numbness that hovers around us and gnaws within us. It releases women for rebirth and empowers them to reclaim their female legacies. In remembering their mothers, daughters grow in their capacities for relating more authentically to their self, to others, and to God. Pastoral caregivers are privileged, indeed, to be midwives to this process in their ministry.

## BIBLIOGRAPHY

Ainley, R., ed. 1994. *Death of a Mother: Daughters' Stories.* San Francisco: HarperCollins.

Bell-Scott, P., et al., eds. 1990. *Double Stitch: Black Women Write about Mothers and Daughters.* Boston: Beacon Press.

Boszormenyi-Nagy, I., and G. Spark. 1973. *Invisible Loyalties.* New York: International Universities Press.

Bowlby, J. 1980. *Attachment and Loss,* Vol. 3: *Loss.* New York: Basic Books.

Boyd-Franklin, N. 1989. *Black Families in Therapy: A Multisystems Approach.* New York: Guilford Press.

Davidson, R. 1983. *The Courage to Doubt: Exploring an Old Testament Theme.* London: SCM Press.

Edelman, H. 1994. *Motherless Daughters: The Legacy of Loss.* New York: Addison-Wesley Publishing Co.

Freud, S. 1915/1957. "Mourning and Melancholia." In J. Strachey, trans. and ed., *The Standard Edition of the Complete Psychological Works of Sigmund Freud,* vol. 14. London: The Hogarth Press, 243–258.

Gilligan, C. 1982. *In a Different Voice.* Cambridge: Harvard University Press.

hooks, bell. 1993. *Sisters of the Yam: Black Women and Self-Recovery.* Boston: South End Press.

Imber-Black, E. 1989. "Rituals of Stabilization and Change in Women's Lives." In McGoldrick, Anderson, and Walsh, eds., 451–469.

———. 1991. "Rituals and the Healing Process." In Walsh and McGoldrick, eds., 207–223.

Keller, C. 1986. *From a Broken Web: Separation, Sexism, and Self.* Boston: Beacon Press.

Laird, J. 1989. "Women and Stories: Restorying Women's Self-Constructions." In McGoldrick, Anderson, and Walsh, eds., 427–450.

Lowinsky, N. 1992. *Stories from the Motherline.* Los Angeles: Tarcher.

Marris, P. 1986. *Loss and Change.* 2d ed. London: Routledge & Kegan Paul.

McGoldrick, M.; C. Anderson; and F. Walsh, eds. 1989. *Women in Families: A Framework for Family Therapy.* New York: W. W. Norton & Co.

Myers, E. 1986. *When Parents Die: A Guide for Adults.* New York: Viking Press.

Rich, A. 1976. *Of Woman Born: Motherhood as Experience and Institution.* New York: W. W. Norton & Co.

Robbins, M. 1990. *Midlife Women and Death of Mother: A Study of Psychohistorical and Spiritual Transformation.* New York: Peter Lang.

Ruddick, S. 1989. *Maternal Thinking: Towards a Politics of Peace.* New York: Ballantine Books.

Ruether, R. R. 1983. *Sexism and God Talk: Toward a Feminist Theology.* Boston: Beacon Press.

Saussy, C. 1991. *God Images and Self Esteem: Empowering Women in a Patriarchal Society.* Louisville: Westminster/John Knox Press.

Strachey, J., trans. and ed. 1957. *The Standard Edition of the Complete Psychological Works of Sigmund Freud,* vol. 14. London: The Hogarth Press.

Vozenilek, H., ed. 1992. *Loss of the Ground-Note: Women Writing about the Loss of their Mothers.* San Diego: Clothespin Fever Press.

Walsh, F., and M. McGoldrick, eds. 1991. *Living Beyond Loss: Death in the Family.* New York: W. W. Norton & Co.

# 10

# Manna in the Desert:
# Eating Disorders and Pastoral Care

JANE E. DASHER

*Grady Memorial Hospital, Atlanta*

Dieting consumes women and yet the United States leads in the consumption of food and is the most overweight country in the world. Models model thinness rather than the clothes that are worn. Children's books start shaping minds and bodies at an early age.

One woman describes her struggle:

> I go through periods where if I'm not able to be alone or I don't have my privacy, I'm anorexic. And when I'm in a tense situation or at home, I become bulimic where I binge and purge—that whole cycle.
>
> I started restricting my food when I was eleven—just like becoming a vegetarian and going on a microbiotic diet—but it wasn't weight control related. It was more just health conscious.
>
> When I was a senior in high school, I thought I overate one day, and I had heard about people throwing up, so I attempted to do that, but it didn't really work. A week later I had overeaten again, and I just really felt bad, so I tried it [throwing up] again and it was easier.
>
> It got really severe this last summer where I was bingeing and purging two or three times a day . . . almost every day.
>
> It was just my only release for the rage I felt.
>
> Kathryn, age 20[1]

It is clear that women are overly concerned with weight and weighty proportions. How does a pastor, counselor, or friend give hope to women who are engaged in what seems to be a never-ending battle with food?

If Kathryn's story or the stories of friends and family are not convincing enough that weight is of great concern in American society, in 1990 Americans spent $33 billion on diets and services related to dieting compared to $29 billion in 1989 (Rodin 1992, 166). The long-range estimate through the end of this century is that $77 billion a year will be spent to "lose those unwanted pounds."

In 1978, 56 percent of female respondents to a Nielsen survey between the ages of 24 and 54 were on a diet; that percentage rose to 72 percent by the late 1980s (Rodin 1992, 166). Not only are large numbers of females on a diet, "nearly 95% of adult women overestimate their body size; 75% of adults within the 'ideal' range of weights for their heights still think they need to be thinner" (Bringle 1992, 25).

These statistics indicate that women not only are concerned with their weight and body image but spend billions of dollars a year on reducing the national debt of being too fleshy. In the search for the thin body, eating disorders often result rather than the goal of the perfect body.

Laura, now eighteen, is in her fourth eating disorders treatment program. She became anorexic when she was fifteen and lost twenty pounds and became very ill. She is also at times bulimic. She has had many physical problems and complications as a result of her eating disorder.

> I know a lot about it and have done so much research, and I've done so many reports on it, but it doesn't stop me. I kept doing it still. I've always been the bulimic person: I've never been Laura [emphasis mine].

Kathryn and Laura clearly show that what began as a concern with weight loss has now turned into a more serious problem than simply wanting to lose a few pounds. The concern has turned to utter chaos. Eating disorders are reflective of a concern gone to seemingly uncontrollable proportions resulting in anorexia nervosa, bulimia, and sometimes obesity. These eating disorders often do result in a thin body. They also result in serious illnesses and often death—the opposite of what is promised by American society if one is thin (being thin = being healthy = eternal life).

Eating disorders and their treatment have received more recognition over the last few years. It seems that the medical side effects of eating disorders, which includes a rise in deaths related to eating disorders, as well as the feminist movement have given room for naming and talking about eating disorders. An estimated eight million persons (seven million women; one million men) are being treated for eating disorders. That estimate does not include those who do not seek treatment.

The age of persons who are dieting and the age of those who are developing eating disorders is decreasing in this generation. Professionals such as pediatricians, child psychologists and teachers report that more preteens are being seen with anorexia nervosa and bulimia. What was once a disorder found mainly in teenage girls and young women is now found in elementary schools along with recess. What was also once a white, middle-class problem now knows no boundaries—it crosses all race, class, gender, and sexual orientation lines.

The focus of this chapter is on women with eating disorders because anorexia nervosa and bulimia occur almost exclusively in females. Cases involving men are reported occasionally but are on the increase. With obesity, men and women are almost equal in number, but an estimated 80 to 90 percent of those seeking treatment are women (Brownell and Foreyt 1986, 507).

## OPPRESSION RESULTING IN OBSESSION: WHEN AND HOW DID IT BEGIN?

How did American society become so overly concerned with body image and weight, and how did this concern spark the rise of eating disorders? Different theories have been developed as to why and when this oppression began.

Self-inflicted starvation and weight loss are found in literary accounts that date back to the Middle Ages, but dieting as a national pastime in America began in the 1920s. As the medical profession saw a correlation between being overweight and certain health problems, dieting was recommended for a longer life. But excessive dieting began several decades before this correlation was popularized by the medical profession. The dieting rage began for reasons other than fear of a shorter life span.

Others attribute the rise of eating disorders to technological ideas developed in the early 1800s.[2] As machines became streamlined and efficient, the body was also expected to be capable of the same. By simply counting calories and expending so much energy per day, it was understood at this time that one could design the shape of the body to one's desires. Control was sought through exercise and controlling the amount of food taken into the system or "machine" in order to maintain health.

Reasons for dieting over the last three decades have shifted. Now a thin body is wanted without concern for a person's health or how that thin body is achieved. Forget only calorie counting and exercise. Much more sophisticated methods are being used not to attain health, but to achieve an appearance—a thin, waiflike appearance. Cosmetic surgery such as facelifts and nose jobs increased radically in the 1960s, as old age and old bodies became seriously devalued in the baby boomer era. Now extensive cosmetic surgery from liposuction to breast reductions to body contouring, which smoothes out trouble spots, is used to carve the body to fit the desired thin mold. The standard for beauty is now at a surgeon's fingertips.

With the 1970s the women's liberation movement became more widespread. Equality in the workplace to the bedroom became the focus. Women became more assertive. Some suggest that as women did so, they were left searching for new ways to care for the self since the traditional ways were changing. Women turned to food as a way to care for themselves.

Food provided the security, comfort, and pleasure that was not found in their lives. It provided stability in an unstable world. One woman says, "And the one thing I know I can do when I come home is cook me a pot of food and sit down in front of the TV and eat it. And you can't take that away from me until you're ready to give me something in its place" (Avery 1994, 7). Eating disorders occur for various reasons which predominantly are caring for ourselves and the search for the thin appearance.

This search for ways to care for ourselves as women and the search for the thin appearance are still on today. Now in the 1990s, 72 percent of women work outside the home. What it means to be a woman is today quite different from fifty years ago. Naomi Wolf in her book *The Beauty Myth* (1990) says that eating disorders have grown out of a beauty backlash against women. This backlash has come about to counteract the feminist movement. By tying women's self-esteem to a scale, thinness is valued more than the woman herself. Being thin, therefore, is the only way for women to be valued and successful in our society. And this thinness by those who seek it is achieved through radical means that include extensive cosmetic surgery, eating disorders, over exercising, and malnutrition.

Meadow and Weiss (1992) understand the rise in eating disorders as a shifting from sexual to oral obsessions. While the question thirty years ago was about sex and whether to do "it" or not to do "it," the authors propose that today's question is whether to eat or not to eat.

The different theories all lead to one result: eating disorders with an emphasis on thinness. In a land of oppression, thinness is valued and America has become a slave to this idol.

While the emphasis is clearly on thinness, women daily receive mixed messages. It is ironic that a company most well known for its production of chocolate bars and other candies (which could make one "fat") now also makes chocolate-flavored diet products (with promises to make one "thin"). And if the myth is true that women are to be thin and that to get thin they must eat healthy foods, why is there a fast-food restaurant, well known for unhealthy foods, on every street corner?

### Eating Disorders Defined

It is important to identify the types of eating disorders that exist and to establish definitions of these types for the rest of this chapter. Three types of eating disorders are identified in most of the literature: anorexia nervosa, bulimia, and binge eating disorder.

Anorexia nervosa has simply been defined by Hilde Burch (1988) as the "relentless pursuit of thinness." Anorexics literally starve themselves. The amount of food intake is greatly restricted by the individual in order to achieve thinness.

Bulimia is a binge-purge cycle where diuretics, laxatives, and vomiting are used to purge food from the body after consumption. Large amounts of food with "a high caloric content, sweet taste, and a texture that facilitates rapid eating" (*DSM*-III 1980, 69) are usually consumed during the binge.

A recently named disorder, binge eating disorder is the name for the consumption of large amounts of food without purging and often results in obesity. The next section examines issues related to eating disorders and different methods used in the treatment of eating disorders.

## TREATMENT OF EATING DISORDERS

Eating disorders are very difficult to treat because of the complex issues involved: spiritual, psychological, and medical. Some of the issues are low self-esteem, shame, guilt, anger, rage, incongruent beliefs regarding self and food, body image distortion, and mind/body dualism. Also found are issues of control and power, trust, fear of food, and fear of being empty. There is also a high correlation between eating disorders and having been sexually abused. Medical problems include heart problems, anemia, an erosion of the stomach lining and bleeding, brittle hair and loss of hair, and, least of all, death.

The Twelve Steps program has been adapted to treat eating disorders. Some programs are hospital-based and have in and out patient services. In these types of programs, eating disorders are understood as an addiction and are treated with the same principles as alcoholism or drug addiction. The emphasis is on addiction not to food but to specific behaviors such as bingeing or purging. Therefore, it is these behaviors that treatment tries to reduce or eliminate completely.

Using a cognitive-behavioral approach to treatment, the program focuses on beliefs, faulty thinking patterns, and self-esteem and self-awareness. The focus on behavior includes relearning how to eat in "normal" patterns as well as eating "normal" amounts of food. Treatment also includes examining how the person has used food in the past (that is, comfort, love, to dispel boredom, and others) and how not to use food to get these needs met in the future.

This treatment approach focuses on the individual with the eating disorder. Families are invited to participate in sessions specifically for training the family about the "disease." This approach does not address the connections between self and other systems (that is, cultural, family, social) that contribute to addiction. It is seen as a personal problem. Not only are systems not addressed, the person is not empowered to change systems. The focus is totally on healing the self in spite of the system.

The healing of the self is in terms of very traditional gender roles. Stereo-types of women are perpetuated in twelve-step programs. Admitting power-lessness over an eating disorder (one of the twelve steps) is problematic for women who understand their eating disorder as the one thing in their lives they control while living in the midst of an oppressive "Egypt." Further powerlessness complicates and disempowers.

When the women interviewed for this chapter were asked to describe their higher power, who, for most of them, was God, traditional male lan-guage was used as well as male images of a transcendent, all-powerful dis-tant God. Again, one has given up control to One who seemingly has all the control and power. This is a familiar pattern for most women raised in a submissive culture and is not helpful in order for liberation from an eat-ing disorder to occur. The one overriding consensus from those in this type of treatment program is that the group meetings are powerful in knowing that one is not alone in her eating disorder.

Another treatment model similar to the Twelve Steps in its understand-ing of an eating disorder as an addiction is based on family systems ther-apy. "The attempt to have power or control over some aspect of oneself through the use of some external agent which ultimately renders a person powerless and dependent" (Bepko 1989, 406) is the primary characteristic of an addiction in this model. The addiction actually is reflective of and as a result of a systemic power differential. This model, unlike the Twelve Steps, is sensitive to power differentials especially among genders as well as family and social orders. Restoration of systems to a more functional balance is the goal of family systems therapy.

An approach such as this one developed by Claudia Bepko (1989) treats not only the family system but the addiction as well. The addiction has its own meaning and function for the person and these must be examined as well as the systemic power differentials.

A feminist psychotherapy approach developed by Ellyn Kaschak (1992) proposes that eating disorders are women's embodiment of societal con-flicts regarding women's body and appearance. Women's worth, as defined by men in a patriarchal society, is judged by their appearance which is val-ued more than life itself. "Appearance *is* life" (Kaschak 1992, 201). Hunger therefore becomes symbolic rather than what it really is—physio-logical—and the body becomes separated from hunger.

Kaschak's feminist psychotherapy focuses on making visible that which is invisible, self-esteem, reconnecting with other women, identifying mul-tiple meanings and changing meanings in a patriarchal society, and sense of self. Also important is the bringing together of mind and body to avoid dualistic splits. Self and context are examined because each defines the other and contributes to the other. Since there is a constant interplay between the two, self and context cannot be separated in feminist therapy.

Like Kaschak's feminist psychotherapy, Larry Kent Graham's (1992) psychosystemic approach is inclusive of the interplay between self and social and cultural orders. In addition, connections with the natural order and how it is impacted by change are part of this approach. How is the environment impacted by eating disorders? Impacts include natural resources that are wasted to develop and produce diet-related products, overconsumption of resources including food, overproduction of food, and overworking the land to produce food. Death of persons from eating disorders disrupts the natural order.

For women with an eating disorder to understand the disorder psychosystemically is to understand relatedness and interconnections between the self and the surrounding world. One is not alone in the disorder. This does not in any way diminish an individual's responsibility for eating patterns. What is helpful in this model is that the individual is not labeled as "sick." What is "sick" are the systems that facilitate and perpetuate eating disorders.

The understanding of interconnectedness allows for a pastoral care of healing, guiding, reconciliation as well as emancipatory liberation, and justice-seeking. Also possible are public advocacy and ecological partnership. This occurs in a trusting therapeutic relationship where persons are heard into speech. It is empowering to the individual as well as larger systems to realize that change in one part of the system also impacts other systems. Change in one produces change in another—which can be hopeful and hope filled change. Caring for persons creates new worlds and caring for the world creates new persons.

## "FOOD IS MEANT FOR THE STOMACH AND THE STOMACH FOR FOOD" (1 CORINTHIANS 6:13)

What does the Christian tradition say about food? Does food have any spiritual significance? What are the implications of a spirituality of food for a woman with an eating disorder? Eating has always been a central activity of humanity. A shared apple by Adam and Eve is a focal point of the Christian tradition. Eating "is a ritual that includes sharing, comfort, satisfaction, pleasure, creativity, sustenance, and nurture" (Juengst 1992, 15). Unfortunately for most, eating is understood more as deadly sin.

Gluttony has long been named as one of the seven deadly sins or capital sins in the Christian tradition. A deadly sin is one that most seriously threatens the divine spirit within humanity so that humanity is no longer any likeness to God. The seven sins are the source of all sins, and all other sins grow from these deadly sins.

As defined by Brian Grant, gluttony is "suicidal activity with a knife and fork" (Grant 1982, 35). Gluttony is equated with overindulgence, an over-riding of innate self-regulation, and a lack of appreciation for the aesthetic value of food and self.

In modern interpretations of gluttony (Grant 1982; Capps 1987), glut-tony is understood as a conscious choice made by a person in order to receive gratification. The person who chooses gluttony also has the capa-bility and the responsibility to change or claim a preferable method or virtue. Through self-control, gratification is to be sought in moderation. An emphasis is placed on body size where one is known as a glutton because of being a certain size or weight.

Mary Louise Bringle (1992, 53–86) in her research of Scripture, patris-tic and monastic writings, and other historical writings on gluttony, chal-lenges the modern interpretations. Rather than being concerned with body shape and size, she finds that historically gluttony is concerned with pat-terns of eating and drinking. Patterns are problematic when the acquisition and ingestion of food are valued above all else.

The context that most closely resembles that of the current American society is the medieval context of the holy anorexics. The point of connec-tion between persons with eating disorders and the holy anorexics is a fear of food and bodily abundance of flesh. There is one important distinction: holy anorexics did it to be holy; in the American context, persons do it to be beautiful or as a way to care for the self.

The modern interpretations of gluttony place emphasis on gluttony as individual sin. The glutton is the one who has the capability and the responsibility to change her behavior. Little is said about other factors out-side the individual that contribute to individual sin. In order to understand gluttony and eating disorders, sin must also be understood corporately. The sinfully constructed systems that contribute to individual sin must also enter into the conversation. How does patriarchy contribute to how women understand themselves (body and mind)? How does a political sys-tem that does not give women choices regarding their bodies contribute? How does the church contribute to perpetuating women as other and less than? How does defining persons in terms of difference ("fat" versus "thin") contribute to the sin of eating disorders?

As for the capability and responsibility to change body size, researchers are finding that humans are less self-determining than was previously thought. Genetics and neurochemicals are found to have great impacts on body shape and size. Yes, persons are responsible for eating patterns, but they cannot control shape and size as much as society would have persons think.

An idolatrous element to eating disorders is also found. Women are liv-ing in an Egypt where they are often not aware of their socialization by an oppressive society. In this Egypt, thinness is valued as godliness. When enslaved to the "god of thinness,"[3] worship of idols replaces worship of God. One woman described her enslavement as falling into evil: "It was almost like I was tempted by evil, and I fell in a way. I got so far away from God and fell into myself. I wouldn't accept help from anyone."

This idolatrous element also impacts how food is understood. Categories of foods are labeled as "sinful" and "nonsinful." Food that often is pleasurable to taste and high in calories is labeled as "sinful." Those foods which are "good," that is, those which have high nutritional value and low caloric counts, are "nonsinful" or "holy." All food is not seen as created good by God.

The woman with an eating disorder has a distorted view of food as well as of body image. She focuses on food as sinful, while at the same time food competes with God for worship. Food is also the idol that is thought to fulfill empty needs and to be a way of caring for the self. The woman with an eating disorder is very rigid and restrictive in her dieting rituals. In her search for perfection, bingeing and purging become a ritualistic part of eating. Food might provide comfort and joy, but these are short-lived.

The woman with an eating disorder does not really "know" much about hunger. The body is usually seen as something foreign that must be controlled and what is put into the body must be constantly controlled. Bodily sensations are misperceived, mistrusted, or not felt at all. The mind is thought to have total control over the body. A mind/body dualism is found.

The saying "Eat only when hungry," meaning eat only when physiologically hungry, makes no sense to one who is not aware of a sensation of hunger. As Sally Tisdale (1993, 51) observes, this saying also assumes that eating is purely physiological and emotions have nothing to do with hunger. Contradictory to this, some of the greatest feasts are at very emotional times of persons' lives: weddings, funerals, Christmas, and so forth.

Eating and the rituals associated with eating are done in isolation by a woman with an eating disorder. An eighteen-year-old described her eating in isolation as "it was something I had, and I didn't want anyone else to have it. It was the only thing I felt I controlled, and I wanted it all to myself." Isolation, secretiveness, and control are important. "I was very careful about it [bingeing and purging] with all these little rituals I did to prevent anyone from knowing," says Barbara. The very thought of eating with others or being "caught" eating can be overwhelming. The secret would be exposed and a loss of control experienced. There is a fear of not having enough food, and to think of sharing food is threatening.

The women interviewed who were in a treatment program also felt as if they did not belong and were outsiders in a society that values thinness as godliness and devalues women. They are persecuted and despised by their neighbors, and they internalize persecution and being despised, to follow these gods. But they can never be thin enough and never achieve perfection to belong with those who worship this god. Food will never fill the emptiness that is felt. The incongruent message is that they can't be like all other women as if all other women are thin and not empty. Laura says, "[I] thought I'd be happy [when I got thin]. But you never become happy, because once you set your weight and you get there, it's not good enough. You keep going and keep going and you're never really happy with it, but you think once you get there you will be happy . . . but it just keeps on going down the line." It is a vicious cycle of frustration and rage trying to attain the unattainable.

Eating disorders feed on hopelessness. Hopelessness that doesn't trust God or anyone else will sustain and feed. Hopelessness that says one cannot be full without food. Hopelessness that one doesn't belong and is "bad." It is in this hopelessness that one cannot hope for a place of restoration and liberation from the disorder. Kathryn, looking back on her hopelessness, says, "There was no way I could see escaping it or getting out of it [her eating disorder], and it was horrifying for me."

## RECLAIMING THE SPIRITUAL SIGNIFICANCE OF FOOD

A reclaiming of the "spiritual significance of food" (Juengst 1992) is necessary in order to claim a healthy perspective of food and offer hope to those with eating disorders. Most of the spiritual significance has been lost in the busyness of everyday life.

In reclaiming the spiritual significance of food, food is understood as God's good gift. God is nurturer, sustainer, and provider. Bodily and spiritual needs are met by God, the one who feeds and provides manna in the deserts of people's lives. Just as the god of thinness is not to be worshiped, a healthy perspective of food must be kept so that food is not worshiped.

Transformative possibilities are alive in the gathering together for a shared meal. In the breaking of bread, strangers become friends, families put aside differences, and the chaos of the day is stilled. People and God come together in relationship to enjoy God's expression of grace and celebrate and affirm God's good gift and the joy that food brings to lives. In the midst of this togetherness, the God of the exodus, the one true liberating God who frees us from bondage to idols, is remembered.

Food, a gift to those who hunger, renews and restores. When food is shared in compassion, no one hungers. Justice is restored as people share the gift of food with those who have hunger.

At the Lord's Table, the joyful feast prepared for all is one of renewal and remembering, a table of hospitality, bonding, and celebration. At this table, all belong to Christ and to each other.

At table, all await the messianic banquet where there will be no more hunger. With hope in God's promises, it is at this banquet where restoration will be found. At this ultimate meal, all will meet in Christ. It is here that total restoration and peace will be found.

## HOPEFUL ENDINGS

In reclaiming the spiritual significance of food as well as having an awareness of the systemic issues involved, the church can be a place of hope, liberation, and healing for a person with an eating disorder. As pastoral caregiver, one can offer a proper perspective of food and self and assist women in finding a place of comfort with eating and body image. By examining idolatrous issues found with eating disorders, one can find the liberating and transforming God who frees from an enslaving land of Egypt.

In a theology where mind and body are brought together as one, women can understand themselves as a whole self. This whole self is connected with other people and systems. In these interconnections is found a sense of belongingness rather than isolation. For one who is alone in her eating disorder, this connectedness brings the world's brokenness together. Change is possible as change in one system brings about change in another, and this possibility offers hope.

Forming a support group for women can offer a safe place where a woman can belong and a place of acceptance where she can be known as a person, not as an object seeking to be controlled. It is also important to assist those with eating disorders in discovering new ways of caring for self other than relying solely on food. Eating a meal together or celebrating the Lord's Supper in worship has transformative possibilities. Facilitate a time of reflection on these shared experiences and the impact these experiences have on the persons who share them.

Addressing the secret of eating disorders can break the silence and offer opportunities for conversation and connection. This can occur in many contexts. A sermon on eating disorders or an educational series on the spiritual significance of food or on the theology of the Lord's Supper can be places to name issues and explore them. It is important to keep in mind how far-reaching eating disorders are. All ages, races, sexes, and classes are touched in some way. This is not a topic for adults only, because minds and bodies are shaped at early ages.

Examine the impacts of eating disorders on the self, social, cultural, and natural orders. Be an advocate for change. Write editors of magazines that present only thin images of women. Speak out against those systems which devalue women. Refuse to buy dieting products.

Also helpful is the recognition of transitional points in the lives of the women to whom one ministers. Periods of transition can be very stressful times and trigger an eating disorder. Periods of transition may be puberty, going to college, a new joy, the death of a loved one, or giving up harmful eating patterns. Develop rituals that recognize these moments and give larger meaning to them as well as offer transformative possibilities.

These acts of pastoral care help women to know that God is present in their lives and in the world. God is actively seeking and desiring transformation for us and the world. The God of the exodus offers liberation from eating disorders through hope that restoration and peace will come— restoration and peace from physical, psychological, and spiritual problems associated with eating disorders; restoration and peace from systems that sacrifice humans and creation for the sake of consumerism and other destructiveness. The messianic banquet "will be a feast to end all feasts, one that satisfies our deepest hungers and thirsts" (Juengst 1992, 99). Human emptiness will be filled to overflowing. At this feast of restoration and peace, one will not be known as the bulimic or anorexic or obese one. All will be known only by name. Just as at the beginning of this chapter Laura said she has always been the bulimic person and not known as Laura, it is here at this feast that Laura will finally be Laura.

Until this delectable feast, women can rely on God's bountiful gift of grace in healing from an eating disorder. Where they are broken, they can rely on the transformative power of God in order to live new lives. In the midst of the desert, God's manna of grace rains, immersing those in their brokenness with food for the journey. This journey may at times seem hopeless with no end in sight for one with an eating disorder, but God comes in the midst of the desert and says, "I am the Lord who heals you" (Exodus 15:26).

## Notes

1. Interviews were conducted with women from an in-patient hospital based eating disorders program. The names and identifying details of the persons have been changed to assure anonymity. I am grateful to these women for their stories of courage and the use of their voices within this chapter.

2. See Mary Louise Bringle's *The God of Thinness: Gluttony and Other Weighty Matters* (1992, 87–118) for an excellent summary of the historical development of eating disorders.

3. The phrase "god of thinness" is one that Mary Louise Bringle (1992) uses to describe her worship of a false god that promises thinness. "Thinness can become a 'god' only in a context from which other more potent gods have disappeared" (Bringle 1992, 100).

## BIBLIOGRAPHY

American Psychiatric Association. 1980. *Diagnostic and Statistical Manual of Mental Disorders.* 3d ed. Washington D.C. (*DSM*-III)

Avery, B. 1994. "Breathing Life into Ourselves: The Evolution of the National Black Women's Health Project." In White, ed., 4–10.

Bell, R. M. 1985. *Holy Anorexia.* Chicago: University of Chicago Press.

Bepko, C. 1989. "Disorders of Power: Women and Addiction in the Family." In McGoldrick, Anderson, and Walsh, eds., 406–426.

Bringle, M. L. 1992. *The God of Thinness: Gluttony and Other Weighty Matters.* Nashville: Abingdon Press.

Brownell, K., and J. Foreyt, eds. 1986. *Handbook of Eating Disorders: Physiology, Psychology, and Treatment of Obesity, Anorexia, and Bulimia.* New York: Basic Books.

Burch, H. 1988. *Conversations with Anorexics.* New York: Basic Books.

Capps, D. 1987. *Deadly Sins and Saving Virtues.* Philadelphia: Fortress Press.

Curtin, D., and L. Helke, eds. 1992. *Cooking, Eating, Thinking: Transformative Philosophies of Food.* Bloomington, Ind.: Indiana University Press.

Graham, L. K. 1992. *Care of Persons, Care of Worlds: A Psychosystems Approach to Pastoral Care and Counseling.* Nashville: Abingdon Press.

Grant, B. 1982. *From Sin to Wholeness.* Philadelphia: Westminster Press.

Juengst, S. C. 1992. *Breaking Bread: The Spiritual Significance of Food.* Louisville, Ky.: Westminster/John Knox Press.

Kaschak, E. 1992. *Engendered Lives: A New Psychology of Women's Experience.* New York: Basic Books.

McGoldrick, M.; C. Anderson; and F. Walsh, eds. 1989. *Women in Families: A Framework for Family Therapy.* New York: W. W. Norton & Co.

Meadow, R., and L. Weiss. 1992. *Women's Conflicts about Eating and Sexuality: The Relationship between Food and Sex.* New York: Harrington Park Press.

Rodin, J. 1992. *Body Traps.* New York: Wm. Morrow & Co.

Tisdale, S. 1993. "A Weight That Women Carry: The Compulsion to Diet in a Starved Culture." *Harper's Magazine* vol. 286, no. 1714: 49–55.

White, E. C., ed. 1994. *The Black Women's Health Book: Speaking for Ourselves.* Seattle: Seal Press.

Wolf, Naomi. 1990. *The Beauty Myth.* New York: Anchor.

# 11

# Hysterectomy and Woman's Identity

BETH ANN ESTOCK

*Druid Hills United Methodist Church, Atlanta*

I first began researching the topic of hysterectomy while working as a chaplain on the gynecology unit of Baptist Medical Center in Birmingham, Alabama. I found myself feeling uncomfortable being with women who had just had hysterectomies. What do I say or do? What words or gestures of comfort can I bring? How can the patient and I acknowledge this loss together? I then realized that hysterectomy is a difficult subject to talk about, let alone to try to minister to a woman who has just had her operation.

While I was finding out more about hysterectomy, one of my friends inquired about the stack of books and articles on my desk. I told him about my research and he replied, "What is the big deal about having a hysterectomy? It is just an operation like taking out an appendix." I responded, "How would you like your penis removed?" Naturally, he looked at me in shock, but when he regained his composure he said, "But that's different, the uterus is inside a woman's body. It doesn't stick out for all to see. A man's penis is a source of pride, a symbol of his manhood. I couldn't imagine being in the men's locker room without one."

Just as my friend could not imagine himself without his symbol of manhood, some women have difficulty imagining themselves without their symbol of womanhood—regardless of whether or not it is "exposed for all to see." I believe just as the womb is hidden, so is woman's reaction to hysterectomy. In many ways, the response to hysterectomy is multidimensional and difficult to process.

When a woman's womb is removed, she may call into question her self-image and wonder how to define herself without that which she believes makes her uniquely woman. She may be shamed into silence about these struggles by her church, her family, and her culture as others treat hysterectomy as though it were routine surgery.

A sampling of five women's experiences with hysterectomies has served as a tool in my research and has provided insight into the complexities of this subject. These women had their hysterectomies at least two years before they were interviewed, and thus they had a more integrated perspective of their experience.

Throughout this chapter, I will offer a variety of definitions that have helped to form our image of "woman" from the dictionary to Freud, from the Bible to modern women writers. I will be discussing the ways in which the Judeo-Christian tradition has helped to shape woman's image as child bearer and the ways in which women are reinterpreting this tradition to allow for other creative expressions of woman's self-identity. It is only when both men and women begin to understand how they have been shaped by their histories—past and present—that they can begin to create their own images for the future. Finally, I will offer ways in which ministers can be supportive of the hysterectomy patient with her own unique struggles.

## WOMAN BY DEFINITION: FROM THE DICTIONARY TO FREUD

"Woman" in *Merriam Webster's Collegiate Dictionary,* Tenth Edition, is defined as "an adult female person," "distinctively feminine nature," "mistress," and is a derivative of an Old English word, "wifman" which means "wife of man." The first two definitions categorize woman by her gender—female. The last two definitions reflect woman in relation to her counterpart—man.

The dictionary states that "female" designates the sex "that bears young or produces . . . eggs." For a woman who has had a hysterectomy and is in her natural childbearing years, this definition falls short because she can no longer bear young, or in cases of radical hysterectomy, she can no longer produce ova. Granted she still belongs to the sex that bears young and produces ova, but she can no longer be defined as a child bearer. The dictionary offers only one more possibility: A woman can be defined by what she is not, man, and her relation to man, wife or mistress.

The image of woman as deficient compared to man continues to influence our culture and ways of relating to one another. Sigmund Freud was shaped by this image and his psychoanalytic theory perpetuates this concept. Freud, in his essay "Femininity," defines woman as a disadvantaged man with no status of her own. She is defined only in relation to man—his negative. This approach is evident in Freud's concept of penis envy. He believes that a little girl finds herself castrated and feels devalued as a result of her lack of a phallus, a symbol of the penis. He uses this theory to explain how a girl moves from her first object of love, her mother, to desire for her father. He writes the following concerning castration complex.

> No doubt her turning away from her mother does not occur all at once, for to begin with the girl regards her castration as an individual misfortune, and only gradually extends it to other females and finally to her mother as well. Her love was directed to her phallic mother: with the discovery that her mother is castrated it becomes possible to drop her as an object. . . . This means, therefore, that as a result of the discovery of woman's lack of a penis they are debased in value for girls just as they are for boys and later perhaps for men. (Strouse 1974, 85)

Freud brings forth the masculine ideology implicit in traditional psychoanalytic theory and in Western discourse in general. I believe that we, along with Freud, have been shaped and continue to be shaped by this male "naming" system—a system that defines woman as a lack, based on negation instead of creation.

However, I think Freud can offer us insight into what it might mean to lose that which is unique to woman, her womb. Luce Irigaray, a psychoanalyst and philosopher, in her book *Speculum of the Other Woman*, evaluates Freud's castration theory in light of his thoughts on mourning and melancholia. Irigaray states that if Freud's theory of castration were carried through to its logical conclusion, a girl's only recourse would be melancholia. Therefore we might ask ourselves: Could it be that melancholia is experienced by some women who have had hysterectomies?

Freud writes that with melancholia what is lost is not tangible and even the patient has difficulty consciously perceiving what was lost. This may be the case even when the patient is aware of the loss that has made her or him melancholic but not able to pinpoint exactly what she or he has lost. Freud then suggests that "melancholia is in some way related to an object-loss which is withdrawn from consciousness" (Irigaray 1985, 68). These are the symptoms of melancholia: profound sadness, low self-esteem, lack of energy, loss of interest in the outside world, and loss of the capacity for love.

Freud comments that after a girl has discovered that she does not have the same genitals of a boy (who has far superior equipment), she believes herself to be a mutilated creature and develops, like a scar, a sense of inferiority. She then realizes that she is castrated and inferior to the male (Irigaray 1985, 67). A woman who has had a hysterectomy could be perceived as mutilated in a way that Freud's women were not unless they happened also to have had hysterectomies.

Many of the women I interviewed felt this inferiority. Reflecting upon her experience after a hysterectomy, Martha, a fifty-one-year-old woman, married for thirty-six years, with four adult children, who calls herself a "housewife" said, "I felt ugly. I didn't want my husband to look at me, and I thought other people thought I was ugly too. I felt something was missing. God put my uterus there for a reason. It is part of a woman that a man doesn't have, and it's not just 'a box for babies' (this is how her doctor explained the function of her uterus). When you breast-feed a baby you can feel your uterus contract. It is all tied together. It has to be or you couldn't feel that." This same woman said that she had a difficult time coping with her family after her hysterectomy. She could not be in the same room when all of them were together. She went into a depression and cried frequently. However, this was difficult to share with her family. She said, "They never knew the extent of the turmoil I was going through. I felt like no one understood or cared." She also commented that she felt a loss of strength with the loss of her uterus that she has never regained. Her hysterectomy had been sixteen years earlier.

It seems that this woman experienced what Freud terms melancholia, not according to Freud's definition of castration complex, but due to the "castration" of her womb. Freud distinguishes grief from melancholia. With grief, one knows what one is losing and can attach an object/phallus to it. The loss is more concrete/exposed and therefore easier to work through and accept. But with melancholia, the loss is much more subtle, hidden, less concrete, and on a more unconscious level.

Sixteen years later this same hysterectomy patient remarked, "Through counseling I am beginning to think better of myself, but I still have a long way to go." I am not implying that the cause of this woman's lack of self-esteem was due entirely to her hysterectomy. However, I believe that hysterectomy is a loss that radically escapes any representation and for a large part remains unconscious. One of the most frequently asked questions of hysterectomy patients according to a nurse specialist with whom I talked was, "What will they do with my uterus after they take it out?" What does the loss of the uterus mean? Does it mean the loss of so called "femininity," the loss of womanhood? What does the woman grieve?

## THE LOSS

A critical review of the psychological reactions of hysterectomy patients by the Department of Psychology at Northwestern University states that a woman finds her identity through her femininity. What constitutes this femininity are such things as physical attractiveness and the ability to bear children. "Therefore, woman's breast, genitals and reproductive organs are probably essential to her adaptation and self-evaluation as a woman. Because of the psychological importance of these organs, a threat to them can easily constitute a threat to a woman's whole self-concept" (Polivy 1974, 417).

A survey of historic literature shows that most women regard femininity as a positive quality and that the loss of reproductive organs produces feelings of loss of femininity. Numerous studies of hysterectomy patients have found that after a hysterectomy women were more likely to have postoperative depression. In some studies they reported a two to four times higher incidence of depression than occurs in the general population (Drummond and Field 1984, 264).

Understanding the process of loss following hysterectomy can prove to be beneficial to counselors working with hysterectomy patients. Jane Drummond, R.N., and Peggy-Anne Field, Ph.D., report they have observed four stages of loss that a woman may experience after having a hysterectomy: (1) impact, (2) retreat, (3) acknowledgment, and (4) reconstruction. The impact stage occurs when the problem arises in the consciousness. This does not necessarily occur at the time of surgery. Retreat, the second stage, is when the woman depersonalizes her uterus, denies that this event is significant, and makes light of her experience. Drummond and Field comment that the purpose of the joking and the denial is to give time for reflection on the meaning of the uterus and to provide energy for the next stage, which is acknowledgment. It is in the acknowledgment stage that the woman talks about her uterus, its meaning, the surgery, the course of the illness, and her recovery. The last stage is reconstruction, when the woman can begin to think about a new self-identity (Drummond and Field 1984, 264).

Drummond and Field state that it is important that the woman's family and friends accept her new identity. If her new identity is not validated by her significant others, then her chances of depression are greater. "Hysterectomy, to the woman who became depressed postoperatively, came to mean rejection from the social milieu in which she had previously functioned" (Drummond and Field 1984, 264). It must be noted that Drummond and Field state that at any time during this process of loss the woman can become depressed. After sixteen years, Martha is finally approaching the self-identity stage. For some, it can be a long process, maybe one that is never completely resolved.

Drummond and Field report that women who have traditionally defined themselves in terms of their childbearing potential, who have many children and no work outside the home, often have a more difficult time recovering from hysterectomy. Therefore it is important to discover how and with what diversity and satisfaction women form their identity. First it will be helpful to consider how the Judeo-Christian tradition has generally defined women and their roles, and then discover some ways women are recovering biblical images and stories in their renaming process.

## THE OBJECTIFICATION OF WOMAN

Julia Kristeva, a French feminist and psychoanalyst, offers an enlighten-
ing interpretation of women's function in the Judeo-Christian tradition. In
her writings, she analyzes the development of Judaism, a patriarchal and
monotheistic religion, over an earlier maternal, fertility-oriented religion.
She states that the negative consequences of monotheism for woman is
that she is reduced to the role of silent object (just as her womb is hidden/
silent object). She argues that in Christian ideology pregnancy is perceived
as a sign of woman's pleasure that must at all costs be controlled to ensure
the life of the community. Sexual promiscuity, she adds, has no place in a
community struggling for survival and order. Therefore the power/function
of procreation is subordinated to the rule of the Father.

Kristeva comments that women in the Bible are generally portrayed as
wife, daughter, or sister and they rarely are acknowledged by their names.
Woman's primary purpose is to preserve the race through procreation.
God is portrayed as generally only speaking to men, who are the keepers
of the law and the religion of the community. Women have no power or
voice in this realm. This is ironic, given the fact that women are intimately
connected with the Creator through procreation—their body and sex. It is
this connection that maintains the existence of the community and "man's
very dialogue with his God" (Kristeva 1986, 140).

Women have a precarious role in such a culture. Their ability to bear
children has to be valued but not to the point of anarchy/polytheism. If
woman discovers her power as pro "creator" and with it the experience of
bodily/sexual pleasures, then it would be impossible to "isolate the principle of One Law—the One, Sublimating, Transcendent Guarantor of the
ideal interests of the community" (Kristeva 1986, 141). Kristeva asserts
that monotheism was rooted in a will to create a community in the face of
the unfavorable circumstances of nomadic communities coming together
with different beliefs and political organizations. In such an environment
God acts as the unifying force in the community and helps ensure the survival of the group through the word/law. In such a system, women have no
access to this God, but they are perceived as the ones who embody desire,
desire to seize the word/law, to control God, to continue the species and
man's relation to God. If there is to be a unified community, women's
power as pro "creator" has to be controlled. Consequently, monotheism
represses the agrarian traditions and their ideologies rooted in the lives of
women and mothers (Kristeva 1986, 141–142).

Therefore sexual difference is made clear. Woman is separated from her
body and its pleasures and excluded from the Word, knowledge, and
power. If she is not wife, she is virgin and can atone for her desire for car-

nal pleasures through martyrdom. This separation is made manifest in patrilinear transmission of the name of the father to his children. In essence this symbolizes the order's refusal to recognize the growth of the child in the mother's body and with that the mother's desire for orgasm. Consequently, woman is treated as object, not as subject. She is to be wife and mother, and only if she is virgin (without sex), can she be "bearer" of the Word. We know her as the Virgin Mary.

In some theological circles the presumption of woman as silent object still exists. Martha commented that her pastor was not helpful during her recovery, instead he intensified her feelings of guilt. She said, "My pastor told me, 'Go till you drop.' I cried. I was angry and hurt that he didn't understand me and discounted my feelings. He also told me to trust in God. Then I felt like I wasn't a good Christian, because if I was, I would have been able to overcome this." She stated that her minister didn't see her as a person. "He acted as if women should be submissive to men." If Christianity cannot recognize woman as "subject," how can a pastor minister to a woman who is struggling with her own identity?

In the Hebrew Scriptures we find that God has the power to open and close wombs in judgment, in blessing, and in mystery. Phyllis Trible, an Old Testament scholar, comments in her book *God and the Rhetoric of Sexuality* that the wombs of women belonged to God. In the story of Sarah and Abraham (Genesis 20:1–18), when Abimelech takes Sarah into his harem, God acts to save Sarah by threatening the king and closing the wombs of the house of Abimelech. Later in Genesis 21, when Sarah is ninety years old with no children, God remembers her, opens her womb, and she gives birth to Isaac. We find in 1 Samuel 1:1–20 that Hannah is sad because "Yahweh had closed her womb." After she prays to God and enlists the support of the priest, Yahweh remembers her, and she conceives a son. Wombs were controlled by and under the power of the patriarchal, monotheistic God.

Similar thoughts were expressed with some of the women who were interviewed. Cindy, a thirty-two-year-old homemaker and former nurse who had her womb and ovaries removed, looked upon her hysterectomy as a blessing. She had prayed for God's direction in deciding whether to have another child. When she had to have a hysterectomy, she felt that this was an answer from God that two children were enough and that "He" did not want her to have another. She said, "l had an inner glow throughout my recovery because God gave me a direct answer. There was no second-guessing this one." She commented that her faith was strengthened because "God answered my prayers and protected me from evil and harm." For Cindy, God closed her womb as a blessing .

Diana, a twenty-eight-year-old nurse with one child and a stepson, felt that her hysterectomy was God's way of punishing her and changing her into the better person that she is now. She comments, "I don't know why God did it, but 'He' did it for a reason. I used to think it was because 'He' thought I was a bad mother, but now I don't blame myself anymore for what happened." Now, five years after her surgery, she says that her faith is probably stronger. She came to realize that she did not have to worry about "all these things" because God would take care of her burdens. For Diana, God was closing her womb in judgment. Both Cindy and Diana epitomize the idea that their bodies are controlled by a mythical man in heaven—a transcendent, hierarchical God. Although Cindy and Diana's faith in God's will for their wombs may have brought them a sense of resolve concerning their hysterectomies, I wonder how they can embody a positive and integrated sense of self with an image of a distant, male God that defines them as an object, a child bearer.

I believe a maternal image of comfort and connection to woman's body and the earth could offer women a better way to integrate their experience and sense of self with their life of faith. An image that conveys the sense that God is with them, blessing their bodies and comforting them through their pain, their questions, and their sense of loss can empower women to give voice to and to make sense out of their experiences. Such a holistic image can provide a way of integrating their faith stories with their lives instead of feeling alienated, guilty, and silenced by the incongruities between their image of God, themselves, and their life experiences.

## IN SEARCH OF MOTHER-GOD

Proper spiritual care for women includes being open to different images and stories that speak to women's experiences and that help to empower women to live out God's call for them in their lives. Phyllis Trible and Elisabeth Moltmann-Wendel recover some helpful images from the Bible, while Joseph Campbell offers an image of the Goddess.

In Trible's attempt to recover images of a Mother-God, she studied the word "womb" in Hebrew. The noun *rehem* means "womb" or "uterus" in its singular form. In the plural, *rahmim* expands its meaning to include compassion, mercy, and love. In essence, the womb is a way to compassion. "The womb protects and nourishes but does not possess and control" (Trible 1978, 33). Trible states that we can see glimpses of this God of the womb in the Hebrew Scriptures. "Yahweh merciful and gracious" appears throughout the Old Testament in a variety of forms and "belongs to recitals of the saving acts of God in history, acts freely given for individuals and corporate liberation (Psalms11:4; 145:8; Nehemiah 9:17)" (Trible 1978,

39). In Second Isaiah, Yahweh uses the image of the womb to express with what compassion and love God bears Israel.

> Hearken to me, O House of Jacob, all the remnant of the house of Israel, who have been borne by me from the womb, carried by me from the womb; even to your old age I am he, and to gray hairs I will carry you. I have made, and I will bear; I will carry and I will save. (Isaiah 46:3–4, RSV; altered by Trible 1978, 38)

These images bring us back to the earth, to the cycles of birth and death, to the goodness of our bodies and sexual pleasure, to a female image of God. In mythology she is known as the Goddess, the one who embodies everything. Joseph Campbell in *The Power of Myth* comments on the image of the Goddess: "She is time and space itself, and the mystery beyond her is beyond all pairs of opposites. So it isn't male and it isn't female. It neither is nor is not. But everything is within her, so that gods are her children. Everything you can think of, everything you can see, is a production of the Goddess" (Campbell and Moyers 1988, 167). The Goddess gives us a sense of flowing movement; she brings things into shape and creates. And each form that is created has its own intentions, its own possibilities that is sustained by the energy of the Goddess. In recovering this more maternal image of God, woman can begin to recover her body and her unique identity as subject. This recovery of God as Mother is not meant to usurp the traditional male image of God but rather an attempt to offer a more complete image of God. God is indeed beyond all opposites and therefore cannot be contained by any one image, including the image of God as Father.

There are plenty of stories and images in the Bible that women may look to for sustenance in their self-discovery process. Several of the five women interviewed mentioned the story of Ruth and Naomi as one that gave them strength. Naomi and Ruth's friendship and commitment to each other enabled them to stand up for themselves and prosper in a foreign land against enormous odds. They were strong, brave women who demonstrated love and trust for each other. It is also a story of a man, Boaz, who was able to love and appreciate the unique qualities of these women in a time when women were considered property. In other words, these two women modeled a different way of being; instead of being passive, they turned to each other for strength and fought to overcome their plight.

Another favorite Bible story is that of the woman with the issue of blood for twelve years (Mark 5:25–34). She approaches from the midst of the crowd around Jesus, grasps his garment and is healed. She was the active one, and Jesus passively felt his power go out from him. What a change in roles! This is a story of a woman who became empowered and who was healed from her powerlessness, that is, her role as silent other.

Theologian Elisabeth Moltmann-Wendel realizes that women have traditionally failed to realize their whole selves. Women tend to be viewed as passive, self-sacrificing mothers and wives. They have been taught that the mind is to be treasured over the body. Accordingly, Moltmann-Wendel's doctrine of justification—"I am good, I am whole, I am beautiful"—is a very liberating call for women. She is interested in helping persons claim their status as "children of God," which does not destroy the human self. She uses the parable of the Prodigal Son as her source for God's unconditional acceptance of "searching, immoral, doubting human beings" (Moltmann-Wendel 1986, 152). The prodigal son was one who accepted the inferior part of his self and returned to his father with nothing but trust. He was not only accepted but was deeply loved.

Moltmann-Wendel states that the expression "I am good" refers not to a moral quality but to our being, our existence which is legitimate and full of quality. So "I am good" means "I am good as I am. . . . I am made by God for pleasure, I am loved, freed. And it follows from this that I also act in this power of God, in the power of this goodness" (Moltmann-Wendel 1986, 155). Wholeness has three elements according to Moltmann-Wendel. These include (1) living from the senses, (2) accepting the allegedly inferior parts of our persons, and (3) integrating them and becoming "body"—rediscovering the earth and our nature. It means that we do not have to be perfect. Moltmann-Wendel comments on "I am Beautiful." "We need a fascinating, transforming, creative feeling of self, of being beautiful—over against all opinions and experiences which we encounter" (Moltmann-Wendel 1986, 161). She believes that if woman can find herself beautiful and turn self-hatred into self-love, then woman's perceived weaknesses can become her strengths.

One of the common threads with the women I interviewed was that the more self-esteem they possessed the less they struggled with their self-image after hysterectomy. Ann, a fifty-eight-year-old administrative secretary with five grown children, stated that she had an optimistic attitude about herself and life in general. "I'm not a worrier and I have a lot of faith." She defines herself as a wife and mother. "Even though I enjoy my job, my family is still number one in my life." She did not think that her hysterectomy changed her identity as a woman. Judy, a forty-nine-year-old minister with four adult children, echoed similar sentiments. She defined herself as a loving person filled with joy and peace. She felt complete and total as a woman. However, both women said that if they hadn't already had children, they would have reacted differently to having a hysterectomy.

Diana, who got divorced shortly after having her hysterectomy, said that she did not feel complete. After she had lost her procreative power, she felt awkward dating men. "I didn't feel like I had the ability that made you different from men." She was quick to share with her dates that she was unable to have children. When she remarried, it was to an older man who already had a family. She says she was intentional about marrying an older man because she did not want to feel guilty about not being able to provide him with children.

After being remarried she said, "I began to make the qualities I did have better." She became an aerobics instructor and often goes to the hairdresser and gets a manicure. She said she does little things for herself that make her feel more attractive and more "like a woman." She commented, "I even became a better nurse. I decided to put energy into my work and my hobbies." Now she says of herself, "I feel good about myself. If I don't like myself, no one else will. I have to depend on myself to find happiness. I just started realizing that this year." She describes herself as self-confident and independent. During the five years since her operation, she has progressed from her original feelings of being punished as a bad mother by God to a sense of being a more self-confident, whole woman. These women are beginning to name themselves, their own experiences, and are finding their own power in that process. They are turning their perceived weakness into a celebrated strength.

## LUSTY WOMEN

Helene Cixous, a French feminist scholar, has begun to question the assertion that woman's difference/identity is anatomical, that is, having or not having a phallus. She comments that this is a "voyeur's theory." She writes, "It is at the level of sexual pleasure in my opinion that the difference makes itself most clearly apparent in as far as woman's libidinal economy is neither identifiable by a man nor referable to the masculine economy" (Marks and de Courtivron 1981, 36). Cixous uses the French word *jouissance* to refer to woman's experience of orgasm as an intense, rapturous pleasure that is diffuse, long-lasting, and fluid. She believes woman's experience of sexual intercourse is one of a giving and dispensing of pleasure without concern for closure (Marks and de Courtivron 1981, 36). Some women who were interviewed expressed joy in having their hysterectomy because they could then enjoy sexual intercourse worry-free and without pain. It is this expression of women's sexual pleasure that has been suppressed for so long in our Judeo-Christian culture. Only recently has woman begun to claim herself as "lusty woman."

Mary Daly, a feminist philosopher, uses the word "lust" to refer to an intense longing or craving. A lusty woman embodies eagerness and enthusiasm. She is full of vitality and strives for abundance of her very being without imposed limits (Daly 1984, 3). Daly comments the following on her image of a "lusty woman."

The word "woman" Names the alienating archetype that freezes female be-ing, locking us into prisons of "forever feminine" roles. But when we wield words to dis-close the inner beauty, the radiance of the Race of Lusty Women, we/they blaze open pathways to our Background/homeland. Thus "woman," wisely wielded, Names a Wild and Lusty Female claiming wisdom, joy, and power as her own. (Daly 1984, 4)

For Daly, this new race of lusty women realizes that there is a great diversity among women when we reject man-made confinement. No two women have to be defined in the same way. There are many creative ways in which women experience themselves. Anatomy does not equal destiny anymore!

Carolyn G. Heilbrun, in her book *Writing a Woman's Life,* examines how women's lives have been shaped unconsciously without recognizing the process. She states that in the past women have seen marriage and child-bearing as their destiny without giving thought to any other options. If a woman didn't get married, she was looked upon as being an unfortunate lonely old maid who was never able to win the love of a man. It was virtually inconceivable to think that a woman would chose a single lifestyle and freedom from the responsibility of raising children. Heilbrun looks to women writers of the nineteenth and early-twentieth centuries who tried to break loose of their "destiny." Writers such as George Sand, who cross-dressed and was known as "a woman who was a great man," broke the sexual barrier. By Sand's very presence and writing she called into question the arbitrary roles assigned to men and women in society (Heilbrun 1988, 33–40). When women begin to break loose from their perceived destinies a new world full of creation awaits them.

## THEOLOGY OF THE WOMB

Clarissa Pinkola Estés, author of *Women Who Run with the Wolves,* calls this creative energy part of the wild woman archetype. She uses the word "wild" to refer to a natural life, lived with innate integrity and healthy boundaries. This wildish nature is part of every woman's instinctive psyche, and it animates and informs a woman's deepest life (Estés 1992, 10–11).

I prefer to think of this creative wildish nature as the Holy Spirit—the Spirit who fills us with joy and passion for life, who can be found deep within the center of our beings. This is our spiritual nurturing and birthing place, our spiritual womb, where vitality and creativity are nourished and valued. This is the source of our intuition, our inner voice who tells us when things just aren't right, and encourages us to voice and give shape to who we are and what we believe. This spiritual womb can be a source of strength and sustenance for women who have had hysterectomies. For it is the place where self-esteem and one's identity as God's good, beautiful, and whole sacred creation are birthed.

Rosemary Radford Ruether in her book *Women-Church* offers a liturgy for menopause. I think this liturgy can be adapted to help women who have had hysterectomies. It embodies the belief that everyone has creative and "birthing" energies that take on many forms. Women not only have the power to create eggs and nurture another human being to life in their womb, but they also have many other creative energies that are shared through a variety of gifts and talents—singing, dancing, writing, painting, drawing, thinking, teaching, gardening, cooking, sewing, loving and caring, to name only a few. A woman may have to let go of one kind of birthing energy—the ability to create other human beings, but when she does so, she can enter more fully into other kinds of "birthing" energies (Ruether 1986, 205).

God calls humans to a life of vitality. If we indeed are created in God's image and God continues to create, we are a part of God's creation process. We are not a "finished product"; rather, we continue to evolve—to learn and grow through experiences of all kinds which include times of loss and of fullness. When persons can embrace this call to a vital life they can begin to accept and even enjoy the sometimes gentle and sometimes not so gentle rhythms that are a part of God's creation.

As representatives of this spiritual womb—God's womb—where love and compassion are nurtured, ministers can begin to help the hysterectomy patient to discover her creative powers in a variety of ways. They can do this by embracing a theology that protects and nourishes but does not possess and control—a theology of the womb. I use this phrase as a way of reclaiming the image of a spiritual womb, a place or state of being where hope is born and possibilities are boundless. Ministers can begin by becoming aware of their own spiritual birthing place where their particular story meets God's call for love and compassion for all of humanity. One way to touch upon this place is to ask questions of themselves and to have the courage to answer them honestly. Some of these questions may include the following. How do I define woman: Is she silent object or active subject? How do I feel about hysterectomy? What does it represent to me? How comfortable am I discussing sexual issues? What are my strengths and limitations? When ministers realize how both men and women have been shaped and named by their religion and culture they can be freed to help others discover the person whom God is calling them to be.

The women I interviewed hoped that ministers would be more sensitive to the feelings of a woman after her hysterectomy. They want a pastor to be able to convey to the woman that she is a person, allowing her to be herself and listening to her full spectrum of emotions—anger, guilt, sadness, joy, pain, etc. This begins with admitting our limitations as a pastor. One pastor admitted that he was scared and that he did not know all the answers. This allowed the woman to experience her fear and embrace her feelings. Another minister listening to her parishioner's concerns and needs while in the hospital prayed that her parishioner would "pass gas" as a sign of healing. This was an acknowledgment of the woman's body and her connection to the earth. The woman responded with laughter and a sense of having been blessed.

Diana's advice to pastors is, "Sit and listen and do not make judgments. Do not tell them how they are supposed to feel. Listen to each individual situation and pick up on her particular needs." We need to remember as pastors that each woman responds differently to her hysterectomy. For some, it may mean death, but for others it may mean new life and renewed sexual pleasure. Some women's lives have been saved through hysterectomy because of the threat of cancer, and they are grateful for a second chance at life. Diana continued, "I didn't want to hear about the pastor's mother who had a hysterectomy. The pastor said from that experience he knew how I felt and coached me on how I should feel."

Traditionally the Judeo-Christian culture has defined woman as man's property, embodied desire, or child bearer. This definition has been stifling to women, especially those women who are stretching the bounds of their creative energies This "stretch" comes in many forms: entering male-dominated professions, struggling with issues of being a mother and working outside the home, choosing alternative lifestyles, recovering from addictions or abusive relationships, and healing from losses, including the effects of hysterectomy and mastectomy.

Pastors have an important role to play in the church if they are to take woman's needs seriously. Pastors can be catalysts to help women discover and embrace their many creative energies. There are many ways a minister can begin to do this: encourage the formation of women's support and discussion groups; help women recover images from the Bible that can empower them to embrace their unique identities; be open to hearing stories and images that may be foreign or uncomfortable to the traditional church; invite women to be leaders in services of worship, on boards and in committees; be intentional about including women's experiences in liturgy and sermon illustrations; incorporate an entire spectrum of images for God in their speech such as Holy Mother, Creator, Loving Parent, Shaddai, and Holy Mystery; be open to doubts and questioning and be willing to share their own doubts and fears; celebrate women's creative energies through special worship services and church programs created by women.

The church can take a positive, affirming role in a woman's self-discovery process. The church can help women discover their capacity not only to be bearers of young but also to be bearers of the Word, risking to answer God's call for them in unique and creative ways. Pastoral care for a woman begins with her birth and baptism into the church. It begins with her being included in all aspects of church life. It begins with the blessing of her feelings, her thoughts, her desires, and her dreams, as well as her body.

## BIBLIOGRAPHY

Campbell, Joseph, and Bill Moyers. 1988. *The Power of Myth.* New York: Doubleday & Co.

Daly, Mary. 1984. *Pure Lust: Elemental Feminist Philosophy.* Boston: Beacon Press.

Drummond, Jane, and Peggy-Anne Field. 1984. "Sequelae Following Hysterectomy." *Health Care for Women International* 5: 261–271.

Estés, Clarissa Pinkola. 1992. *Women Who Run with the Wolves: Myths and Stories of the Wild Woman Archetype.* New York: Ballantine Books.

Heilbrun, Carolyn G. 1988. *Writing a Woman's Life.* New York: W. W. Norton & Co.

Irigaray, Luce. 1985. *Speculum of the Other Woman.* Translated by Gillian C. Gill. Ithaca, N.Y.: Cornell University Press.

Kristeva, Julia. 1986. *A Kristeva Reader.* Edited by Toril Moi. New York: Columbia University Press.

Marks, Elaine, and Isabelle de Courtivron, eds. 1981. *New French Feminisms: An Anthology.* New York: Schocken Books.

Moltmann-Wendel, Elisabeth. 1986. *A Land Flowing with Milk and Honey: Perspectives on Feminist Theology.* New York: Crossroad.

Polivy, Janet. 1974. "Psychological Reactions to Hysterectomy: A Critical Review." *North American Journal of Obstetrics and Gynecology.* vol. 118, no. 3.

Ruether, Rosemary Radford. 1986. *Women-Church.* San Francisco: Harper & Row.

Strouse, Jean, ed. 1974. *Women and Analysis.* New York: Grossman Publishers.

Trible, Phyllis. 1978. *God and the Rhetoric of Sexuality.* Philadelphia: Fortress.

# 12

## Matters Close to the Heart: Pastoral Care to Mastectomy Patients

IRENE HENDERSON
*South Carolina Baptist Hospital, Columbia, South Carolina*

### INTRODUCTION

According to the American Cancer Society, one in nine women will be diagnosed with breast cancer during her lifetime. This means that all people ministering to women and families will find themselves dealing often with the myriad of physical, emotional, social, sexual, and spiritual dynamics that may accompany a diagnosis of breast cancer. The purpose of this chapter is to provide a basic overview of these issues surrounding breast cancer that will enhance a pastoral care approach to breast cancer patients and others affected by the disease. The primary resources for this chapter are women who have experienced breast cancer; some who have shared their story through their writing (see the bibliography at the end of this chapter), and others who have personally allowed me to be their chaplain at some point along their journey. My hope is that you will use the information collected from these women's stories, not as a recipe for how a woman should or must approach her experience with breast cancer, but as a background from which to understand and to minister.

While it is true that breast cancer can occur in men, this chapter will specifically address the phenomenon of breast cancer and breast surgery of women in keeping with the overall theme of pastoral care to women. While mastectomy is no longer the automatic or only option available to many women diagnosed with breast cancer, this chapter will deal primarily with the pastoral care concerns and dynamics involved in working with women who have lost one or both breasts from mastectomy.

Because of increased use of the lumpectomy, a surgical procedure that preserves as much of the woman's natural breast as possible, many women are now treated for breast cancer without having to cope with the complete loss of a breast. Even though this chapter will address mastectomy concerns more specifically, the diagnosis of breast cancer and the decision-making process that accompanies such a diagnosis make many of the issues discussed in this chapter applicable to lumpectomy patients as well.

## BACKGROUND OF THE AUTHOR

My interest and limited knowledge into the dynamics of breast cancer and breast loss stem primarily from my two and a half years as an Oncology Chaplain during my Supervisory Clinical Pastoral Education residency. Initially, I worked at Emory University Hospital's Winship Cancer Clinic as an outpatient chaplain to persons undergoing chemotherapy treatments for a variety of cancers. After frequently ministering to women who were undergoing chemotherapy treatment for breast cancer, I realized my purpose as a chaplain might be more effective if I visited with the women first while they were in the hospital for their mastectomy surgery, then followed them through their chemotherapy and subsequent follow-up visits. This shift in becoming more involved in their process was rewarding to me personally and provided a continuity of care and support that proved helpful to many of the women and their families.

I now no longer work directly with breast cancer patients with the same day-to-day regularity as before. Recently, I have been occasionally involved with a monthly breast cancer support group and also counsel female clients who are reconciling issues stemming from breast cancer and breast surgery. Although my primary pastoral responsibilities have shifted to clinical supervision, the previous daily encounters with breast cancer patients and their families provide the base from which this chapter is written.

## FACTS ABOUT BREAST CANCER DIAGNOSIS AND TREATMENT

Women facing breast cancer are often quickly introduced to a new language of medical terminology identifying procedures and physicians that represent the individual components of a larger treatment plan. Breast cancer and subsequent treatment are different for each woman, based on the size of the tumor and the stage of the cancer cells' infiltration into the woman's body. The following is a brief introduction to a simplified version of the routine procedure of diagnosing and treating breast cancer, explaining the different doctors and tests involved.

If a woman suspects or detects a lump in her breast, she should report it to her gynecologist or family practitioner. A lump in the breast is not an automatic indication of cancer; however, it should be taken seriously and checked out medically. If the lump is determined to be abnormal, the physician may order a mammogram for the woman, which is read by a radiologist to determine whether a biopsy of the lump is necessary. The biopsy may be performed by a radiologist (a stereotactic needle biopsy) or by a general surgeon (surgical biopsy). If the lump is determined to be malignant (cancerous), the surgeon and the medical oncologist help the patient determine whether a lumpectomy or a mastectomy is the best treatment in her situation. If reconstruction is to be done at the time of surgery or shortly afterward, a plastic surgeon joins the treatment team prior to the original surgery. Reconstruction is sometimes an option that may be added later in the treatment plan and is not necessarily a decision that has to be made at the initial diagnosis. The medical oncologist supervises any follow-up treatment, such as radiation or chemotherapy.[1]

## MYTHS, ATTITUDES AND ASSUMPTIONS ABOUT BREAST CANCER

One of the most frightening medical words a person can hear is the word "CANCER." A common myth about breast cancer, as with most cancers, is that the diagnosis is equivalent to a death sentence. The prevalence of this myth can affect the mind-set of the pastor being called to visit a newly diagnosed breast cancer patient in the same way it might affect the woman receiving the diagnosis. When people hear the words "breast cancer," their automatic response system kicks in based on their prior knowledge of the disease. A diagnosis of breast cancer is scary for anyone. However, if the person hearing the words has experienced the death of a family member or close friend to breast cancer, the news may be even more overwhelming.

Obtaining all the facts for each woman's particular situation is crucial for the patient, family member, and person offering pastoral care. An important pastoral care technique helpful in talking with breast cancer patients and families is to let them tell you their view of reality rather than assuming how they have heard or interpreted the diagnosis. This enables you, and the person, to discover the emotional meaning of the facts that may be unconsciously influencing how they are interpreting the data.

Even though a cancer diagnosis does not automatically mean death, there are still many women who die from breast cancer. According to the American Cancer Society facts, breast cancer is currently the leading cause of death of women between the ages of thirty-five and fifty-four. To deny the reality of death when working with a person terminally ill with breast cancer would be withholding pastoral support of "walking through the valley of the shadow of death" with her and with her family. This denial on the part of the pastoral caregiver might unknowingly facilitate offering of false hope instead of helping the woman and her family find the real hope that is possible only through being grounded in the reality of the situation.

As mind-boggling as these statistics can be, it is important to remember that breast cancer should no longer carry with it the automatic assumption of death. Increased awareness about breast cancer has successfully led to more educational opportunities regarding prevention of breast cancer, including changes in diet and lifestyle and early detection. Breast cancer detected in the early stages is considered as highly treatable. Early diagnosis and proper treatment of breast cancer increases a woman's chance of complete recovery and survival through a long and healthy life. A preventive pastoral care intervention includes using the educational component of the parish setting as a forum for breast health education awareness. Churches can sponsor classes on breast self-exam and invite physicians and breast health specialists to lead forums on symptoms and risk factors. Churches can be intentional about planning activities during October, which is national Breast Cancer Awareness Month.

Another myth about breast cancer treatment revolves around the age of the patient. A common, yet frequently erroneous assumption in working with women with breast cancer is that older women do not struggle with issues around body image and sexuality. I have experienced this many times in working with older women whose loss of breasts was oversimplified by their doctors and/or family because they were told "you don't *need* them anymore." For some women, this is true; however, when that happens, it is a truth that comes from within the woman's life experience and inner sense of wisdom about her individual situation, and not from what she is told or expected to feel. Some women personally reconcile their breast loss through a process of seeing losing a breast as being less destructive or invasive to their sense of self than perhaps another illness or surgery would be for them and their lifestyle. It is not uncommon for older women to report a sense of relief that for them it was "only" a breast and not something like eyesight which would more significantly impair their daily routine.

However, not all older women feel this immediate sense of relief when faced with losing a breast. Assumptions on how a woman will or should react based on age can cause the pastoral caregiver to miss many women in their pain. Many older women, like many younger women, consider losing a breast a very intimate and personal loss, one that requires a complex grieving process.

This prejudice based on age assumptions is too often the case when older women have to plead their case to be considered as a candidate for reconstructive surgery. One of my memories is working with June*, a seventy-year-old-woman, after her mastectomy. June was a retired nurse who wanted the option of reconstructive surgery but met resistance from her doctor, her husband, her adult children, and her sister. Each thought she should be thankful to be alive and not worry about losing a breast at her age.

With a growing sense of personal empowerment that is often one of the benefits women derive from their encounter with breast cancer, June continued to make her case. A year later, after winning her right to make the decision herself rather than have it arbitrarily made for her based on age, she chose not to have the surgery. By that time, June had grown used to her prosthesis (an artificial breast form worn under clothing) and was making peace with her new body image. She was also learning to value life through her newly awakened sense of empowerment and appreciation for life that came out of her struggle with breast cancer. As it turned out, the main issue for June had been the experience of being denied the opportunity to chose an option that might have been routinely offered to her if she had been younger. Once the option of reconstructive surgery was granted to her, June was able to study the material and assess the situation personally and professionally, enabling her to make a well thought out, informed, and very personal decision.

## COMMON ANXIETIES AND REACTIONS

One common phenomenon is that the diagnosis of breast cancer, whether terminal or not, catapults the woman and her loved ones into facing her and their mortality in ways that change her forever. Most women emerge from their experiences of facing breast cancer stronger and more self-assured than ever before. Before they get to that peak, however, they often go through intense valleys of confusing and painful experiences. Pastoral care to persons who are facing, treating, recovering, or dying from breast cancer includes patience and an awareness of the complexities of the normal grieving process. As in any grief situation, reconciliation takes time and takes place over a sporadic course which can be confusing to the woman and to her loved ones. Women who take chemotherapy after breast surgery often have their grief process intensified by the emotional reactions such as depression, mood swings, and fatigue that are common side effects to the drugs. The pastoral caregiver needs to take into consideration the impact of these side effects when working with breast cancer patients.

In her resourceful book *Spinning Straw into Gold*, psychotherapist Ronnie Kaye shares two lists that she compiled based on five years of working with breast cancer patients and from her experience as a breast cancer patient. The first list is Kaye's understanding of the issues that surround having breast cancer. These include death, body image, sexuality, differentness, communication, self-worth, recurrence, femininity, isolation, fatigue, treatment concerns, side effects and relationship problems (Kaye 1991, 17).

A prerequisite for offering effective pastoral care to women with breast cancer is for the minister to be able to *listen* to the woman as she wrestles with, and voices, her changing perspective on these very personal and complex issues without the minister needing to "fix" the situation for her. Parish pastors may want to include within their working file of interdisciplinary resources a counselor who specializes in breast cancer recovery or a qualified breast health specialist for making appropriate pastoral referrals for specialized care. The prevalence of breast cancer in our society and the sheer numbers of women affected by the disease can create a natural resource base in parishes in which breast cancer is made speakable. This provides the groundwork for potential support networks within the congregation when newly diagnosed breast cancer patients can be put in contact with members who have similar experiences.

The second list is what Kaye discovered to be the common feelings that may be part of a woman's response to breast cancer. These include fear, grief, depression, envy, powerlessness, vulnerability, guilt, betrayal, self-hate, anxiety, anger, sadness, loneliness, shame, and resentment (Kaye 1991, 17).

It is important for the pastoral caregiver to understand and bless these intense emotions as being normal. Quite often, the woman feels lost in the chaos of the many unknowns suddenly facing her, and wonders whether she is "crazy" or abnormal in her experiences and reactions. The pastoral care intervention of "normalizing" the woman's experiences for her by placing them in a larger, shared context can have the empowering effect of helping her move into, and subsequently through, the intensity and uncertainty. As Christian ministers, we have the example of the death, burial, and resurrection model of salvation (reconciliation) as a guide that undergirds our pastoral care and facilitates our invitation to the woman to move through the pain and emptiness as the pathway to reconciliation and resolution.

Women facing breast cancer are often women who have been socialized to be "pretty" or "nice," characteristics that are stereotypical of a woman's femininity in this culture. The emotions previously mentioned as "normal" reactions to breast cancer are in no way "pretty" or nice." For many of these women, coping with breast cancer gives permission to break free of the molds placed on them by society and/or family and accepted by themselves for whatever reasons. This concept of permission giving is often the catalyst for a powerful metamorphosis a woman with breast cancer may undergo over a period of time. Even though facing breast cancer is an enormous crisis that may shake all the foundations in a woman's life, she can possibly emerge more aware of her femininity and her personal power as a woman—with or without breasts. The challenge for pastoral caregivers is to equally attend to the woman's grief issues and support her transformation of self-empowerment and attitude that can take place only with time and hard work. This transformation may be symbolized by an awakened sense of spirituality that also emerges from the crisis of facing breast cancer and the life/death priority issues that accompany it.

Pastoral care to breast cancer patients involves being able to explore and listen to expressions of guilt and confessions of real or perceived mistakes the woman has made especially relating to her health and the care of her body. Too often, well-meaning pastoral caregivers want to help people talk themselves out of their guilt rather than talk themselves through their guilt. Some guilt stems from legitimate misdeeds from which forgiveness and healing can evolve when confession is encouraged and allowed. For example, a woman who ignored a lump that could have been treated differently if caught earlier has legitimate guilt to confess and reconcile within herself and with her God. Learning to face one's mistakes and regrets is an important part of the empowerment growth process.

There are other times when confessions are more about shame than about guilt. Confession is still good for the soul in cases of shame, not so much for forgiveness but for release from the binding effect that shame can have on a life. Lending an understanding and supportive pastoral ear to a woman's ponderings about the possible causes of her cancer can facilitate her facing and resolving deeply embedded shame issues. This can manifest itself, for example, when a woman who has been sexually abused, or was sexually promiscuous, develops breast cancer and wonders whether God is punishing her because of her "sins." Rather than moving too quickly into introducing her to a God image that doesn't punish through breast cancer, the pastoral caregiver can be more helpful to first stand with her while she voices her inner sense of wrongdoing. My experience is that most people who approach an illness wondering whether God is punishing them have some hidden reason that warrants punishment, at least in their mind, that is usually not too far under the surface waiting to be released. Having the opportunity to make the hidden transgression speakable in the company of a trusted pastor is often a key event in the transformation process.

Women facing a diagnosis of breast cancer may be overwhelmed and angry at all the important decisions and choices they are asked to make in what feels like a whirlwind of time. Breast cancer is one of those crises in life that is never planned and instead comes as an unexpected and untimely intrusion. All of a sudden, the woman's life is turned upside down, and instead of being able to process what is happening, she is suddenly faced with life-changing and life-threatening decisions about things she has never had to consider before.

In many situations, the woman wants to make wise decisions and be an active part of her treatment planning but finds herself in very unfamiliar territory that has a language all its own. At other times, a woman may be so overwhelmed that she is tempted to have someone else (usually a doctor or her spouse) make the decisions for her in an attempt to get it over with.

Many of the women to whom I ministered reported that in retrospect they regretted acting too quickly, mostly out of a sense of panic. Most health care experts agree that decisions needing to be made as a result of a diagnosis of breast cancer do not have to be made immediately. Instead, the decision-making process can wait long enough to allow second and third opinions, as well as to allow for consultations with other professionals to enable the woman to ask pertinent questions and therefore make informed and well-processed decisions.

One strategy that pastoral caregivers can offer women caught in the decision-making whirlwind is to help them slow down and find the stillness needed to think through what they are facing and feeling. This slowing down phase enables the woman to connect with the important persons in her life who may be trying unsuccessfully to offer her support. Another intervention is that of appropriate and informed referral. The minister should be knowledgeable of some of the resources available to women in this situation and refer them to information hot lines and breast health resource centers. Several of the books listed in the bibliography have suggested questions that women can use as a guide in knowing who and what to ask.[2] The books also list procedures for obtaining important information in a relatively short period of time. Several of the national cancer organizations have hot line or toll-free numbers for patients and family members to receive updated information on treatment decisions, current options, and referrals for second opinions. The listing of these numbers, as well as newsletters and pamphlets from reputable cancer organizations, should be a visible part of church libraries and resource centers.

The loss of a breast is often not the only physical loss accompanying breast surgery. Some chemotherapy treatments cause the woman to lose all or part of her hair as one of the temporary side effects of the powerful drugs taken to stop the cancer growth. It is common for women to report a sense of devastation and powerlessness as emotional reactions to the physical loss of hair. Many women initially grieve hair loss more than the loss of a breast because it is so exposed, whereas breast loss can be kept hidden at least from the public eye. Several women shared with me that it was easier for them to allow their husbands to see their scar from their breast surgery than it was for them to be seen without their wig. For some of these women, it is not until six or seven months later after their hair grows back that they begin to recognize and grieve the loss of their breast—

which, unlike their hair, will not grow back, unless they go through the added surgery of reconstruction.

Friends and loved ones are often caught without knowing what to say to a woman who has lost her breast. People who know how to respond to other losses withhold verbal support for fear of saying the "wrong" thing. For whatever reason, hair loss can elicit a more sympathetic response from others. The painful aspect of this phenomenon was illustrated to me in my encounter with Tammy*, a patient I met at the clinic when she was receiving her first chemotherapy treatment. Tammy had thick, luscious auburn hair. In my conversation with her, I asked her about her feelings concerning losing her hair. She said, "Well, the doctor said it would be the greatest loss to mankind [*sic*] if I lost my hair." Inwardly, I was angered by the doctor's choice of gender insensitivity in the use of language and thought to myself, What about the loss to womankind? Trying to contain my anger, I said to Tammy, "You do have pretty hair, and it's sad to think about your losing it. But I was just wondering . . . what did the doctor say in response to your losing your breast?" She looked at me with a startled look, then began to cry. Finally she said, "*Nobody* has ever said anything at all to me about losing my breast. You are the first person to even acknowledge that I may have lost something very important to me when they took off my breast." We continued our conversation, exploring ways she could have a "funeral" (her words) for her breast.

## THE SIGNIFICANCE OF BREASTS

Breasts are visible signs of womanhood that are simultaneously private and public. One does not have to look far into magazines or television advertisements to realize that we are a culture focused on women's breasts as important symbols of womanhood or femininity. From even before the onset of puberty and into mid-life and sometimes beyond, girls and women are measured by themselves and by others on their breast size. Awkwardness and embarrassment often accompany falling on either end of the development scale—the girls and women who develop late or who have very small breasts and the girls and women who develop very young or very fully.

Because of this emphasis on breasts as an indicator of femininity, women facing breast surgery often experience a loss of their sexuality and their womanhood. Sometimes, for women on either side of the development scale, their loss may paradoxically include a relief from a deeper sense of shame or embarrassment. They may also experience some underlying guilt stemming from the irrational fear that their lack of acceptance of their too large or too small breasts somehow contributed to their having breast cancer.

A story shared recently by a chaplain colleague poignantly illustrates the significance of breasts in gender identity that knows no age boundaries. This particular chaplain was visiting a woman who had had a radical mastectomy a few days prior to the visit. The two women exchanged general pleasantries for a little while, followed by a lull in conversation. The patient teared up and began to cry. After she regained her composure, the following conversation took place:

| | |
|---|---|
| Patient: | You know, I had my breast cut off. |
| Chaplain: | Yes, ma'am, I knew that. That is why I came to see you. |
| Patient: | I didn't think anyone would want to see me—I'm not a woman anymore. My pastor hasn't been to see me. I think he is just too embarrassed to see me like this—no breast and just not whole anymore. I can't blame him, though.[3] |

The woman in that visit was in her early eighties. For her, losing a breast meant being cut off from her own sense of womanhood as well as from significant relationships that supported her image as a woman in relationship to others—in this case her pastor. This scenario serves as a reminder to all ministers about the importance of making regular contact with breast cancer patients especially during the recuperation and adjustment period following surgery. Here the ministry of presence and the ministry of relationship validate a woman's sense of relational attractiveness at a time when her self-esteem and gender identity may have suffered a serious blow. Part of the strong pull into isolation that can accompany losing a breast comes in the days and weeks immediately after surgery when women are apprehensive about reentering life with an altered body image.

Just as a woman's particular personality and coping style are indicators of how she might uniquely react to breast cancer or to loss of a breast (Kneece 1993, 1), the meaning that a woman's breasts have for her (past, present, and future) is also very important in helping her understand and process her particular reaction to the loss, or threat of loss. One common error any pastoral care provider can make is to assume we know how a person feels or thinks about her illness or its ramifications in her life. This is also true with body image and, particular to this case, breasts as an important part of one's body image. Oftentimes, the woman may not understand what meaning her breasts have to herself and to her significant relationships; in addition, she may be experiencing intense feelings of loss that stem from unrealized sources within her identity as a woman. A pastoral care intervention may be to help the woman discover and articulate the meaning of her breasts and the meaning of the loss of one or both of them for her. In a society that disrespectfully refers to a woman's breast as a "boob," facilitating the personal awareness of the meaning of one's breasts may take time and involve reframing as well as the renaming of body parts.

Important pastoral care questions that facilitate discovery of meaning in working with a woman with breast cancer or breast loss include helping her to articulate what breasts mean to her: What have her breasts meant to her in the past? What have they meant to her in her relationships to others (especially with spouse/lover, children/ grandchildren, family, friends, God, and others)? How does she anticipate that those relationships will be affected by the loss of a breast? And what do her breasts—and loss of them—mean to her identity as woman? These meaning questions help uncover sources of loss that then need to be grieved as part of the reconciliation process.

As a woman minister who values the body as part of one's spirituality, ministering to breast cancer patients called forth in me the tension of helping women learn to value their bodies while also helping them to move beyond seeing their identity as a woman defined only by the presence or size of a particular body part, such as a breast. The paradox, both for the minister and for the woman, is to honor the loss of something very sacred (the breast) and recognize the grief that is a normal response to that loss, while at the same time moving toward an awareness of the holy that allows for and embraces imperfect bodies as also being sacred and sexual. It also involves redefining womanhood and femininity to be inclusive of loss.

## THE RELATIONAL ASPECT OF BREASTS

Because women find identity and value in their relationships with others, and because women are bodied persons in those relationships, the loss of a breast is very often a shared loss. In addition to breasts being an outward, physical, and sexual symbol of being female for the woman, they also have particular roles and functions for those in relationship with her. When a woman is facing and recovering from breast surgery, the memories of these various functions are often part of the grieving process for her and for the persons close to her.

An important role of the breast is being a sexual organ. Nerve endings in the breast and nipple can be important sources of sexual pleasure and stimulation for the woman and for her partner. Women facing a mastectomy, and their partners, usually have questions about sexual functioning and sexual attractiveness. Women wonder whether their partners will still find them desirable. This is also true for single women who wonder how and when to tell a new or potential partner about their breast surgery. Many of the books listed in the bibliography at the end of the chapter are written by women who have faced breast cancer and breast surgery. They deal candidly with the sexual component of losing a breast and describe the normal hesitancy inherent in accepting the newly altered body as being sexually desirable.

In sexual relationships, the loss of the breast is often a significant loss for the partner. Most partners can accept the changes very graciously with time but need permission and room to grieve their version of the loss. A partner may not know how or when to approach the woman about resuming sexual relations and may be hesitant as a way of attempting to show care and concern. The woman may interpret the hesitancy as rejection or as an indication that she is no longer sexually attractive. A pastoral intervention would be to encourage the couple to talk to, and listen to, the other as openly and honestly as possible. Referral to some of the books listed in the bibliography might be helpful. It might also be helpful to encourage the couple to become involved in a support group. Many cancer support groups routinely address the issue of sexuality and cancer and can be valuable resources for couples facing breast cancer as a shared experience.

Breast-feeding children is a relational and functional role of breasts for many women. For women who did not have children, losing a breast may involve facing any resurfacing or newly experienced regrets of what might have been. Part of the bittersweet ritual of letting go of her breast for mothers who breast-fed their children often include reawakened memories of the specialness of breasts in their identity as a nurturer-provider.

Because of the relational connection between women's breasts and significant relationships, the loss of a breast may evoke unresolved grief that comes as a surprise to the woman and to those close to her. Jaime* was a patient who introduced me to this connection between unresolved grief and breast loss. When I met Jaime in the hospital the day before her mastectomy, I expected to have a pastoral visit addressing the "normal" anxieties and fears that usually accompany such a situation. When I walked in and found her crying, I assumed she was crying about her upcoming surgery. Instead, I discovered a mother who was in deep grief over the death of her first child who had died at the age of two over twenty years prior to our meeting. The anticipated loss of her breast and the myriad of emotions surrounding it brought forth unresolved maternal feelings that gave her the courage to walk down the street and visit the children's hospital prior to checking in for her surgery the next day. As the story unfolded, I listened to a mother talk about going back for the very first time in twenty years to the place where her child had died. She had somehow managed to accomplish something that had haunted her for years. Mingled with the tears of sadness were also tears of tenderness and maternal bonding as she shared with me stories of remembering being with her child at the children's hospital and the events that led up to the death.

In the months that followed, Jaime used our relationship as a place to work through her unresolved grief and to begin to look more honestly at how it had affected her current relationships with her husband and remaining children. Instead of getting in the way of her grief work related to her mastectomy, her newly tapped sense of courage to face the difficult things in life enabled her to combine past and present losses while she did some intense grief work.

Seven months later, she reminded me of a female "Samson" whose return of strength was symbolized by the return of hair growth. As Jaime celebrated the slow but sure return of her hair following the end of her chemotherapy, her strength also began emerging in ways that signified the growth and integration that had taken place within her as a result of facing her losses. Jaime, like many women emerging on the other side of facing breast cancer, discovered that her breast cancer was an opportunity for making major changes in relationship patterns and in recognizing herself as a person with limits and worth. In facing the possibility of her own death, she had discovered the strength to finish facing her daughter's death. When I asked her how she understood her sense of timing (doing something so painful the day before surgery), she replied, "I realized I might not get another chance, and that I didn't want to run from it forever."

As in any pastoral care situation, it is important for the pastoral caregiver to assess her or his personal thoughts and feelings regarding body image and the significance of breasts to a woman's identity and function. This self-awareness increases the ability to work through one's own prejudices or stereotypes that may inadvertently prevent effective pastoral care. It also allows for a greater capacity of listening to the breast cancer patient or loved one talk openly and honestly about the way they find meaning and/or make sense of the situation.

## RITUAL AND BREAST LOSS

One function as ministers is to facilitate ritual as a way of discovering meaning in a situation. Women facing breast cancer often go through several rituals as they grieve and reconcile their loss. Some of these rituals are immensely private, such as the last shower they take before their surgery, looking at their breasts for the last time and saying "good-bye."[4] While we as pastoral caregivers will not participate personally in many of these sacred rituals, we can openly bless their existence and place in the grief process. We might also invite the woman to share them with us in the context of a trusted, well-established pastoral relationship or invite them to write prayers or poems that express the significance of the ritual.

Other rituals are more communal and involve participation from others.

One form of ritual that is ongoing is the support group. These groups may meet weekly or monthly, and they may be for women only, spouses only, or mixed. Support groups facilitate healing by offering a ritual of shared experiences—a meeting on common ground to question, explore, cry, rejoice, pray, socialize, and of course "support" all in the context of community.

## CONCLUSION

A diagnosis of breast cancer affects many lives. Pastoral care to breast cancer patients involves honoring the individual and private nature of the disease as well as the relational aspect of the illness. As stated earlier, pastoral care in these situations involves embracing grief and hope simultaneously as we embark on a pastoral relationship with a woman in transition. It also calls for us to use our prophetic voices to speak against the culture that elevates the significance of a woman's breasts to the point that they define her and her value to society rather than allowed to be but one part of this beautifully complex body, mind, and soul experience called womanhood.

## NOTES

* An asterisk after a name indicates that the name has been changed to protect confidentiality.

1. The concise form of this information is my summary of an interview of Isabel Law, R.N., Breast Health Patient Educator at Baptist Medical Center, Columbia, S.C.; quoted in "Physicians Present Update on Breast Cancer," *House Calls,* fall 1994 edition, a publication of Baptist Medical Center Public Relations Office.

2. Examples of this from books listed in the bibliography include Appendix E "Questions to Ask the Doctor at the Time of Diagnosis," in *Spinning Straw into Gold,* 210–214; and "Scripts: Questions to Ask Your Doctors," in *Women Talk about Breast Surgery,* 282–285.

3. Personal story shared by Rev. Elaine Greer, Chaplain for Women's and Children's Services, Baptist Medical Center, Columbia, S.C.

4. A poignant example of this ritual told in a woman's own voice is recorded by columnist and cancer spokesperson Erma Bombeck in *A Marriage Made in Heaven or Too Tired for an Affair,* 241–242.

## BIBLIOGRAPHY

American Cancer Society. *The Impact of Breast Cancer on Sexuality, Body Image and Intimate Relationships.* Publication #3496-PE.

————. *Sexuality and Cancer.* Publication # 4657-PS.

Bombeck, E. 1993. "After 60, It's Patch, Patch, Patch!" In *A Marriage Made in Heaven or Too Tired for an Affair,* 241–247. New York: Harper-Collins.

Dackman, L. 1990. *Up Front: Sex and the Post-Mastectomy Woman.* New York: Viking Penguin.

Greenberg, M. 1988. *Invisible Scars: A Guide to Coping with the Emotional Impact of Breast Cancer.* New York: Walker & Co.

Greer, A. 1994. "Physician's Present Update on Breast Cancer." *House Calls.* Columbia, S.C.: Baptist Medical Center Public Relations Office.

Gross, A., and D. Ito. 1990. *Women Talk about Breast Surgery: From Diagnosis to Recovery.* New York: Clarkson Potter Publishers.

Kahane, D. H. 1990. *No Less a Woman: Ten Women Shatter the Myth about Breast Cancer.* New York: Prentice Hall Press.

Kaye, R. 1991. *Spinning Straw into Gold: Your Emotional Recovery from Breast Cancer.* New York: Simon & Schuster.

Kneece, J. 1993. *Helping You Face Breast Cancer Treatment.* Columbia, S.C.: Publication of Women's Place, Baptist Medical Center Public Relations Department.

Mayer, M. 1993. *Examining Myself: One Woman's Story of Breast Cancer Treatment and Recovery.* Boston: Faber & Faber.

National Cancer Institute. *Mastectomy: A Treatment for Breast Cancer.* Publication #91-658, U.S. Department of Health and Human Services Public Health Service.

————. *What You Need to Know about Breast Cancer.* Publication # 93-1556.

————. *Facing Forward: A Guide for Cancer Survivors.* Publication # 90-2424.

Wadler, J. 1992. *My Breast: One Woman's Cancer Story.* New York: Addison-Wesley Publishing Co.

Winkler, W. A. 1976. *Post-Mastectomy: A Personal Guide to Physical and Emotional Recovery.* New York: Hawthorn Books.

## TELEPHONE HOTLINES

American Cancer Society National Information Hotline: 1-800-525-3777.

National Cancer Institute National Telephone Service: 1-800-4-CAN-CER.

Y-ME National Breast Cancer Information & Support: 1-800-221-2141.

# 13

## Daughters of Tamar: Pastoral Care for Survivors of Rape

S. AMELIA STINSON-WESLEY
*Founder of Response: A Religious Response
to Violence against Women and Children*

> . . . He [Amnon] took hold of her [Tamar], and said to her, "Come, lie with me, my sister." She answered him, "No, my brother, do not force me, for such a thing is not done in Israel; do not do anything so vile! As for me, where could I carry my shame? And as for you, you would be as one of the scoundrels in Israel. Now therefore, I beg you, speak to the king; for he will not withhold me from you." But he would not listen to her; and being stronger than she, he forced her and lay with her. (2 Samuel 13:11-14 NRSV)

Sexual assault and rape have been recorded since Old Testament times. Probably the most famous Old Testament story dealing with rape is 2 Samuel 13:1-22. How many people have either preached or heard a sermon based on that text? The church does not deal well with the concept of violence against women, particularly sexual assault or rape. Most congregants believe that only bad women are raped, while most pastors believe that no one in their congregation has ever been subjected to that kind of violence.

Incidents of sexual assault and rape are quite common. The statistics are overwhelming. The National Victim Center and the Crime Victims Research and Treatment Center estimate that one out of every eight adult women has been the victim of forcible rape sometime in her lifetime. Using U.S. Census estimates of the number of adult women, that means that 12.1 million American women have been the victims of forcible rape in their lifetime.[1]

Statistically speaking, pastors and counselors can assume that either we, ourselves, or someone we know has been victimized by sexual assault or rape. Victims and survivors[2] of violence are all around us—even if we don't know it about that person. Perhaps you have already counseled a survivor of sexual assault. Perhaps a colleague has shared such a counseling experience with you. Regardless, it is safe to assume that at some point most pastoral counselors will counsel someone who has experienced rape.

Providing pastoral care for those who have survived any type of violence is an exhausting and time-consuming task and should be done only by those who are knowledgeable about the topic and willing to become very involved with the survivor. Initial reactions and subsequent actions will greatly influence the survivor, her spirituality, and her sense of church, particularly if the pastoral counselor is the first contact the survivor has with any religious professional. Unfortunately, most seminaries offer little or no training on the subject of pastoral care with victims of violent crime in general. Usually if the topic of rape *is* addressed, it is hidden in a course specifically about women, making rape a woman's problem alone. In fact, rape and sexual assault are society's problem, and the church is not absolved from responding to that problem.

Merely citing statistics is not enough. Simply tracking the problem to know how often rape occurs is not enough. Providing adequate pastoral care for survivors of rape and sexual assault requires knowing the definitions and consequences of rape and sexual assault; what constitutes rape trauma syndrome; how to respond to survivors; and what spirituality crises arise when one has experienced such violence.

## WHAT IS RAPE?

Rape is defined as "any sexual act that is attempted or completed by force, threat of force or coercion against another person's will. "[3] Simply put, "if she says no, then it's rape!"[4] Rape can be attempted or completed against anyone. Age, race, education, geographic location, economic status, religious convictions, marital status, and gender are not factors in rape. Rape is the most common term used, but other words or phrases include "sexual assault or aggravation" and "forced sexual activity." Words and terms vary according to the legal statutes in each state. The term "sexual assault" will be used interchangeably with "rape" in this chapter. It is important to continue to use the term "rape" despite the fact that some people see it as a dirty or disgusting word. Rape is both a dirty and disgusting subject and should not be sugar-coated. It is also important to use the word "assault" which emphasizes the criminal aspect of rape. Sexual assault is a crime and should not be treated lightly simply because of the intimate nature of the violence.

Despite the fact that rape has been happening since before biblical times and numerous women have survived it, myths continue to surround rape. Many people see rape as sex. They think that men rape to relieve their sexual urges or that rape is sexually motivated. Rape is even sometimes viewed as "a lonely man's response to a lack of love."[5] In reality, rape is not sexually motivated; it is neither sex nor love. Rape is violence. It is about power and control, the use of the body in a violent and violating way. It is an expression of some men's need to dominate women.

Studies show that rape is a planned act of violence against a woman. Most rapists decide *to* rape before deciding *whom* to rape. Yet women are often blamed for rape by those who think that a woman asks to be raped by the way she dresses. Victims who believe this myth may wonder what they did to provoke the attack. They may feel guilty and distraught and may be afraid to report the attack. Some people also believe that women secretly desire to be raped and actually enjoy it. Just as no one wants to be robbed or murdered, no woman wants to be violated in that manner. Rape is not enjoyable; it is a horrible and terrifying experience for anyone.

Victims are also blamed by those who believe that a woman can prevent the rape if she really wants to. Almost all reported rapes involve threats of physical harm or the actual use of physical force. Women often submit to a rape to prevent more severe bodily injury or death. If we believe that any woman can prevent rape, then we can expect some victims to be brutalized for their resistance. Only the victim can know what amount of resistance is possible in each case.

Even when people believe that rape happens, they often minimize the extent to which it occurs and consequently do not believe women who have been raped. The FBI estimates that one in three women will be raped or sexually assaulted sometime in their lives. Rape is a crime affecting a huge number of people.

Unfortunately there also remains the racist myth of the "black rapist" who rapes white women. In the past, men of color who were accused of raping white women were often convicted without a trial. Some argue that there exists a racial prejudice in rape trials today, although it is difficult to prove. Actually most rapes occur intraracially, or between members of the same racial group, although some rapes are interracial, or between members of different races. In fact, over half of reported rapists are known by the victim. Another myth about rape is that all rapes are "stranger rapes," meaning that the victim does not know the assailant. Most rapists are known by their victims. Date rape, acquaintance rape, and marital rape occur more often than stranger rape.

By believing these myths, others may blame the victim for the rape or she may even blame herself. Dispelling the myths surrounding rape is vital to meeting the needs of rape victims and preventing further victimization of those already injured.

## RAPE TRAUMA SYNDROME

There is no prescribed way to react following a sexual assault or rape. Every woman has her own set of emotions and reactions. However, there are several stages that usually follow an assault. These stages are known as rape trauma syndrome. Rape trauma syndrome affects every person who has been raped or sexually assaulted. The effects may be extreme or not so extreme, but everyone who has been a victim of a sexual assault experiences some type of trauma. In some ways rape trauma syndrome is very similar to posttraumatic stress disorder. Posttraumatic stress disorder is often used to describe symptoms found in those who have been held hostage or those who have fought in a war or who were prisoners of war. The same set of symptoms often appear in women who have been raped.

There are two phases to rape trauma syndrome. The first one is the immediate or acute phase. The second is the long-term process of reorganization. Not all victims display all aspects of each phase, but they do experience both phases. No "textbook" example of how a rape victim reacts exists, because different people have various reactions to trauma.

The first phase of rape trauma syndrome is the immediate emotional reaction to rape. There may be expressed emotional reactions or controlled emotional reactions. If a victim expresses her emotions, she may display shock or disbelief initially, followed by anger, fear, and anxiety. The victim may cry or sob uncontrollably. If the victim's emotions are controlled, she is usually very calm, composed, even subdued and quiet. A victim may not display emotions in an attempt to control herself, her life, her surroundings. Rape takes away the sense of control over body and life, and the victim needs to regain control.

In the first hours following a rape, medical needs and safety needs are of primary concern. Injuries and the possibility of pregnancy, abortion, sexually transmitted diseases, and AIDS must be addressed. The victim needs to be told that the hospital will use a rape kit to collect evidence in case she decides to press charges. The use of a rape kit can be a very unpleasant and dehumanizing experience. Rape kits involve taking a complete medical history, pubic hair combings, pubic hair pulling, vaginal, oral, and/or rectal swabs and smears, a pelvic exam, anatomical drawings of bruises or other physical injuries, head hair pulling, saliva and blood samples, and the collection of all clothing worn at the time of the attack. The woman needs to have the procedure explained to her in detail because it may be seen as an invasive revictimization if she is not prepared for it. She also needs to know what additional medical procedures will take place. She may also need to shower and sleep. She may need to talk or be with someone she trusts. During this crisis time, the victim needs support and acceptance. She needs to be assured of her physical safety. She should be told that reporting the assault (if she chooses) is not the same thing as pressing charges. However, if she decides to press charges at a later date, having filed a report will increase the possibility of a conviction. She needs to be told of the law enforcement policies and legal procedures that are involved with sexual assaults. Any local rape crisis center will have this information.

During the days and weeks after the assault, underlying stress emerges. The victim is likely to be very anxious and may experience a number of fears. The fear of being alone is very common. She may be afraid of being with others, particularly those who remind her of the attacker in smell, dress, or sound. She may not want to be in the location of the attack or in places that remind her of the rape. She may have a difficult time trusting anyone. Remember that, temporarily, a victim's whole life is controlled by the experience of being assaulted. She is concentrating on simply coping. She may repeat tasks in order to make sure they were done. She may repeat details of the assault again and again. Doing these things is normal; assure her that her coping mechanisms are part of healing; she is not losing her mind. The victim may also feel guilty or ashamed that the rape happened to her. It is important to tell her that she is not to blame for the attack.

Some physical reactions usually occurring in rape trauma syndrome include:

- Physical pain, especially in areas of the body that received the brunt of the assailant's force such as throat, chest, arms, and legs
- Sleep patterns disturbed by wakefulness, insomnia
- Loss of appetite, stomach pains, nausea

Also in phase one, the victim may experience rapid mood swings and may feel anger out of proportion to situations (such as getting extremely angry over a wrong turn or a dropped lunch tray or something else that may seem minor to those around her). Victims may become easily irritated. They may try to block out all thoughts of rape from their minds. They may be unable to perform tasks from their regular routine. This may also include anything forced upon them or those around them (such as an agenda for a meeting or a work or school assignment).

Several weeks following the rape the victim may appear to be fine. She may look as if she is functioning normally and fully recovered. Then, somewhat suddenly, she may experience violent nightmares, recurring dreams, very intense feelings, and even relive the rape. These symptoms are part of the second phase, called reorganization. It is long-term and may take a lifetime to complete. It may never be complete. Rape is a devastating crime; victims need a great deal of support and time to heal. Many factors affect the speed and the effectiveness of the victim's recovery. These include the victim's personality, the amount of support available from her particular community of relatives and friends, of her church, and the attitudes of the officials and colleagues with whom she must deal after the rape.

These are four areas of long-term stress that may need attention:

- *Physical.* These symptoms include muscular and skeletal pain, sleep pattern disruption, and chronic gynecological and menstrual problems.
- *Psychological.* These symptoms include having violent dreams and nightmares, new phobias, or being overly suspicious and paranoid of other people.
- *Social.* Victims may return to work or school routines after the rape but may be unable to participate in other activities. They may be absent from or drop out of work or school. Victims may change residences or telephone numbers, especially if they were assaulted at home or knew their attacker.
- *Sexual.* Women may develop a fear of sex after rape, whether or not they were sexually active previously. Victims who are sexually inexperienced have no positive experience with which to compare it, and those who were sexually active may fear being intimate with their partner. A victim may be unable to engage in sexual activity. This inability is connected to being unable to trust anyone; it is not related to distrusting one's partner.

## PASTORAL CARE AND COUNSELING

Caring pastorally for those who have experienced sexualized violence is very focused. Although insomnia or depression or uncontrollable rage may be the presenting problem, entire psychological makeups are not the issue with rape survivors. The pastoral counselor should assume that the woman was functioning adequately before the rape. She is seeking help for the impact that a specific trauma has had on her life. The counseling is oriented toward a single issue, that of meeting the needs of a victim of a violent crime and empowering her to move beyond victimhood into survivorhood. It is not psychotherapy where one's childhood, relationships with others, life experiences, and other issues are discussed.

Carol Adams maintains that "three qualities of the pastoral counselor are essential when survivors disclose their experiences: the ability to process the information about the dehumanizing violence enacted by one person against another; the ability to provide practical assistance; and the ability to reflect theologically."[6] Any counselor must take an active role to enable the woman to make the transition from victim to survivor. Being active in a victim's recovery may involve helping her to the hospital or the police station and providing information about legal assistance if she so chooses.

Being active does *not* include making decisions on behalf of the woman or presenting her with limited options. Counselors can help her identify and sort out different options, their advantages and disadvantages, but only the victim should make decisions. Remember that the assault robbed her of much of the control she felt over her life. Making her own decisions about her body, her life, and her environment are ways to regain that control.

It is vital that a counselor believe the victim. If a victim perceives she is not being taken seriously at any point, her self-blame and guilt may increase. She may not receive the help she needs if her experiences are discounted or minimized. All disclosures of an experience of sexual assault deserve to be heard and believed.[7] Emphasize the fact that she *survived* the rape. Any rape victim has survived a violent crime and is, or has been, in a severe crisis.[8] Almost all survivors of sexual assault report thinking that they were going to die (be killed) during the attack. To face one's own death is indeed traumatizing, and to survive that kind of terror takes a great deal of strength. Enabling her to see that she used her resources to live through such a harrowing experience is an empowering step toward recovery.

Simply listening to her story is a way of restoring some of that control that was taken from her. Some counselors tend to refrain from reacting at all when listening to parishioners. Others use reflective listening skills, or active listening, when a person is sharing her story. These listening techniques, although they have their place in counseling, are not helpful when working with rape survivors. If a counselor just repeats or rephrases what she or he hears, the counselor may be perceived as reinforcing the victim's feelings of guilt or of self-blame. Exploring ways she could have avoided the rape is also not helpful because she will continue to think she could have prevented the assault, which is another way of blaming herself. Reassure the woman that she was not at fault for the rape. Assist her in turning her feelings of self-blame, guilt, and powerlessness into control over her life again.

One caution regarding listening. Do not ask too many specific questions related to the attack unless the victim freely shares that experience. As Jane Boyajian states, "Hearing too much can magnify the power we have over her [the victim]. . . . We enhance our own power by hearing another's secrets."[9] It is important to let the victim know that she is believed and she will be helped without having to share every detail of her horror. However, if she needs to share a detailed experience, react in such a way that does not convey shock or being overwhelmed. Reactions are important because pastors and pastoral counselors may be representing the church's reaction to the victim. If she thinks that her congregation or faith community will be too horrified by her experience, she may never reach out and receive the love and support of that community. Do express sorrow and outrage that such a tragedy has happened to her.

All counseling and pastoral care relationships are filled with a power imbalance. When someone is in need of care and counseling, that person is less powerful than the one from whom help is sought. When counseling someone who has experienced the complete loss of power that rape brings, remember that the counselor's role is as much about restoring power and control to the victim as anything else. Giving the victim as much say as possible about what happens within the counseling relationship is a good way of sharing the power that a caregiver possesses.

The concept of power must also be reconstructed. Power "over" someone or being able to "get" power are inappropriate ways of thinking about power. Power must not be taken *from* one and *given* to another as if there is a set amount to be dispersed. Rather, power should be something to which all have access. This relational power is particularly important when counseling those who have been raped and had all power taken from them. Touch is related to power, particularly in relation to those whose power has been stripped by the touch of another. It is crucial to remember that a counselor placing a hand on the victim's shoulder or on top of the victim's hand is perceived as "power over" by the victim, especially if the counselor is male.[10] Never insist on touch of any kind.

The myths that surround rape have an impact upon victims. Victims may believe myths about rape or may be affected by others who believe the myths. The counselor is responsible for being knowledgeable and well informed about the facts concerning rape and sexual assault. Dispel myths with accurate information so that the victim has a realistic understanding of her experience. Also, educate congregations and faith communities about rape and sexual assault before even being confronted with a survivor. Informed and knowledgeable members of her community are often the best support a victim can have, but only with the victim's consent should anyone be told of her experience.

Offer her comfort. Recognize her pain. Hear her suffering. In short, care for her. Give her warmth in whatever way she can receive it. Through tone of voice, body language, words, and even touch (if she requests it), share kindness and show compassion for the woman. Be available for her. As anyone who works in crisis counseling knows, crises do not always come at convenient moments. Being available shows you care.

Safety is a major concern for survivors. Ask whether she feels safe—in a counselor's office, in her home, in her car, at church, in the mall, at work or school, alone, in crowds. Ask what should happen for her to feel safe. Help her attain as much security as possible.

Empowering someone who has lost a significant amount of power is not easy. It is important to affirm that person. Concentrate on the positive. This may be easier to do if you already know this person, perhaps if she is in your congregation. If you do not already have a relationship, encourage her to remember positive things about herself. Realize that it may be very difficult for her to see anything positive about any aspect of her life, especially the first few weeks following the rape. Continue to ask her questions, particularly about what would make her feel more comfortable or what needs she has.

Encourage her to vent any anger she may have about the attack. It may be directed at the perpetrator, but she may also be angry with those who surround her daily, her friends or family, or even those who are trying to help her. Anger is very empowering. Rage can be healing and comforting. It can also be scary, since women are usually socialized to refrain from expressing anger. Reassure her that anger is very normal and is healthy.

When counseling a rape survivor, remember the stages of rape trauma syndrome. She may feel as though she is going crazy or is losing her mind, particularly since the emotions associated with surviving rape are so intense. Reassure her that she is experiencing normal reactions to a trauma. Allow her to ask questions and provide her with accurate information, especially regarding medical and legal issues. Also remember that, as with any trauma, reactions may include an impulse to commit suicide or to entertain suicidal thoughts. Be prepared to deal honestly and openly about this possible reaction.

At any point during contact with a survivor of sexual assault, it is always appropriate to suggest calling a rape crisis center. It is not feasible to expect that one person can provide all different types of assistance a rape survivor will need. In fact, pastoral counseling may be inadequate for the victim. Use a local crisis center for referrals. If the community does not have a rape crisis center, check the local domestic violence shelter (shelters often cover both populations). Consider also calling the National Coalition Against Sexual Assault or the National Coalition Against Domestic Violence, whose addresses are listed at the end of this chapter, for information on a crisis center near you. Also, if you are in a counseling relationship with a survivor of violence, use the crisis center for yourself. Most centers will recognize you as a "secondary," and there may be a support group or advocate who would be willing to talk to you about your feelings, thoughts, and ideas. It is important to know that once you begin working with a survivor of sexual assault, it can dominate your view of the world for a while. You may even experience some of the symptoms of rape trauma syndrome to a certain degree. It is a good idea to find a safe and affirming place for you to express your own emotions about the work you are doing.

The transformation from victim to survivor is a long process. It usually takes years. Recovery from a criminal assault must take place at the woman's pace. Respect her timetable and do not impose your own schedule for healing. Realize that recovery and healing are not the same for each woman. Recovery is not moving beyond the experience but rather integrating it into one's life. After rape the victim will always see the world through the eyes of a survivor of sexual violence. She has changed. She has experienced a loss, the loss of the woman she was before the rape. It is appropriate and often helpful to mourn the loss of the person whom she lost.

## SPIRITUALITY ISSUES

Mourning a loss is one of the best ways to begin discussing spiritual issues related to surviving violence. Although no survivor's experience is exactly like that of another, most women do have a tremendous sense of loss: of safety, of control, of their lives to a certain degree, of their bodies, of hope. There may be a loss of friends who cannot handle the fact that she was raped. She may lose relationships because of the rape. She may be shunned, disbelieved, or blamed. She may lose her husband or boyfriend or partner because of the rape and the chaos it brings to her life. She may lose her innocence, her trust, her belief in a loving and protective God. Recognize whatever loss she has experienced.

Remember that the survivor probably thought she was going to die during the assault. As Mary Pellauer states, "Death is a religious issue."[11] If one's life has been threatened, one has confronted death. Therefore one must face religious issues that result from that experience. Any survivor who has faced her own death will never be the same and will never view the world the same again. She has realized her own mortality in a way many people never have. She has a very different experience of the world now.

Survivors also have a number of very difficult questions such as:

Why me?
Was it my fault?
Was God testing me?
Was God punishing me?
Was God strengthening me?
Why did God let this happen to me?
Does God still love me?
Can God forgive me for this? (Evidence of self-blame on the part of the survivor)
Why is there suffering?
Where was God?

As Carol Adams says, "If she feels abandoned by God we need to ask,

'What kind of God do you feel has abandoned you?' Before her images of God are refuted, she must have the space to describe just how she has experienced God during her victimization. Feelings such as betrayal and anger at God are legitimate and should not be short-circuited by attempting to substitute a benign and loving God for the punishing or absent God she has experienced."[12] Give her the freedom to express her doubt of God's presence, but reassure her that God continues to love her. It is normal and healthy to be angry with God. Give her permission to be angry with God and to express that anger. Remind her that God can handle her anger and rage.

Marie Fortune relates the story of a young woman who realized that her prayers changed after she was raped. Her prayer "Dear God, take care of me" became the prayer "Dear God, please help me remember what I have learned." Fortune accurately states that the woman "had moved from a passive, immature relationship with God, in which she expected God to protect her, to a more mature, assertive relationship in which she recognized her own strength and responsibility to care for herself with God's help."[13] Reassure the survivor that God suffers with the children of God. God does not promise to provide protection from all evil and violence, but God does promise to be a creative partner with us. Remember that God does not promise a life without pain, but God does promise a partnership through pain and suffering.[14]

Prior to the rape she may have believed that those who are good are rewarded and those who are bad are punished. If she perceives herself as basically good, that belief is now shattered. If she perceives herself as basically bad, she furthers her self-blame. Enable her to redefine her ideas about human nature. Talk to her about God as an interactive, loving presence, not a cause or effect.

Do not encourage her to forgive and forget. Forgiveness is an issue over which only the survivor should have control. She knows if and how she will forgive. Do not impose an external standard or schedule for her forgiveness. Do not impose the idea that she must forgive in order to be healed. Forgiveness may be necessary for the healing of some survivors; it may not be essential for the healing of others.

The survivor may need forgiveness, not for the attack, but for blaming herself for the attack. Offer her forgiveness for self-blame and encourage her to forgive herself as well.

Creating a service of healing is often helpful for the transition from victim into survivor. Any healing service should certainly have an aspect of mourning or loss or lament in it. Healing services may also include a cleansing, a time for anger, or an empowering action or speech. Healing services can be any ritual act or intentional time of remembering and honoring her experience, her pain and survival. Suggesting a healing service is a delicate matter. Be careful not to insist upon anything or any form. Let the survivor decide whether and when and how any ritualized form of healing will take place. Offer resources such as prayers, litanies, and songs related to the surviving of violence. Help her plan, but do not create the entire service without her contribution.

Spirituality issues for survivors of violent crimes such as rape and sexual assault often remain unresolved even after years of thought and processing. Giving the time and space necessary for healing is essential in enabling a woman to move from victim to survivor.

## CARING FOR SECONDARY VICTIMS

Survivors of an assault need the assistance of many professionals, including rape crisis advocates, psychologists, the police, lawyers, and doctors. However, pastors and pastoral counselors are usually the only resources available for the persons who live with or love the victim. Secondary victims (parents, siblings, other relatives, lovers, partners, spouses, children, co-workers, or other friends) also need support during this crisis. A pastor or pastoral counselor should take the time to check on those persons who are close to the victim and who know that she was raped (be sure that you first ask the victim if that is acceptable to her). Do not assume the responsibility of informing these people of the assault. However, help the victim decide whether she wants to share her trauma, when and with whom she will share it, and how she wishes to continue.

If secondary victims already know about the rape, they may want information such as the legal process for prosecuting a rape in the state in which it occurred or the components of rape trauma syndrome and what reactions and emotions to expect from the victim. Provide that information if needed.

Secondaries, as they are called, often have their own issues related to the assault. Male secondaries (fathers, boyfriends, spouses, and brothers) usually react in one of two ways to hearing about the assault. These reactions fall into the categories of "traditional" and "modern."[15] The "traditional" reaction of some men is that they act as though *they* have been injured because "their" woman lost value as a result of the rape. These men view a woman as their property, and anything that happens to her is an affront to them. They then blame the victim for their loss. They may feel betrayed, ashamed, or repulsed by the woman. The "modern" reaction is that a woman is injured in her own right. The men feel concern for woman's welfare. In either case, men need to have a safe place to discuss their own feelings and emotions following the rape of someone they love.

One of the most common impulses a male close to a survivor of rape will have is that of wanting to kill the rapist. These men wish to match violence with violence. Usually the last thing the survivor wants is more violence, and if her partner or father gets angry and goes to look for the assailant, then she feels as though she is to blame for further violence. This reaction also places an additional hardship on the survivor who feels she must be the one to prevent more violence.

Most parents, particularly fathers, feel guilt for not protecting the woman. They may feel as if they have let their little girl down. These feelings are normal. However, it is important for parents to realize that they cannot always protect their children from evil. It is also important for parents to remember that continuing to view their daughter as a little girl further disempowers her and impedes her recovery. She needs to concentrate on the strength she has, not be told that she is a child or powerless.

Daniel Silverman does an excellent job of listing some of the responses of male partners. He states that besides the possibility that he may think his "property" was damaged, the male partner may share a sense of devaluation and shame. He may believe some of the myths about rape and be angry at the survivor because he thinks she could have prevented it if she wished. He may wonder whether she enjoyed it, or he may feel sexually inadequate. [16] The counselor must educate the partners and friends and family of the victim. They need to know the facts, not the myths, surrounding sexual assault. It will also be helpful to identify for them the symptoms of rape trauma syndrome. You can let those around the survivor know how she may react to this crisis. Encourage emotional reactions and the open sharing of feelings on the part of family and friends. Offer direct counseling for the secondary victims as well.

Reactions of female secondaries (mothers, sisters, friends, and partners) may be similar to reactions of male secondaries. All persons close to a victim may experience intense emotional, even physical reactions.

Family members may also feel shock, numbness, a sense of lost power or helplessness, anger, or shame. They may even develop the fears associated with rape trauma syndrome. Some friends and family will be able to be supportive. Others may distance themselves from the survivor. Some family members or friends may minimize the attack or try to keep the rape a secret in order to protect themselves from dealing with the horror; others will respond with true compassion. Some may distract the woman to keep her from discussing the rape. Some may abandon the woman because they do not know how to react to her now. Counselors must help the survivor's support system understand that keeping the rape a secret will add to her sense of shame, self-blame, and guilt.

It is vital that the survivor feel she can trust the persons around her.

Enable her partner, her family, her church community, and her friends to understand exactly what has happened and how they can offer the most support to her. Be available to meet their needs so they do not rely on the survivor to take care of them.

The Church has long ignored the issue of violence against women. (When was the last time you heard a sermon preached on the text that began this chapter?) Offering pastoral care and counseling for survivors of sexual assault and rape is one step the Church can take toward recognizing the pain and suffering of women who have been violated. Only when those in the Church begin to meet the needs of those who have suffered sexual assault can true healing take place.

## CRISIS GUIDELINES

If someone you know is raped:

Ask first, "Are you in a safe place?" If not, help her make arrangements to get to safety.
Help her organize her thoughts, but let her make decisions about how to proceed.
Encourage her to preserve evidence.
Take her to a hospital.
Encourage her to report the crime to the police and take her to the station.
Call the rape crisis center.
Help her get psychological and legal help.

If you are raped:

Go to a safe place.
Do not shower, bathe, or douche.
Save all clothing and personal items from the time of the assault.
Do not disturb anything at the site of the assault.
Go to a hospital emergency department for medical assistance and evidence collection.
Report the assault to the police.
    (Reporting is not prosecuting and you can decide later what you
    wish to do)
Call your local rape crisis center.
    (Look under crisis counseling or even domestic violence in the
    phone book)
Get counseling.

Take the necessary time to heal.
Talk with other women.

If you have been raped, remember, rape or sexual assault is not your fault, no matter what you were doing or wearing, no matter who you were with or where you were going. It can happen to anyone, anytime, anyplace. If you have been sexually assaulted, know that you are not alone. Sexual abuse or assault happens to one in three women during their lifetimes.

Please seek help. Trained counselors and advocates are available to help you through this crisis. If you cannot locate your local rape crisis center, contact one of the national offices:

> National Coalition Against Sexual Assault:
> 912 North Second Street
> Harrisburg, PA 17102-3119
> Phone: (717) 232-7560

> National Coalition against Domestic Violence:
> PO Box 18749
> Denver, CO 80218-00749
> Phone: (303) 839-1852

## Notes

1. *Rape in America: A Report to the Nation* (National Victim Center and Crime Victims Research and Treatment Center, 1992).

2. Those who have experienced rape or sexual assault are often called both victims and survivors. In many ways both labels are correct. They *have been* victimized, but they *did* survive. Recovery is a process in which victims can move toward seeing themselves as survivors.

3. Kathryn M. Johnson, *If You Are Raped*, 2. It should be noted that men, as well as women, are and have been raped. In fact, male rape is even more underreported than female rape. However, in view of the title of this book and the subject matter it covers, the language used in this chapter will reflect the vast majority of rape scenarios which involve a male perpetrator and a female victim.

4. Originally a syndicated column by Ellen Goodman, now chap. 3 in Pellauer, *Sexual Assault and Abuse*.

5. Johnson, *If You Are Raped*, 13. Case in point: In Chattanooga, Tennessee, criminal court judge Doug Meyer suggested that a man charged with raping a local woman and forcing her daughter to watch only needed a girlfriend. The judge even offered to arrange a dating service for the suspect. Later, Judge Meyer admitted he made a mistake. In *Ms.* May/June 1994, 94.

6. Carol J. Adams, "'I just raped my wife!'" 79.

7. Only 2 percent of reported rapes are false reports, which is the same percentage as other felonies. Statistically you will be dealing with a true report, and it is important to treat it as truthful.

8. More than likely you, as a pastor or pastoral counselor, will not be the initial contact a rape victim makes following an attack. If you are, however, follow the crisis counseling guidelines outlined at the end of this chapter.

9. Jane Boyajian, "Standing By Victims of Sexual Violence," 118.

10. Ibid.

11. Mary Pellauer, "A Theological Perspective on Sexual Assault," 86.

12. Adams, "'I just raped my wife!'" 81.

13. Marie Fortune, *Sexual Violence*, 199.

14. Linda Braswell, *Quest for Respect*, 57.

15. Lynda Lytle Holmstrom and Ann Wolbert Burgess, "Rape: The Husband's and Boyfriend's Initial Reactions." *The Family Coordinator*, July 1979 (a), 321–330, as discussed in Judith H. Katz, *No Fairy Godmothers, No Magic Wands: The Healing Process after Rape*, 88–89.

16. Daniel Silverman, "Sharing the Crisis of Rape: Counseling the Mates and Families of Victims," in Pellauer, et. al., *Sexual Assault and Abuse*, 141–144.

## INTERNET RESOURCES

The Survivor's Page is dedicated to survivors of sexual assault and abuse:
   http://Cam043212.studen.utwente.nl/
Sexual Assault Information Page contains the most complete set of web
   links: http://www.es.utk.edu/~bartley/saInfoPage.html
Domestic Violence Hotline Resource List contains all of the 24-hr crisis
   phone numbers in the United States and lists them by state:
   http://www.feminist.org/911/crisis.html
Domestic Violence Information Center provides general information:
   http://www.feminist.org/other/dv/dvhome.html
Internet Resources lists all sites related to domestic violence:
   http://www.feminist.org/other/dv/dvinter.html
Abuse Resources contains websites and email lists:
   http://www.crl.com/www/users/th/thefly/abuse.html

## BIBLIOGRAPHY

Adams, Carol J. 1993. "'I just raped my wife! What are you going to do about it, Pastor?' The Church and Sexual Violence." In *Transforming a*

*Rape Culture,* edited by Emilie Buchwald; Pamela R. Fletcher; and Martha Roth. Minneapolis, Minn.: Milkweed Editions.

Boyajian, Jane. 1987. "Standing By Victims of Sexual Violence: Pastoral Issues." In Pellauer, Chester, and Boyajian, eds.

Braswell, Linda. 1989. *Quest for Respect: A Healing Guide for Survivors of Rape.* Edited by Eugene D. Wheeler. Ventura, Calif.: Pathfinder Publishing.

Fortune, Marie M. 1983. *Sexual Violence:The Unmentionable Sin.* New York: Pilgrim Press.

Johnson, Kathryn. 1985. *If You Are Raped: What Every Woman Needs to Know.* Holmes Beach, Fla.: Learning Publications.

Katz, Judith H. 1984. *No Fairy Godmothers, No Magic Wands:The Healing Process after Rape.* Saratoga, Calif.: R & E Publishers.

Koss, Mary P., and Mary R. Harvey. 1991. *The Rape Victim: Clinical and Community Interventions.* Newbury Park, Calif.: Sage Publications.

Pellauer, Mary. 1987. "A Theological Perspective on Sexual Assault." In Pellauer, Chester, and Boyajian, eds.

Servaty, Chris. 1987. "Support Counseling with Victims of Sexual Assault." In Pellauer, Chester, and Boyajian, eds.

Silverman, Daniel. 1987. "Sharing the Crisis of Rape: Counseling the Mates and Families of Victims." In Pellauer, Chester, and Boyajian, eds.

Warshaw, Robin. 1988. *I Never Called It Rape:The Ms. Report on Recognizing, Fighting, and Surviving Date and Acquaintance Rape.* New York: Harper & Row, Harper Perennial.

Wiggen, Cooper. 1987. "The Male Minister and the Female Victim." In Pellauer, Chester, and Boyajian, eds.

Wilson-Kastner, Patricia. 1987. "Theological Perspectives on Sexual Assault." In Pellauer, Chester, and Boyajian, eds.

### Other Suggested Reading

Blumenthal, David R. 1993. *Facing the Abusing God: A Theology of Protest.* Louisville, Ky.: Westminster/John Knox Press.

Brown, Joanne Carlson, and Carole R. Bohn, eds. 1989. *Christianity, Patriarchy, and Abuse: A Feminist Critique.* Pilgrim Press. 1989.

Horton, Anne, and Judith A. Williamson, eds. 1988. *Abuse and Religion: When Praying Isn't Enough.* Lexington, Mass.: Lexington Books.

Schüssler Fiorenza, Elisabeth, and Mary Shawn Copeland. 1994. *Violence against Women.* Concilium.

Trible, Phyllis. 1984. *Texts of Terror: Literary-Feminist Readings of Biblical Narratives.* Philadelphia: Fortress Press.

## General Bibliography

Adams, Caren; Jennifer Fay; and Jan Loreen-Martin. 1984. *No Is Not Enough: Helping Teenagers Avoid Sexual Assault.* San Luis Obispo, Calif.: Impact Publishers.

Apsler, R., and Ellen Bassuk. 1983. "Are There Sex Biases in Rape Counseling?" *American Journal of Psychiatry* 140 (March 1983): 305–308.

Bateman, Py. 1982. *Acquaintance Rape: Awareness and Prevention for Teenagers.* Alternatives for Fear.

Elwood, Douglas, and Bruce Larson. 1981. *Same Sex Assault: A Handbook for Intervention Training.* Minneapolis: Park Ave. Clinical Services, Minneapolis Program for Victims of Sexual Assault.

Finkelhor, David, and Kersti Yllo. 1985. *License to Rape: Sexual Abuse of Wives.* New York: Holt, Rinehart & Winston.

Fortune, Marie M. 1984. *Sexual Abuse Prevention: A Study for Teenagers.* New York: United Church Press.

Frieze, Irene H. 1983. "Investigating the Causes and Consequences of Marital Rape." *Signs* 8 (spring 1983): 532–553.

Gager, Nancy, and Kathleen Schurr. 1974. *Against Rape: A Survival Manual for Women.* New York: Farrar, Straus & Giroux.

Glass, Lola, and Janet Yassen. 1984. "Sexual Assault Survivors Groups: A Feminist Practice Perspective." *Social Work,* May-June.

Heggen, Carolyn Holderread. 1993. *Sexual Abuse in Christian Homes and Churches.* Scottdale, Pa.: Herald Press.

Ledray, Linda. 1986. *Recovering from Rape.* New York: Henry Holt.

Levy, Barrie, ed. 1991. *Dating Violence: Young Women in Danger.* Seattle: Seal Press.

McCombie, Sharon L., ed., 1980. *Rape Crisis Intervention Handbook: A Guide for Victim Care.* New York: Plenum Press.

McEvoy, Alan, and Jeff Brookings. 1984. *If She Is Raped: A Book for Husbands, Fathers, and Male Friends.* Holmes Beach, Fla.: Learning Publications.

New York Radical Feminists. 1974. *Rape: The First Sourcebook for Women.* New York: New American Library.

Pellauer, Mary D.; Barbara Chester; and Jane Boyajian. 1987. *Sexual Assault and Abuse: A Handbook for Clergy and Religious Professionals.* San Francisco: Harper & Row.

Poling, James Newton. 1991. *The Abuse of Power: A Theological Problem.* Nashville: Abingdon Press.

Russell, Diana E. H. 1982. *Rape in Marriage.* Macmillan Publishing Co., Collier Books.

Schecter, Susan. 1982. *Women and Male Violence.* Boston: South End Press.

Silverman, D. 1977. "First Do No More Harm: Female Rape Victims and the Male Counselor." *American Journal of Orthopsychiatry* 47 (1977): 91–96.

# 14

# Pastoral Care and Older Women's Secrets

EMMA J. JUSTES

*Northern Baptist Theological Seminary*

She began, "I thought I would take this to my grave with me. I've never told anyone before." These are the words of a seventy-six-year-old woman speaking to her pastor. This was the way she began to tell him how her father had sexually abused her from the time she was seven years old until she left home in her late adolescence. She went on to describe her memories of her father's abuse of her and her suspicions about his abuse of some of her six siblings. She expressed feelings of disgust and anger only after she paused and asked the pastor, "Well, what do you think of me now?" Even though she was a constant and beloved member of the congregation, she still felt very unsure about continued acceptance by the pastor once he *knew.* After all, she had never had the experience of telling anyone. What could she expect regarding a response? For many years she had imagined how someone would react to such a revelation.

This encounter was only the beginning of a long series of conversations between this woman and her pastor. The conversations extended over the remaining eight years of her life. The numbers of women who have never told anyone their secrets are legion.

Today we have a greater awareness of sexual and other abuse of children, so that many of us know these abuses exist. We know that we may even talk about them. Persons who are victims have begun to speak out in public about their experiences. Such abuses have shaped the lives of a multitude of women who fill churches and synagogues, nursing homes and retirement centers. Many of these women still have not told anyone. Older women have kept and continue to keep secrets about experiences that have profoundly shaped and altered their lives. Persons who are in positions of caring for older people have discovered the importance of the telling of life stories. Life review enables elders to tell stories. The telling of stories enables people to fit pieces of their lives together to make a whole picture with integrity and peace within it. In the process, previously unresolved conflicts may be brought to the surface and resolved and unanswered questions may be answered.

My thesis for this chapter is that many older women have lived their lives with the burdens of kept secrets that have deeply affected their lives. These experiences remain unresolved pains in the lives of women. These secret experiences have played important roles in shaping the lives of women (and their children) in the areas of spiritual and emotional wholeness and in self-fulfillment.

Cultural differences influence the way secrets are held, and even what matters will become secret. Women of every racial, ethnic, religious, geographical, and economic background are victims of experiences that lie behind the secrets discussed here. Every woman will not see her experience in the same way. Cultural diversity should be part of the caregiver's awareness in the process of thinking about and working with older women and their secrets.

The pastor, chaplain or pastoral counselor who is working with an older woman needs to examine the woman's issues and concerns with awareness of the social system that has shaped who this person is and whom she can consider becoming. Failing to hear the pain in her reality will reinforce its domination in her life and fail to support her for who she really is. The focus of this chapter is to aid caregivers to help women to break the silence regarding secrets that have diminished their lives and that now prevent them from experiencing integrity in their later years. The persons offering ministry to older women need to realize the impact of kept secrets on the lives of women, even when the women's secrets have been kept from themselves. The concern of this chapter is that if the secrets of older women are not addressed, the barriers to wholeness also will remain unbroken. The breaking of silence means that what is secret is recognized and acknowledged. The gate-keeping work and energy expended to maintain the silence can be redirected. The struggle with the pain of the secret's contents enter a new arena. Even in the final years of life, new life becomes possible.

## THE REALITY OF WOMEN'S SECRETS

The woman described above shared a painful memory of an experience of incest that occurred seventy years earlier. Other women carry secrets that are equally painful and equally enduring. Some women, now widowed, spent their entire lifetimes of marriage experiencing emotional and/or physical abuse from their husbands. They may never have told anyone. Still other women have lived married lives raising children with a nagging awareness that their true sexual identity was lesbian (even if they had no such label for it). Still others may carry secret experiences of rape or other forms of sexual abuse outside the family. Some women have taken on roles of caregivers in their families of origin, forgoing a family of their own to tend the needs of ill or aging parents, while other siblings married, moved away, and raised children of their own. While women graciously take on this role, some of them may hold secret regrets or resentments. What might they have done had they not been limited by this or that? This may be the focus of some women's secrets. Still other women hold secrets about pregnancies that were ended in abortion, about children who were offered for adoption, or about the true paternity of children who were raised as children of their husband.

While research has shown that men are also victims of abuse, men play a key role both in inflicting the pain and in maintaining the secret. Ironically it may be the abused women who are called upon to offer support and comfort for the same parent when he or she is older, infirm, and in need of caretaking. Mrs. Gray was both physically and sexually abused as a child by her father. Like many women, she did not tell anyone, even her sister. Recently, Mrs. Gray's mother died and she is now in the position of having to become the primary caregiver for her father, who has Alzheimer's disease. When Mrs. Gray came to her pastor for help, she was aware of her rage but not of the reasons for it. She noted that she particularly got angry when she had to help her father in matters of personal hygiene. Only when she got in touch with her own pain from her childhood could she face caregiving for her father in a more realistic manor.

Early sexual abuse, battering throughout the lifetime of a marriage, secrets of paternity, denial of one's sexual identity, or living with the memory of rape have shaped the lives of older women behaviorally, economically, relationally, emotionally, psychologically, and, especially, spiritually. The issues these experiences present are not likely to have been part of the pastoral care that women have received. These secrets add up to an enormous amount of unfinished business for aging women.

Research on the sexual abuse of female children has presented a wide range of results (Russell 1986), but a current figure claims that 30 percent of female children experience some form of sexual abuse (Poling 1991, 260). The reported incidence of childhood sexual abuse of women over sixty was not as great as that reported by women in subsequent age groupings (Russell 1986, 77). The lack of reporting among older women may not be a true reflection of the reality for older women. While hard statistics are not available as to the prevalence of this problem, anecdotal evidence from therapists, chaplains, and pastors suggests that this is a problem in need of being addressed.

Secrets that women hold regarding childhood sexual abuse, incest or otherwise, reflect only one category of secrets that contain unfinished business for older women. There are other categories of secrets kept that have some similar dynamics and bear similar consequences (many have some relationship to sexuality).

Research by Straus, Gelles, and Steinmetz (1980) indicated that almost two million American wives are beaten by their husbands every year. Because of underreporting and different definitions of what constitutes violence, the true figures may be closer to 50 or 60 percent (Clarke 1986, 15). This happens today in a time when women have more rights and awareness of their rights than at any time in history. Many of the older women with whom we do ministry or to whom we offer care were born before women had the right to vote in the United States. Beating of wives is not a new phenomenon. The frequency with which it is reported and public awareness of the presence of such behavior is more common today. It would not be surprising to discover that many older women have hidden the fact that they were beaten by their husbands much of their married lives.

As many as 50 percent of women may be victims of attempted or completed rape through the course of their lifetimes (Crooks and Bauer 1990, 710). Researchers have suggested that the age of the victim is no barrier to the rapist, as women and girls of all ages have experienced rape. Today rape is much more in our public awareness. In the early decades following the turn of the century this was not the case. Many women being cared for today as elder women could say about experiences of rape or attempted rape (which could have occurred at any age in their lives), "I have never told anyone before." Rape long ago or from more recent time and kept secret becomes a burden that can form barriers to wholeness.

Gay Pride and gay and lesbian activism have become a part of common public experience as people in the United States recognize the presence of persons who identify themselves as homosexual. Because of increased awareness and openness, it may seem to some that homosexuality is a new phenomenon, certainly not previously a part of human experience to the extent that it seems present today. However, the reality and presence of those persons whose affectional attraction is to persons of the same gender is not a new creation of our "free" society. It is estimated that approximately 10 percent of any human population will have a homosexual orientation (Crooks and Bauer 1990, 318). If this statistic is true, many of our foremothers must have been lesbian. They were not always women who remained single or who shared a life with another woman throughout adulthood. Many were women who married and raised children and lived the life of heterosexuality, fulfilling the expectations for women to be wives and mothers. Now in their old age many women are becoming able to redefine or identify their sexuality for the first time.

As women approach their latter years of life they begin to "process" their lives, considering the events, achievements, losses, pains, and joys of life in light of their faith and their understanding of the meaning of life. This is a positive process that can be done with relative ease and comfort or can become a major internal battleground. In the midst of this "processing," many women deal with secrets kept for years and even for decades of their lives. If the secrets can be realized and shared with a trusted caregiver the process is facilitated. When the processing must include some way to continue to keep the secret, the struggle is magnified and its resolution may become, in the end, elusive. For each of these categories of secrets kept, the struggle exists for some women. For the women who carry these secrets, their lives have not gone unmarked by the presence of the secrets and the experiences they represent. How have these kept secrets shaped lives of women? What will their telling mean?

Kept secrets create divided lives and preclude wholeness. Pain and memories that are shut away mean that the woman's life is split rather than whole. Some women so divide themselves from the pain and memories that the secrets are kept even from themselves. In other instances, women participate in a denial of what has happened to them. They are able to remember, but they deny and create different scenarios for their lives that are not faithful to their true experience. The secrets, divisions, denial, and façade prevent a movement toward spiritual well-being and wholeness.

Divided lives are often diminished lives. The gifts of the women are not put to full use because of the attention that must go to maintaining the denial, keeping the secret, and sustaining the façade. Divided lives do not remain divided only internally, but the women often are divided, separated from other people—there are limits to the genuine intimacy they are able to share and experience. Spiritual life lived in a cloak of secrecy is stunted and crushed rather than full and rich. Rage that smolders throughout life and resentment that gradually emerges both take a severe toll on one's spiritual life.

Kept secrets mean that the woman denies not just what happened in her life, it also means that she denies her *self*. Who she is includes the experience that preceded the secret keeping and is not exclusive of that part of her life. Wholeness requires acceptance of self. This is not possible when a piece of one's life and self is relegated to nonexistence, whether that nonexistence is internal, external, or both.

The business of keeping such secrets diminishes a woman's view of herself. Not only are gifts denied and events "forgotten" but she also has feelings of guilt, if not for what happened, then for not being true to herself. In some ways she has answered the question, "Why me?" in ways that put her at fault. Why couldn't she stop what happened? The answer may have to do with her not being good enough. A high sense of self-esteem is seldom compatible with kept secrets like those named here.

The fact that she gets a great deal of support from her religious community for *keeping* the secret further diminishes her self-esteem and reinforces her guilt. Churches and synagogues have been in the forefront of maintaining secrets, particularly those related to sexuality. "What is impressive is the enormous control that silence retains in the sexual area" (Nelson 1978, 41). Support for breaking the secret seldom seems to be available among those with whom we worship.

In a discussion of aging and human fulfillment, Bernie Lyon identifies fulfillment as referring to "the process of finding out who one really is" (Lyon 1985, 11). Women who participate in keeping deep life secrets are shut out of this process. Caregivers can enter into a process with aging women to enable them to find out who they really are.

## PASTORAL CARE AND OLDER WOMEN'S SECRETS

A pastor who had served a particular church for several years initiated a series of adult classes dealing with human sexuality. Approximately a dozen adults attended the series. Their ages ranged from the early twenties to the seventies. Following the series, a woman who was about sixty years of age told the pastor that when she was a young girl some older boys from the neighborhood had gotten her alone and fondled her. She was not raped or physically hurt but the terror and shame of the experience never left her. She remembers how they laughed at her and how embarrassed she was later whenever she would see those boys. She told her pastor that after that experience she never could trust men. She thinks now that it was why she never did get married. She said to her pastor, "I have never told anyone about this." This woman is aware of some of the ways this experience (which some would see as harmless) has affected the living of her life. One can only wonder whether there is not more that she may not have yet connected to the experience. I wonder how the keeping of the secret itself added to the burden of the event and how it diminished her ability to relate to men, and thus also diminished her life.

In the context of the adult class that focused on human sexuality, her pastor, who was a woman, raised issues of sexual abuse. This and the trust relationship she had with her pastor probably made it possible for her to break a secret of more than fifty years. She had never had a female pastor before this woman began to serve their church. She may not have been able to trust the men who had been her pastors with her spiritual growth because of her secret and its impact on her life and her relationships with men.

This first telling of her story was only the beginning of what needs to happen for her to heal the wound of her secret. Her telling was received with understanding, so she may be able to continue. For her experience to have been viewed as unimportant would have meant that it would return to secret status and any processing would be put to rest.

The pastor of the woman with whom we began this essay described the woman as having very low self-esteem. The woman continued to struggle to the end of her life to assimilate her experience of abuse into her life story. Each time she had a private conversation with her pastor she would return to the topic. Sometimes she repeated the same story. Other times she went further to talk about her feelings of rage. To see this loving and beloved old woman express such deep rage at her father was startling and revealing for the pastor. How had feelings toward her father and about herself shaped her life? What possibilities were never realized? She had refused all of her adult life to take any leadership role in the church because she would not "get up in front of people." Feelings of not wanting to be "seen" (exposed?) persisted throughout her life. Her inability to assert herself meant that she had been repeatedly taken advantage of by others, a pattern learned from her abuse and an identity developed for herself out of her abuse.

The secrets that have in some sense broken the lives of older women have to be broken. The women face the ending years of their lives and the secrets still form barriers to their spiritual wholeness. Care for these women involves care about these secrets and willingness to face them with the women. It is not only the women who have to be willing to face their secrets but those who offer them care have to be willing to come face-to-face with the secrets with them. Clergy and other caregivers are capable of communicating that they do not want to face some of these secrets, or that they will walk with the women in this new territory. There are ways to facilitate the telling and the recognition of the secrets.

## DIMENSIONS OF CARE

There are three stages that can be considered as involved in care related to older women's secrets. First, caregivers must communicate some willingness to hear about the secret. This can be in the form of a topic on which a sermon is preached, an adult class on human sexuality, a prayer that addresses the issue involved in the secret, any way the caregiver can convey a willingness to deal with sexual abuse. If caregivers are not able to mention the issue of sexual abuse, then they cannot expect others to risk raising the issue. Somehow this willingness to hear ought to communicate a freedom from blame or judgment. "I can talk about sex and I will not judge your behavior or your experience." This is the message that may form the foundation for the breaking of a secret. Behind this message there probably needs to be a foundation of trust in the caregiver, a sense that the message is true and the person will be faithful to her or his word.

For some of the secret keepers, there may still remain strong barriers to sharing their secrets with male caregivers which may not be overcome by any degree of trust and willingness to hear. For others, the gender of the caregiver may not be an issue.

Second, the secret must be heard. Even though the event occurred long ago, even though it may not sound very significant in the context of world affairs, and even though it may seem like something that should and could have been resolved long ago, the caregiver must receive the secret with seriousness and concern. If the caregiver does not readily understand, the woman could be encouraged to explain more. If it seems as though she should have done something about it at the time, the caregiver still should give the secret every respect and should not ask questions such as, "Why didn't you tell your mother?" The woman has probably asked herself that question over and over through the years and will tell the caregiver her own curiosity about it as she or he is open to listen. On the other hand the woman may have told her mother and the reality was denied even then. As the caregiver listens, she or he should convey to the woman concern and willingness to talk about it again (and again). Affirmation and continued acceptance of the woman is necessary at the time of the telling. Making this *explicit* is important. The woman is not likely to *assume* continued acceptance and care after the telling. "What do you think of me now?" is at the heart or under the surface of every secret telling.

Third, it is important to be willing and able to *continue* to hear about the secret—to hear it as it evolves from hidden to open status, to assist with the exploration and examination of the experience and its lifelong impact, to help fit this piece of life into the whole life picture, to enable the woman's new movement toward wholeness and spiritual fulfillment. For some women this is a process of several years. The assurance of continued acceptance and care must be an explicit part of the ongoing telling of the secret. There is theological work involved for religious care givers as women need to discover where in their faith there is room for this part of their life.

This ongoing telling and hearing of the story of the secret can have a place in a context of life review. The process of sorting out one's whole life may be a helpful context for continuing the unpacking of secrets kept in hiding during that life. Life review also could encourage the assessment of the ways in which the secret experience had affected the woman's life, for good or for ill.

It is often difficult for caregivers to be able to receive anger from people.

They often just do not want to hear about anger. To care for the woman who carries secrets of abuse they must be able to hear her anger and acknowledge it and accept it without deflating it or turning it aside or denying it. They need to be willing to work with her to incorporate anger into the whole of her life story and not to let her or help her turn it into denial.

A temptation, particularly for religious caregivers, may be to encourage women abused as children to forgive their abuser. While this could be a desirable goal, it is an issue that should not be forced on the woman. Forgiveness more appropriately flows from one in power toward one with less power (as in God's forgiveness of us). A lifetime of pain over abuse cannot be instantly put aside with a word of forgiveness. The focus would be more appropriate in terms of enabling the woman to "let go" of the power the experience has over her rather than encouraging her to "forgive" her abuser. Many times, the abuser will no longer be alive. In other cases, the abuser may not have *asked* for forgiveness. To push a woman toward forgiveness under circumstances of years of pain and no remorse from the abuser is not a healing approach, no matter how much one values forgiveness. The issue must be what the woman needs and wants to do in order to move toward wholeness and not what a caregiver needs, wants, or expects her to do.

## SOME PROCESSES

There are ways in which the caregiver can communicate that she is willing to hear about a secret. There are also ways in which she can more actively enable the revealing of secrets. This is not to imply that one should ever *push* the revealing of secrets or demand in any way that someone tell her secrets. It does mean that caregivers can play a role of providing the avenue for someone to be able to recognize a secret hidden from themselves or to reveal a secret to others.

The study of Scripture can be one way of providing an arena for women to be able to talk about their secrets. Specific passages may be useful as well as themes that can be studied in various passages of Scripture. There are some benefits to such study being done with a small group of women of similar age. The experiences of one woman may be expressed and enable the telling or even recognition of secrets that another woman has hidden from herself. In the telling of stories the women are also available to provide acceptance and support of one another.

Betrayal is a theme that runs throughout Scripture from Adam and Eve's betrayal of God in the Garden through the betrayal of Joseph by his brothers when they sell him into slavery all the way through to Judas' betrayal of Jesus in another garden. A study of Scripture that would focus on any of the stories of betrayal could provide a backdrop for the telling of a secret. Specific stories of denial and secret keeping also provide fertile ground for the breaking of secrets. A theological discussion of the commandment to "Honor your father and your mother" could be another kind of approach to enabling women to face their secrets.

The study of Scripture that would enable secrets to be revealed or considered would not be the kind in which a leader of the study would explain the Scripture. It would need to be a study that engages the participants in seeing the Scripture in relation to their own lives. One caregiver gave an example of using the story of the blind man by the side of the road (Luke 18:35-43). In this story the blind man is crying out to Jesus, and others around him are trying to keep the man quiet. The caregiver's suggestion for using this Scripture was to begin with a more distant view of Scripture and then move closer to home. The questions for participants' reflection could first be, "What is going on in this story?" then, "Does that ever happen today?" and finally, "Has that ever happened to you?" When the participants in the Scripture study reply that the people are trying to get the man to be quiet and then think about whether it still happens to people today, the next step toward thinking about their own experience with being kept quiet may allow or open up reflection on their kept secrets. The Scripture plays a role in revealing their own lives while connections between the lives of the women and the Scripture are drawn more strongly.

Scripture may also be approached in terms of gender issues. A group of women could be asked, "What if Abraham had been a woman? What would she have done?" This question could be asked with any biblical character. This approach can raise the difference in life experiences that women perceive from their own lives compared to their perception of the lives of men they have known.

Life review has been appreciated for its value in enabling older people to do the life sorting and storytelling that will help them to draw together the pieces of their lives to form a coherent whole. Life review may be pursued in ways that will be more likely to help women recognize and express their kept secrets. Questions that ask, "What difference has it made in your life that you were a woman?" or other specific questions related to gender issues or even sexuality may help women feel free to reveal secrets they have carried through a lifetime. Taking another direction, one could ask, "Are there things you have been angry about for a long time?"

## SOME POSSIBILITIES

It is not possible when working to enable women to face and deal with life secrets to expect them to "get rid of" their painful experiences, memories, and secrets. This is what they have tried to do their whole lives. Instead, there is the possibility of creative transformation of the past. This does *not* mean a rewriting of history. It *does* mean that the experience, moved beyond being a secret held in the woman's life, can take another place. It is often out of pain and struggle that human beings can discover or create the most valuable blessings. To say this is not to make light of the pain and the struggle but to affirm that the action of faith within a supportive context can have transforming power. New life is possible out of old secrets.

Women's experiences with keeping secrets are not lived in isolation. The women have raised children of their own, related to siblings and a range of other family members who themselves may have been their abusers. They have related to others out of the structures that their secret keeping imposed upon them. This is particularly true of the children of mothers who kept secrets of early childhood sexual abuse.

The secrets of the mother can also become dynamics and secrets of the family. A woman who was sexually abused as a child, and who marries as an adult and raises children, carries into the parenting relationship a mistrust of men, rage toward, perhaps, her own father, and low self-esteem and depression. She is likely to be alienated from her sexual self and passes on to her children attitudes about sex and themselves that are shaped by her secret. The son has difficulty feeling accepted. The daughter cannot welcome intimacy with men. Neither son nor daughter can easily feel good about themselves. Perhaps the mother's unlocking of her secret can become a gift to children who have received an experienced mystery as a legacy of their mother's secret. Care for the older woman and the benefits this care brings to her are valuable enough. There may be additional possibilities for new life even in the next generation.

One adult daughter welcomed her mother's "confession" of her secret of having been sexually abused by her own father with expressions of relief. The daughter realized that she had been trying to discover the secret through the way she had been living her life. The daughter then had the possibility of reconstructing her own life in more positive directions.

Is it ever too late to bring up the pains from secrets of the past? Isn't it too much to deal with at the end of one's life? Do old women have enough time and energy left to struggle toward resolution of issues related to their kept secrets? Is it worth the struggle that follows revelation of a secret? Caregivers sensitive to the women with whom they work raise questions like these out of concern for the women who have long-kept secrets. A seventy-five-year-old woman answers them: "Tell everybody its never too late." She had recovered the memory of abuse when she was seventy-one years old after having endured four failed marriages. When she spoke these words she was in a new and fulfilling relationship, the first in her lifetime. Where there is a possibility of redeeming women from the burdens of damage caused by pain-filled kept secrets, it is never too late. It is never too late to take more steps toward fullness of life and wholeness in spirit.

Care that includes awareness of secrets kept by older women and the barriers these secrets create in women's lives also needs to include awareness that there are sometimes powerful reasons for women not to remember or not to reveal secrets. There is pressure from family expectations (whether expressed by the family or merely assumed by the woman). There may be a feeling that her life—all the years she had lived—would be seen as a lie if she revealed her secret. She may anticipate religious judgment because of the contents of the secret. Some women have to wait for the death of a parent, sibling, or spouse in order to be freed to tell.

Some women may be aware of the degree of emotion involved in the secret and not want to face what that may mean, what it would take to face and deal with. In old age, women deal with a great burden of often accumulated grief. Too many friends and relatives die in too short a period of time. Too many things in life are lost in too short a time. To face the grief or loss of one's life of a "life that might have been" had the experience of a kept secret not happened, may be more than a woman wants to face. Women need to be their own judges of what they are able to do and when. Their secrets must be freely shared and never sought after. In every instance of which I have heard the woman's revelation of her secret was a surprise to the caregiver who received it. This is as it probably should be. Caregivers can pave the way. They can signal willingness and ability to hear and respond. They can provide a setting for the telling and avenues for realizing what has been hidden. The women must determine whether to tell or not without persuasion or manipulation or probing. It is the woman's secret to keep or to expose.

## CONCLUSION

One of the most crucial factors in the excavation of secrets by older women is that women be helped to move toward compassionate attitudes toward themselves. To be able to feel compassion toward the wounded child of the past, to feel compassion toward the younger self who was not able to rescue herself from the trauma that has lasted a lifetime, to feel compassion toward the adult woman who has suffered under the burdens of the secret is essential in the movement toward the healing of old wounds that extend into the present. Caregivers can be instrumental in helping women to move in this journey as they express compassion for her self now and her self of the past.

Throughout this essay the focus has been on women who may be seen as wounded and limited people. Caregivers may feel sadness at the losses the women have experienced as the result of different forms of abuse. What remains to be said is that some of these women are women who have accomplished remarkable things. Out of their pain and, perhaps, with denial intact, women have continued to struggle through life and become significant contributors to society. Caregivers would do them a great injustice to see them as weak, incomplete, and useless women, wounded and never healed. This is, in part, certainly true but it is not the whole picture of these women. It is not all there is to them. Even among those who have accomplished a great deal throughout their lives as they carried burdens of secrets there is still a need for healing. As women face the closing years of their lives and raise up secrets long kept as part of their movement toward wholeness and integrity it may be very exciting to see what they will do when their burden of silence has been removed.

## BIBLIOGRAPHY

Bass, E., and L. Davis. 1988. *The Courage to Heal: A Guide for Women Survivors of Child Sexual Abuse.* New York: Harper & Row.

Bass, E., and L. Thornton, eds. 1983. *I Never Told Anyone: Writings by Women Survivors of Child Sexual Abuse.* New York: Harper & Row.

Brownmiller, S. 1975. *Against Our Will: Men, Women and Rape.* New York: Simon & Schuster.

Clarke, R. 1986. *Pastoral Care of Battered Women.* Philadelphia: Westminster Press.

Crooks, R., and K. Bauer. 1990. *Our Sexuality.* 4th ed. Redwood City, Calif.: Benjamin-Cummings Publishing Co.

Dobash, R. E. 1979. *Violence Against Wives.* New York: Free Press.

Fortune, M. 1983. *Sexual Violence: The Unmentionable Sin.* New York: Pilgrim Press.

Ledray, L. 1986. *Recovering from Rape.* New York: Henry Holt.

Leehan, J. 1989. *Pastoral Care for Survivors of Family Abuse.* Louisville, Ky.: Westminster/John Knox Press.

Lyon, B. 1985. *Toward a Practical Theology of Aging.* Philadelphia: Fortress Press.

Macdonald, B., and C. Rich. 1983. *Look Me in the Eye: Old Women, Aging and Ageism.* San Francisco: Spinsters.

Nelson, J. 1978. *Embodiment.* Minneapolis: Augsburg Publishing House.

Poling, J. 1991. *The Abuse of Power: A Theological Problem.* Nashville: Abingdon Press.

Russell, D. 1986. *The Secret Trauma: Incest in the Lives of Girls and Women.* New York: Basic Books.

Straus, M.; R. Gelles; and S. Steinmetz. 1980. *Behind Closed Doors: Violence in the American Family.* New York: Doubleday & Co.

Walker, L. 1979. *The Battered Woman.* New York: Harper & Row.

# Part Three
# Visions of Home

From the visions of women, pastoral insights emerge. Elizabeth Liebert writes of a spiritual care that removes the cataracts of silence, invisibility, passivity, low self-esteem, depression, inability to trust, and isolation. This spiritual care attends to the experience of women and engages both the woman's story and the structure that surrounds, perhaps entraps, the narrative. Liebert offers insight as well into the caregiver's spirituality.

A vision of home includes networks of support and community for women. Paul Buford points to the inadequacy of traditional pastoral care and counseling for women and recommends widening the theological parameters of care with enlarged systems of support as contemporary women grow, heal, and mature in connection and relationship.

As women remain connected and maintain relation, they will feel the cultural tug to sacrifice themselves and their needs. According to Brita Gill-Austern, women are motivated toward self-sacrifice and self-denial by the unholy trinity of self-abnegation, self-doubt, and false guilt. Much of this is encouraged by the Christian tradition. Gill-Austern offers a liberating understanding of self-giving love modeled on the Holy Trinity. This understanding is essential in a pastoral care of women.

In closing, stories from the depths of a woman's personality that have shaped and reshaped her psychosocial development will be examined as "core moments" of insight in a pastoral care. These "core moments" are revelatory and prophetic. They can serve as transitional moments as they illumine the eyes of the heart. Jeanne Stevenson Moessner expands on such "core moments" in a pastoral relationship and shows how these moments of insight contribute to a woman's coming home to herself—with journey mercies.

# 15

## Coming Home to Themselves: Women's Spiritual Care

ELIZABETH LIEBERT

*San Francisco Theological Seminary*

"Why can't a woman be more like a man?"
—Henry Higgins, in *My Fair Lady*

Why indeed? Because, simply, she isn't a man. Henry Higgins voices one aspect of the conundrum in which women find themselves in a society in which the implicit—and often explicit—rules have been made by and serve the purposes of the white, male, Euro-American dominant group. This dominant group offers women two choices—actually, two versions of the same thing. Women can strive to become like men, an option the dominant culture will tolerate only for a few women, Henry Higgins's plea notwithstanding. Or, women can reconcile themselves to the ideal of woman as defined by the dominant culture; becoming a "good woman" is by far the most acceptable option to the dominant group.[1] Neither choice honors the unique experience of women in their own right.[2] This conundrum affects women's spiritual care, the focus of this chapter.

Examining issues surrounding women's pastoral care must, I believe, include addressing women's spiritual care. If women are to be served as deeply as they deserve, their care must extend to the transcendent as well as the mundane, to meaning, significance, and ultimate direction as well as to problem solving and crisis resolution. Thus this chapter builds on the axiom that the church's healing, sustaining, guiding, reconciling, and nurturing of women—their pastoral care—must include women's spiritual well-being, as well as their physical, emotional, economic, and cultural well-being. It asserts that, while spiritual care may originate in pastoral care, it moves beyond much pastoral care by its explicit and intentional focus on the Ultimate and the woman's relationship to this Ultimate, how-

257

ever she conceives it.[3] It further asserts that pastoral care itself reaches its completion not simply when persons function better, valuable as this is, but when they are set free to live the gospel more fully within the context of their lives (Duffy 1983). This assertion implies that pastoral care necessarily involves prophetic efforts toward emancipatory liberation, justice seeking, public advocacy and ecological partnership, as Larry Kent Graham (1992, 20) puts it—and that these prophetic acts comprise essential aspects of women's spiritual care.

Spiritual care of women, then, is at the heart of their pastoral care, building upon it, when appropriate, but explicitly including the woman's relationship to God. This chapter will examine the tensions around and possibilities for nourishing women's spiritual lives within a church in which their unique experience and personhood before God is only gradually becoming recognized and celebrated.

I believe that women's spiritual care cannot simply be forced into molds made by and for men. Nor can it remain always within the parameters defined as safe and feminine—that is, orthodox as defined by the dominant group—assumptions that have undergirded the church's ministry to women. Instead, a life-giving spiritual care for women must be created, perhaps painstakingly, by women as they carefully listen to their experience, do theology from that personal and communal experience in dialogue with the church's often ambiguous theological heritage, create their own experiences and practices of prayer, ritual, and healing, and determine their own spiritual goals and evaluate their progress toward these goals. By these criteria, an adequate understanding of the spiritual care of women has yet to be articulated.

This chapter does not propose a product, "the spiritual care of women," but uncovers underlying assumptions and proposes a *process* which I hope will assist women toward the spiritual care of themselves and each other. The process can be adapted by men in coming to understand their own spiritual care, and it is equally useful for men and women caring for each other. In other words, the process itself is not gender specific, although it is woman-friendly.

Some preliminary steps will set the context for the process. This chapter examines, in turn, the contemporary problem in caring for women spiritually, some cautions about generalizations, and the notions of "spiritual" and "spiritual care." It concludes with an example of a particular women's spiritual support group and a discussion of the spirituality of the caregiver.

## THE PROBLEM

The issue of women's spiritual care must be set within the place of women within a particular culture and time. Hence, many of the following contextual observations concern the situation in which women find themselves in North America in the waning years of the twentieth century. These conditions deeply affect the spiritual lives of women by creating the horizon within which women imagine the possibilities, struggles, and goals of their lives. In comparison to their sisters in many parts of the world, North American women may appear to "have it all." Yet, as the proverb warns, appearances deceive.

The consequences of treating women as if they were merely appendages of men rather than persons in their own right are amply chronicled in women's tendency toward silence, invisibility, passivity, inability to trust their own experience and authority, feelings of low self-worth, depression, and alienation from church and society. Let us examine two symptoms, silence and depression, in order to get a sense of the situation in which women find themselves.

The first symptom, silence, may be literal or figurative. Mary Belenky and her colleagues (Belenky et al. 1986, 22–34, 157–64) describe some women who, quite literally, carry on no interior dialogue with themselves. They swim in a sea of words that make no sense, which they cannot negotiate and which have been used against them. Although these silent women do develop language as such, they do not develop inner words and conversation; without such representational thought, they are limited to the present, the concrete and the specific. Significantly, without this inner "I-ness," they do not develop a sense of "we-ness." Furthermore, they have no sense of agency and depend on someone outside themselves to tell them what to do. They are passive, subdued, subordinate. They see life in terms of simple polarities. They cannot describe themselves to themselves. These "mute" women were disproportionately represented among the most socially, economically, and educationally deprived of those whom Belenky and her colleagues interviewed and came from families that were also silent or where words and speech were punished. They are also the women who conform most clearly to the society's most rigid stereotypes of what "good" women are to do—be seen but not heard.

Women's silence is also figurative. Carol Christ opens her study of women writers and the spiritual quest with the following words:

> Women's stories have not been told. And without stories there is no articulation of experience. Without stories a woman is lost when she comes to make the important decisions of her life. She does not learn to value her struggles, to celebrate her strengths, to comprehend her pain. Without stories she cannot understand herself. Without stories she is alienated from those deeper experiences of self and world that have been called spiritual or religious. She is closed in silence. The expression of women's spiritual quest is integrally related to the telling of women's stories. If women's stories are not told, the depth of women's souls will not be known. (Christ 1980, 1)

Carol Christ uses the word "story" to include all articulations of experience that have a narrative element, including fiction, poetry, song, autobiography, biography, and even simple talk between friends. While her description of the effects of silence is strikingly similar to the muteness of the deprived women of the study by Belenky and her colleagues, the scope of Christ's use of the word "story" extends to *all* women to some degree. Stories give shape to lives; without authentic stories, women lack imaginative possibilities to try out in their own lives. Stories reveal the powers that provide orientation in people's lives; without stories, lives appear empty and meaningless. Certain religious stories provide orientation to sources of meaning, and many other seemingly mundane stories also have a sacred meaning that grounds existence in ultimates. Thus, Christ concludes that the depth of women's souls will not be known if their stories are not told (Christ 1980, 1–4).

The second symptom is depression. Christie Cozad Neuger (1993, 201) notes that depression is at an epidemic level among women, with the incidence steadily rising. Although there are several theories advanced to account for this disturbing statistic, feminist researchers generally agree that this differential is exacerbated, if not caused, by women's abiding rage at their oppression without any viable way to extricate themselves from it. In other words, women's optimistic perceptions about the options available to them and about the very power to make choices concerning these options do not match the reality. Women's rising expectations without the means to fulfill them contribute to the frequency and severity of depression.

Dana Crowley Jack (1991, 5, 16, 21) claims that (non-biochemical) depression arises from fundamental inequality of power. In women, depression is based on failure of connection within a system that institutionalizes this power differential. Depression cannot be understood in traditional categories based on male experience but must be understood by examining the forms of connection that result in "loss of self." When women are depressed, look first to the quality of the woman's relationship with her partner.

Depression in women, then, has a structural and societal foundation; it is not simply a given woman's personal problem, weakness, or illness. Along with such other "women's disorders" as hysteria, phobias, and eating disorders, depression is rooted in the typical development and socialization of women in this society, Ellyn Kaschak (1992, 170–83) has demonstrated; the woman who experiences depression is well attuned to the psychological and social environment. Depressed women are done a disservice when their depression is "treated" from a purely intrapsychic perspective while ignoring the overarching system that breeds and perpetuates a power differential in which women never "catch up" no matter how their situation "improves."[4]

As this brief sketch of two symptoms suggests, women are not just like men, to the serious detriment of their psychospiritual health. If women are not appendages of men, still less are women the property of men, perpetual minors, disenfranchised from direct participation in the present and future manifestations of the reign of God. The propensity to think of women this way (by either men or women) appears to be directly linked to sexual and physical violence directed against women, children, and dependent adults. As in earlier ages, sexism undergirds and contributes to many contemporary forms of domination (Nelson 1978, 65–67).

The notion that women are property is very much alive today. It appears in economic arrangements that keep women dependent and poor in disproportionate numbers. It appears in cultural permission to perpetrate violence upon them. Susan Faludi (1991, xiii) questions that, if women "have it all," why don't they, for example, have the most basic requirements for achieving equality in the workforce, namely, equal pay for equal work, adequate child care, and adequate programs for eliminating discriminatory practices? Why do three-fourths of all high schools still violate the federal law banning sex discrimination in education? Why do undergraduate women receive only 70 percent of the aid that undergraduate men receive, and women's sports programs, a pittance compared with men's? Why do more than three hundred thousand women who seek emergency shelter to escape domestic violence find none? And why is it that between 40 and 50 percent of all homeless women are fleeing domestic violence (Robb 1993, 150)?

We begin to see the structural relationships between women's invisibility, proneness to depression, economic powerlessness, and violence directed against them and their children. While individual women vary in the power they have to overcome these structural and systemic blocks to their full personhood, this situation deeply pervades the climate in which women seek their deepest yearnings. Since both silence and structural inequality permeate women's lives, their pastoral and spiritual care must necessarily engage both story *and* structure if it is to address their deepest aspirations.

Religious traditions have been an ambiguous force in the lives of women.[5] While there have been prophetic moves on behalf of women's full personhood, religious traditions also have consistently contributed to the oppression of women. In Christianity, women's narratives have been omitted in the formation of the biblical texts; the stories of women that do occur have often been reified into symbols of evil and seduction or of impossibly idealized self-sacrifice and perfect love and used to characterize women and define their role in society and church. Women have generally been excluded from worship leadership and decision making within Christian denominations; even where access to these roles has occurred, they are still denied positions and salaries comparable to those of male religious leaders, and they often have to contend with sexual assault and harassment in common with their sisters in other professions (Neuger 1993, 187).[6]

The alternative to treating a woman as an appendage or property of a man, namely, treating her as if she were a man, has long historical precedent within Christianity. The holier a woman, the more she became like a man; she exhibited "manly virtues." As the apocryphal *Gospel of Thomas* puts it:

> Lo, I will draw her
> so that I will make her a man
> so that she too may become a living spirit
> which is like you man;
> for every woman who makes herself a man
> will enter into the kingdom of heaven. (Grant and Freedman 1960, 197)

But let her really put on men's armor and literally act like a man, as did Joan of Arc, and it becomes all too clear that there are limits to manly behavior from a woman.

Being accorded the status of a man could be realized by only a tiny minority of women by virtue of a heroic degree of sanctity. The rest of the women, and indeed women's nature itself, were seen to be inferior, following the thought of Aristotle. James Nelson comments on the institutionalization of the Aristotelian view of women through the theology of Thomas Aquinas:

> Aquinas borrowed directly from Aristotle's biology and from that philosopher's definition of women: the female is a "misbegotten" or "defective" male. Nature always intends to produce males, so a woman is a man gone wrong. Thus, Aquinas could say, "man is the beginning and end of every creature." So embedded in Western thought was the notion of the man's superior biological function in reproduction, that for centuries after Aquinas early microscopists were picturing spermatozoa as containers with homunculi (miniature, fully formed males) sealed up inside. (Nelson 1978, 63)

This perspective is not just a quaint notion gleaned from antiquated biological and theological thinking; it is very much alive today, although in subtler forms. The dualities set forth by the ancient and medieval theologians hardened into the modern split between the "softer" private virtues of the home for women and the "tougher" public virtues of the marketplace for men. These splits were—and often still are—sanctioned by the churches in official writings and sermons, supporting a gulf between the private and the public realms and a narrowly limited women's "place" within the wider male "world" (Carr 1988, 16).

Consider, for example, the assumption, based on male experience, that the root sin is pride; yet for most women, the underdevelopment of the self, in all its various forms, is more virulent and destructive (Saiving 1979, 37). Consider the vociferous insistence in some quarters of the church that women should be silent—although of course they may volunteer to do the behind the scenes work that keeps the church functioning. Consider the underrepresentation of women on finance committees and the invisibility of women in centers where decisions about the life of the church are routinely made. Consider the long and painful struggle for women's ordination and the lack of advancement for women who are ordained.

The church may no longer state that women are misbegotten males, but it still acts as if women are less valuable and effective than men, both in the pews and behind the altar. We will not be able to assume that the church's tradition will offer sufficient guidance on women's spiritual care.

## CAUTIONS ABOUT GENERALIZATIONS

Before we proceed to the heart of the issue of women's spiritual care, some cautions are in order. First, the category of our discourse defies easy naming. As Sandra Schneiders (1991, 9-15) notes, while the women of every class experience more discrimination than the men of the same class, women cannot be considered a class as such but are a part of all classes. What women have in common is not class but sex. Therefore class analysis, while it may assist us in uncovering the situation of women, does not precisely situate women's predicament in contemporary culture, and it tends to pit the interests of one class of women against those of women of another class. On the other hand, gender analysis, based on the assumption that women are not just like men, runs the risk that women will be defined only in terms of gender and can lead to new versions of "the good woman" who complements and is defined only in relation to men. In constructing an understanding of women's spiritual care, I shall build upon the belief that both women and men have individual rights *and* relational responsibilities and insist on equitable rather than identical access to the goods of society and the ministrations of the church. A vision of a human social order where women are self-determining and fully participative grounds this vision of women's spiritual care.

Second, women share certain experience by virtue of being women (for example, the effects of a normative violence against women and economic disparity in earning power compared to men of the same education, job preparation, and race), but at the same time each woman is a unique individual, formed in a matrix of race, class, sexual orientation, family background, age, life experience, and personal choices (Neuger 1993, 186). Hunches about women as a group may arise from careful listening to many women recount their experiences, but these generalizations must not over-shadow the particularities of each woman's spiritual care.

Finally, my own social location (white, middle-aged, educated, academic, Roman Catholic, celibate member of a religious congregation) will influence my perspectives on the situation of women and their appropriate spiritual care. This social location is as likely to distance me from aspects of the situations of persons different from me as it is to assist me in situations similar to mine. I offer a particular perspective, which can only be enriched by conversation and critique of women from other social locations.

If a woman, then, is neither exactly like a man, a "misbegotten man," nor adequately understood as a member of a class of human beings called "women," how shall we understand her spiritual care? We begin to answer this question by examining the terms "spiritual," "spirituality," and "spiritual care."

## THE ASSERTION

"Spirit" and "spiritual" are mystifying terms for many contemporary persons. As I use them here, these words do not connote the ethereal or otherworldly. Rather, they point to that intangible reality at the core of the person, the animating or life principle, the life breath as a graced human being among other creatures. "Spirit" and "spiritual" are simply words that alert us to look for the deepest and most authentic dimension of human experience in all its aspects. That dimension is not restricted to what we ordinarily think of as holy. Rather, the spiritual suffuses all life. It can be uncovered in what is said and not said, in the way one moves and holds oneself, the way one "lives in" and cares for one's body, the way one enters into intimate relationships, the way one uses time or spends money—as well as the way one prays and worships.

As a Christian, I bring a theological tradition to these words as well. From this perspective, the word "spiritual" alerts me to look for the presence and action of the Holy Spirit. A deep strand of the Christian tradition speaks of the Holy Spirit as the animating Person of God: The Holy Spirit is God's active presence on our behalf. The Holy Spirit teaches humankind the meaning of the life, death, and resurrection of Jesus of Nazareth, calling to mind what Jesus said while he was present on earth, bringing understanding about who the Christ is for us today. The Holy Spirit names the indwelling, re-creating presence of God within all of creation, in communities of faith and, particularly and uniquely, within each human heart. Thus, the deepest reality of one's being lies where the Holy Spirit and one's human spirit intersect (Liebert 1992a, 10–11).

The term "spirituality" builds upon this base of meaning within the Christian tradition, although its referent is no longer limited to Christian religious experience. Sandra Schneiders (1986, 684) speaks of spirituality, in its widest sense, as the experience of consciously striving to integrate one's life in terms of self-transcendence toward what one perceives to be of ultimate value. It can be specified by a variety of religious or nonreligious contexts and theologies but is distinguished by its reference to issues of ultimate concern.[7] From a theistic starting point, Maria Harris (1989, 67) understands spirituality as (at least) our way of being in the world: surrounded, held, cherished, touched by, bathed in the mystery of God. And if we understand God as the ground of all reality, then Carol Ochs' (1983, 114) description of spirituality as "coming into relationship with reality" bridges theistic and nontheistic understandings of spirituality.

In these terms, a specifically Christian spirituality would relate the human capacity for self-transcendence to God as revealed in Jesus Christ and communicated by the Holy Spirit to the church (Schneiders 1993, 14). Since my perspective is grounded in Christian spirituality, in what follows I will refer to the ultimate as the God understood and experienced in the Christian tradition. By doing so, I do not mean to predetermine certain conceptions of God or certain required responses to that God on the part of others. I do not assume, for example, that Christian baptism or accepting Jesus as one's personal savior is a requirement or a necessary outcome of spiritual care.

Adequate spiritual care of women will include assisting women to become more deeply in touch with reality, however it is expressed in a given woman's life situation. It will assist women in their moves toward self-transcendence and will help them come home to themselves as creative, autonomous and life-giving members of human communities. It will deal, at moments, with beliefs, convictions, and patterns of thought, with emotions, with desires, and with behavior, all in relationship to what the women themselves judge to be Ultimate.

To reiterate, then, women's spiritual care is at the heart of their pastoral care because of its focus on self-transcendence in light of the woman's relationship to God. It is not sufficient simply to relieve an individual woman's symptoms or even to work to change the structures that systematically oppress women, as valid and necessary as both of these may be. Spiritual care of women consists in creating or restoring the conditions in which a particular woman—and by extension, all women—may become more deeply in touch with and live out her deepest call as a human being before God. The goal in women's spiritual care is their self-transformation based on a vision of the realm of God.

Thus women's spiritual care is a part of the church's mandate to nurture all its members, whether or not they arrive at the office of a pastoral care-giver expressing some problem or discontent with an aspect of their lives. The spiritual care of women goes far beyond problem-oriented pastoral care.

## STARTING POINTS

If we have not yet arrived at an adequate understanding of women's spiritual care, neither are we without resources for creating a process. Two psychologically oriented starting points that can serve to reinforce and summarize many of the points developed above can be found in feminist therapy and structural developmental theories. We turn briefly to these perspectives.

Several principles of feminist counseling as articulated by Christie Cozad Neuger (1993, 188–197) can provide a feminist orientation to our caring. Although the context and goals of spiritual care and psychotherapy are quite different, the principles can still illumine women's spiritual care.

The first and most basic consideration concerns our own consciousness: we must become aware of patriarchy and its relation to the issues the woman articulates. Seeing the systemic grounds for a given woman's impasse helps break the isolation so many women feel in their pain and helps avoid "blaming the victim." It also encourages us in the search for structural as well as individual approaches to these issues.

Within the context of an awareness of patriarchy, we must attempt to create an egalitarian relationship between the caregiver and the seeker that is characterized by empowerment, advocacy, and appropriate self-disclosure. All these qualities are not only possible but essential elements of effective spiritual caring relationships, whether of women or of men. They are especially important for women, given the highly unequal distribution of power that characterizes most other professional relationships in which women find themselves.

Third, we can explore the benefits of a group context as a source of empowerment. Social arrangements frequently work to isolate women from other women and encourage them to compete with each other. Groups can bring women together in an environment where they feel safe enough to share pain, struggles, successes, and hopes—that is, safe enough to tell their stories.[8] Such communities of women who validate the lives of each other provide a powerful context for mutual spiritual care.

Finally, effective care for women assumes a woman-centered approach: that is, it begins from the individual woman's experience in her social context and considers the particularities of her race, class, sexual preference, age, and other personalizing characteristics. All of these characteristics apply equally to women's spiritual care and can serve as a foundation for constructing a spiritual care process.

A second starting point arises from developmental theory. Harvard-based developmentalist Robert Kegan (1982) investigated the kind of climate in which development took place without conscious attention and intervention around developmental progression. He isolated three dynamics that must occur in appropriate degree and timing: confirmation, contradiction, and continuity.[9]

A developmentally useful environment confirms the person, her assessments of what is going on around her, and her deep desires. When sufficient confirmation has occurred to ensure that she need not protect herself unduly, a developmentally useful environment works to contradict entrenched views of the world, excessive need for security and safety, and a perception of the world as always predictable. This disconfirmation may propel the individual toward a deep reexamination of what is most meaningful to her—a *kairos* moment spiritually. But, at the same time, a developmentally useful environment contains enough continuity that the individual is not abandoned in midcourse, prematurely cut adrift from the significant relationships that propelled the reorganization. These three dynamics, in the appropriate degree and timing for each individual, and set within a community of support, challenge, and commitment such as may occur in a women's spiritual support group, can create a powerful context for women's growth in self-transcendence before God.

By introducing a developmental perspective into this discussion, I do not mean to imply that spiritual care can be reduced to good developmental techniques or that the goal of spiritual care is (simply) a more humanly developed person. Rather, the dynamics that characterize developmentally useful environments also create a climate encouraging other kinds of transformations, including, I believe, growth in relationship to God, and thus may serve the enterprise of creating a process for women's spiritual care.

These two starting points, principles of feminist psychotherapy and developmentally helpful environments, suggest, then, that spiritual care will most effectively occur in an environment that is egalitarian, person-centered, and safe, but also appropriately challenging. In such an environment, women can pay attention to their experience, learn to name it through narrative, obtain validation for it, and learn to give and receive mutual care. They can also receive appropriate challenge to deal with blocks to their self-transcendence and nudges to move, however haltingly, toward their visions of ultimate good.

Such environments can occur in many contexts. Some women's Bible study groups, for example, have grown into this kind of committed context for personal and communal growth. Some consciousness-raising groups have served just this purpose in recent years. Certainly some twelve-step groups have re-created such optimal conditions for moving toward self-transcendence without explicit use of Christian theological concepts. Our grandmothers and their mothers may have participated in the same dynamics in their quilting parties and female charitable societies as well as in their classes, bands, and prayer meetings of the last century. What settings will serve to nourish women in the future remain to be discovered.

## A PROCESS FOR WOMEN'S SPIRITUAL CARE

With these supporting perspectives from feminist psychotherapy and developmental theory in place, I propose the following process for women's spiritual care. In outline form, this process consists in the dynamics of contemplative attending, mutual accompaniment, critical analysis, and authentic action.

Note that these dynamics need not occur in a particular order; in "real life," things are hardly ever so tidy. But explicating them in this order offers a certain logical progression that allows us to illuminate the dynamism of effective caring for women. Note, as well, that this process applies alike to both caregiver and receiver, and to one-to-one and group situations. What it states in barest outline will take a variety of forms with particular women. In other words, this process is not to be treated as a recipe to be applied in some "add and stir" fashion, and it implicates the caregiver simultaneously with the seeker.

### Contemplative Attending

Since experience of the transcendent is the raw material of spirituality, the first and most basic moment of spiritual care happens in the act of attending to this experience.

Experience, says Thomas Clarke (1983, 20, 22), has to do with the *perception* of reality, with *receptiveness* toward the real in all its dimensions. Experience is the initial aspect of our encounter with life, the phase where we feel the touch of life. The building up of an authentic spiritual consciousness in any individual or community is contingent on the quality of paying attention. Since the distancing of women from their own experiences and from their history as women essentially denies them authentic spiritual consciousness, the basis for all spiritual care of women lies in effective attending to women's experience.

Each party in the spiritual care relationship must *listen* to her own experience in all its aspects, not just in areas she would name as "religious."

Such listening to one's experience is by no means automatic, especially when the culture denies women's experience in very subtle ways; many women must learn this skill. Next, she must *name* these experiences and give them life outside herself. Simultaneously, she must receive validation that her experiences are not idiosyncratic to her alone but that she belongs to a community of shared experience, of which she articulates one unique aspect.

Attending to experience applies to all parties involved in the spiritual care of women, whether seeker or caregiver. Indeed, caregivers' helpfulness will be severely curtailed, if not completely vitiated, without attending to and articulating their own experiences. Seeker and caregiver alike must ground themselves in reality if they are to grow in authentic spiritual consciousness. The caregiver has the additional task of attending to the seeker's experience: the quality of the caregiver's attending facilitates the seeker's attending.

The adjective "contemplative" may sound strange in this context. Yet, suitably demystified, contemplation offers a means from within the Christian spiritual tradition to ground our listening in attentiveness to the sacred.

Contemplation is a basic attitude of radical openness. Contemplation is being before someone or something with pure immediacy (Jones 1992, 145), "a long, loving look at the real" (Burghardt 1989). In the Christian spiritual tradition, contemplation names the attitude of receptivity to God's action toward us. It is the prayer of waiting and receiving whatever comes to us as God's gift. It may be wordless or may evoke words. It flourishes within and itself nourishes a rich inner silence and centeredness that are qualitatively different from the muteness and invisibility which leave women cut off from their own inner wisdom.

Contemplation, says Gerald May (1991, 193), occurs in everyone's life. "It happens in moments when we are open, undefended, and immediately present. People who are called contemplatives are simply those who seek the expansion of the moments, who desire to live in that quality of presence more fully and continually." Such natural contemplation lies in direct continuity with spiritual contemplation, as Brenda Meehan notes:

> Some people, including many artists and mystics, consciously nurture the natural gift of contemplation, developing an intentionality about it; those people who direct their intentionality toward love transform natural contemplation into spiritual contemplation. (Meehan 1993, 147)

Thus the contemplation that grounds attentiveness to women's experience is both an attitude of radical receptiveness to life as it is experienced and a spiritual practice of honoring this experience. Such contemplative attending literally "hears another into speech," in Nelle Morton's felicitous phrase. It bonds persons to one another and to God in profound community through uniting them at their very ground and center.[10]

To reach its fullest power, contemplative attending must extend beyond individual women to include what is happening in our society and culture. Such listening must encompass historical sensitivity to how things came to be the way they are; it must also include hopeful imagination in order to create alternative visions for the future of humankind.

Storytelling has proven to be one of the most effective avenues for women to attend to their experience, name it in each other's presence, and create a community of solidarity with respect to their experience. Storytelling, engaged in contemplatively, can become a privileged medium of women's spiritual care.

In what do the stories consist? Women's present experience, surely, both outer and inner.[11] But through the medium of memory, stories can bring the past into the present (Clarke 1983, 20–25). Through storytelling and creative midrash, women can *re-member* that which has been severed from their consciousness and speak themselves back into sacred stories. They can begin to hear themselves present there, perhaps for the first time. Through storytelling, women can reconnect themselves with their foremothers, near and distant. Without living memory of one's history, no future is possible.

Stories also provide a vehicle for the imagination, which brings the power of the future to bear on present struggle. Through imagination, we can envision a future different from the present. Dreaming, by both day and night, is an essential ingredient in healthy human beings. When imagination becomes blocked in individuals, communities, and cultures, trouble lies ahead.[12]

An example of such contemplative attending in service of women's spiritual growth occurred in the context of a women's retreat. A small group of three women took an afternoon to reflect on the midwives of the first chapter of Exodus. As they pondered the nine verses that recount the story of Shiphrah and Puah, these formerly overlooked biblical women took on texture, imagination, integrity, and courage. The group analyzed the social situation in which these biblical women found themselves and compared it to their own. They saluted the simplicity and effectiveness of their passive resistance and gained a greater sense of their own power within social structures. They created their own rereading of this passage which they styled as a Greek tragedy, complete with a chorus of voices representing the forces of society aligned against the women and a competing chorus representing the liberating insights of the midwives. At the end of their afternoon's reflection, they shared their rereading with the other women on the retreat, including the sense of energy and power they had gleaned from their connection to these largely invisible biblical women.

## Mutual Accompaniment

As we have seen, spiritual care flourishes in relational contexts, if for no other reason than that personality development occurs interactively. But the end of spiritual care requires a further rationale for accompaniment. Here I suggest a theological one: even a community of two embodies the conviction that Christian community is the context for living out one's baptism and growing in one's relationship with God, oneself, the human, and even the nonhuman community. Graced community fosters deeper interdependence.

Effective accompaniment in women's spiritual care relationships will be consistent, faithful, nonjudgmental, supportive, and challenging. Consistency and faithfulness mark spiritual care contexts for two reasons. We have seen that developmentally useful environments remain constant during the course of a transition in order that new and broader relationships become fully integrated into the emerging horizon on the other side of the transition. But even more important, the self-transcendence in relationship to the Ultimate which is the end of spiritual care is a lifelong matter. The need for spiritual care does not cease when a given problem is solved, when pain is eased, or when a developmental transition is negotiated. It follows each human being throughout life because the possibility for further self-transcendence exists as long as life does.

Effective spiritual accompaniment does not judge women whose life may have been lived out of others' expectations. The ethical reflection of many women has been driven by moral judgments formed by others, often without consideration of the contexts in which the subjects of the reflection find themselves. But self-transcendence requires that moral decision making flow from internalized and self-validated moral principles formed in relationship to the Ultimate. These grow slowly, if at all, if the climate is frosted by judgment. Yet it is equally important that women receive sufficient and appropriately timed and personalized challenges; without such discomfiting experiences, little growth occurs. In a society that socializes women to compete with each other, the art of women effectively challenging other women comes slowly. A committed context of mutual vulnerability offers its best climate.

Any mutual accompaniment must take seriously the theological setting in which it occurs. Two clergywomen colleagues, each working with women's spiritual care groups, illustrate this need. In one case, the women who come are largely estranged from traditional churches and from theological language in general; this group struggles to create rituals and processes that empower them to relate to the transcendent without relying on traditional Christian images, symbols, and rituals. The other clergywoman's theological context differs radically. The women in her congregation, equally hungry for spiritual nurture, respond most readily to a context that honors their traditional Christian background. They do not trust any materials that carry the adjective "feminist" because of their perception of feminism's ideological and political cast, even though much of that material might be helpful if presented in a different context. This clergywoman's challenge is equally to facilitate a climate of safety and trust where the women are free to explore their experience of God, but for this group, that will occur within specific theological constructs. In either case, to ignore these theological "boundaries" will be to move too far outside the range of tolerable disconfirmation and cause excessive and non-productive anxiety, hardly conducive to exploring experiences of the transcendent.

Much of women's spiritual care occurs without the intervention of a pastor, a minister, or a spiritual director. Yet these "professional" caregivers will also be involved in women's spiritual care. This context alters the traditional understandings of care somewhat. Without abrogating their relatively greater responsibility for the tenor and parameters of the relationship, spiritual caregivers respond in a more mutual and egalitarian fashion than usually occurs in other helping relationships. This relative equalizing of power arises from the conviction that the relationship of spiritual caregiver to seeker is itself set within the more basic relationship of all humans to the Ultimate, all Christians to God. A conviction that God is the effective agent in spiritual growth relieves the spiritual caregiver of any need to fix or change others. Both spiritual caregivers and seekers participate in the healing, renewing, and empowering action of the Spirit of God.

Effective spiritual accompaniment can occur in a variety of situations. Some of the more traditional occasions for women's care have succumbed to the rising demands of employment outside the home on top of homemaking and child care. New possibilities for spiritual accompaniment will rely upon careful attention to natural contexts of women's relationships. Since many women struggle with relationships with their mothers, situations that bring together women from several generations may prove especially fruitful.

### Critical Analysis

As the first section of this chapter suggests, women's growth in self-transcendence is no less a systemic than an intrapersonal and interpersonal issue. The feminist claim that "the personal is the political" underlines this simultaneity as well as an understanding of the basic unity of the human person. Therefore effective spiritual care includes critical analysis of the systems and structures in which women live: family life, economic arrangements, political structures, health care, arts, religion, law and law enforcement, international relations.

Many Christians are unused to thinking of structures as a theater of God's action. They have assumed that spiritual care occurs in intrapersonal and interpersonal dimensions of human experience; that is, spiritual care deals with relationship to God and to ourselves and to immediate, face-to-face relationships of family, work, and church. Beyond that, secular takes over from spiritual, or so they assume. They do not consider one's call with respect to, for example, workplace, child-care arrangements, rising homelessness in the community, free-trade agreements, and health care policy. Yet these social arrangements affect the possibilities for women's self-transcendence with respect to the Ultimate and thus inevitably have spiritual implications.

A spiritual practice that examines and acts on systems may be especially helpful to those women who feel particularly disenfranchised from them. Perhaps systems seem impenetrable, operating on their own mysterious rules unaffected by any single person's attempts to change them. Or perhaps the centers of power and decision making within a system are closed to women, who thus experience themselves as powerless to affect even a system such as family, which touches them moment by moment. Or systems are perceived to be "unspiritual" and therefore not recognized as a theater for the transformation of themselves before God. In each of these cases, experiencing God working through systems, discerning God's call with respect to a given system and acting on that call can be exquisitely liberating to women's spiritual lives.

## AUTHENTIC ACTION

Action emerging from prayerful reflection completes the dynamic process of women's spiritual care and prepares for its reemergence. This is true whether the action emerges from a formal spiritual practice such as that suggested above or as the result of more general spiritual development. Response embodies one's self-transformation; response actualizes the Spirit's work in us. Responsive action bridges the inner moment of conversion to the outer moment of mission. Authentic action places one in solidarity with others in their attempts to live the transforming power of the gospel. Authentic action is orthopraxis.[13]

Several areas of authentic action are particularly nourishing to women's spirituality; here I underline ritual, prayer, discernment, and action on behalf of justice. Since women have largely been excluded from ritualizing their religious experience publicly, ritual created by women for their own use often carries particular transformative power (Cady, Ronan, and Taussig 1989). These rituals may look like nothing they inherited from their religious traditions, such as rituals to celebrate menarche or menopause, to mourn the surgical removal of organs or to heal from sexual abuse. But also, rituals central to the woman's own tradition, if not freighted with too much oppressive baggage, can also come alive as women generate their own metaphors and exercise leadership.

Prayer can provide an authentic response to the action of the Spirit in a woman's life; it will grow out of her own experience rather than being an imposed structure from without. It may involve reimaging God, reinterpreting Scriptures, drawing authority from new places in the tradition, and seeking images and mentors from a variety of nontraditional sources. Those who accompany women in their prayer experiences need to be comfortable pushing out the boundaries of "acceptable" or "orthodox" prayer.

As women reflect on their experiences and responses, they will grow in their ability to discern for themselves how God is acting in their lives and in the world. Not only will they be able to distinguish for themselves ever more subtle movements of the Spirit of God, they will gradually transform the very process of spiritual discernment.

I have already touched upon the transforming power of acting concretely upon a carefully discerned call. Here let me further assert that authentic action on behalf of justice for all undergirds women's spiritual transformation. As the literature on recovery from physical and sexual abuse reveals, the transformation from victim to survivor often results in direct service to other abused women or commitment to working for more adequate, empowering, and just systems. Action on behalf of justice is both a means to and the fruit of empowerment.

These actions need not be earthshaking in their scope. They can be as ordinary as the way in which one changes a diaper or answers one's spouse. They can be public and observable, as in writing a letter to one's congressperson or lessening one's reliance on fossil fuels by joining a car pool. Likewise, they can be private and hidden, as in the decision to pray for one's nemesis in the workplace. Since spirituality involves the deepest aspects of all that is human, the scope of authentic action is unlimited.

Caregivers cannot assume that they are free of this requirement to act on behalf of justice; as has so often been the case in women's spiritual care, the caregiver is as deeply implicated as the seeker. Women's spiritual care is inevitably a reciprocal process. And caregivers do well to heed the warning: participating in women's spiritual care may very well require the caregiver's own renewed conversion.

## FINDING GOD IN THE MIDST OF STRUCTURES AND SYSTEMS

In this chapter, I have attempted to reflect on the underlying dynamics that effectively assist women in their spiritual growth. These dynamics can be—and have been—applied in widely divergent social, cultural, theological, and ecclesial contexts. Each woman or group's own context must dictate the particular expression of spiritual care. Thus it is impossible to suggest a "typical" process or experience. Yet a concrete example of one woman's experience may help embody the above discussion.

Because structures are so seldom seen as a theater of God's action, and because women's lives are so frequently constrained by structures for which they tend to assume personal responsibility, I will illustrate the dynamics of women's spiritual care by describing a retreat experience that expressly engages structures as a locus of prayer and reflection. This particular experience has been created around the "pastoral circle," the process of attending, in turn, to experience, structural analysis, theological reflection, and pastoral response made familiar through Christian base communities.

The pastoral circle offers a systematic way of incorporating structural analysis into spiritual care and thus offers the possibility for a spiritual practice that takes structures seriously (Holland and Henriot 1983; Shea 1985; Liebert 1992b). John Mostyn and Elinor Shea have developed a retreat experience based on the pastoral circle, which has proven effective for enabling women to incorporate structures and systems into their spirituality.[14] It is expressed in explicitly Christian terms but may be adapted, I believe, to other religious contexts. I will follow one woman through such a retreat, interweaving her experience with the description of the retreat dynamics based on the pastoral circle.

### Attending to Experience of Structures

The first locus of attention helps bring one's experience of a given system or structure into focus. At this point, the task involves examining the current situation and one's feelings about it, noting the people, behaviors, physical environment, interpersonal connections, and estrangements and any other aspect of the system that would deepen one's understanding of it, all in the context of prayer and mutual sharing. It is important to pay attention to one's own feelings at all points—these interior responses reveal much about the spiritual issues involved and will point toward avenues of self-transcendence. There is no need to judge oneself or the structure; one simply notices, contemplatively, one's multifaceted experience of and within this structure.

The post-Christmas "low time" was the setting for a women's retreat called "Finding God in Everyday Life." About fifteen women gathered for an extended weekend, including a woman whom I shall call Christine, a member of a Roman Catholic teaching community that staffs several elementary and secondary schools in the area. Other women represented Presbyterian, Methodist, and United Church of Christ denominations. The first evening of the retreat focused, appropriately, on the relationship and the trust building of leaders with the group and of the women with each other. A brief overview of the process, several exercises designed to assist the participants to begin to notice and to take seriously both the inner and the exterior world in which they live, and simple ritual comprised the "opening exercises" of the retreat. The women began to create a safe and sacred space among themselves. They began to expect that their time together might bear rich fruit in the Spirit.

The stress of the few days prior to the retreat was the substance of Christine's initial sharing. She had come from an especially intense several weeks of parent conferences. She was relieved to notice that the leaders did not expect her to be filled with insight about her situation as fatigued as she was. The leaders simply suggested that she and the other women prayerfully select a "structure" that they would focus on during the next few days, defining "structure" as a system of relationships that continues with or without the presence of individual persons. Structures that the women might select include their families of origin or marriage, their work situation, their church community, their civil community, a particular organization to which they might belong, and so on. The leaders suggested that they ask for the assistance of the Holy Spirit in allowing the appropriate structure to surface in their quiet time this first evening.

The first sharing in the morning took place in a smaller group of three, which remained consistent for the duration of the retreat. Christine deepened her connections to her two companions in the context of describing the respective structures that they had chosen for their prayerful reflection. As she reflected during the evening and early morning, Christine realized that she was experiencing considerable tension within her living community and decided to focus on the unnamed assumptions within that group. The overt issue concerned the unnamed expectations that were making it difficult for the newest member to settle comfortably into their group. As Christine related her experience of this structure, she noticed that there was a good bit of tightness and anxiety contained in her body, which she identified as related to her sense of frustration that things could be any different in this community. The leaders encouraged her to notice those feelings but not to judge or try to fix them.

### Critically Analyzing Structures

Once the experiences of a particular structure are clear, the facts and structural connections operating in this reality become the focus of attention. In this step, one recalls the history of the structure, identifies the traditions that undergird it, names the assumptions that the participants hold and examines the power arrangements, noting any trends that emerge. As an integral part of this step, one then examines one's own participation in this structure, taking care to attend to feelings evoked.

Christine's afternoon prayerfully focused first on her own five-year experience of her living group. She noted the high points of life and energy during those years but also remembered her own struggles to gain entry into the long-established dynamics of the group during her first years. She remembered several painful confrontations with various members of the community over "rules" that she didn't know existed until she had violated them. She noticed her complicity with this covert system and her tendency to collude with it by not challenging either the "rules" or their covert nature.

Next, Christine ranged farther back into the group's history. She recalled several incidents that preceded her arrival and that influenced the relationship between the community and the present school administration that administered the convent living space. She noted how the configuration of the personal and shared living space played into the situation as she now experienced it. She recalled some of the particular stresses sustained by other members of the community. All of these realizations, and others, helped her to understand how thing came to be as they were. Yet at the same time, she found herself even more discouraged about the prospects for change. She found the process at this point strangely unsettling.

### Prayerful Consideration of the Data

The next movement of the retreat process requires a spirit of openness to God's reality and a willingness to engage the issues in light of one's relationship to God. After such an interior climate has been established, one then brings to God in an attitude of prayer all the feelings and thoughts that the above process has stirred. It is not necessary to focus explicitly on the structure; it is only necessary to focus on God and let God's power form and transform one's vision and choices. Out of the deepest center of oneself, where God's Spirit resides, flows the response most true to the individual person at this moment in time.

By the time Christine and her two group members had reflected on and shared their respective structural dynamics with each other, the afternoon had grown late. All the women reported fatigue but at the same time a kind of awareness of the complexity of the structures. They began to claim their own responsibility for their participation in their structures and experience some empathy for other actors in the system. Upon resuming in the evening, the leaders directed them to set aside for the time being all the work they had been doing. Instead, they were to turn explicitly toward God, becoming aware of God's presence. The leaders offered some simple suggestions on how to release any burden that the structure seemed to impose as well as how to relax into their bodies and then into God's presence. This gentle reflection ended their day.

In the early part of the following morning, Christine returned to her sense of God and God's call to her. She asked for, and after some minutes began to experience, a desire to do and be for God whatever God desired in her living group. In that spirit, she just "rested," believing that the next "move" belonged to the Spirit of God. Some minutes into her quiet waiting, Christine experienced the following awareness: "If you speak the assumptions, they are no longer unspoken."

This simple insight struck her with great power. Without arguing, without trying to change any of the members of the community, she did have power with respect to the unnamed assumptions: she could, quite simply, voice them. Once they were named, then the group could choose to deal with them—or not—but the dynamics of the group would be substantively different because the assumptions would no longer be functioning unconsciously. The more Christine reflected on this simple truth, the more she felt the power and energy of a "word of God" around it. The heaviness that she had experienced the previous day began to fall away. Christine shared her experience with her two colleagues and they confirmed Christine's sense of breakthrough.

### Embodying a Response

The final movement of the retreat leads toward informed action. It involves examining any personal responses that suggest themselves during and after one's prayer. If several possibilities have opened, one selects an action that seems to express most closely the sense of call which emerged in prayer, and determines a first, do-able step. One imagines how to evaluate that action. As before, one continually notes the quality of the experience and the feelings that the action generates. In other words, one moves, in a spirit of prayer, toward a concrete embodiment of the new call. Such concreteness issues in taking a step, however small, toward actualizing the vision. Repeating the process as experience grows and circumstances change enhances a sense of efficacy with respect to systems.

Christine's final reflections considered prayerfully how God might wish her to embody her insight about speaking the unspoken assumptions. She determined one occasion in which she would speak her perception of her living group's unspoken assumptions, knowing that too global a resolution could place the entire insight at risk of paralysis. She offered that "resolution" to God for confirmation; the sense of rightness that she experienced, combined with her group members' affirmation, gave her that sense of confirmation.

Christine noted with some surprise that almost every woman's prayer had yielded an insight that was simultaneously simpler yet more profound than her initial inclination. She could see that the other women were also experiencing a surge of energy and sense of competence with respect to their own structural realities. The elation with which they concluded their sharing was palpable. Christine's group spontaneously committed themselves to write to each other in one month, sharing their struggles and successes in carrying out what they discerned in the context of their time together.

Why did this experience move Christine so deeply? Although many persons feel more comfortable *thinking* about the spiritual implications evoked by systems than actually *praying* them, the power for spiritual transformation is seldom sufficiently engaged at an intellectual level. Rather, spiritual transformation is more effectively evoked through prayerful openness to God's action. Consequently as essential as theological reflection may be, it is rarely sufficient to affect the necessary insight and inner conversion, nor to support wise responses to structures. The spiritual effectiveness of this method relies on wedding critical thinking and prayerful openness to God and a commitment to embodying a response to one's prayer. In addition, the community of support created an environment of safety, trust, discernment, challenge and confirmation. The women knew they were not alone either in their struggles or in their successes.

## THE CAREGIVER'S SPIRITUALITY

In any helping relationship, the person who is performing the caregiving carries certain responsibilities for the quality and duration of the relationship. Those who assist with women's spiritual care are no exception. But once this additional qualification based on function is noted, the spirituality of the caregiver and the seeker differ little in essence. Our description of spirituality and women's spiritual care, I believe, fits caregiver and receiver alike.[15]

Much that nourishes women's spiritual life takes place serendipitously, using whatever resources are at hand. Some aspects of women's spiritual care resist categorizing. Many persons involved in the process would not recognize themselves if they were called spiritual caregivers. But there are particular qualities that foster women's spiritual care, and their presence increases the possibility that spiritual care relationships will yield fruit.

The persons to whom women frequently entrust their spiritual lives have learned to respond to life as a process. They compose their lives out of the many interruptions and contingencies that life brings them, garnering meaning where they can find it. Or another metaphor: they sew together the scraps as well as the choice cloth of their experience, creating a unique and beautiful quilt out of the large and small pieces of their lives. Or a third: when the music outstrips the dance step, they learn to improvise (Bateson 1990).

They are transparent. They do not hoard their struggles and their successes, or their hopes and their dreams, as if either their persons or dreams would diminish by sharing them. They know when to offer a dream, and when to wait patiently for another to dream her own dream.

They are healers who have become so through their own wounds. They have faced their share of the blows and benefits of human existence but have grown despite and through the struggles. The wisdom they have gained belongs to their sisters as well as to themselves.

They are willing to risk conversion, having found that the struggles bear valuable fruit. They are willing to receive help themselves, recognizing that giving and receiving require each other for their completion. They are also willing to risk the pain of entering into and staying with another's pain and the shared pain of all women.

They are willing to stand alongside rather than in front, pulling, or behind, pushing. They enter into relationships from a stance of empowerment.

These qualities—and there are surely others—are gifts. They may come unbidden as a result of personality. More often, they appear as the fruit of struggling with the circumstances of lives as they unfold. They are, I believe, signs of deepening spirituality, deepening self-transcendence before God.

## NOTES

1. Ellyn Kaschak (1992, 20) discusses the logical typing error in women's status within "mankind," which renders woman either a subset of man or totally invisible. Mary Catherine Bateson (1990, 106–109) considers the power differential between men and women. Susan Faludi (1991, 70–72) chronicles the current cultural trends toward women.

2. The situation is more complex for women of color, who must deal with the culture of their racial-ethnic or national group and its assumptions about gender,

as well as with those of the dominant white culture. These women often face situations of double or even triple discrimination.

3. I do not intend to imply that pastoral care and spiritual care are completely discrete; their respective concerns clearly overlap. Rather, my intent concerns figure and ground: to shift focus from a largely implicit "*context* of ultimate meanings and concerns," as Clebsch and Jaekle (1964, 4) put it, to explicit attention to the ultimate at all the points where it might be discerned.

4. See Christie Cozad Neuger (1991, 146–61) for suggestions about pastoral counseling with depressed women.

5. Elisabeth Gössmann (1991, 50–59) provides an accessible summary of the Christian theological tradition's tendencies either toward making women into men or toward keeping them unequal and subservient. This article also traces the alternative women's traditions, ignored in the mainstream of Christian theology, which sought to develop a dual (not dualistic) notion of human nature which we still lack today.

6. For a hermeneutical perspective on the treatment of women in the Bible, see the ground-breaking works of Elisabeth Schüssler Fiorenza (1983) and Phyllis Trible (1978). For the situation of women in early Christianity, see Rosemary Ruether and Eleanor McLaughlin (1979). For a discussion of the ordination of women in Christian theology, history, and ethics, see Ann Carr (1988). For the contemporary experience of ordained women, see Judith Weidman (1985) and Lynn Rhodes (1987).

7. The difficulty with this definition, of course, is that by stressing consciousness this definition seems to leave out of bounds any spirituality of children before they are self-consciously able to appropriate it as well as any of the spiritually formative, but not always conscious, effects of living within a spiritual community and absorbing its ethos. See Bradley Hanson (1994, 5).

8. See Patricia Berliner (1992) for an example of a therapeutic model carefully adapted to women's spiritual care.

9. For a more extensive discussion of these and other developmental change principles, see Liebert (1992a, 55–76).

10. See Kathleen Fischer (1990) for a more extended discussion of contemplation and relationship and (1988) for a discussion of contemplative prayer on women's experience and naming of God. This earlier work extends several aspects of my treatment here, including ways of remembering and retelling the biblical tradition, possibilities for reconnecting with mothers and grandmothers, and discernment with women.

11. Mary Catherine Bateson (1990) deals extensively with the process of women reflecting with other women on the experiences of their lives. She finds the metaphor of "improvisation" especially fruitful for encouraging women to ponder the discontinuities and continuities of their lives.

12. Gail Ranadive (1992) offers a gentle series of writing exercises specifically designed to tap what already exists within women themselves, waiting to be reawakened and given a voice. These exercises may be pursued by an individual woman alone, or, preferably, a group may convene around writing and sharing the results of the creative process.

13. "Praxis" refers to intentional social activity directed toward emancipatory transformation; "orthopraxis" refers to that Christian praxis directed toward transforming the historical conditions that in turn lead to the realization of freedom (Downey 1993).

14. This reflection process is based on materials from the workshop "Integrating Spirituality and Justice," facilitated by John Mostyn and Elinor Shea at San Francisco Theological Seminary, January 1993.

15. Kaschak (1992, 23) notes that current masculinist epistemologies are based on the drawing of boundaries, which include, in the case we are considering, the boundary between caregiver and receiver: "While it is probably impossible to work without some sort of boundary by means of which to organize experience, it must be acknowledged that any distinction between figure and ground is arbitrary and a function of the epistemology of the maker of that boundary." In other words, the distinction between caregiver and receiver serves the caregiver by obscuring her or his similarity with the person receiving care.

## BIBLIOGRAPHY

Bateson, Mary Catherine. 1990. *Composing a Life*. New York: Penguin Books.

Belenky, Mary; Blythe Clinchy; Nancy Goldberger; and Jill Tarule. 1986. *Women's Ways of Knowing: The Development of Self, Voice and Mind*. New York: Basic Books.

Berliner, Patricia. 1992. "Soul Healing: A Model of Feminist Therapy." *Counseling and Values* 37 (October): 2–14.

Burghardt, Walter. 1989. "Contemplation." *Church* (winter): 14–18.

Cady, Susan; Maria Ronan; and Hal Taussig. 1989. *Wisdom's Feast: Sophia in Study and Celebration*. San Francisco: Harper & Row.

Carr, Ann E. 1988. *Transforming Grace: Christian Tradition and Women's Experience*. San Francisco: Harper & Row.

Christ, Carol. 1980. *Diving Deep and Surfacing*. Boston: Beacon Press.

Clarke, Thomas E. 1983. "A New Way: Reflecting on Experience." In *Communities of Social Action and Theological Reflection*, ed. James E. Hug, 13–37. New York: Paulist Press.

Clebsch, William, and Charles Jaekle. 1964; 1967. *Pastoral Care in Historical Perspective: An Essay with Exhibits*. New York: Harper & Row.

Downey, Michael, ed. 1993. *New Dictionary of Catholic Spirituality*. Collegeville, Minn.: Liturgical Press. S.v. "Praxis," by Rebecca Chopp.

Duffy, Regis. 1983. *A Roman Catholic Theology of Pastoral Care*. Philadelphia: Fortress Press.

Faludi, Susan. 1991. *Backlash: The Undeclared War Against American Women*. New York: Crown Publishers.

Farganis, Sondra. 1986. *Social Reconstruction of the Feminine Character.* Totowa, N.J.: Rowman & Littlefield Publishers.

Fischer, Kathleen. 1988. *Women at the Well: Feminist Perspectives on Spiritual Direction.* New York: Paulist Press.

———. 1990. *Reclaiming the Connections: A Contemporary Spirituality.* New York: Sheed & Ward.

Gössmann, Elisabeth. 1991. "The Construction of Women's Difference in the Christian Theological Tradition." *Concilium* 6: 50–59.

Graham, Larry Kent. 1992. *Care of Persons, Care of Worlds: A Psychosystems Approach to Pastoral Care and Counseling.* Nashville: Abingdon Press.

Grant, Robert, and David Freedman. 1960. *The Secret Sayings of Jesus.* New York: Doubleday & Co.

Hanson, Bradley. 1994. "Theological Approaches to Spirituality: A Lutheran Perspective." *Christian Spirituality Bulletin* 2 (spring): 5–8.

Harris, Maria. 1989. *Dance of the Spirit.* New York: Bantam Books.

Holland, Joe, and Peter Henriot. 1983. *Social Analysis: Linking Faith and Justice.* Maryknoll, N.Y.: Orbis Books/Center of Concern.

Jack, Dana Crowley. 1991. *Silencing the Self: Women and Depression.* New York: HarperCollins.

Jones, W. Paul. 1992. *Trumpet at Full Moon: An Introduction to Christian Spirituality as Diverse Practice.* Louisville, Ky.: Westminster/John Knox Press.

Kaschak, Ellyn. 1992. *Engendered Lives: A New Psychology of Women's Experience.* New York: Basic Books.

Kegan, Robert. 1982. *The Evolving Self: Problem and Process in Human Development.* Cambridge: Harvard University Press.

Liebert, Elizabeth. 1992a. *Changing Life Patterns: Adult Development in Spiritual Direction.* New York: Paulist Press.

———. 1992b. "Spiritual Formation in a Reformed Context." In *Justice and Spirituality: The First Consultation on Practical Theology, Nae Jang, Korea, October 26–28, 1992* by Ecumenical Doctor of Ministry Studies in Korea, 88–104.

May, Gerald. 1991. *The Awakened Heart: Living Beyond Addiction.* New York: HarperCollins.

Meehan, Brenda. 1993. *Holy Women of Russia.* San Francisco: Harper & Row.

Nelson, James. 1978. *Embodiment: An Approach to Sexuality and Christian Anthropology.* Minneapolis: Augsburg Publishing House.

Neuger, Christie Cozad. 1991. "Women's Depression: Lives at Risk." In *Women in Travail and Transition: A New Pastoral Care,* edited by Maxine Glaz and Jeanne Stevenson Moessner, 146–61. Minneapolis: Fortress Press.

————. 1993. "A Feminist Perspective on Pastoral Counseling with Women." In *Clinical Handbook of Pastoral Counseling,* vol. 2, edited by Robert J. Wicks and Richard Parsons, 195–209. New York: Paulist Press.

Ochs, Carol. 1983. *Women and Spirituality.* Totowa, N.J.: Rowman & Allanheld.

Ranadive, Gail. 1992. *Writing Re-creatively: A Spiritual Quest for Women.* Boston: Skinner House Books.

Rhodes, Lynn N. 1987. *Co-Creating: A Feminist Vision of Ministry.* Philadelphia: Westminster Press.

Robb, Carol. 1993. "Principles for a Woman-Friendly Economy." *Journal of Feminist Studies in Religion* 9 (spring/summer): 147–60.

Ruether, Rosemary, and Eleanor McLaughlin. 1979. *Women of Spirit: Female Leadership in the Jewish and Christian Traditions.* New York: Simon & Schuster.

Saiving, Valerie. 1979. "The Human Situation: A Feminine View." In *Womanspirit Rising: A Feminist Reader in Religion,* edited by Carol Christ and Judith Plaskow, 25–42. San Francisco: Harper & Row.

Schneiders, Sandra. 1986. "Theology and Spirituality: Strangers, Rivals or Partners?" *Horizons* 13 (fall): 253–74.

————. 1991. *Beyond Patching: Faith and Feminism in the Catholic Church.* New York: Paulist Press.

————. 1993. "Spirituality as an Academic Discipline: Reflections from Experience." *Christian Spirituality Bulletin* 1 (fall): 10–15.

Schüssler Fiorenza, Elisabeth. 1983. *In Memory of Her: A Feminist Theological Construction of Christian Origins.* Philadelphia: Fortress Press.

Shea, Elinor. 1985. "Spiritual Direction and Social Consciousness." *The Way Supplement* 54 (autumn): 30–42.

Trible, Phyllis. 1978. *God and the Rhetoric of Sexuality.* Philadelphia: Fortress Press.

Weidman, Judith, ed. 1981. *Women Ministers: How Women Are Defining Traditional Roles.* Rev ed. San Francisco: Harper & Row.

# 16

# Women and Community: Women's Study Groups as Pastoral Counseling

PAULA BUFORD

*Pastoral Counselor, Atlanta*

## THE PROBLEM OF COMMUNITY FOR
## CONTEMPORARY WOMEN

Despite the liberating tradition of women's inclusion within the ministry of Jesus, women have often been omitted from true community[1] within contemporary church structures. Many women are caregivers but not carereceivers within their church families. They are taught about redemption but not given the opportunity to experience it fully. Others attend worship services where their models for God are male—an all-male ministerial staff who utilizes noninclusive language for God and humankind and preaches primarily on male biblical characters.[2]

Women often feel they are in a double bind socially. They perceive having to choose between having a self or living in community, between having autonomy or relationship.[3] Some women are forced to choose between relating to families and structures that use them up or leaving these structures out of a healthy self-love or healthy narcissism.[4]

While Freud extolled that healthy persons need both "love" and "work" in their lives, women may be criticized when they want both. Women who work "outside the home" and seek a career often lack energy to develop significant female friendships.[5] More traditional women, who combine their work and love in full-time parenting, may devalue themselves as being "only housewives." Generations of poor, working-class women have never had the option of "full-time homemaking" and often carry full responsibility for the financial and emotional support of their households.

Women clergy have unique problems in balancing work, family, and friendships. Growing numbers of women are training for professional ministry within environments that foster open inquiry and feminist thought. But after graduation, these same women may find themselves pastoring churches, with little support from their own congregations and the larger social context for their work.[6] Female pastoral counselors may find themselves well trained and employable yet paid significantly less than their male colleagues.[7]

In addressing this problem of community for women, this chapter has two constructive objectives: to advocate that local ministers and pastoral counselors offer women's study groups and to develop a feminist pastoral theology of community. In this chapter, I will reflect theologically on the importance of community within the ministry of Jesus; challenge the adequacy of traditional pastoral counseling for women; name three historically significant communities of American women; offer a case study of a women's study group in Dalton, Georgia; and develop a feminist pastoral theology of women and community.

This chapter is written from the perspective of an educated, middle-class, southern, Caucasian woman who primarily works with other middle-class Caucasian women.

## THEOLOGICAL REFLECTION ON COMMUNITY

We are created in God's image to be in relationship, to embody God's acceptance within our own human relationships. Paradoxically, only through community with others do we truly understand ourselves as individuals. We are more fully ourselves together than we are apart. Although we need space to be separate and alone, we were never created to be isolated persons.

Within the biblical story, God's chosen communities of Israel and the church were to be instruments of blessing and grace to others, not hoarders of divine truth and love. As a pastoral counselor, I understand the radical nature of Jesus' ministry as that of creating new community for all persons, regardless of their personal histories and current problems. Jesus was especially touched by the "outcasts" of society and challenged his disciples to go out into the "highways and hedges" to invite folks to his banquet table of grace and relationship.

In the Gospels, Jesus clearly elevated women as full members of his radical community,[8] one in which all persons are equally accepted by God.[9] To the Samaritan woman at the well (John 4), Jesus offered "living water," despite his knowledge of her past. To the woman caught in adultery, he offered grace by challenging those who were ready to stone her: "Let anyone among you who is without sin be the first to throw a stone at her"

(John 8:7). Additionally, he added his own exhortation, "Has no one condemned you? . . . Neither do I condemn you" (John 8:10,11). Jesus responded to the gentle touch of a sick woman's fingers on the hem of his garment, despite a crushing, shouting crowd who vied for his attention: "'Take heart, daughter; your faith has made you well.' And instantly the woman was made well" (Matthew 9:22). These marginalized women, alongside their more socially acceptable sisters, were called into the covenant community of early believers, which practiced radical inclusion and equality.

The role of community has always been prominent for feminist theologians. "Self-in-relation" is an ongoing focus for Jean Baker Miller and associates at the Stone Center. Carol Gilligan (1982) and Nel Noddings (1984) envision responsible relationship as the central ethical dilemma for women. Sallie McFague (1987) understands the earth to be the body of God and challenges us to work together in mutual interdependence to care for ourselves, each other, and the earth. Mary Hunt (1991) and Janice Raymond (1986) insist on the primacy of friendship for women, and McFague (1987) reinterprets the third person of the Trinity as friend. Marjorie Procter-Smith offers an engaged, corporate spirituality that celebrates both women's power and the "whole web of life" (1990, 172). Jim Poling (1991) and Carrie Doehring (1995) challenge caregivers to attend to power dynamics within their relational webs.

Thus, in referring to the need for community for women, I am drawing on the biblical image of community within the ministry of Jesus and the early church, and contemporary feminist understandings of community, self-in-relation, friendship, spirituality, and power dynamics within relationships.

## THE INADEQUACY OF TRADITIONAL PASTORAL COUNSELING FOR WOMEN

As can be seen in the previous section, community was offered by Jesus to all persons and is paramount in feminist thought. Yet, for some contemporary women this community seems elusive. In this section, I will show how traditional pastoral counseling does not adequately meet women's needs for community.

In *The Dictionary of Pastoral Care and Counseling,* John Patton defines pastoral counseling as a relationship that is initiated by persons "who can articulate the pain in their lives and [are] willing to seek pastoral help in order to deal with it" (Patton 1990, 849). Implicit in the definition of pastoral care and counseling is the minister's offering of self to the other in love and mutuality. It is hoped that as an intimate pastoral relationship develops, healing and enlargement of the counselee's relationships outside the structured therapy will occur in a parallel process.

There are several problems with this traditional understanding of pastoral counseling as it applies to women—first in its assumption that women are able to "articulate the pain in their lives and [are] willing to seek pastoral help in order to deal with it." Many women are unable to articulate their pain. Even in the 1990s, women continue to suffer from "the problem without a name"[10] in silent anguish and self-blame. Depressed women may feel shame for their unhappiness. They may see themselves as selfish persons, undeserving of their family's love, of God's love, of the special attention of a pastoral counselor—certainly unworthy of spending money on themselves if a fee is involved.

Second, in its focus on individual and/or family systems' pathology apart from cultural factors, traditional pastoral counseling has often been inadequate for women's healing process. Feminist scholars have offered an important corrective by looking at women's problems through the lens of larger patriarchal culture. Their voices, alongside those of other minorities, have helped mainstream pastoral theology begin to formulate new paradigms of care. However, even some seasoned pastoral practitioners who are open to "women's issues" have never read a single book by these scholars to critically inform their budding feminist consciousness.[11]

In addition to these first two concerns, traditional pastoral counselors may not understand why many of the needs of women cannot be met through the local church. Because they have been deeply injured by the church (or by persons claiming to be religious), some women may never be able to embrace religion in its traditional sense, although they may be deeply concerned with "ultimate" issues of life and are seeking a balanced spirituality in their lives.[12] Any woman who seeks to make meaning of her individual life and corresponding social structures—and is open to personal and social change—is on a spiritual quest. Ironically, this spiritual movement may occur in women who dare to rebel against ideologies of the institutional church.[13] Ideally, Sunday school classes, Bible study groups, prayer groups, women's "circles" or missions groups, and other small groups within the local church should be places where women can "be themselves" and be accepted. Sometimes they are safe havens for women. However, all too often church members have difficulty in being vulnerable and honest with each other in the very settings where they could receive the most love and affirmation.[14] The proliferation of twelve-step groups is an evidence that people are hungry for authentic relationships and personal growth within an affirming and challenging community, which is absent within many churches.

Fourth, the pastoral counseling field, although somewhat prolific in its writing on group work in the church in its formative years, has failed to address adequately the need for support/therapy groups.[15] Many pastoral counseling centers require their residents to co-lead inpatient psychiatric groups within their training programs. Yet these centers may fail to integrate this therapeutic model into their professional structures, seeing group therapy as a "stepchild" to individual and family work.

In summary, my concerns are as follows: pastoral counselors assume that women can articulate their need for help; some pastoral counselors have not integrated feminist theory into their practice; some ministers do not understand women's need to find spiritual healing outside traditional church structures; and not enough emphasis is given to group therapy for women.

In addition, I believe that a sole emphasis on group therapy to address women's special needs for community is inadequate. For many women, group therapy is the preferred mode of treatment. But for others, a referral to any kind of therapy may reinforce their self-blame and cause them to pathologize their relational alienation.

Women who engage in traditional psychotherapy often have to alter dramatically their personal relationships and understanding of social structures to sustain any level of personal change and differentiation. Thus, in their beginning efforts for change, women may be intensely lonely and depressed, though paradoxically they have begun a powerful journey toward individual health and integration.

Other women, who continue to be repeatedly damaged by their own families, may have to "cut off" entirely from these destructive systems for their very survival, a "cutoff" that some family systems purists do not support.[16] All women participate in relationships that are tainted by patriarchal influence and power imbalance if they are unexamined. Thus, women may leave a long-term psychotherapy process of many years with an "intact ego" and a "sufficient self" but with virtually no community to sustain them in their ongoing movement toward wholeness. Is that what health is really about?

In a clinical case conference several years ago, a colleague presented his concerns about his long-term female client who was close to termination. She had made tremendous personal progress, yet was uncomfortable within an institutional church setting. What was to be "church" to her now that she had outgrown her old support structures? That question for her, for my own clients, and for myself continues to haunt me.

As a partial response to that question, and out of my belief that traditional pastoral counseling is inadequate to meet women's needs for community, I offer a historical overview of three significant communities that

American women have created for themselves. Out of these female traditions, I will develop a feminist theology of community for women that can be incorporated into women's study groups.


## WOMEN'S COMMUNITIES IN AMERICAN HISTORY

Throughout history, small groups of women who longed for more meaningful lives have initiated larger social change. As women migrated to America from Europe, they brought the art of quilt making with them. Colonial women pieced together scraps of old clothing into intricate patterns in quilt making. And they taught their daughters this art form to prepare them for the "profession of marriage." Women's friendships were cemented as they sat around quilting frames in one another's homes. While they made rows of tiny stitches that held the three quilt layers together, they offered care to each other. Women who moved from their communities were given a symbol of this care: a friendship quilt on which their female friends signed their names and addresses.

Alongside quilting, a second source of community for women evolved in the late 1700s to mid-1800s in women's missionary societies. Thousands of women were converted to the faith, supported anew in their roles as Christian wife, mother, and teacher (Solomon 1985, 16). Some expressed their newfound religion by becoming evangelists and ordained ministers.

Other churchwomen banded together to form interdenominational missions groups to financially support foreign missionaries. Most societies had simple goals for women of simple means.

In these "public" missions groups, women began to search the Scriptures together, to pray aloud, and to focus on helping women in "heathen" lands (Hill 1985, 61). They soon discovered their collective power in fundraising and began to speak or pray in church on behalf of their missionary endeavor. As their mission groups grew, women also grew as orators, organizers, and self-fulfilled persons. They extended their roles from "homemakers" to "housekeepers of the world."

A new professional role emerged for women—that of missionary. These women exercised a role of ministry overseas that no laywoman or pastor's wife dared undertake in America, challenging the social roles of their American sisters.

Parallel with their concern for "heathen" women, women also began to work for social reform in the United States. As they worked with "ladies of the night," former slaves, immigrants, and residents in housing projects, they became astute in analyzing systemic problems and sought to change "evil" systems that were the bedrock of corrupt society. Gradually women began to realize that they, too, were a culturally disenfranchised group.[17]

In addition to quilting bees and missionary groups, a third source of community for women in American history was the consciousness-raising group, which had its inception in the mid-1960s second-wave feminism.[18] Seeking a collective understanding of their common plight in society, women struggled to buy back the self-esteem and individuality that had been robbed from so many of them in the isolated years of the "feminine mystique."[19]

During this "backlash" period in American history between the two waves of feminism (from 1920 to the mid-1960s), women failed to utilize their communal strength. After their employment during World War II as "soldiers without guns" in munitions factories and all areas of industry, they were relegated anew to the "private sphere" of domesticity when the men returned from war. As modern technology created more laborsaving devices, women raised the standard of the "perfect homemaker" to an all-time high. Even college women were challenged by educators to assume their rightful role as wives and mothers, one that required their undivided attention. Thus, women's community was shattered as they tended to their individual homes, often in quiet isolation and desperation.[20]

Consciousness-raising groups evolved in the late 1960s with the goal of changing women's understandings about what it meant to be male or female.[21] The "learned helplessness" that many of them experienced was a natural response to social systems that defined them as inferior.[22] When they discussed their common experiences as a minority group, many grew into a new perception of themselves, which in turn led to changed behavior and activism (Harris 1978, 177; Chafe 1977, 103). In summary, consciousness-raising groups defined "the personal issues of daily life —housework, childrearing, sexuality, etiquette, even language—as political issues susceptible to collective action and solution" (Rix 1988, 61–62).

Thus, in three disparate time periods in American history, women discovered unique ways to be together which empowered them both personally and socially. The quilting bees and mission groups both began as service enterprises, focusing on an external "mission" of providing material and spiritual resources for their families and larger community. These groups were often centered in the church or had traditional religious overtones. In contrast, the consciousness-raising groups of the 1960s were secular in nature, with the sole task of helping women to work together for their own self-actualization and personal healing.

Unfortunately some contemporary women have never experienced female communities such as the quilting groups, the missions groups, and the consciousness-raising groups in which they could experience authentic relationships with each other. To a particular group of these women in Dalton, Georgia, we now turn for a contemporary case study.

## WOMEN'S STUDY GROUPS IN DALTON, GEORGIA: A CASE STUDY

In 1987, I was assigned by Georgia Baptist Medical Center to work as a pastoral counselor in our satellite center one hundred miles north of Atlanta in the First Baptist Church of Dalton, a town of about seventy-five thousand persons. A rural community, Dalton suddenly emerged as the "carpet capital of the world" from mom-and-pop chenille bedspread factories. Currently, it is an interesting mix of millionaires, mill workers, rural southerners, and persons from all over the country who migrated there to work in the burgeoning carpet mills. It has a small-town conservative atmosphere where persons are concerned with outward appearances, along with a narcissistic streak which is encouraged by prosperity. Alongside traditional marriage and gender roles, there is a high incidence of depression, extramarital affairs, and divorce.

Early on in my practice, I taught a continuing education class at the college in town, which focused on gender differences. Although many of the women in the group volunteered in their churches and worked professionally with helping agencies, most had done little formal reading in feminist thought. Some of them seemed to be living out the "feminine mystique," with no awareness of the 1960s feminist wave. It was as if feminism had passed them by.

Within my psychotherapy practice, I kept hearing the same themes from female clients: depression, self-sacrifice, self-blame, guilt, religiosity, or alienation from religious structures. I found myself wishing that these women could find a way to support each other in their common experiences.

So, I began to focus my continuing education groups on feminist psychology.[23] Yearning to make this study group a formalized ministry of the pastoral counseling center, I moved its meeting place to the local Baptist church. I felt a shift both within myself and the participants about the meaning of our group. Therefore I publicly acknowledged my belief that institutional religion had silenced and harmed as well as helped many women. My hope was that we could maintain our honesty now that we were in a church setting.

I brought myself and my personal motivation into the group. My "calling" to work with women had been born out of my own struggle with Southern Baptist systems for professional affirmation and out of my struggle to be a whole woman in a patriarchal culture. I explained that I understood pastoral counseling to be a holistic ministry that encouraged persons to grow in grace and self acceptance—a journey that we would undertake together.[24]

Participants began to offer support, intimacy, honesty, humor, challenge, and care to one another. A core group of women elected to take every short-term offering (twelve to fourteen weeks), thus maintaining group cohesion when topics of study change.[25]

Over the years, many women stated that this group was the highlight of their week—"a place where I can be accepted"; "a place where I feel 'normal'"; a place to be "real" in a town that supports "appearances" over happiness. One woman voiced that this group felt to her what Sunday school should be like. All have agreed that the group has provided the basis for special friendships to develop among them—collectively and individually.

Many poignant experiences have occurred over the years. When I had participants draw what it was like to be a woman in our culture, one woman drew the head of a pin, stating that women were about that significant. Another woman drew an angel in a "superman" cape. Most drew six or eight different roles, which together were impossible to fill.

"You're an answer to my prayers!" a woman exclaimed to me after an initial class on anger. And indeed this woman was angry. Wishing to leave an unhappy marriage to a wealthy man, she felt no support for her own well-being from her religious community or family. As a female pastoral counselor, I embodied a prophetic role that both challenged her religious/social structures and also provided a sacred place for her to explore her anger with other uneasy pilgrims.[26]

Another woman dropped out of this same class: "I was in such a painful place in my marriage, I just couldn't hear what the group was processing about making a firm stand on issues." After working in marital therapy to develop a better relationship with her husband, she then felt free to rejoin our group.

Early on, much anger and sarcasm were expressed about men. When I challenged the women to think of relationships that were mutual, they would tell me they knew few decent men! There was much criticism of males, supported by articles and comics that the women spontaneously brought to the group. For a number of months, the women talked more about men/patriarchy than they did about themselves, even when we were studying books that focused on women's self-exploration. I repeatedly raised the question: "What does it mean that we talk so much about men and other persons in our lives and say so little about ourselves?" For some, their silence about themselves was a self-definition.

Not all of the women had invested themselves in being defined by others. One woman could not relate to the pain of some of the women who were "other" focused. Widowed with young children, she had developed a successful business career for herself and never had difficulty being honest with others. She enjoyed the group because honesty was not only accepted but encouraged.

The women in the group have tempered the pain of looking closely at themselves and their personal relationships by engaging in a lot of humor and by caring deeply for each other—inside and outside the group. They have shared meals together and vacationed together. When one woman acknowledged a personal crisis at the end of a group meeting, the members initiated meeting her for dinner later in the week to offer their support.

Participants in their mid-forties to mid-seventies struggled to see how they had sacrificially given themselves over to their husbands, families, and larger culture. One woman jokingly referred to herself as the "death-and-dying cook for the neighborhood." While she meant to say that she cooked and ministered to neighbors with special needs, her unconscious statement was more about the cost of her service: *She* was the "dying" cook.

Though grieving, participants challenged each other to concrete action and change. One woman "hid out" in her bedroom while her teenagers got ready for school so she could set limits on her caretaking. Another woman in her seventies, who cared for two generations in her home, confessed she had never taken a vacation by herself. After taking a huge risk, she reported her enjoyment of her trip. This new behavior showed others that they, too, could discover new possibilities for their lives.

Contemporary fiction and cinema provided challenge for the group. We saw *Fried Green Tomatoes, The Color Purple,* and *Thelma and Louise.* Our group made a major shift toward self-direction and intimacy when we decided to study women's history. Members took turns presenting a woman of their choice from history, politics, contemporary fiction, or from their own families. Interestingly, most chose to tell about women in their families.

Our first presenter began with her mother's and aunt's experiences as "Rosie the Riveter"s during World War II, and other women followed suit.

Another woman told of her grandmother, who married at age fourteen and had sixteen children. Her daughter (the group member's mother) was raised in a Christian fundamentalist environment and was not allowed to attend school after the eighth grade. Her strict religious upbringing and her lack of education constricted her potential; however, she encouraged her children to aim for more in life. Her daughter, our group member, became a nurse and converted to Judaism.

After about three years of facilitating this women's study group at the First Baptist Church, I left the Dalton area. Although initially resisting the idea of shared leadership, the group has maintained its autonomy by electing a facilitator who helps rotate leadership of the group among its members. Because it is smaller, the group has moved toward more intimate sharing. They have more of a support-group personality than a study-group personality, even though they still have focused reading.

One woman, who is trained in developmental psychology, explained her understanding of how the group has been able to be so honest and confrontational with each other, alongside offering care. The age of the group is very mature, with the women's ages from the thirties to the eighties. Developmentally, she said, because our members have a firm sense of self and are comfortable with who they are, they can differ with each other without injury.

One woman voiced that this group has offered her a place where she could trust other women. In addition to having a mother with no close female friends, she was told by the significant men in her life to view other women as competitors and enemies: "This group has opened up a whole new world to me!"

Another woman told us that the support she experienced in the group empowered her to share a "family secret" with her children and thus begin a healthier relationship with them.

Another woman proudly told us that she had consulted a therapist for a few sessions before attending our group. When she returned to therapy a year later, the therapist exclaimed that she was a different person.

One member had just vacationed with her family and brought back quilts that were made for her by family members. Opting for a more professional and independent life, she had differentiated from her family's lifestyle and values. But she felt sad that she had not learned the art of quilting—something of value in her family legacy. As she shared her quilts with us, we all affirmed her desire for connection with her family and suggested that she return to her home for several weeks to learn this age-old family skill from her mother and her aunt.

## AN EMERGING FEMINIST PASTORAL THEOLOGY OF COMMUNITY FOR WOMEN

In building a feminist pastoral theology of community, I will offer a conversation between my Dalton study groups and significant elements from the historical quilting, missions, and consciousness-raising groups.

The consciousness-raising group has had the most straightforward agenda for helping women to examine their own roles within a patriarchal culture and to strategize for change. But the work of consciousness-raising groups has only reached a small segment of women. A whole generation of younger women is beginning to seek out its place in this world, naively assuming equal power with males. Many middle-aged and senior-adult women have been either unaware or afraid to engage in the transforming power of "feminist" ideas and/or support groups.

This consciousness-raising has been vital to my Dalton group, for without it we might have become just another group of women seeking to bolster ourselves to "overfunction" more efficiently in our familial and communal settings. Efforts to achieve a more balanced care of self and of others for women is not a "selfish" endeavor. Women's individual growth does not occur in a vacuum. From a family systems perspective, individuals' growth effects a change in their larger family systems and larger community. A redefinition of womanhood effects a redefinition of gender, family, and the use of power.

Second, akin to the early women's missionary groups, we are a "mission society" of the First Baptist Church, Dalton, and of the Georgia Baptist Medical Center. This small women's group has far-reaching repercussions for helping the community to understand the gospel as "good news" with a prophetic and transforming voice. We have helped to birth new women's groups—two formed in New York and one in a nearby town.[27] Also, a previous member of the group, now employed in the school system, began support groups with mothers, seeing that their children's academic problems could not be isolated from their mother's emotional, social, and financial needs.

Theologically, women's groups often struggle with balancing self-denial, servanthood, and self-worth in a positive way—dilemmas that many Christians face. Love of God, others, and self can be complementary, not hierarchical.[28] Embodying a theology of grace and wholeness can be a "mission" or "ministry" that women can carry to their families, friends, and larger communities.

Third, these women's study groups embody many of the characteristics of quilting groups of Colonial America.[29] With the original intent of meeting household needs by recycling scraps into something usable, quilters were working on a different kind of quilt than they had originally envisioned: a quilt of self-affirmation and community.

Within women's study groups, pastoral counselors can engage women in the art of "quilt making"—helping them to see the beauty in their own lives. Within my women's groups, we are "quilting" together. We are developing group coherence and a transitional space in which we can all grow to fuller personhood. As ministers to each other, we are collectively reconstructing our lives with the belief that God is active among us.

We help each other to become active "life historians" and revisionists of our own family stories. By sharing the battered, torn, devalued scraps of our lives with each other, we work together to cut, shape, and piece these rags together into a quilt that has a unity, beauty, and meaning both for individuals and for the group as a whole. We build on our past identities without totally discarding them.

Even fabrics that are "horrible" to look at may be the very thing that we need in our quilts for balance. Each member of the group has scraps in her life story that she has to piece into a harmonious and acceptable whole. The work of the group is to move our cloth around; share our piece goods with others; and accept their offerings to us. Quilting is work; rearranging our lives together is the corporate work of the group.

So we continue to quilt our fabric together, working and reworking, with a balance of anger and hope. We sew together and mend the broken relational threads from whence we all come.

Through women's study groups, even the most unassuming woman can come to see that she is a minister to others. As she helps others to grow, she becomes more valuable in her own eyes.

## SUMMARY

As more women are ordained, they are starting women's groups within their ministry settings. Pastoral counselors are becoming more concerned with providing community for their female clients. Academically, the field of pastoral theology is exhibiting a growing interest in and body of knowledge about culturally informed pastoral care and counseling. But there is still much to be done.

The aim of this chapter has been to challenge traditional pastoral counseling to become intentional in developing communities for women as an extension of the ministry of empowerment to all persons. After all, with women doing so much of the work of the church, why wouldn't the church offer groups for women to learn to give out of fullness? Why not offer women a "sacred space" in which to nourish their souls?

Ongoing groups that assist women in developing friendships and community at a deep level are both a spiritual enterprise and an expanded form of traditional pastoral counseling. By "evangelizing" or raising the consciousness of the larger community about the special needs of women, and in dealing with social justice issues, private pastoral counseling can thus be transformed into a public, prophetic voice for social change.[30]

## NOTES

1. Within some religious traditions, the term "fellowship" is more commonly used than "community."

2. Cf. Carroll Saussy (1991) for the correlation between inclusive images for God and women's self-esteem.

3. This is the thesis of Harriet Goldhor Lerner's *Dance of Anger* and many other feminist works.

4. Many feminist scholars see this bind as more acute for women than for men because of the central concept of "self-in-relationship" for women. Cf. Jean Baker Miller (1976) and the Stone Center articles, Carol Gilligan (1983). Catherine Keller (1986), Maxine Glaz and Jeanne Stevenson Moessner (1991) for a further development of this concept.

5. Cf. Bonnie J. Miller-McLemore (1994).

6. Edward Lehman's research (1985) shows that female pastors tend to be assigned to smaller congregations initially and progress at a slower pace in their career tracks than their male counterparts.

7. Research shows that female psychologists in private practice charge less than male therapists. I assume this phenomenon occurs with pastoral counselors also (Burnside 1986).

8. Cf. Stagg and Stagg (1978).

9. Liberation theologians even note a "hermeneutical privilege to the poor," a privilege that feminist liberation theologians would extend to women as a disenfranchised group (Dorothee Soelle, 1990).

10. Betty Friedan's term in *The Feminine Mystique* for the depression and alienation that many women in the 1950s and early 1960s suffered when they made their families an all-consuming focus.

11. Cf. Glaz and Moessner (1991), DeMarinis (1993) for feminist pastoral care. Cf. Wimberly (1979 and 1991) for African American pastoral care. Patton (1983), Graham (1992), and Doehring (1995) discuss sociological/cultural issues as well as individual concerns in their introductory texts on pastoral care.

12. Cf. Joann Wolski Conn (1986) for a critique of patriarchal religion and for a holistic approach to women's spirituality.

13. This is especially true of female incest survivors whose "Christian" abuser fathers used patriarchal religion as a tool to dominate their daughters' lives. Many other women are emotionally abused by "fundamentalist" husbands and fathers who exact unquestioning obedience from females.

14. Some traditional women's groups in local churches are marvellous places of honesty and openness for women. My argument, however, is that the church needs to offer groups whose primary focus is on women's sharing their personal stories and seeking to understand themselves from a larger cultural perspective.

15. In a survey of *Pastoral Psychology* and the *Journal of Pastoral Care,* I discovered 34 articles on group therapy in the church written before 1967. Cf. Kew and Kew (1951), Edgar (1964), Leslie (1964), and Reid (1967).

For additional resources, cf. Baranowski (1988), Brody (1987), Jackson (1969), and Yalom (1985).

16. For a brief discussion of Murray Bowen's concepts of "emotional cutoffs," cf. Michael Kerr 1981, 249–250.

17. See Hill (1985) and Beaver (1980) for more about the women's missionary movement.

18. "First-wave" feminism describes women's fight for suffrage from 1848 to 1920.

19. "Feminine mystique" was coined by Betty Friedan in her 1963 book with the same title.

20. Brett Harvey challenges us to see that women were given the message that "achievement and autonomy were simply incompatible with love and family. The equation was inescapable: independence equalled loneliness" (1993, xviii). Cf. Ehrenreich and English (1978), chapters 7 and 8, for the "experts' advice" to women during this period of time.

21. As in abolitionist times, feminist consciousness sprang in part from women's attempts to assist in the Civil Rights movement of the 1950s.

22. Cf. chapter two, Lenore Walker (1980) for the psycho-social theory of "learned helplessness."

23. We studied Miller (1976) and Gilligan (1982).

24. Seven out of eight women who returned surveys about the Dalton study group process agreed that there were spiritual elements in our being together. All eight affirmed that this group served significant functions that were lacking in their local churches, such as "being myself without being judged," "ability to disagree with some" and to "discuss controversial topics," to have a "feminist perspective," and to "relate to a woman minister."

25. No matter what the topic, the agenda of the group was consistent: to offer community and friendship to participants and to offer understanding of how societal definitions of gender and power shape personal relationships.

26. In her response to my chapter, she requested that I explain that when her anger and pain were accepted by our group, her resolve was strengthened to make a new life for herself and her children. She divorced, remarried, and has started her own business. Although she considers herself a "spiritual person," she is still leery of institutional religion, after being told by religious leaders that her "feelings [of unhappiness within her previous marriage] were sinful."

27. The daughter-in-law of one of our members visited our group and subsequently started two women's study groups in her psychotherapy practice in New York.

28. For example, the teaching that "JOY in the Christian life means Jesus first; others second; yourself last."

29. I am indebted to professors Brian Childs and John Patton for the dilemma of pastoral counseling as "private" vs. a "public" form of ministry.

Cf. Pam Couture (1991) for an expansion of the essential link between pastoral care, public policy, and social justice issues.

30. I am indebted to those persons who have been community to me in my ministry in Dalton, Georgia: Murphy Martin, Andrew Gee, Martha Hughes, Billy Nimmons, Annette and Alan Stout, Carole Whaley, my counselees, and especially the women's study group. The following group members collaborated with me on the final draft of this chapter: Andrea Aaron, Carol Bell, Beth Haney Bennett, Sue Cochran, Lillian King, Liz Raisin, Nancy Reynolds, Beulah Rodstein, Katie Strals, Hilda Tennenbaum, and Sarah Tester.

## BIBLIOGRAPHY

### General References

Beaver, Pierce. 1980. *American Protestant Women in World Mission: A History of the First Feminist Movement in America.* Grand Rapids: Wm. B. Eerdmans Publishing Co. Reprint of *All Loves Excelling.*

Burck, J. R. 1990. "Community, Fellowship, and Care (Christian)." In *Dictionary of Pastoral Care and Counseling,* Rodney J. Hunter, general editor. Nashville: Abingdon Press.

Burnside, Mary A. 1986. "Fee Practices of Male and Female Therapists." In *The Last Taboo: Money as Symbol and Reality in Psychotherapy and Psychoanalysis,* edited by David W. Krueger, 48–54. New York: Bruner/Mazel.

Chafe, William H. 1977. *Women and Equality: Changing Patterns in American Culture.* New York: Oxford University Press.

Conn, Joann Wolski, ed. 1986. *Women's Spirituality: Resources for Christian Development.* New York: Paulist Press.

Couture, Pamela D. 1991. *Blessed Are the Poor? Women's Poverty, Family Policy, and Practical Theology.* Nashville: Abingdon Press.

DeMarinis, Valerie M. 1993. *Critical Caring: A Feminist Model for Pastoral Psychology.* Louisville, Ky.: Westminster/John Knox Press.

Doehring, Carrie. 1995. *Taking Care: Monitoring Power Dynamics and Relational Boundaries in Pastoral Care and Counseling.* Nashville: Abingdon Press.

Ehrenreich, Barbara, and Deirdre English. 1978. *For Her Own Good: 150 Years of the Experts' Advice to Women.* New York: Doubleday & Co.

Friedan, Betty. 1984. *The Feminine Mystique.* 20th Anniversary ed. New York: Dell Publishing Co.

Glaz, Maxine, and Jeanne Stevenson Moessner, eds. 1991. *Women in Travail and Transition: A New Pastoral Care.* Minneapolis: Fortress Press.

Graham, Larry Kent. 1992. *Care of Persons, Care of Worlds: A Psychosystems Approach to Pastoral Care and Counseling.* Nashville: Abingdon Press.

Harris, Barbara J. 1978. *Beyond Her Sphere: Women and Professions in American History.* Contributions in Women's Studies, no. 4. Westport, Conn. Greenwood Press.

Harvey, Brett. 1993. *The Fifties: A Women's Oral History.* New York: HarperCollins.

Hill, Pamela R. 1985. *The World Their Household: The American Women's Foreign Missionary Movement and Cultural Transformation, 1870–1920.* Ann Arbor: University of Michigan Press.

Hunt, Mary E. 1991. *Fierce Tenderness: A Feminist Theology of Friendship.* New York: Crossroad.

Keller, Catherine. 1986. *From a Broken Web: Separatism, Sexism, and Self.* Boston: Beacon Press.

Kerr, Michael E. 1981. "Family Systems Theory and Therapy." In *Handbook of Family Therapy,* edited by Alan S. Gurman and David P. Kniskern, 226–264. New York: Bruner/Mazel.

Lehman, Edward C. 1985. *Female Clergy: Breaking through Gender Barriers.* New Brunswick, N.J.: Transaction Books.

McFague, Sallie. 1987 Models of God. Philadelphia: Fortress Press.

Miller-McLemore, Bonnie J. 1994. *Also a Mother: Work and Family as Theological Dilemma.* Nashville: Abingdon Press.

Noddings, Nel. 1984. *Caring: A Feminine Approach to Ethics and Moral Education.* Berkeley: University of California Press.

Orlofsky, Patsy and Myron. 1974. *Quilts in America.* New York: McGraw-Hill Book Co.

Patton, John. 1990. "Pastoral Counseling." In *Dictionary of Pastoral Care and Counseling,* Rodney J. Hunter, general editor. Nashville: Abingdon Press.

———. 1993. *Pastoral Care in Context: An Introduction to Pastoral Care.* Louisville, Ky.: Westminster/John Knox Press.

Poling, James Newton. 1991. *The Abuse of Power: A Theological Problem.* Nashville: Abingdon Press.

Procter-Smith, Marjorie. 1990. *In Her Own Rite: Constructing Feminist Liturgical Tradition.* Nashville: Abingdon Press.

Raymond, Janice G. 1986. *A Passion for Friends: Toward A Philosophy of Female Affection.* Boston: Beacon Press.

Rix, Sara E. 1988. *The American Woman 1987–88: A Report in Depth.* New York: W. W. Norton & Co.

Saussy, Carroll. 1991. *God Images and Self Esteem: Empowering Women in a Patriarchal Society.* Louisville, Ky.: Westminster/John Knox Press.

Soelle, Dorothee. 1990. *Thinking About God: An Introduction to Theology.* Philadelphia: Trinity Press International.

Solomon, Barbara Miller. 1985. *In the Company of Educated Women: A History of Women and Higher Education in America.* New Haven: Yale University Press.

Stagg, Evelyn and Frank. 1978. *Woman in the World of Jesus.* Philadelphia: Westminster Press.

Walker, Lenore E. 1980. *The Battered Woman.* New York: Harper & Row.

Wimberly, Edward P. 1991. *African American Pastoral Care.* Nashville: Abingdon Press.

### Groups within the Church/Group Psychotherapy

Baranowski, Arthur R. 1988. *Pastoring the "Pastors": Resources for Training and Supporting Pastoral Facilitators for Small Faith Communities.* Cincinnati: St. Anthony Messenger Press.

Brody, Claire M. 1987. *Women's Therapy Groups: Paradigms of Feminist Treatment.* Springer Series: Focus on Women. Vol. 10. New York: Springer Publishing Co.

Edgar, Robert A. 1964. "The Listening Structured Group." *Pastoral Psychology.* 15 no. 145 (June): 7–13.

Jackson, Edgar N. 1969. *Group Counseling: Dynamic Possibilities of Small Groups.* Philadelphia: Pilgrim Press.

Kew, Clifton E., and J. Clinton. 1951. "Group Psychotherapy in a Church Setting." *Journal of Pastoral Care* 1, no. 10: 31–37.

Leslie, Robert. 1964. "The Uniqueness of Small Groups in the Church." *Pastoral Psychology* 14, no. 145: 33–40.

Reid, Clyde H. 1967. "Pastoral Care through Small Groups." *Pastoral Psychology* 18, no. 172 (March): 14–21.

Yalom, Irvin D. 1985. *The Theory and Practice of Group Psychotherapy.* New York: Basic Books.

### Suggested Resources for Women's Study Groups

Bender, Sue. 1991. *Plain and Simple: A Woman's Journey to the Amish.* San Francisco: Harper & Row.

Bepko, Claudia, and Jo-Ann Krestan. 1990. *Too Good for Her Own Good: Breaking Free From the Burden of Female Responsibility.* New York: Harper & Row.

Bohler, Carolyn Stahl. 1990a. *Prayer on Wings: A Search for Authentic Prayer.* San Diego: LuraMedia.

———. 1990b. *When You Need to Take a Stand.* Resources for Living, Andrew D. Lester, general editor. Louisville, Ky.: Westminster/John Knox Press.

Campbell, Cynthia. 1987. *Theologies Written from Feminist Perspectives: An Introductory Study.* New York: Council on Theology and Culture and the Advisory Council on Discipleship and Worship of the Presbyterian Church (U.S.A.).

Delany, Sarah, and A. Elizabeth with Amy Hill Hearth. 1994. *Having Our Say: The Delany Sisters' First 100 Years.* New York: Kodansha International.

Ehrenreich, Barbara, and Deirdre English. 1978. *For Her Own Good: 150 Years of the Experts' Advice to Women.* New York: Doubleday & Co.

Gilligan, Carol. 1982. *In a Different Voice.* Cambridge: Harvard University Press.

Glaz, Maxine, and Jeanne Stevenson Moessner, eds. 1991. *Women in Travail and Transition: A New Pastoral Care.* Minneapolis: Fortress Press.

Lerner, Harriet Goldhor. 1985. *The Dance of Anger: A Woman's Guide to Changing the Patterns of Intimate Relationships*. New York: Harper & Row.

Mairs, Nancy. 1993. *Ordinary Time: Cycles in Marriage, Faith, and Renewal*. Boston: Beacon Press.

Milhaven, Annie Lally, ed. 1991. *Sermons Seldom Heard: Women Proclaim Their Lives*. New York: Crossroad.

Miller, Jean Baker. 1976. *Toward a New Psychology of Women*. Boston: Beacon Press.

Sanford, Linda Tschirhart, and Mary Ellen Donavan. 1985. *Women and Self Esteem*. New York: Penguin Books.

Saussy, Carroll. 1991. *God Images and Self Esteem: Empowering Women in a Patriarchal Society*. Louisville, Ky.: Westminster/John Knox Press.

Tan, Amy. 1991. *The Kitchen God's Wife*. New York: Ivy Books.

Tannen, Deborah. 1990. *You Just Don't Understand: Women and Men in Conversation*. New York: Ballantine Books.

Trible, Phyllis. 1978. *Texts of Terror: Literary-Feminist Readings of Biblical Narratives*. Philadelphia: Fortress Press.

Viorst, Judith. 1986. *Necessary Losses*. New York: Simon & Schuster.

Walker, Alice. 1982. *The Color Purple*. New York: Simon & Schuster.

# 17

# Love Understood as Self-Sacrifice and Self-Denial: What Does It Do to Women?

BRITA L. GILL-AUSTERN

*Andover Newton Theological School*

The equation of love with self-sacrifice, self-denial, and self-abnegation in Christian theology is dangerous to women's psychological, spiritual, and physical health, and it is contrary to the real aim of Christian love. This chapter will examine three primary questions: What motivates women toward self-sacrifice? What are the negative effects of self-sacrifice on women? What is the distinguishing characteristic of Christian love? These questions have far-reaching consequences for women's lives that must be examined through psychological, cultural, and theological lenses. The lens through which women address these questions will be part of creating a pastoral theology that is life-giving to women and men.

As background to writing this chapter, I asked many women—colleagues, students, staff persons, relatives, and friends—the question, "What does love understood as self-denial and self-sacrifice do to you?" When I asked this of my sister-in-law, a perpetually self-giving and self-sacrificing person, she said, without a moment's hesitation,

"It turns you into mush!"

"Mush?" I said.

"Yes, Mush!"

"Penny," I said, "you will have to exegete mush. I can't just say 'mush,' I will have to describe the ontological character of mush. What do you mean by mush?"

"You know," she said, "everything falls on top of you, you have no control of yourself, your self goes out the window, you lose patience, temper, sight. Your wick is used up and gone. There is no time for *you.*"

Later that weekend the subject came up again, this time with my brother Michael present as well as my sister-in-law, Penny. When Michael heard the question and Penny's response, he said,

"Of course you will feel like mush. You'll give anyone the shirt off your back, but then you won't ask anyone to do anything for you."

"I know," Penny said. " I don't want to put anyone out."

This conversation typifies a common pattern among women; they give, give, give, but are incapable of asking anything for themselves.

Jean Baker Miller tells us that women in therapy often are preoccupied with the questions: Am I giving enough? Can I give enough? Why don't I give enough? (Miller 1976, 49). Only recently has another question begun to surface: Are women getting enough?

## PSYCHOLOGICAL, CULTURAL, AND THEOLOGICAL ISSUES THAT MOTIVATE SELF-SACRIFICE AND SELF-DENIAL

To respond to the question, "What does love as self-sacrifice and self-denial do to women?" I want first to name some of the psychological, cultural, and theological issues that motivate self-sacrifice and reinforce this behavior. Why is it that women are so prone to self-sacrifice and self-denial, and why do they continue to act in ways that are often detrimental to self and other?

*First, such behavior is deeply rooted in women's experience of identity as essentially defined in connectivity and relation; and in a culture that substantially informs this sense of self by raising women to consider the needs of others, to take care of men, and to care for children.*

Jean Baker Miller and the Stone Center theorists have shown that women develop their sense of self, not by separating out from relationships as male developmental theory describes it, but through the process of building on affiliations, creating increasingly complex webs of relation (Miller 1976; Jordan et al. 1991). This defining centrality of relationship in the lives of women often exacts a high price because our culture has defined relationship for women as caregiving.

Jeanne Stevenson Moessner in *Women in Travail and Transition* tells of a conversation with Ann, a nurse who entered group therapy after leaving her job in a detoxification unit. As was customary at the beginning of each group session the patients and counselors introduced themselves. When Ann's turn came, she had difficulty with the counselor's request: "Tell us about yourself."

| | |
|---|---|
| ANN: | "I take care of people. I'm a nurse. I'm a mother. I take care of my daughter; I am a daughter. I take care of my mother, who has Alzheimers. She lives with us." |
| COUNSELOR: | "Tell us about yourself." |
| ANN: | "I can't, I don't know who I am." (Glaz and Moessner 1991, 198) |

One of the risks of caregiving is losing one's life without ever finding it. Whereas men have been encouraged to bolster the "I" at the expense of responsible connectedness to others, women have learned to sacrifice the "I" for "we."

Sanford and Donovan argue in their book *Women and Self Esteem* (1984) that girls learn from their mothers that mothers must not expect to have their needs met; they must learn to meet others' needs and make others feel especially loved. Women, by and large, are not only raised to see affiliation and relation as central but are socialized to create and maintain emotional ties, and to expect their needs to be subservient to the needs of others. As Jean Baker Miller puts it, "Women are taught to center around others, men around the self" (Miller 1976).

*Second, women are motivated toward self-sacrifice because they have grown up in a culture that gives them the message that in order to remain connected and maintain relation they must sacrifice themselves and their needs.*

Carol Gilligan and her colleagues at the Harvard School of Education have studied how girls' sense of self and relationships develop. They have found in their research on more than a hundred girls of many economic and racial backgrounds that a fundamental shift occurs around adolescence.

What seems to happen in adolescence is that girls find themselves caught in the paradoxical belief that they can establish and sustain relationships only by refusing to enter fully into relation with their authentic selves (Gilligan et al. 1988, 23).

Relationships are primary to girls; yet in their desire to keep friends and be desired, they negate what they know about self and others. They come under the spell of the ideology of feminine goodness, what Gilligan calls "the tyranny of kind and nice." Love becomes associated with selflessness, relationship with lack of conflict. As they struggle to conform to society's vision of the "good girl," the real self, the authentic "I," goes into hiding and they begin to substitute fraudulent relationships for authentic relation (Brown and Gilligan 1992). They learn not to want what they want if it brings them into conflict with others.

The dilemma that this presents for a woman is that her desire for connection and relation is one of her greatest strengths and, as Miller reminds us, central to social advancement. Yet it is also inevitably the source of many of women's current struggles and their greatest vulnerability.

*Third, self-sacrifice is motivated by women's economic and social dependence.* The fact is that most women are still economically dependent upon men, even when they work. For many, security requires the maintenance of the relation as it is, which means a continuation of self-sacrificing behavior. A fear for their children's financial well-being and their own financial survival is one motivation that keeps many women in abusive relationships. Many women live with the reality that they are one check away from welfare. The truth is that many women feel that they can find and keep men only through patterns of self-sacrifice.

*Fourth, women are motivated toward self-sacrifice by the unholy trinity of self-abnegation, self-doubt, and false guilt which is always knocking on the door of women's lives.* Women often behave in self-sacrificial ways because they believe they are less important, less valuable, and less essential than men. Low self-worth is endemic to people socialized in structures of domination and subordination; and they come to believe that they will feel better about themselves if they give. Because women often do not feel lovable, they settle for being needed. Women often feel they are worth something only if they do something for others. Legal scholar Catherine MacKinnon raises a question that women must consider: "Do women value care because men have valued women according to the care they give them?" (MacKinnon 1987, 39).

Jean Baker Miller points out that women have developed a sense that their lives should be guided by the constant need to attune themselves to the wishes, desires, and needs of others and often cannot allow themselves activities that are "only" for themselves (Miller 1976). When women have received little real nurturing in their lives they try to meet this need through caregiving, ameliorating their own pain by identifying with the pain of another. Not believing deep in their souls they are good, women try to appear good.

Because women's perceptions, insights, and experiences have frequently not been taken seriously or affirmed, women are filled with self-doubt. Self-doubt fuels women's desire to please and to win approval. Women all too often seek the cause of all ill within themselves. Women attribute it to not being smart enough, pretty enough, quick enough, astute enough. Self-doubt leads women to believe they are not entitled, that their needs, desires, and perceptions are somehow less legitimate than those of men. Self-abnegation, self-doubt, and false guilt lead women to hold themselves responsible, but too often women do not hold the other accountable.

Because women come to believe in their souls that they can never do enough, they are plagued with false guilt. The idealization of feminine goodness and motherhood leads inevitably to the inescapability of guilt whenever women fall short of the ideal.

*Fifth, women are motivated toward self-sacrifice not primarily because of distortions of caring and love which are individual neuroses but by the structural inequalities in which they are embedded.* When women are deprived of a sense of power or control over their own lives, it is understandable that they will subtly seek ways to control others and deny their own pain. Women who are autonomous and self-assertive are not only unrewarded, they are often penalized. Self-sacrifice can be a means of controlling as much as of loving. A sign on an office door speaks simply of the reality underlying much of women's self-sacrificing behavior. The sign is a circle divided into two halves, the top yellow, the bottom black. It reads, "Help is the sunny side of control." With women having so little socially conferred power and control, it is not surprising that they seek to find it where they can.

*Sixth, women are motivated toward self-sacrifice because their identities as women and Christians have been shaped by a theological tradition that views self-denial and self-sacrifice as the defining attributes of Christian love.* This notion derives from the classical understanding that Jesus' suffering was required by God as atonement for human sin and so was fundamental to salvation. Within the interpretive framework set by this defining notion, the story of Jesus came to be understood principally in terms of sin, guilt, sacrifice, and forgiveness (Borg 1994, 127). The emphasis is placed on the crucifixion as the supreme act of love, and suffering love becomes identified with the Christian ideal. Feminist theology rejects the interpretation that Jesus' death was ordained by God and required as payment for sin (Brown and Bohn 1989; Harrison 1985; Johnson 1993). When Jesus' passive victimization is seen as necessary to salvation, it is a small step to the belief that to be of value is to sacrifice self for others.

> The values that Christianity idealizes, especially for women, are also those of the victim: sacrificial love, passive acceptance of suffering, humility, weakness, etc. Since these are qualities idealized in Jesus who died for our sins, his functioning as a model re-enforces the scapegoat syndrome for women. (Daly 1973, 77)

The Christian understanding of love as self-sacrifice and self-denial has taken on its power in a tradition that has too often glorified suffering. At its extreme, Joanne Brown says, women have become acculturated to accept abuse, because they come to believe it is their place to suffer and therefore it is justified (Brown and Bohn 1989).

This acceptance and glorification of suffering can result in theological masochism. Carter Heyward jolts us to remember that, "This notion of welcoming, or submitting oneself, gladly to injustice flies in the face of Jesus' own refusal to make concession to unjust relation" (Heyward 1982, 58). The glorification of Jesus' suffering also leads to a theological sadism and an image of God as a violent, angry, sadistic father. When the cross becomes the goal of love, love is distorted and perverted.

The image of the suffering servant has reinforced for some, the belief that suffering is good per se, rather than what happens when love is committed at all costs. The suffering servant is a role that women have played in family and society at large. When the crucifixion is used as the paradigm for ultimate loving, rather than being understood as what Beverly Harrison calls "the tragic consequence of Jesus' faithfulness and his refusal to give up his commitment in the face of Roman oppression," we run the risk of furthering theological masochism (Harrison 1985, 18–19).

Self-sacrifice is also motivated by the notion that ideal love, true Christian love, is agape—disinterested, sacrificial love, as distinct from and purer than eros, erotic, mutual, desiring love. Anders Nygren speaks of agape as "a love that gives itself away, that sacrifices itself, even to the uttermost" (Nygren 1953, 117). One Roman Catholic sister spoke of this in her training as a nun as the teaching that "we must live like candles that burn before the altar and leave no trace of themselves." Nygren says that "agape and the theology of the Cross are . . . quite simply one and the same thing. It is impossible to think of either without the other" (Nygren 1953, 117). This ideal of love as selflessness and self-sacrifice rests on the assumption that Jesus' love was never motivated by self-concern. Although the ethical norm for the Christian has always been *imitatio Christi,* this has been understood too narrowly. Thomas à Kempis, the fourteenth-century monastic, proclaimed, "Oh, how powerful is the pure love of Jesus, free from all self-interest and self-love!" *Imitatio Christi* meant a complete denial "retaining no trace of self love" (Thomas à Kempis 1952, 83–84). But Jesus' teaching was simply not disinterested or devoid of all self-concern. He wanted to show others how their life might be enhanced if they followed in his way. His way entailed suffering and required sacrifice, but its promise, its ultimate destination, was abundant life and joy. Jesus' first intention was not to suffer or die. He said, "Strive first for the kingdom of God and his righteousness, and all these things will be given to you as well" (Matthew 6:33) and "Those who want to save their life will lose it, and those who lose their life for my sake will save it" (Luke 9:24). Paradox, but not self-sacrifice, is at the center of Jesus' teaching. Neither his teaching nor his life was devoid of self-concern. Stephen Post argues persuasively that clearly Jesus did not want his love to be rejected and unreciprocated. Rather, he lamented over a people who "did not recognize the time" of their visitation from God (Luke 19:44). He was concerned for his Father and himself: "I have come in my Father's name, and you do not accept me" (John 5:43). Mutual love, not sacrifice, is the desire and norm here. Jesus yearns for response and personal communion; only after this becomes impossible does he undertake the radical act of self-abnegation (Post 1994, 218).

Jesus' teaching about self-denial needs also to be put in context. When New Testament scholar Krister Stendahl is asked about why the Bible talks so much about self-denial, his answer is that "the people who wrote it were usually the people in power. They were speaking to themselves, reminding themselves to be humble" (Boyd 1994, 22). Women who experience little sense of power, who are victimized, who have not utilized their gifts, do not need to be preached self-denial as the central aspect of love.

## THE NEGATIVE EFFECTS OF SELF-SACRIFICE AND
## SELF-DENIAL ON WOMEN

I have named some of the major theological and cultural motivations for self-sacrifice, although my list is certainly not exhaustive. I cannot speak about the theme of love as self-sacrifice and self-denial without also naming some of the negative effects on women and the institutional and systemic inequalities that give birth to such behavior.

Women place particular emphasis on sacrifices they make for men, and they speak little about what they give up for their children. This tendency indicates that women do not expect mutuality with children, but they continue to long for it with men.

*First, women whose loving has consistent patterns of self-sacrifice commonly lose touch with their own needs and desires.* Acculturation to their subordination to men often leads women to be silent about what they need. Even though women will go to great lengths to please others, they frequently do not know or attend to what pleases themselves. As one woman put it, "Women are not supposed to do what they want to do. Much of their life is dictated by a should mode—such that they operate out of a doing versus a being mode."

I remember one former member of my parish saying that the most liberating experience she had in the church was my giving her permission to say no without feeling guilty. This was a radically new experience for her. Women have no chance of finding and being in touch with their own needs, desires, and directions unless they have permission to say no to some of the demands that pull them in directions in which they really do not want to go.

In my years of working pastorally and therapeutically with women I have found again and again that the hardest question for women to answer is "What do you want?" "What do you need?" Women will frequently look at me stunned and say, "No one ever asked that of me before. I don't know. I have no idea what my needs are." Women, so tuned to the needs of others, simply draw blanks when asked to name their own. To state boldly their own needs throws women into potential conflict with the needs of the others, and it can feel like a threat to the relationship, for it changes the balance. It is difficult to talk about women counting themselves in the equation of those who deserve care if we cannot even begin by naming our own needs and desires.

*The second pervasive effect of self denial and self sacrifice on women is that it often leads to a loss of a sense of self and a loss of voice.*

One woman, Diane, described to me how she had put her husband through two master's programs and worked so he did not have to. They had agreed that when he finished his master's program, it would be her turn to go to graduate school. When she decided to go back to school, he left her.

"The deal was broken. So there I was working three jobs, taking care of my two kids and going back to school. One morning I looked in the mirror and saw nobody. I had sacrificed down to nothing, there was nothing to see."

Self-sacrifice that requires the subjugation of one's own needs and desires contributes to a loss of voice. When one's own needs and desires are not seen as valued, one learns to silence the self. The silencing of the self is one of the major contributors to depression in women, for if one cannot even voice one's desires, needs, or opinions, one certainly will not be able to be brought into the equation of those for whom care is to be shown (Jack 1991).

Part of the difficulty for women is that they are acculturated to see options in terms of mutually exclusive alternatives. So women feel forced to choose between self-sacrifice and egoism—between giving up what they have a right to and being primarily concerned with their own interest; between taking seriously others' rights and ignoring the rights of others; between showing too little interest in themselves and taking too little interest in the welfare of other people.

The real question is not whom do I put first, but how do I care for the other and myself? Some of us develop such capacities very early. Carol Gilligan tells the story of two four-year-olds, a girl and a boy who were playing together and wanted to play different games. In this version of a common dilemma, the girl said,

"Let's play next-door neighbors."
"I want to play pirates," the boy replied.
"Okay," said the girl, "then you can be the pirate that lives next door."

Self and other find a way into the equation. There is compromise and accommodation, but not self-sacrifice.

*Third, the fall-out from self-sacrifice is often a reservoir of resentment, bitterness and anger as women come more and more to feel victimized.* Anger is a signal that something is amiss in relation and that some change is called for. Beverly Harrison has stated with forceful conviction that "where anger is hidden or goes unattended, masking itself, there the power of love, the power to act, to deepen relation, atrophies and dies" (Harrison 1985, 15).

Unexpressed anger often turns frozen and becomes the ice of resentment that turns women cold and withdrawn. When women orient themselves totally toward the needs of others and the harmony of relation, they repress negative feelings that might threaten the relationship. Innumerable studies show the disastrous consequences to mental and physical health when people repress their true feelings. Depression is the common outcome when one's own needs and feelings have been denied over time.

*Fourth, love as self-sacrifice frequently leads to overfunctioning on behalf of others, underfunctioning on behalf of self, which contributes to a loss of sense of self- esteem and a sense of one's own direction.* Continual focus on others can lead people to abdicate responsibility for themselves and their own direction and goals. Self-sacrifice often prevents women from taking the risks required to become fully themselves. The less responsibility one takes for one's own life, the more need there is to control others. Although the need to control may masquerade as helpfulness, it is often motivated by a lack of security. Karen Horney reminds us that female altruism has an underside, an overwhelming sense of responsibility that is based on culturally reinforced dependency (Horney 1967). The underlying purpose of such behavior is to do, to care, to be for others, but for the purpose of winning approval, affection, and help. Women may use others to bolster their own sense of self-esteem. Whereas this doing may temporarily bolster a sense of self, it ultimately lowers self-esteem, for it is a pseudo or false self that is bolstered. It is also understandable that the overly responsible one will carry more guilt and blame in the relation, allowing herself to be taken advantage of and allowing others to avoid responsibility. Overfunctioning can also lead to help that treats the other as incompetent.

Underlying this deep desire to be "helpful" may be the psychological equivalent of works righteousness. Women who are "helpers" may justify themselves by their acts of care—if I care, I will be valued. Caretaking, especially self-sacrificing, may lead to codependency. Melody Beattie describes codependency as:

> thinking and feeling responsible for other people
> feeling anxiety, guilt and pity when others have a problem
> feeling compelled to help a person solve a problem
> anticipating others' needs
> finding the self saying yes when they mean no
> not knowing what they want or need
> feeling safest when giving
> focusing on others gives little opportunity to live your own life. (Beattie 1985, 37)

Although this may fit the description of codependent behavior, which is very close to what passes in our culture for self-sacrificing love, it also describes how women are socialized to being attuned to the needs of others. Such behavior has recently been labeled pathological, even though the social and theological reinforcement for it is overwhelming. Gilligan would remind us that dependence can also mean a healthy reliance on others; it can signify the conviction that one is able to have an effect on others (Gilligan et al. 1988, 13).

*Fifth, self-sacrificing love can undermine the capacity for genuine mutuality and intimacy.* Without the capacity to bring the fullness and authenticity of the "I" into relation, mutuality and intimacy are both limited. Moreover, self-denying love may lead to patterns of caretaking that cripple and inhibit another's initiative and lead the caretaker into the successive roles of rescuer, persecutor, and victim. The rescuer takes responsibility from another, implicitly calling into question the other's competence. The rescuer is likely to slip, in short order, into the roles of persecutor and victim, lashing out in anger and then passing into hurt and self-pity when the person she rescues is insufficiently grateful. Finally, the caretaker feels used and abused and void of self. Self-sacrificial love turns to resentment of those who have exacted the sacrifice.

Women who continually take a subservient place to others' needs become incapable of developing into full selfhood. They become what they have been driven to become: tentative, insecure, and excessively vulnerable. So the cycle of dependence is perpetually renewed. Recognition of this self-perpetuating cycle may have led Elizabeth Cady Stanton to say, "Self- development is a higher duty than self-sacrifice. The thing that most retards and mitigates against women's self-development is self-sacrifice." Many women have experienced this truth.

*Sixth, love as self-sacrifice and self-denial creates great stress and strain.* Modern women find themselves torn by conflicting social pressures. They are expected to strive for self-development and self-fulfillment, while continuing to fill their traditional role as self-sacrificing caretaker. Women who seek these mutually exclusive aims are dubbed "superwomen." Women strive to strike an impossible balance which the social structures demand and simultaneously undercut by not providing systemic supports to make it possible.

The conflicts, tensions, double binds, and ambivalence that lurk beneath love as self-sacrifice are in some degree responsible for many of the physical disorders affecting women today such as digestive problems, allergies, high blood pressure, strokes, nervous ticks, insomnia, and sheer exhaustion. Such complexes of conflicting pressures are the stuff out of which depression is made; over a long period of time they can radically affect women's health.

*Seventh, love understood as self-sacrifice can lead women to abdicate their public responsibility to use their God-given gifts on behalf of the greater community and for the common good.* It can lead them to idolize the needs of the family and to undervalue the importance of work and creativity as vehicles not only of self-expression but also as expressions of the love of God and others. Women caught in the web of traditional expectations can be seduced into believing that family must always come first and therefore women's needs for self-expression must be sacrificed to the good of the family. If a woman is unable to use her own gifts and abilities, she may turn in upon herself. Although she may continue to do caretaking, the actual caring may really disappear (Noddings 1984, 127). Unable to give from the fullness of her self, she has nothing finally to offer others. So caretaking becomes less a contribution to the well-being of loved ones than a paradoxically self-centered search for some recognition and credit—some compensation for her loss of self.

Central to the Christian tradition is the call to self-denial as a counter to the fundamental sin of pride. Calvin implored us to remember "that those talents which God has bestowed upon us are not our own goods, but the free gifts of God; and any persons who become proud of them show their ungratefulness" (Calvin 1960, 695). And Paul asked, "If you received [all things], why do you boast as if [they] were not given to you?" (1 Corinthians 4:7). But for women, not pride but timidity, pride's underside, is likely to be the basic sin (Saiving 1960); so a more appropriate question for women might be, "Why are you hiding your lamp under a bushel?" Calvin warns us that according to Scripture "whatever benefits we obtain from the Lord have been entrusted to us on this condition: that they be applied to the common good of the church" (Calvin 1960, 695). Hiding our gifts, no less than flaunting them, is refusal to open ourselves to the free flowing of God's grace. In order then to be faithful to God and to the gifts we have been given, we must sacrifice outmoded and outlived images of the self that hold us back from sharing and the living out of our gifts.

Calvin names a life-giving aspect of self-denial when applied to women today: "Self-denial gives us the right attitude toward our fellow men [sic]" (Calvin 1960, 693). What is essential here is that Calvin underscores that "denial of self has regard partly to men [sic], partly, and chiefly, to God." Whereas his concern was to ensure that persons do not esteem themselves too highly, the aim of giving us the right attitude toward our fellow human beings would also protect women from thinking too little of themselves. Self-denial for women in this regard might mean risking the displeasures of men and the sacrifice of one's image for a higher good that one feels called to in faithfulness to God. Self-denial in this sense might require women to deny themselves the approval, the praise, and the sense of belonging that comes when we give up pleasing the other. Self-denial must ultimately lead to loving and just relation that brings one in closer faithfulness to God. Self-denial is not first and foremost about meeting another's need before our own but rather aligning oneself and one's will to God so that every part of one's life might be governed by God.

Self-denial can be understood as a form of self-transcendence that is at the heart of the gospel. Self-denial is not primarily self-deprivation but is the self-abandon (that paradoxically is simultaneously the deepest kind of self-fulfillment) that we reach when we are focused on a higher good.

*Last, but certainly not least, love understood as self-sacrifice and self-denial can unwittingly contribute to exploitation and domination of relationships by the more powerful party.* Unexamined patterns of self-sacrifice on the part of women contribute to the perpetuation of patterns of domination and subordination between men and women. Elizabeth Cady Stanton clearly saw the danger and criticized male clergy for making self-sacrifice a central virtue for women. She wrote, "Men think that self-sacrifice is the most charming of all the cardinal virtues for women . . . and in order to keep it in healthy working order they make opportunities for its illustration as often as possible" (Andolsen et al. 1985, 75).

## A WORD OF CAUTION—LOVE IS SELF-GIVING

A complex web of social forces compels women to sacrifice themselves in ways that can do great damage to their lives and the lives of the people they touch. Nevertheless, women need to resist the increasingly widespread tendency to condemn all forms of self-giving. Self-sacrifice is not pernicious by definition; it is not always a manifestation of codependency. Self-sacrifice can be an essential element of authentic, faithful love—the self-fulfilling self-transcendence to which Jesus calls us.

In the United States, the individualistic orientation of this culture contributes to an understanding of success which is defined in terms that glorify the self through the worship of the idols of autonomy, independence, and self-sufficiency. The danger to women is to be co-opted by the predominating values of this society that have in fact largely been shaped by men. Bonnie Miller McLemore reminds us that "women fall prey to two impulses: not only collusion with limited definitions of womanhood, but also with patriarchal ideals of adulthood" (Glaz and Moessner 1991, 69).

Adult male power in our society is identified with a powerful, autonomous, and fulfilled self, one who is in control, competitive, hierarchical, and more self-seeking than self relinquishing. In contrast, women's traditionally instilled feminine powers are ones committed to the nurturing of others and facilitating and empowering the growth of others. This power is grounded in generosity, empathy, yielding, receptivity, and sometimes relinquishment and can be a life-giving form of self-giving. Women need to distinguish self-giving that is life-giving from unhealthy, life-denying forms. Women cannot in our critique of self-sacrificing love devalue all that we have acquired in the importance of caregiving, participation in others' development and cooperating in the preservation and nurturance of human life.

Self-development within the context of faithfulness to God is not to be equated with anxious striving to obtain the goods of this world whatever they be: wealth, prestige, knowledge, or power. We need to be cautious that we do not judge too quickly as sacrifice of self as only that which turns away from our societies most cherished values, achievement, productivity, and competitiveness for a sense of self that society continues to devalue, where relationality, being, and attention to the present is foremost. Jean Baker Miller has stated powerfully that male-led society has delegated to women not humanity's lowest needs but its highest necessities (Miller 1976)—necessities that are needed not only in the private world of home and family but also in the public world.

How shall women preserve the value of these highest necessities? How can women continue to hold in tension the terms of the paradox that those who lose their lives will find them? How can women's sacrifice of self be made in ways that fulfill rather than diminish their lives and the lives of the people around them? How can women continue to affirm the importance that the meaning of life cannot be sought with the self at the center of the world? How can women continue to affirm the delicious self-abandonment that can come in self-forgetfulness when they are dedicated to a larger purpose than self alone? How can women continue to affirm also that the healthiest people psychologically, spiritually, and often physically are those who are centered upon something larger than the self and have learned a discipline of self that allows a sublimation of one's own ego needs?

I begin with the premise that Jesus' central and deepest desire was that in following him we might have life and have it in all its abundance. Self-giving in whatever form it takes must ultimately be for the sake of helping to create, redeem, and sustain love that furthers abundant life. Does the form of self-giving enhance the capacity for love and care for self and other, or does it reify patterns of exploitation and domination?

## HEALING IMAGES OF SELF-GIVING IN THE NEW TESTAMENT

Three healing images from the New Testament give us ways of conceiving self-giving love as life-enhancing, for both giver and receiver.

*First, a new reading of the story of the Good Samaritan gives us an important metaphor for life-generating love and care.* Jeanne Stevenson Moessner has pointed out that in this story we have a model of love that is based on interdependence. The good Samaritan was not called to extraordinary self-giving. He did not cancel his journey. He did not give up his plans or sacrifice all his needs to the needs of the occasion. Rather, he met the need of the wounded one on the road, but then also relied on some communal resources, represented by the innkeeper at the inn. He then continued on his journey. The work of compassion often begins with the act of joining with, accompaniment, solidarity, rather than self-sacrifice (Glaz and Moessner 1991, 209–210). Caring requires effective action, and effectiveness demands the sharing of burdens and allowing others also to assume responsibility.

Women and men are called to care, but care does not mean a relinquishment of all their own needs or agendas for the sake of the other, nor does it mean that we are required to care alone. Caring in our time requires mobilizing community and relinquishing involvement in the caring when it is not needed.

*The second healing image for loving relation is the story of Mary and Martha.* The metaphor of Mary and Martha complements that of the good Samaritan for a holistic understanding of what is required by Christian life. Such a life honors, values, and invites both Mary and Martha into the center. It requires active doing, and it also requires time to sit, to be nurtured, and to receive love. Love in the story is not related simply to serving but also to receiving and knowing what is required when. Attentive love has a sense of timing. There is a time to give and a time to receive, a time to serve and a time to learn, a time to do and a time to be, and all are part of the work of love. If caring and love are to be maintained, then the one caring must be maintained (Noddings 1984, 105). An ethic of caring needs to be able to sustain the caring attitude (Noddings 1984, 112). The story of Mary and Martha reminds us that for love to be sustained, one must also receive the love of the other. The cared for contributes to the act of caring by her responsiveness to the other (Noddings 1984, 145). Just as Jesus often withdrew from the crowd in order to restore his energy and commitment, so women are encouraged to receive whatever it may be that feeds their spirits so that they may authentically give to others out of their fullness.

> The one caring properly pays heed to her own condition. She does not need to hatch out elaborate excuses to give herself rest, or to seek congenial companionship, or to find joy in personal work. . . . To go on sacrificing bitterly, grudgingly, is not to be one caring, and when she finds this happening, she properly but considerately withdraws for repairs. When she is prevented by circumstances from doing this, she may still recognize what is occurring and make heroic efforts to sustain herself as one caring. (Noddings 1984, 112)

For caring to be sustained, attentiveness to the one who is doing the caring is essential. Women will continue to give powerfully when they are "strong, courageous and capable of joy" (Noddings 1984, 100).

*We find the third image in the Gospel of John where Jesus says to his disciples:* "No longer do I call you servants, but friends. All that the Father has shared with me I have shared with you" (John 15:15, para.). The paradigm he seeks for Christian love is characterized chiefly not by sacrifice but by the mutuality of friendship. If mutuality is one of the aims of love between adults, then people need to ask themselves how their own acts of self-sacrificing love either further mutuality or reinforce roles and structures of domination and subordination.

As Elisabeth Schüssler Fiorenza has written (1983), Jesus instituted a discipleship of equals. He desired to move love toward mutuality. One of the resources that can help women move in this direction of life-giving love is friendship with other women. It is in the context of friendship that many women are "heard into speech" (Morton 1985) and learn what it means to recognize themselves as persons with their own needs, wants, and desires. Friendship is one of the places where women have the opportunity to clarify their beliefs, values, and life goals, to learn the places of their own deepest gladness and passion so they may give out of their own sense of fullness. It is often in the context of female friendships that self-acceptance and self-love are fostered; and this love of self is the seed from which genuine love of other can grow. It is within the nourishing bonds of female friendship and support groups that women are often given the courage to make transformative changes in their lives.

Mutuality may be the aim of mature adult love, but it is not its eternal resting place. No relationship can exist in a perpetual state of perfect mutuality. We sacrifice in the short term for others, when we are committed to a greater good and believe in a balancing over time. Relation that is always weighing or measuring the exact extent of the equality and mutuality operates only by a language of rights and not also with a language of care. Selflessness is not the final goal of love, but without a capacity to practice it, love's possibilities are diminished.

Adult relationships built on mutuality will take seriously that the care of children requires self-denial and the sacrifice of the kinds of ego gratification that the world of work may bestow. Parental love's highest aim is not mutuality but the nurturing and protecting of another's life for the sake of his or her fullest development. "Women have paid and continue to pay for nurturing children, costs that men have not had to bear in the same measure as it comes to self development" (Miller-McLemore 1994, 83). Mutual love will require men's nurturing of women as well as children and the realization that a woman's creative work, like a man's, sometimes requires the protection of her solitude. Mutual love will also require men's capacity to sacrifice ego gratification and some measure of self-development for the sake of spouse and children. On the other hand, if men engaged in what T. Berry Brazelton calls the "moral practice of attunement to an infant, "they might have less conscious anger and driven need to acquire, cope, win and be first" (Miller-McLemore 1994, 161). Joy is often the outcome that comes from deep relatedness; this kind of joy has been too scarce in the lives of men.

## SELF-GIVING LOVE AS MODELED IN THE TRINITY

To be human is to care and to be cared for, to love and to be loved. But what is the distinctive mark of Christian love if it is not self-sacrifice and self-denial? What is most distinctive about divine love is not first and foremost self-sacrifice but rather a total and mutual self-giving. Women may find a liberating understanding of self-giving love if they look to the Trinity rather than to the atonement (Andolsen 1980; Johnson 1993). A pastoral theology that takes seriously women's experience and their way of seeing will turn for one of its resources to the more holistic model of self-giving love found in the Trinity rather than to the crucifixion as the premier symbol of ultimate self-giving. The Trinity offers important insights concerning the nature of divine love.

First, self-giving is not about denial of self (there is no withholding of the self), but rather an offering up of one's very fullness. The Trinity reveals that the inner life of God is marked by a total and mutual self-giving (McGill 1982, 74). Full becoming requires the presence of an other. The decisive mark of the Son, as Athanasius argued, is the love by which he gives all glory back to the Father (McGill 1982, 75).

Second, in the Trinity there is no pattern of domination or subordination, no quelling of individuality or uniqueness. "In this vision personal uniqueness flourishes not at the expense of relationship, but through the power of profound companionship that respects differences and values them equally" (Johnson 1993, 219). The Trinity as a model of self-giving love safeguards difference while maintaining connection.

Third, the Trinity affirms persons' need for one another by showing us that wholeness is a relational concept, not something that one achieves on one's own. The God revealed to us here is a God who is needy and needs the other. At the heart of divine love is reciprocal giving. As Elizabeth Johnson says, "Being in communion constitutes God's very essence. Divine nature exists as the inescapable mystery of relation" (Johnson 1993, 227). But it is self-giving without domination or subordination. "At the heart of holy mystery is not monarchy, but community; not an absolute ruler, but a threefold koinonia" (Johnson 1993, 216).

The traditional understanding of agape has been based on the assumption of the radical separation from us of a God who has no need of humanity and is lacking any self-concern. Such an understanding has encouraged the prevalence of the themes of masochism and domination within Christian theology. The doctrine of the Trinity reminds us that the God who loves the world is a God who draws near to people in intimate communion, where both giving and receiving are the aim of love, in order that persons might have life and have it in all its abundance.

Women's hope for loving and just relationships lies not in self-sacrifice but in seeing clearly that mutual self-giving and receiving are at the heart of divine love and in women's courage and strength in insisting upon and working for mutual loving relation. Such love may require self-sacrifice as a step on the journey to mutual love, but never as its ultimate aim.

## BIBLIOGRAPHY

Andolsen, Barbara H. 1980. "Agape in Feminist Ethics." *Journal of Religious Ethics* 8, no. 1: 83–99.

Andolsen, Barbara, et al., eds. 1985. *Women's Consciousness, Women's Conscience: A Reader in Feminist Ethics.* San Francisco: Harper & Row.

Borg, Marcus. 1994. *Meeting Jesus Again for the First Time.* San Francisco: Harper & Row.

Boyd, Jeffrey, M.D. 1994. *Affirming the Soul.* Cheshire, Conn.: Soul Research Institute.

Beattie, Melody. 1985. *Codependent No More.* New York: Pocket Books.

Brown, Carole, and Carole R. Bohn, eds. 1989. *Christianity, Patriarchy and Abuse.* New York: Pilgrim Press.

Brown, Lyn Mikel, and Carol Gilligan. 1992. *Meeting at the Crossroads.* Cambridge: Harvard University Press.

Buber, Martin. 1958. *I and Thou.* Translated by R. G. Smith. New York: Macmillan.

———. 1965. *Between Man and Man.* Translated by R. G. Smith. New York: Macmillan.

Calvin, John. 1960. *Institutes of the Christian Religion.* Translated by Ford Lewis Battles. ed. 1559. Philadelphia: Westminster Press.

Daly, Mary. 1973. *Beyond God the Father: Toward a Philosophy of Women's Liberation.* Boston: Beacon Press.

Gilligan, Carol, et al. 1990. *Making Connections.* Cambridge: Harvard University Press.

———. 1988. *Mapping the Moral Domain.* Cambridge: Harvard University School of Education.

Glaz, Maxine, and Jeanne Stevenson Moessner. 1991. *Women in Travail and Transition: A New Pastoral Care.* Minneapolis: Fortress Press.

Gudorf, Christine. 1985. "Parenting, Mutual Love and Sacrifice." In Andolsen et al.

Harrison, Beverly. 1985. *Making Connections.* Boston: Beacon Press.

Heyward, Carter. 1982. *The Redemption of God.* Lanham, Md.: University Press of America.

Horney, Karen. 1967. *Feminine Psychology.* New York: W. W. Norton & Co.

Jack, Dana. 1991. *Silencing the Self.* Cambridge: Harvard University Press.

Johnson, Elizabeth. 1993. *She Who Is: The Mystery of God in Feminist Discourse.* New York: Crossroad.

Jordan, Judith, et al. 1991. *Women's Growth in Connection: Writings from the Stone Center.* New York: Guilford Press.

Kaplan, Alexandra G. 1991. "The Self-in-Relation: Implications for Depression in Women." In Judith Jordan et al.

MacKinnon, Catherine. 1987. *Feminism Unmodified: Discourses on Life and Law.* Cambridge: Harvard University Press.

McGill, Arthur. 1982. *Suffering: A Test of Theological Method.* Philadelphia: Westminster.

Miller, Jean Baker. 1976. *Toward a New Psychology of Women.* Boston: Beacon Press.

Miller-McLemore, Bonnie. 1994. *Also a Mother: Work and Family as Theological Dilemma.* Nashville: Abingdon Press.

Morton, Nelle. 1985. *The Journey Is Home.* Boston: Beacon Press.

Noddings, Nel. 1984. *Caring: A Feminine Approach to Ethics and Moral Education.* Berkeley and Los Angeles: University of California Press.

Norwood, Robin. 1985. *Women Who Love Too Much.* New York: Pocket Books.

Nygren, A. 1982. *Agape and Eros.* Translated by Philip S. Watson. Chicago: University of Chicago Press.

Post, Stephen G. 1994. "The Inadequacy of Selflessness: God's Suffering and the Theory of Love." *Journal of the American Academy of Religion* 56, no. 2: 213–228.

Ruether, Rosemary Radford. 1988. *Womenguides.* Boston: Beacon Press.

Saiving, Valerie. 1960. "The Human Situation: A Feminine View." *Journal of Religion* 40 (April 1960): 100–112.

Sanford, L. T., and M. E. Donovan. 1984. *Women and Self Esteem.* Middlesex, England: Penguin Books.

Schüssler Fiorenza, Elisabeth. 1983. *In Memory of Her.* New York: Crossroad.

St. Athanasius. 1970. *St. Athanasius on the Incarnation.* Translated and edited by a Religious of C.S.M.V. London: A. R. Mowbray & Co.

Thomas à Kempis. 1952. *The Imitation of Christ.* Translated by L. Sherley-Price. Middlesex, England: Penguin Classics.

# 18

# From Samaritan to Samaritan: Journey Mercies

JEANNE STEVENSON MOESSNER

*Columbia Theological Seminary*

Love your neighbor *as yourself.* Women have traditionally had difficulty hearing the last two words in this biblical injunction found in Luke 10:27. This injunction is followed by a parable of a Samaritan who stopped to help a wounded person. The parable has usually been understood by commentators to be an elaboration of "love of neighbor" with love of God intimately connected. The interconnection in Luke 10:27 is to love God with all your heart, and with all your soul, and with all your mind, and your neighbor as yourself. Pastoral care as developed in *Through the Eyes of Women: Insights for Pastoral Care* never loses sight of the more subtle interconnection in the text: Love your neighbor *as yourself.*

It is only from the periphery of the parable, from the side of the road, stripped, beaten, half dead, as one receives the mirroring of God's perfect healing love through the compassion of the good Samaritan, that a person has a kairotic moment of understanding that she or he is of cosmic concern and of immense worth to God (Glaz and Stevenson Moessner 1991, 207). This is the foundational understanding of a loved self. It is a core moment in a person's journey of awareness.

Love of self in interconnection with love of God and neighbor is a goal of pastoral care. Love of self includes the acceptance of one's anger, aggression, sexual identity, and secrets as the contributors of this volume have discussed these aspects of pastoral concern. Love of self eventually embraces loss and grief, especially loss of significant others such as mother. The "woundedness" found in the Lukan parable can certainly include eat-

Sections of "Core Moments in the Journey," "Failed Core Moments," and "Well Women" were originally published in *Sewanee Theological Review* 36:3 (Pentecost 1993), published by The School of Theology, The University of the South, Sewanee, Tennessee.

ing disorders, hysterectomy, mastectomy, and rape. Love of self as presented in this book reenvisions the role of self-sacrifice and self-denial. It is only a female-friendly pastoral care that will be inclusive of those "by the side of the road" of society's main thoroughfare of care.

Another crucial aspect in the narrative of the Good Samaritan is difficult for many women: the Samaritan finished his journey. The Samaritan finished his journey while meeting the need of a wounded and marginal person. The Samaritan did not give everything away; in this enigmatic parable, he did not injure, hurt, or neglect the self. He relied in a sense on the communal, on a type of teamwork as represented by the host at the inn. For women who have excelled at self-denial, self-abnegation, and self-sacrificial care of others, an understanding of the shared responsibility and the networking necessary in pastoral care is a liberating perspective. This distribution of responsibility for caring frees women for an exploration of boundary issues needed in the balance between care of self and care of others.

The good Samaritan cared for the wounded person and transported him to an inn. He told the innkeeper to take care of him, left money for this care, and promised to return with additional funds. *Through the Eyes of Women: Insights for Pastoral Care* has developed the realities and possibilities of the "inn" in contemporary settings. Sometimes, the "inn" is the church. Other times, it is resources such as a battered women's shelter, a rape crisis center, an eating disorders clinic, a support group such as Reach for Recovery or Bosom Buddies. Always, when the teamwork between the Samaritan and the innkeeper becomes obvious, there is great relief. Particularly, there is appreciation from the African-American women who have often carried much upon their matriarchal shoulders as in the parable and image of the shepherd with a heavy, stray sheep.

Pastoral care has traditionally operated in an individualistic society. The emphasis in this volume on "the living human web" and on "weaving the web" is a way of countering this individualism. Community and the role of support groups have been highlighted in this text as a way of envisioning the teamwork and interconnectedness possible in pastoral care. It is a contemporary application of the relation between Samaritan and innkeeper.

The journey mercies that are received from the parable of the Samaritan in Luke 10 are these: love of self as interconnected with love of God and neighbor; shared responsibility and networking in pastoral care; the experience of community; and the finishing of one's journey while caring for others. When the Samaritan in Luke 10 is imaged, usually the Samaritan is a male. Therefore I would like to transverse the biblical text to another Samaritan, the woman of John 4. It is there that another core moment in the pastoral care of women is revealed. First, what are core moments in pastoral care?

## CORE MOMENTS IN THE JOURNEY

There are core moments in pastoral care that are revelatory, prophetic, and transitional. These moments are not to be missed, for they convey to the caregiver, to the pastor, or to the counselor which patterns, relationships, traumas, and experiences have stamped or stigmatized the one who is speaking. One counselee disclosed the death of his eight-month-old son which had occurred fifteen years earlier. The grief had been largely suppressed for a decade and a half. In recapitulating his wife's total investment in the critically ill infant and her immediate pregnancy following the death of their son, the counselee stated: "This is where I got lost." Another counselee recounted the afternoon she had been urged by neighbors to call 911 as her father almost fatally beat her mother. The police intervention, the bloody maternal figure on the kitchen floor, and the ride in the police car were all told with a freshness of recent memory although the incident had been twenty years previous. These core moments retold in therapy or in a pastoral setting are stories from the depths of the narrator's personality, stories that have shaped and reshaped psychosocial development. When they are told, time stands still, and all space is centered on the speaker's memory. These moments are revelatory and prophetic in both the pastoral care and the counseling process. With understanding interpretation, these core moments can be transitional and healing agents. It is to these moments that pastors and counselors can bring both feminist sensibility (Luepnitz 1988, 231) and feminine empathy and offer a resistance to the overused label "hysterical women." This resistance counters the tendency of the traditional male analytic establishment to reduce many such core moments to female hysteria or histrionic traits (Myers 1992).

Feminist sensibility has been defined by Deborah Anna Luepnitz and distinguished from feminist techniques.

> Feminism is not a set of therapeutic techniques but a sensibility, a political and aesthetic center that informs a work pervasively. One does not merely make clinical interventions in the family as a feminist; one also greets the family and sets the fee as a feminist. The words spoken during the session that catch one's attention or that slip by, the things that make one feel warm toward the family, and the things that offend are all determined in part by this sensibility. (Luepnitz 1988, 231)

This is best illustrated in Luepnitz's case study of the McGinn family as she deals with "irrational Mom," Mrs. McGinn. Margo McGinn arrives early and angry at the adolescent inpatient center where her son is a new patient. Mrs. McGinn shows up in the reception area and demands to see the therapist. Luepnitz reflects in a variety of ways on an appropriate response to Mrs. McGinn and intuits that there is something wrong in the family's "holding capacity."

This led me to think that Mrs. McGinn herself might be overburdened and exploited in the family, and that it might actually be good that she was reaching out for help independently. Since it is something of a historical novelty for mothers' needs and protests to be considered important, I allowed myself to feel comfortable and even pleased to take the opportunity to offer her some extra support. (Luepnitz 1988, 232)

Refracting the notion of the family's sense of overwhelmedness through her feminist sensibility, Luepnitz greeted Mrs. McGinn in the waiting area. Luepnitz as therapist rewarded a mother's open expression of anger. Ten months later, on the day of termination, Mrs. McGinn recounts this initial meeting: "I felt so selfish, and here you were taking me in. I felt, 'Lord, bless this woman,' because I could count the times someone had made extra time for me.'" (Luepnitz 1988, 271)

In another case involving an African-American family, the Johnsons, Luepnitz effects a dramatic intervention with Ms. Johnson, the mother and single parent of inpatient Leroy, when she tells Ms. Johnson that Leroy's problems are not her fault:

She had received messages for ten years like a ticker tape coming in from schools, guidance counselors, judges, and relatives saying that she had destroyed her child and that if he was on his way to prison, this too was her doing. She sat now looking thoughtful. (Luepnitz 1988, 285)

This moment of feminist sensitivity became a pivotal and transforming moment in the therapy; it was a core moment inaugurated by the therapist. Feminine empathy occurs when we too, as caregivers, have experienced the situation, for example, of being overburdened and exploited as a woman (Mrs. McGinn) or of being scapegoated (Ms. Johnson). Feminist sensibility can occur without feminine empathy. Both bring to a "core moment" a nontraditional and novel perspective.

## FAILED CORE MOMENTS

Failed core moments in a traditional pastoral care with women can occur when a woman is not understood as a *self-in-relation*. This understanding can only be explicated with feminist sensibility which includes cultural analysis. An example of failure to receive a core moment will be illustrated from Seward Hiltner's *Pastoral Counseling*.

In Hiltner's evaluation of a student's initial pastoral visit with the widow Mrs. Tompkins, Hiltner commented on two specific counseling errors. However, in this study of grief, a feminist sensibility goes even farther to underscore the core moment: A bereaved Mrs. Tompkins puts her head down on her arms, sobs, and cries, "I'm so lonesome. My husband was all

I had" (Hiltner 1949, 230). The cosmic loneliness surrounding the recent widow, a loneliness symbolized by her standing in the separate apartment at the rear of her house, contextualizes the statement: "I'm so lonesome." With cultural analysis we can more clearly formulate the developmental theory that women's intimacy issues often precede their identity formation. Women frequently understand their identity through relational attach-ment. For better or worse, and with varying definitions of the term, they are a *self-in-relation*. In the grief process, the loss of the significant rela-tion(ship) effects an identity crisis of vast existential proportions. The remainder of the interview with Mrs. Tompkins testifies to her wrenching emptiness and her subsequent shame about these feelings (Hiltner 1949, 229–231).

In the case of Mr. and Mrs. Goodheart, failure to receive another core moment in its cultural context is evident (Arnold 1982, 153–160). It is noteworthy that numerous details of Mr. Goodheart's business profile are given. He is a successful corporate executive on a new corporate assign-ment to South America. Both Goodhearts are extremely active in the church, serve as a model church family, and give generously to missions. After Mr. Goodheart's absence of four weeks, Mrs. Goodheart—in crisis—calls the pastor: Mr. Goodheart had only written one-third as many letters as she had written, a loan from the bank was due, she was overdrawn in her checking account, and the car had broken down. She did not know how to transfer funds; she also did not know how to cope with car problems. Furthermore, the husband's secretary *did* know how to transfer funds and had the power of attorney over the checking account. Mrs. Goodheart wavered between despair and rage: "It is ridiculous for a forty-one-year-old woman not to know how to transfer funds into a bank account or how to deal with automobile problems" (Arnold 1982, 156). However, given the reality of Western culture, it is not so ridiculous in a society where female and male responsibilities are traditionally delineated along the lines of the Goodheart marriage. It is only with a cultural analysis of the case that we see how much power resides in the finances: power in the nuclear family and in the family of faith, the church. We are aware early on that the Good-hearts have given generously. Mr. Goodheart and his secretary held the positions of financial power and expertise so valued in the United States. The automobile in American Western culture is also a treasured symbol of prestige and control. It is not the case that Mrs. Goodheart is infantile or necessarily overly dependent. She has probably been left with numerous responsibilities—children, schooling, aging parents, clothing, home, and social commitments—that would have put Mr. Goodheart under stress had Mrs. Goodheart been in South America. The industry that Mrs. Goodheart has most likely excelled in is rendered inferior by North American society. This is not to say she should not learn to fulfill "male" responsibilities in assuming more responsibility and independence. However, to label her helpless, out of control, indecisive, and dependent is insufficient and, at points, inaccurate (Arnold 1982, 156). To suggest the resource of "confession" even when it is seen as guiltless "admission" of what is happening is inadequate as Arnold would surely concur in our contemporary context (Arnold 1982, 157). It is the confession of a culture that is needed. Mrs. Goodheart has succeeded well in performing in a way her society expected. An awareness that she has played traditional feminine roles, a consciousness that she is now uncomfortable, and a willingness to change are appropriate to feminist therapeutic goals. This case connotes more than a "pastoral approach to stress." Following Mrs. Goodheart's lead, it is a pastoral approach to the ridiculous. "It is ridiculous for a forty-one-year-old woman not to know how to transfer funds into a bank account" (Arnold 1982, 156).

## WELL WOMEN

A woman once told a group of people: "Come, see a man who told me all the things that I have done." What exactly had been told her? She had been told that she had five husbands and that the current man in her life was not her husband. The woman called the spokesman a prophet. This interchange between a woman at the well in Sychar, Samaria, and the man called Christ was revelatory, prophetic, and transitional. It was a core moment in the exchange between the one who claimed, "I am he," meaning Messiah, he who is called Christ, and the woman who identified herself: I am a Samaritan woman. This narrative is recorded in the fourth chapter of the Gospel of John. The discourses in this Gospel present Jesus Christ as revealer, or as the proclaimer who is revealing his identity (Kysar 1976, 8). Identity is disclosed through statements of "I am." In the midst of the "I ams" of Jesus, we have the "I am" of a woman. Her identity is also revealed.

I am he.      <—>      I am a Samaritan woman.
(John 4:26)                              (John 4:9)

Rather than reading this text from the traditional viewpoint with a focus on the person of Christ, we can read it from the viewpoint of the marginal person, the woman. To do this, the first-century cultural context with its dualistic worldview is acknowledged, a dualism that creates insiders and outsiders.

| Christians | <—> | Jews |
| us | <—> | them |
| I am he | <—> | I am a Samaritan woman |

The narrative of the woman of Samaria as found in John 4 can be approached in a variety of ways and used as a paradigmatic text in pastoral care. Women come to the biblical text by differing paths. Some do not come at all. Some feel so marginalized by the text that they do not come to read. The diversity of textual interpretations of John 4 can be illustrated with two examples. One adult survivor of child sexual abuse read the text and described her thirst for living water. It is like receiving a little water in her empty well, then the water leaks out again. To her, even "living water" leaks out, but living water is at least growing. "You wouldn't have to drag it from someone else's well." This woman sees her own recovery as taking forever. The pattern for abused women can be repeatedly picking the same type of male as the woman looks for love in a relationship. This adult survivor of child sexual abuse comes to the text of John 4 and sees Jesus as a male who breaks the abusive pattern. "Come, see a man who told me all the things I *have* done." Note, she does not say: "Come, see a man who told me all the things I am." Rather, this man, Jesus, recognizes her false patterns of connectedness. This is not done in an accusatory way but in a grace-filled core moment of insight, a gift of living water.

Another woman, a pastoral counselor and minister, reads the John 4 text as a story of empowerment. Emphasizing the unlikeliness of the meeting between the Jew and the Samaritan, the man and the woman, and underscoring the mysteriousness of the statement, "Go, call your husband, and come here," she interprets the encounter as an occasion of empowerment.

> Jesus also was not limited by the woman's own defenses or limited self-image. She did not expect much of herself. Her life was probably without hope of being better. Since she went her own way and spoke her own mind, she must have appeared to many as arrogant, cynical, indifferent to the opinions and feelings of others. They may even have been angry that she could act as if the rules didn't apply to her. This is not what Jesus saw. He saw her hurt, her loneliness, her isolation, her fear that there was no one she could trust. . . . Acting out of Jesus' empowerment of her, she returned to her community. (Tyner Canzoneri 1990).

God is presented in this interpretation as redeemer of broken people and as comforter and encourager. Christ is presented as an extension of this relationship and, as such, as living water to a thirsty person.

Other women today will have difficulty coming to the text of John 4. The three main areas of difficulty have to do with biblical authority, Christology, and theodicy. First, as Christine Smith has so aptly illustrated in *Weav-*

*ing the Sermon,* "Christian feminists no longer assume that the Bible has ultimate authority, nor do they agree that all texts should be understood as God's revelation" (Smith 1989, 94). Second, some women consider Jesus' maleness as problematic and do not wish to receive empowerment from any male. Other women see Jesus as healer, companion, loving presence, and counselor, but only one of many examples of this (Smith 1989, 87). Third, some women emphasize the God within, or the Goddess within themselves. This can be done to the exclusion of an external manifestation of the divine, for example, in the person of Christ. James Bugental, a psychologist and proponent of existential-humanistic psychotherapy, has described the search for the god within:

> Thus when I speak of a search for the god hidden within the person, I mean quite literally that I believe that within each of us is the divine—the potential to create and the awareness of knowingly contributing to the determination of what will be real. . . . I believe God is identical with man's [woman's] deepest longings for his [her] own being. (Bugental 1976, 295–296)

We come to the text of John 4 in different ways, if we come at all. The narrative of the Samaritan woman as a centering, paradigmatic text sets forth themes of pastoral concern: core moments, false patterns of connectedness, relationship-attachment, cultural analysis, the internal thirst of women, emptiness and loneliness, the significance of female anatomy, autonomy, identity, self-esteem, and love of self.

Whereas one commentator has described the woman of Samaria as mincing and coy (Brown 1975, 175), she could alternatively be seen as sarcastic (John 4:15) and assertive, and curious (John 4:11). She begins the narrative in a servile position, not only drawing water but standing ready to serve a male, and ends the narrative as a leader of the community, a spokeswoman. Using a feminist ideological critical approach, Sandra Schneiders shows that "the consistent identification of the Samaritan Woman in John 4 as a duplicitous whore whom Jesus tricks into self-exposure and then, presumably, converts, both violates the text and allows the woman's role in the evangelization of Samaria to be minimized while the (presumably male) townspeople emerge as virtual self-evangelizers" (Schneiders 1991, 186). The little that we have of the Samaritan's story illustrates a typical pattern for traditional women, for example, that women's identity is understood through relationship-attachment or intimacy of sorts. Infantile development occurs in *relation* to another person or persons (Chodorow 1978, 77). This raises the question of what it means to be a *self-in-relation*, a term brought into prominence through the research and lectures of the Stone Center in Wellesley, Mass. In speaking of the divine as Relation, the theological question is posed: What does it mean to be a self-in-Relation (to the divine)?

John 4 can be used to establish numerous themes pertinent to women today. First, the woman of Samaria discloses in the core moments of the exchange a repetitive pattern of relationship-attachment: five husbands and a sixth male who is not a husband. She can be used to illustrate a self-in-relation who is so enmeshed in the relations that she loses a sense of self. She cannot say: I am she. Much like Hiltner's Mrs. Tompkins, her identity has accrued through investment in relationships. Like the widow Mrs. Tompkins, we discern between the lines: "I'm so lonesome." The repetitive relational pattern of the woman of Samaria, five husbands plus one more male, offers a false paradigm of connectedness.

Second, we come into the dialogue with a cultural analysis. As in the case with Mrs. Goodheart who excels in a culturally reinforced and societally rewarded dependency within certain marital roles, the woman of Samaria is enacting her part as a serving woman and as a marginal person. Jesus prods her: "Give me a drink." The woman points to the inevitable racism involved: "How is it that you being a Jew, ask me for a drink since I am a Samaritan woman?" Classism, racism, and sexism impinge on an understanding of the exchange. A cultural analysis is always necessary in understanding women past and present.

Third, the woman of Samaria communicates an internal thirst of women, an emptiness, a loneliness. On the very scanty information about her in the passage, my tendency would be to see histrionic and dependent traits in this woman intent on filling up her emptiness with relationships, husbands. Relationship-attachment raises secondary issues of permeable self-boundaries. "The firmer a sense of self and the more internally secure about selfhood a person is, the more freely he or she may be to relate to others in an intimate manner and to allow the existence of permeability in relationship boundaries" (Nichols and Everett 1986, 311). How fluid or how rigid are boundaries constructed by the healthy self-in-relation?

The emptiness of women can be expressed in diverse ways. In *The Black Women's Health Book: Speaking for Ourselves,* Byllye Avery states:

> We have to do what is necessary to survive. It's just a part of living. But most of us are empty wells that never really get replenished. Most of us are dead inside. We are walking around dead. That's why we end up in relationships that reinforce that particular thought. (Avery 1990, 6)

In working with obese women in a "self-health" group, Avery found that the women were very aware of health issues. Nevertheless, these severely obese women overate: "the one thing I know I can do when I come home is cook me a pot of food and sit down in front of the TV and eat it. And you can't take that away from me until you're ready to give me something in its place" (Avery 1990, 7).

The woman of Samaria enters the narrative with a water pot on her shoulders. The image of the water pot can symbolize the external pressures and burdens on women today. There are also many internal pressures, metaphorically speaking, "water pots of the psyches." It is into these empty enclosures that women pour anger, guilt, shame, loneliness, and doubt. Many women come to the counseling process as a self-in-relation, saying in subtle or obvious ways: "I'm so lonesome"; "I'm so thirsty"; "I'm so empty." In John 4, Jesus speaks of human beings as a spring (Moltmann-Wendel 1994, 83). "And then as the story goes we are told that the woman leaves her jar, the jar, the vessel, her symbol as a woman, and runs off to tell her fellow-countrymen what she has experienced. She leaves behind her old female symbol, the jar, the vessel, because she may be something different: a source from which ever new, independent and living things can proceed" (Moltmann-Wendel 1994, 83).

Fourth, it is symbolically noteworthy that the woman of Samaria stands at the well of Sychar. This archaeological actuality replicates the anatomical well, the womb, the uterus, the gynecological water pot. "Fill me up," women have erroneously said to men. The emptiness and the thirstiness result when women realize that the relations are not filling enough. Identity is secured when a woman is a *self*-in-relation. Then she can say: I am a woman. More secure in her identity, she can claim: I am she.

Women sometimes disparage themselves by way of introduction. "I am *just* a housewife." If they do not denigrate themselves, they often qualify themselves. "I am a woman minister." "I am a woman doctor." "I am a married woman." "I am a divorced woman." "I am a single woman." Women continue to work on identity issues, self-esteem, and love of self in therapy. Ann France in *Consuming Psychotherapy* discusses her relationship with three therapists, her suicidal impulses, and her therapists' commitment to keeping her alive:

> It only occurs to me some years later, and because someone else pointed it out, that maybe they actually cared whether I were alive or dead. I can see, with my intellect, that this is a likely explanation for their resistance to the topic of suicide. But since I have never considered my own life worthwhile, nor have I ever been able to believe that I could matter to another human being, I still cannot understand this emotionally. (France 1988, 152)

It is a concern in therapy that a woman can say with self-esteem: "I am a woman." It is a further concern that she declare with love of self: "I am she." It is a goal of therapy that a woman state with a profound sense of identity: "I am."

In an empowering core moment, Jesus reminded a woman at the well of her enmeshment in relationships. Although an individuated, nonenmeshed *self-in-relation* model has been embraced by numerous feminist scholars to elucidate women's psychosocial development, "it is essential that we develop models of female autonomy along with the relational perspective" (Jacobs 1992, 37–46). Only then can a woman find a developmental perspective to underscore her sense of reality as a self. Her assertion, I am, is a gift of living water.

## JOURNEY MERCIES ON THE WAY HOME

From Samaritan to Samaritan. The Samaritan of Luke 10 finished his journey while helping a wounded person. He exhibited love of God, neighbor, and self. He relied on a sense of the communal as represented by the innkeeper and the inn. The Samaritan of John 4 encountered on her journey to and from the well One who empowered her. She ran to her community with such a convincing proclamation that many believed her. From Samaritan to Samaritan to samaritans, we receive insights for pastoral care. These insights are the journey mercies as women come home to themselves.

## BIBLIOGRAPHY

Arnold, William. 1982. *Introduction to Pastoral Care*. Philadelphia: Westminster Press.

Avery, B. 1990. "Breathing Life into Ourselves: The Evolution of the National Black Women's Health Project." In E. C. White, ed., 6.

Brown, R. 1975. *The Gospel according to John*. London: Geoffrey Chapman.

Bugental, J. F. T. 1976. *The Search for Existential Identity*. San Francisco: Jossey-Bass.

Chodorow, N. 1978. *The Reproduction of Mothering: Psychoanalysis and the Sociology of Gender*. Berkeley and Los Angeles: University of California Press.

France, A. 1988. *Consuming Psychotherapy*. London: Free Association Books.

Fenn, R., and D. Capps, eds. 1992. *The Endangered Self*. Princeton: Center for Religion, Self, and Society.

Glaz, M., and J. Stevenson Moessner. 1991. *Women in Travail and Transition: A New Pastoral Care*. Minneapolis: Fortress Press.

Hiltner, S. 1949. *Pastoral Counseling*. New York: Abingdon Press.

Jacobs, J. L. 1992. "The Endangered Female Self and the Search for Identity." In Fenn and Capps, eds., 37–46.

Kysar, R. 1976. *John, the Maverick Gospel*. Atlanta: John Knox Press.

Luepnitz, D. A. 1988. *The Family Interpreted: Feminist Theory in Clinical Practice.* New York: Basic Books.

Moltmann-Wendel, E. 1994. *I Am My Body.* London: SCM Press.

Myers, Gary. Conversation with author, May 1992.

Nichols, Wm., and C. Everett. 1986. *Systemic Family Therapy: An Integrative Approach.* New York: Guilford Press.

Schneiders, S. 1991. *The Revelatory Text: Interpreting the New Testament as Sacred Scripture.* New York: HarperCollins.

Smith, C. M. 1989. *Weaving the Sermon: Preaching in a Feminist Perspective.* Louisville, Ky.: Westminster/John Knox Press.

Tyner Canzoneri, T. 1990. Address at the Georgia Baptist Women in Ministry Conference, Savannah, Ga., November 12, 1990.

White, E. C., ed. 1990. *The Black Women's Health Book.* Seattle: Seal Press.

Through the eyes of women :
insights for pastoral care